0125182P

old
Edition

Party Politics in America

PARTY POLITICS IN AMERICA

Frank J. Sorauf
UNIVERSITY OF MINNESOTA

Little, Brown and Company · Boston

For My Mother and Father

PREFACE

I hope my scholarly goals and outlooks in writing this book will be apparent to the reader without any extended prefatory comments. I can only say that I have tried to present a systematic survey of the American parties within a coherent, logical approach to them. The main outlines of that approach are indicated especially in the first and last two chapters and in the introductory pages to the six parts of the book.

Whatever sins of commission I may have been guilty of in this book are on the pages for readers to see. I hope they will not hesitate to call them to my attention. My sins of omission may, however, require a brief comment. With the scholarly literature on political parties expanding so rapidly, it has been impossible to refer to all of it here; I have often been forced to difficult, even arbitrary, selections from it for representation here. In the interests of a unity and logic in the approach to the American political parties, I have also resisted the temptation to dwell at length on interest groups and on American voting behavior. It is a self-imposed limitation which I think can be defended intellectually.

Finally, I should like to acknowledge some of the intellectual debts I incurred in writing this book. Countless students, colleagues, and friends — far too many to list here — helped me in one way or another, and I hope they will forgive such a brief and collective acknowledgment. I am especially indebted to my assistant, Darrell Jensen; to my typist, Marilyn Grosenick; and to my friend and fellow student of American politics, Gerald Elliott. I am also grateful to John Andrews and Donald Hammonds for their help, patience, and understanding during the book's long gestation period. Finally, I should like to thank Demetrios Caraley, Bernard Hennessy, and Allan Sindler for their careful and constructive reading of the manuscript. What merit it may have owes a great deal to their comments; its errors and shortcomings are, of course, entirely of my own devising.

FRANK J. SORAUF
Minneapolis, Minnesota

TABLE OF CONTENTS

PART ONE

Parties and Party Systems

The aggressive and open pursuit of personal advantage will probably never easily win the admiration of any society. It has certainly not won the admiration of ours. We have tended always to consider "politics" a grubby and scarcely ethical business, whether played as "office politics," "academic politics," or as plain and simple "politics" in the political and governmental system. Yet the fact remains that men are ambitious for the scarce rewards their groups, their occupations, and their societies offer. The things men desire in this world — status, acceptance, authority, or money, for example — are in short supply at every level of social organization. Access to the boss's ear in the business office, therefore, has its parallel in access to a governor or an important congressional committee. "Politics," that striving to influence the allocation of the scarce rewards, consequently, is as ubiquitous as ambition itself.

In everyday use "politics" has become an epithet or at the least a term of peevish disapproval. Generally, however, political scientists have tried to strip the term of its uncharitable connotations. And rarely do they use it as broadly as laymen do. In its broadest use "politics" refers to the organizing of any influence, the shaping of decisions allocating any resources. But for the specialist it denotes the particular process of mobilizing influence and shaping decisions within government and the political system.

Popular hostility and indifference to the political processes do not diminish their impact or importance. The growth and pervasiveness of

government remain cardinal facts in the 20th century, and it seems unlikely that the tides of governmental authority will recede to any great
extent in our time. The demands of a complex, increasingly urbanized,
industrialized society — and the dictates of a world beset by international
tensions and dependence — scarcely seem to permit a return to the limited
government of the early years of the American republic. For the present
and the foreseeable future an increasing proportion of the important conflicts over goals and resources in the American society will be settled
within the political system. The really meaningful issues for our time will
surely be those of how influence and power will be organized within the
political system, by whom it will be organized, and to whom it will be
responsible. For it will be increasingly within the political system that we
will decide, in the candid phrase of Harold Lasswell, "who gets what,
when, how." [1]

In the United States this political system operates largely through the
formal, regularized institutions of government set up under the constitutions of the nation and the states. Few Americans and fewer political scientists subscribe to arguments that the "real" and important political
decisions are made clandestinely by murky, semi-visible "elites" and
merely ratified by the governmental institutions they control.[2] It may
happen, to be sure, in a local community that effective political decisions
are made by some informal group of influential local citizens rather than
by a city council or a school board or a mayor. Nonetheless, one is reasonably safe in looking for the substance of American politics within the
complex, often overlapping governmental apparatuses of the nation, the
fifty states, and the localities. The "politics" of which we have been talking concerns the attempts to influence either the making of the decisions
in these governmental units or the selection of the men who will make
them — whether those decisions take the form of laws, treaties, ordinances,
executive orders, judicial decisions, or administrative rules and regulations.

In the American democracy the political party is, of course, one of the
chief instruments through which the politically active organize and mobilize political influence. It is not, however, the only one. Interest groups,
charismatic individual leaders, smaller factions and cliques, and non-
party organizations such as the Americans for Democratic Action and the
American Conservative Union may all mobilize influence. Therefore, we
cannot use the term "politics" simply to refer to the activities of the political parties. A substantial portion of American politics goes on outside

[1] The phrase comes from the title of Harold Lasswell's pioneering book, *Politics:
Who Gets What, When, How* (New York: McGraw-Hill, 1936).
[2] C. Wright Mills in *The Power Elite* (New York: Oxford University Press, 1956)
offers the best known and most influential example of the recent elitist interpretations
of American politics.

of the political parties. Interest groups rather than the parties, for example, bring certain issues and policy questions to legislatures and administrative agencies; non-party organizations may also support candidates for office with money and manpower. Occasionally the individual himself may act without the assistance of a political intermediary; he may write his congressman or otherwise directly attempt to influence the decision-making activity of government. Thus the terms "politics" and "political" embrace the activity of the political parties — which one may conveniently call "partisan" — but they are in no sense limited to partisan political activity.

These political organizations — parties among them — stand athwart complex political systems as intermediaries between the millions of political individuals and the distant seats of governmental authority. They bring together into large and powerful aggregates the many individuals whose political influence is miniscule and insignificant when it stands alone. By attaching the loyalty of individuals to sets of interests, programs, symbols, and leaders, the organizations establish powerful political aggregates and bring them to bear on the selection of policy-makers and on the processes of policy-making. By working between the political individual and the policy-making machinery of government, they aggregate political influence as it moves from individual to government, and they codify and simplify information about government and politics as it moves back to the individual. Political organizations are the informal agents of representation in the complex and enormous representative democracies of our time. In a practical way they permit the individual and small groups to participate in the selection of their representatives and in the formation of the decisions of a usually remote government. They are in the broadest sense both the builders and the agents of majorities.

In any political system the political organizations have developed a division of labor in the business of aggregating political influence. Some of them, and primarily the political parties, concentrate on contesting elections. Others pursue the avenues of direct influences on legislators or administrators. Still others seek mainly to propagate ideologies or introduce voters to the ways of politics and political action. Indeed, the nature of the division of labor among the various political organizations in any political system says a great deal about the system and about the general processes and procedures of mobilizing power within it. The division also speaks meaningfully about the political parties themselves. It is a commonplace that the American political parties are, to an extent unusual among the parties of the Western democracies, occupied with the single activity of contesting elections. Those of Western Europe, on the other hand, have traditionally been more committed to the spreading of ideologies and the disciplining of majorities in legislatures. And those of a country such as India have been more involved with the transmitting of political values and information to a semi-literate citizenry lacking other avenues of political communication and socialization. Political parties may also differ in their long-run success in the competition with the non-party political organizations. It may very well be the case, for example, that the American parties control less of the organizing and mobilizing business of politics than do the political parties of Western Europe or South Asia.

The division of labor or function among the political organizations is, however, neither clean nor clear. There is always an overlapping and a resulting competition among political organizations over the performance of many of the organizational activities. That competition is most obvious when it takes place between two political parties as they contend for the votes and loyalties of a fickle electorate. But it takes place as well among the parties and the other political organizations – in, for example, the competition of parties and powerful interest groups for the attention and support of legislators, or for the right to name candidates in a primary election. Nor is this rough and approximate division of labor a fixed or permanent one. The American parties may find that affluent non-party groups increasingly impinge on their control of election campaigns, and they themselves may begin to impinge on others' activities by concerning themselves increasingly with political ideologies.

In short, this book will reflect a view of the political parties as aggregators or mobilizers of influence in the competition for scarce goals and resources – not merely among themselves, but in competition with a mixed array of other political organizations. These competitions take place at least on three levels (Figure 1):

Figure 1
THE POLITICAL PARTIES:
THREE LEVELS OF COMPETITION

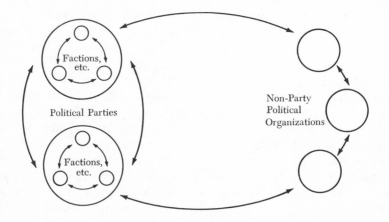

1. among the individuals, groups and factions within the political party.
2. between and among the parties in the "party system."
3. among the parties and the other political organizations (e.g., interest groups, personal followings, local political elites, *ad hoc* issue or election groups).

And for what do they compete? They compete first of all for political resources: for money, for skills and expertise, for the efforts of men and women committed to a political goal. All of these "inputs" are essential for the "fueling" of organizational activity, but none of them is in abundant supply in the American polity (or in any other polity). What resources one organization or type of organization takes may very well deplete the resources of another and thus curtail its capacity for action. Secondly, they compete in the mobilization of the broader American citizenry behind political goals. They may and do differ, of course, in the ways in which they mobilize American adults. Some mobilize through the contesting of elections, and thus the selection of the decision-makers of government; others mobilize significant aggregates of influence by propagandizing an issue position or an ideology, others by bringing influence to bear on the making of public policy. If we combine these two facets of competition among political organizations, therefore, we may summarize by saying that the parties and other political organizations compete for scarce political resources with which to mobilize political influence to capture the scarce rewards the political system allocates (Figure 2).

This book will focus on the most visible, the most celebrated, and the most widely-studied of the political organizations. Its concern with the political parties, however, will always be in the context of their competi-

Figure 2
THE OBJECTS OF COMPETITION
AMONG POLITICAL ORGANIZATIONS

Important

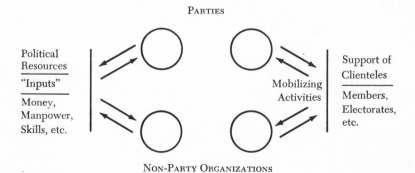

PARTIES

Political
Resources
"Inputs"
———
Money,
Manpower,
Skills, etc.

Mobilizing
Activities

Support of
Clienteles
———
Members,
Electorates,
etc.

NON-PARTY ORGANIZATIONS

tions in the broader political processes. Yet, it is not enough to study merely the inputs and outputs of a political organization. The political party has as well an internal, organizational life. It is men and women making decisions, seeking rewards and goals of their own, and accepting an organizational division of labor and system of authority. As a goal-seeking organization in the political process, the party must, both in its recruitment of resources and the achievement of its goals, meet the personal needs and goals of the activists of the organization. Whether the people of the party organization value the rewards of patronage employment or the triumph of principle, the party cannot ignore their claims. If it does, the party does so at the risk of hurting the organization's vitality and thus its capacity for action.

Much has been made of the central, guiding role of the political parties in the American democracy. It has not been uncommon to view them as the authors — or at least the featured stars — of the democratic political dramas. For many scholars, as well as for many thoughtful citizens, democracy as we know it is unthinkable without the viable two-party system of today. Yet, the major American parties have changed and are presently changing, both in their organizational form and in the pattern and style of their activities. Political parties as they existed fifty years ago scarcely exist today, and it may very well be that the parties as we know them will not exist fifty years hence.

A strong case can indeed be made — and will be made in this volume — that the political parties have lost their pre-eminent position as political organizations over the past century and that they have seen competing political organizations wrest away some of the mobilizing activities we have traditionally thought were prerogatives of the parties. Those changes raise questions of the centrality and indispensability — and the "natural superiority" — of the parties in the competitions of the political process. The final answers to these questions will await the last two chapters, but for the moment they underscore the point that the entire issue of the party's competition with the other political organizations is no less than the question of how political influence will be organized in the American democracy.

Chapter One

IN SEARCH OF
THE POLITICAL PARTIES

Consider the American adult who insists "I'm a strong Republican," or "I've been a Democrat all of my life." It is likely that he never actively worked within the party organization of his choice or made a financial contribution to it. He might be hard pressed to recall its recent platform commitments, and if he did, he would probably feel no binding loyalty to them. Furthermore, he probably never comes together with the other Americans who express the same party identification, and he would very likely find it difficult to name or identify the local officials of his party. In fact, his loyalty to the party of which he considers himself a "member" may involve little more than a disposition to support its candidates for office if all other considerations are reasonably equal. Yet, when the interviewers of the national polling organizations come to his door, he hesitates not at all to attach himself to a political party. And we do not hesitate to credit his word, for it is in the nature of the American parties and politics that we consider a man a Democrat or a Republican merely because he says he is one.[1]

When viewed merely as the total of the loyalties of millions of adults, the major American parties appear as great and formless aggregates united on little more than adherence to a traditional symbol or label. But the American political parties are also organizations. It *is* possible to join them, to work within them, to become officers in them, to participate in setting their goals and strategies — much as one would within a local fra-

[1] In this chapter we deal only with the two American major parties. The "major parties," the Democrats and the Republicans, are so called because they are the only two that can compete for public office with any chances of success. The "minor" ("third") parties will be discussed in the next chapter.

7

ternal organization or machinists' union. They do have the characteristics of stable and patterned personal relationships, the banding together of individuals to seek goals, which we associate with social organizations.

Approaches to a concept or definition of the political party in the United States tend to vacillate between these two conceptual options — one of the party as essentially a body of voters or a loyal electorate, the other of the party as a militant, hierarchical organization (a "machine," if one prefers). Not even the statutory attempts of the American states to define the parties escape the conflict of these two approaches. In their laws on elections any number of states define the parties in terms of the votes cast for candidates at the last election, and yet they set about creating for them (and imposing on them) an intricate organizational framework that rises from the local ward or precinct committeeman to an all-embracing state committee. A third approach — the ideological one — has not engaged or detained observers of the American parties. To think of the parties in terms of commonly-held values or principles has simply seemed to most an exercise too far removed from reality. Ideological unanimity or homogeneity has not been a hallmark of the major American parties.[2]

The problem of identifying the political party is thus an understandably vexing one. The parties are both more and less than the other political organizations; they do have organizational characteristics, but they lack a well-defined concept of membership and an integrated system of authority. Few partisans become party "members" in the conventional meaning of that term. A legislative leader may speak as a member of the party and for the party, even though he won the right to carry the party label in a primary election over the opposition of the party organization. And the wing of the party in one state or section may refuse to accept the authority of the national committee or the national convention of the party. Furthermore, the formal, legal structure, as the fifty states set it up, may bear little relationship to the reality of party organization. Thousands of ward and precinct positions around the country are vacant, and real and substantial power in the party often rests in hands other than those of the duly-elected chairmen of the party committees.

Nor is it any easier to identify the American party by its activities. While it is undeniably true that the American parties spend vast sums of time and money contesting elections, other political organizations are not without a substantial interest in nominating and electing candidates. Other political organizations also propagandize and socialize the American electorate; and they, too, attempt to influence and organize American legislators and executives.

So, one returns to the artless question of who are the Democrats and

---

[2] See page 21 of this chapter for Edmund Burke's classic definition of a political party, probably the most renowned "ideological" definition.

who are the Republicans. What people, what organizations, what relationships are we talking about when we speak of the two major American parties? The party leaders and officials, the hundreds of anonymous activists who work for candidates and party causes, the people who vote for the party's candidates, its actual dues-paying members, the people who have an emotional identification with the fortunes of the party, the men and women elected to office on the party's ballot — all of them, or some of them? To what extent is the political party an organized, goal-seeking apparatus? And above all, is it anything more than a symbol to which its loyalists may give what meaning they will?

THE POLITICAL PARTY AS A STRUCTURE

An old, yet valuable, metaphor suggests that the political party may be visualized as a set of ever-expanding, concentric circles (Figure 1). At the center one would find the formal and active leaders of the party — the ward and precinct leaders, the members of the city, county, state, and national committees, as well as informal but powerful party leaders who operate "behind the scenes." One circle beyond them are the active workers of the party — the men and women who canvass for the party, man its campaigns, help recruit other workers and loyalists, and make financial contributions to it. Beyond them (or with them) one may place the small

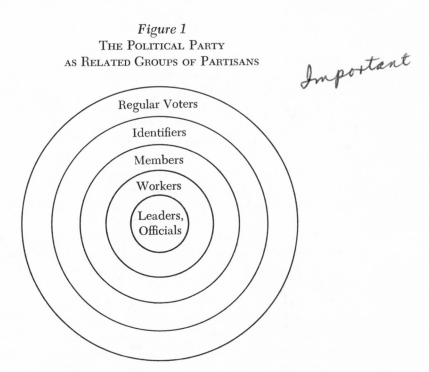

Figure 1
THE POLITICAL PARTY
AS RELATED GROUPS OF PARTISANS

Important

Regular Voters

Identifiers

Members

Workers

Leaders,
Officials

but expanding group of formally-enrolled members of party clubs or organizations. In the two, greatly overlapping, outer rings are the two chief party clienteles: the party voters who vote for the party's candidates by some arbitrarily-set standard of regularity, and the party identifiers who, in response to the queries of the public opinion surveys, express some degree of general preference for the party.

As striking as the image of the concentric circles may be, it has its sharp and obvious limitations. The circles are arbitrarily drawn and placed. Active workers, members, voters, and identifiers overlap, and furthermore, the decision to place one or the other closer to the center of party life and activity is at least partly an arbitrary one. Furthermore, the device suggests a static quality far from reality; it suggests that the circles represent well-defined, stable, and separate sub-groups within the party organization, while the truth is that they overlap and that people move freely from one to another and back again. Nor does the metaphor accommodate the special case of the office-holders elected under the party's aegis; while in some ways they may not be "of" the party, they speak for it and the public identifies them and their actions with it. However, in a rough and approximate way the circles suggest the shades and degrees of involvement and activity which individuals bring to the parties. As with the ripples which result from the pebble thrown into the lake, each successive circle away from the center of impact is less forceful and distinct than the one before it. And the further away one gets from the center of party decision-making and authority, the harder it is to see the relationship to the center and the harder it is to see even the outlines of the partisan ripples.

Perhaps it would be more accurate to think of the major American party as a tri-partite system of interactions, a great and enigmatic three-headed political giant. As a structure it embraces three separate elements (Figure 2).

1. *The party organization.* In the party organization one finds the formally-chosen party leadership, the informally-anointed ones, the legions of local captains and leaders, the members and activists of the party — those who give their time, their money, and their skills to the party, whether as leaders or followers, and who make and carry out decisions in the name of the party. In part, the organization operates through the formal machinery of committees and conventions set by the laws of the states, but in part, too, it has improvised its own informal apparatus. Here we find the centers of party authority and bureaucracy, and here, too, one observes the face-to-face contacts and interactions that bespeak organization of any kind. This is the part of the party which the public, with a good deal of native shrewdness, often refers to as "the organization," or less flatteringly as "the machine."

2. *The party in office.* This is the portion of the party ensconced in

Figure 2
THE TRI-PART POLITICAL PARTY

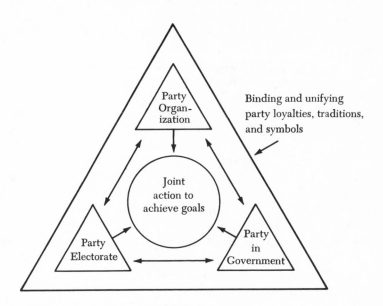

public office: the men who, to put it succinctly, have captured the symbols of the party and who speak for it in public authority. They are the chief executives and the legislative parties of the nation and the fifty states. Although they are not in many ways subject to the control or discipline of the party organization, they are in the broadest sense "spokesmen" for their party. Theirs is a semi-autonomous part of the party, frequently at odds with the party committees and conventions, and often in competition with the organization proper for resources and public attention.

3. *The party in the electorate.* To use an often mis-used term, these are the party's "fellow-travellers," the men and women who affiliate casually with the party, who identify with it, or who may even vote habitually for it. Yet, they do not participate in the party organization, and they do not interact with the leaders and the activists of the party; nor are they subject to the incentives and discipline of the party. They are, in effect, the regular consumers of the party's candidates and appeals. As the party's clienteles they make up the majorities necessary for effective political power in the American political system. But their association with the party is essentially a passive one — accepting here, rejecting there, and always threatening the party with the fickleness of their affections for it.

As structures, therefore, the American major parties are mixed, varied, and even contradictory. They are in part political organizations with active, goal-seeking, even disciplined participants ("members"), but they are also in part aggregates of unorganized partisans who claim to speak for the party and act within it but who may begrudge the party organization even the merest gesture of support or loyalty. The party thus embraces the widest range of involvement and commitment. It is at one and the same time a reasonably well-defined, voluntary political organization and an open, public rally of loyalists. It is both a goal-oriented organization for its activists and a habitual loyalty or reference symbol for many of its supporters.

Perhaps the most telling structural characteristic of the major American party, therefore, is the integral relationship its clientele — its "political consumers" — has to it. The usual political organization — the interest group, the *ad hoc* campaign organization, the informal local political elite — works to attract supporters or converts to its political cause. It must work within the electorate to attract to its banners the popular support necessary if it is to achieve its goals. But this clientele, the object of its mobilizings, stands outside the political organization. Not so with the political party; its clientele (the party in the electorate) is more than an external group to be wooed and propitiated. It is usually permitted a voice in the selection of the party's candidates by virtue of the direct primary, and in most states it helps to select the officials of the party organization (the local precinct or ward committeeman, for example). Consequently, the major American party is an open, inclusive, semi-public political organization. As a political structure it includes both a tangible political organization and its own political clientele; and it must, therefore, act to achieve both the goals of the activists of the organization and the members of the parties in the government and in the electorate. It is this combination of organization and clientele, of exclusive and inclusive groups, that makes the political party *sui generis* among political organizations on the American political scene.

Finally, rather than speak of the two major American parties as political structures, it might be more accurate to talk of the 100 American parties. The Republicans and the Democrats are so decentralized and so diverse that the two parties of each state have different organizational forms, kinds of personnel, and goals and incentives. Each state party has its own distinctive "mix" of the three sectors of the party structure. Party organizations, for example, differ in form from state to state, and in some the party organization dominates the party in government, while in others the reverse is closer to reality. Also, the party electorates differ in composition and in the bases of their loyalties; in some states, the two parties in the electorate divide roughly along social-class lines, but in others they do not. Much, indeed, of the distinctive quality of a state party is a reflection of the form and composition of each of the party sectors and of their relationships with each other.

THE PARTY AS A CONGERIES OF ACTIVITIES

From a discussion of what the political parties are as social structures, one moves easily and naturally to the question of what they do — their role and activities within the American political system. In varying degrees the competitive political parties of every democracy perform three chief sets of activities. They select candidates and contest elections through them, they propagandize on behalf of a party ideology or program, and they organize and attempt to guide the elected officeholders of government. The degree of emphasis which any particular political party puts on any one of these activities varies within and between countries, but no party completely escapes the necessity of any of them. And, indeed, in the different emphasis and priorities the parties of any two countries give to their activities one may discover some of the fundamental differences between them. The fact that the British and continental European parties organize the policy-making machinery of legislatures far more diligently and effectively than do the American parties demands an explanation. And in that explanation — reserved for a later chapter — one learns a good deal about the American parties and the political context in which they function.

PARTIES AS ELECTORS

It often appears that the American parties are little more than grudgingly tolerated, semi-public conspiracies to capture public office. This electoral activity so dominates the life of the American party that a "fever chart" of party activity — or to mix the metaphor, the ebb and flow of party adrenalin — follows almost exactly the cycles of the election calendar. Party activity and vitality reach a peak at the elections, and between them the parties go into a recuperative hibernation. Despite the hurdles and limitations of state laws governing the nomination and election processes, the parties live to mobilize voter support behind their candidates in elections. Only by winning elections do they maintain the allegiance of voters and candidates and achieve the incentives and goals so important to their activists. Party activity is goal-oriented, and most of the party goals depend ultimately on electoral victory. It is, in fact, chiefly in the attempt to achieve their separate goals by winning public office that the three sectors of the party are brought together into a unified whole.

PARTIES AS PROPAGANDIZERS

Secondly, the American parties carry on a loose series of related activities that one can perhaps best call those of education or propagandization. There is, of course, a school of thought which argues that the American parties fail almost completely to function on behalf of ideas or ideologies.

The Democrats and Republicans, to be sure, do not espouse the global, all-inclusive ideologies of a European Marxist or proletarian party. But the American parties do represent clusters or aggregates of interests, and thus in a less precise and less grandiose way they do stand for different policies on selected issues. The advent of Goldwater conservatism in 1964 may even indicate that ideology in the purer sense is coming to the American parties. At the least the American parties do represent interests of, and policy stands congenial to, population groups which identify with them and support them electorally. In this "pseudo-ideological" sense they become parties of "business" or of "labor." And in order to maintain their popular appeal, the parties and their candidates must attempt to popularize their issues. Even where the appeals of the parties are those of tradition or personality, or even of empty symbol, they must project, even "sell," the party image in order to recruit and reinforce their loyalists.

PARTIES AS GOVERNORS

Finally, the successful candidates of the American parties organize the decision-making agencies of government. The legislatures of all the fifty states, even the two which are officially "non-partisan," and the United States Congress have been organized along party lines, and the voting of their members shows to varying degrees the effects of party discipline and cohesion. That cohesion on substantive issues is, to be sure, irregular, sporadic, and imperfect in most of the legislatures. The Congressional Democrats, for instance, do not generally mobilize their Southern contingent to support the President's civil rights bills. Yet, in the aggregate an important measure of party discipline does exist. In executive branches Presidents and governors depend on their fellow partisans as a source of executive talent and count on their loyalty to a party to bind them to the executive and his programs. Only the American judiciary largely escapes the organizing and directing touch of the parties.

These, then, are the chief overt, manifest activities of democratic political parties, the American as well as those of other political systems. They are the activities which the parties consciously set out to perform; they are the task-oriented behavior of the parties — or of sectors of the parties — as they seek their goals openly and consciously in the broader confines of the American political system, and they are mentioned here purely in an introductory sense. Large sections of this, or any other, book on the American parties must of necessity be devoted to these activities of democratic political parties.

To list the activities of the parties, however, is not to suggest that the American parties monopolize any or all of them. Their competition with the non-party political organizations, in fact, is over the ability and the "right" to perform them. The American parties, having organized the American legislatures, battle constantly against interest groups and constituency pressures to firm up party lines in votes on major bills. In attempting to nominate candidates for public office, especially at the local level, the party faces an often insurmountable competition from interest groups, local community elites, and powerful personalities, each of whom may be sponsoring pet candidates. In the statement of issues and ideologies they are often overshadowed by the fervor of the minor ("third") parties, the ubiquitous interest groups, the mass media, pundits and publicists, and political associations such as the John Birch Society.

These patterns of party activity also interact with the party structure. The three sectors of the party structure, even though they may be bound together in the contesting of elections, are unevenly and differentially involved in the various activities. For example, in the American parties:

> the party organization is perhaps more directly concerned with all three activities than are the other two sectors; it tends for that reason to become the core or focal point of the party.

> the party organization and party in government together are the initiators of party activity, while the party in the electorate remains largely a passive political clientele within the party.

> the emphasis on the electoral activities elevates the party in government to a position of unusual power, even dominance within the parties; it frequently competes with the party organization for the favor of the party in the electorate.

Furthermore, individuals from all three sectors of the party may unite in specific activities. Activists of the party organization loyal to an officeholder, a senator for example, may unite with him, with other individuals of the party in government, and with individuals in the party in the electorate to return him to the Senate. When the election is won or lost, they may very likely drift apart again. One finds, therefore, within the parties these functional clusters or "nuclei," these groups of individuals drawn together in a single, concerted action.[3] And so, the parties as structures tend to be shaped and reshaped by the patterns and pace of their activities. Small and informal task groups transcend and cut across the differences in structure and goals which characterize the three party sectors.

THE UNPLANNED CONSEQUENCES OF PARTY ACTIVITY

The goal-seeking behavior of any individual or organization has unplanned and unintended consequences. The hard-driving, competitive salesman, in his aggressive pursuit of new orders and accounts, may alienate his fellow

[3] On the party as a series of task-oriented nuclei, see Joseph A. Schlesinger, "Political Party Organization" in James G. March (ed.), *Handbook of Organizations* (Chicago: Rand McNally, 1965), pp. 764–801.

workers and even disturb the morale of the work group of which he is a part. And it is no different with political organizations and institutions. Congress, by pursuing its political and law-making activities, may be said, depending on the occasion and the observer, either to be resolving or aggravating great areas of social conflict. Interest groups, by pursuing their particular goals in legislatures, have been said to provide an informal, auxiliary route of representation. A similar search for the unplanned consequences of party activities has become an old tradition in the study of the American parties. The tradition is rich in insight into the contributions of the parties to the American political system, and yet it can be frustrating in its imprecision and its elusiveness.

When one makes a statement that a political party is picking a candidate or organizing an election campaign, one makes a statement about overt, explicit, intended party activity. Not so when we make the observation that the same party is organizing consensus, integrating new groups into society, or giving voice to political opposition. These latter statements involve the roles or functions we impute to the parties. They are statements framed in analytical categories rather than in terms of specific activities, and as such they depend on what meaning, results, or consequences of action one observes. Some of them are more easily established or verified by empirical evidence than are others. It is surely easier to adduce evidence to show that the parties contribute to the political socialization of young Americans than it is to demonstrate that they settle social conflict, if only because it is easier to observe the process of socialization. Not surprisingly, then, the eyes of the beholders of the American parties have seen and recorded wildly differing sets of these consequences. They have tended to refer to them as "functions," but that semantic convention is virtually the extent of their agreement.[4]

As we have suggested, the parties participate in the political socialization of the American electorate, in the transmitting of political values and information to large numbers of voters and to-be voters. They preach the value of political commitment and activity, and they convey information and cues about a confusing political system. By symbolizing and representing a political point of view, they offer the uninformed or underinformed citizen a map to the political world. They help him form his political judgments and make his political choices, and in both physical and psychological terms they make it easier for him to be politically ac-

---

[4] Two points should be noted here. First of all, there is considerable debate within political science and all of the social sciences over the definition of these functions and the implications of functional analysis. In the interests of clarity, I would prefer to postpone that debate to the final chapter. Second, the distinction I have made here between the intended, goal-oriented activities and the unplanned results or consequences is similar to the distinction Robert K. Merton makes between manifest and latent function. See his *Social Theory and Social Structure* (Glencoe: Free Press, 1951), p. 19ff.

tive. In short, the parties in the American society traditionally have purveyed the information, the loyalties, and the opportunities for political activity. By their own behavior they have as well encouraged the development of political norms about what kinds of political activities and ethics will and will not be tolerated in any specific locality.

Similarly, in a complex and heterogeneous political system the parties function as political simplifiers or "reductionists." They accumulate massive aggregates of political power behind a few candidates and a few political alternatives. They build meaningful aggregates of power from ineffectual political individuals and groups, and thereby they organize blocs powerful enough to govern or to choose men to govern. For the confused and confounded citizen they simplify, and often oversimplify, the political cosmos into dichotomous choices. By using his attachment to a party as a perceptual screen, the voter has a master clue in the assessment of issues and candidates. Through the party he can relate present political conflicts to those of the past. So, both within the individual and in the external political world the political party operates to focus political loyalties and actions on two great alternatives. If in so doing it does violence to the inherent confusion and complexity of things, it does help prevent what would most certainly be a disastrous atomization of political power. Where the alternative result might well be a deadlock among many centers or foci of power, the American parties at least permit decision.

Furthermore, by contesting elections the American parties recruit much of the American political leadership. One needs only to run down a list of the members of the Cabinet or the Supreme Court to see how many entered public service through a political party or through partisan candidacy for office. The orderly contesting of elections enables the parties to routinize political change and especially the change of governmental leadership. More than one commentator has noted the disruptive measures that are often necessary for the changing of the guard in those countries in which no stable political parties contest in regular elections. And because the American parties pervade all governmental levels in the federal system they may recruit and elevate leadership from one level to another.

Perhaps these recruitment functions can be put another way. In complex political systems like the American some division of political labor is inevitable. Not all men have equal interests in and skills for political activity. Through the political parties we achieve an orderly selection of the political activists, a "political elite," and through party participations in elections the elite can be placed in a regular, responsible relationship to the less active, less interested electorate. By the nature of large organizations — whether they be fraternal organizations, universities, business corporations, or trade unions — an active minority will emerge to direct its affairs. So it is with government. The aggregation of power of which we have spoken demands the initiative and direction of some kind of active minority. Thus, the parties, while recruiting political leaders and office-holders, also recruit and organize the active, participating political minority in the American society.

Finally, the American parties contribute to the functioning of the American political system by providing a unifying focus in a system of vastly dispersed political authority. The basic rationale for both American federalism and the separation of powers is that a society is best able to control the exercise of political authority by scattering it. Whether these institutions do indeed control power by decentralizing and dispersing it is a question we need not explore here. But the decentralization, even fragmentation, of governmental authority is an incontestably crucial fact of American politics. To the fragmentation of the nation and the fifty states multiplied by the three-fold separation of powers in each, the two great national political parties bring a unifying force, a point of focus or center of gravity, which helps to hold the disparate fragments together. In acting as a political "adhesive" the parties bring similar traditions, interests, symbols, and issues to all the parts. They unify with an obviously limited efficiency — they often fail, for example, to bind President and Congress together in a single set of causes that can transcend the national separation of powers. But partially or totally, they *do* constitute a force for unity in an institutional tradition that divides.

PARTIES AND THE OTHER POLITICAL ORGANIZATIONS

Too much has been made of the differences between the major American parties and the other political organizations such as large, national interest groups. To be sure, if the category "political party" is to have any meaning, there must be some differences. But the differences one looks for are those between two species of the same genus rather than between two grossly different genuses.

This question of the differences between the major American parties and the other American political organizations has been explored empirically only rarely. V. O. Key in his classic study of southern politics examined the prevailing one-party systems of the American South in the 1940's and in the process asked whether the factions and cliques of a one-party system came eventually to resemble the political parties of a two-party system. The faction, however, proved to be no real substitute for the political party.

Consider the element of discontinuity in factionalism. Although conditions differ from state to state and from time to time, in many instances the battle for control of a state is fought between groups newly formed for the particular campaign. The groups lack continuity in name — as exists under a party system — and they also lack continuity in the make-up of their inner core of professional politicians or leaders. Naturally, they also lack continuity in voter support which, under two-party conditions, provides a relatively stable following of voters for each party's candidates whoever they may be.

Furthermore, the disorganized politics of factionalism, Key wrote, does not produce the desirable "unintended consequences" that party activity does. For example,

loose factional organizations are poor contrivances for recruiting and sifting out leaders of public affairs. Social structures that develop leadership and bring together like-minded citizens lay the basis for the effectuation of the majority will. Loose factions lack the collective spirit of party organization, which at its best imposes a sense of duty and imparts a spirit of responsibility to the inner core of leaders of the organization.[5]

Stability, continuity, and a sense of responsibility in their mobilizing of electoral groups mark the political parties. But whether one reads the careful scholarly analyses of Key or the more casual impressions of other observers of the parties, the context of the evaluation of the political party remains the electoral process. Nowhere in the scholarly literature on the political party can one escape the special identification of the party with the contesting of elections.

It is feckless to suggest that the major American parties monopolize the contesting of elections. Their pre-eminence as electoral organizations does not rest on such an exaggerated claim. Even though the interest group in the United States has classically eschewed electoral participation for attempts to influence the decisions of public officials after they have won office, interest groups increasingly enter the election lists. In many localities they encourage or discourage candidates, work for them within parties, contribute to party or candidate campaign funds, and help get their members to the polls. Yet it does remain true that in the aggregate the American parties are occupied with the contesting of elections in a way that interest groups and other political organizations are not. Few of the varied goals that attract men into the three sectors of the political party can be achieved without electoral victory.

It is not only the commitment to electoral activity that characterizes the political party, but the structural consequences which flow from it. The party's curious tri-partite structure — the ambiguous combination of organization and clientele, of political activists and the objects of their mobilizing — results from its electoral nature. The three party sectors are, after all, the electoral strategists, the already elected, and the electorate. One finds in the political party, therefore, a complex political organization, a second organization of the elected, and a great clientele relying on the cues and symbols the organizations control to guide its political

[5] V. O. Key, *Southern Politics* (New York: Knopf, 1949), pp. 303–304.

choices. Above all, it is this combination of organization and clientele, and its consequent variety of goals and commitment, that sets the parties aside.

Dependence on the pursuit of its goals through the electoral process has forced major decisions on the political party. Other political organizations may focus on other political avenues — the influence of political opinion through the mass media, for example, or the influence of rulemaking in administrative agencies — that require the support of only small supporting clienteles. But when a political organization chooses to work to its ends in elections, it must recruit an enormous supportive clientele. It comes to depend less on the intricate skills and maneuverings of organization *per se* and more on the mobilization of large numbers, and it thus becomes unusually dependent on and oriented toward that clientele. Party appeals must be broad and inclusive, for the party can ill afford the exclusivity and narrow range of concerns of many political organizations. In diffuseness and decentralization its structural pattern matches the pattern of elections in the localities, states, and nation of the United States. The major political party has, very simply, committed itself to the political mobilization of large numbers of citizens in large numbers of elections, and from that commitment flow most of its identifying characteristics.

In addition, the political party differs from the other political organizations in two other important ways: its commitment to political activity and its enduring stability. The major political parties operate solely as instruments of political action. Not so the interest groups and most other political organizations. They move freely and frequently from political to non-political activities and back again. The AFL-CIO, for example, seeks many of its goals and interests in non-political ways, most especially through collective bargaining. It may, however, turn to political action — to support sympathetic candidates for office or to lobby before Congress — when political avenues appear the best or the only means to achieve those goals. Every organized group in the United States is, as one observer has suggested, a "potential" political interest group.[6] And most of them make good on that potential these days as government grows and involves their interests increasingly in the political process. Still, the interest group maintains some sphere of non-political action, while the political party has on the contrary organized and recruited its members exclusively for political action.

Secondly, the major parties of virtually all the Western democracies have displayed a remarkable stability and persistence. The personal clique, the faction, the *ad hoc* campaign organization, even many interest groups, seem by contrast almost evanescent political will-of-the-wisps which appear as suddenly as they disappear. The size and the abstractness of the

[6] David B. Truman, *The Governmental Process* (New York: Knopf, 1951).

political parties, their relative independence of personalities and leadership, and their continuing symbolic strength for thousands of voters seem to assure them an impressive political longevity. And it is precisely this enduring, on-going quality which enhances their value as reference symbols. They achieve, in a way which few other American political organizations can match, an organizational and symbolic life that survives changes in leadership, issues, or clienteles.

In attempting to distinguish the political party from the other political organizations it is dangerously easy to exaggerate the differences. The other political organizations, like the parties, have identifiable organizational characteristics: lines of authority and responsibility, divisions of labor, formalized decision-making processes. Like the parties, they organize and represent groups of political interests, and often they compete with the parties in so mobilizing political power; they may even achieve a symbolic status; they too give political clues and cues to their members and "fellow-travellers." Like the parties they also put their "seal of approval" on men and policies. Some of them, indeed, such as the Americans for Democratic Action (the ADA) or the American Conservative Union, differ from the parties chiefly in size and influence. They participate in elections, propagate ideologies, and organize office-holders, and like the parties they too operate exclusively as political organizations. They do not, however, offer their names and symbols for candidates to use on the ballot. It is largely that slender difference which separates their activities and political roles from those of the parties.

So similar are the parties to some other political organizations that they resemble them more closely than they resemble the minor or "third" parties. These minor political parties — so-called because they are not electorally competitive — are only nominally electoral organizations; not even the congenital optimism of candidates can lead Socialists or Prohibitionists to expect substantial victories at the ballot. In structure, lacking local organization as most of them do, they resemble the major parties less than do the complex, nationwide interest groups. And their membership base, often related to a single issue, may be just as narrow, just as exclusively recruited, as that of most interest groups. In fact, in structure and activities interest groups such as the U.S. Chamber of Commerce and the AFL-CIO really resemble the Democrats and Republicans far more than do the Vegetarians, the Prohibitionists, and the Socialist Workers.

Definitions and concepts are often as significant for what they exclude as for what they include, and this one is no exception. This simple characterization of the American major party shares little in common with the classic definition of Edmund Burke. The political party, wrote the great Whig leader, is "a body of men united for promoting by their joint endeavors the national interests upon some particular principle on which they are all agreed." To be sure, some men may be drawn to the parties

because of ideology or issue, but no such agreement on principle exists in
the massive and diversified American parties. They are not even agreed on
the pursuit of some national interests or set of goals; many American partisans are merely united in the pursuit of public office *per se*. The Burkean
definition may, therefore, be more nearly applicable to the large American
interest group. In its emphasis on unity and the higher national interest
the Burkean prescription has seemed to some critics to suggest that anomaly, a political party "above politics," a party abjuring the special goals of
groups and rising above the contention and competition of the political
processes. It may in fact embody a non-party ideal of a political party.
Burke's often-quoted words have probably accurately described very few
democratic parties, and they certainly have never described the American
ones.

POLITICAL PARTIES IN THE AMERICAN DEMOCRACY

The American political system is more than a chastely neutral political
mechanism. It establishes, as a representative democracy, a particular distribution of political power in which large numbers of American adults
may effectively register their political demands. It rests on the democratic
assumption that majorities by choosing decision-makers or influencing
their decisions may make government responsive to their goals — that, in
short, they can affect the personnel and the behavior of the institutions of
government. Any of the parts or components of the American political
system may, then, be assessed in terms of its role and function in promoting that democratic process and its enveloping ethos. Scholars of the
American political parties have long argued that the ability of the parties
to promote that democratic representation and choice-making was far
superior to the capacity of other political organizations. Their writings on
the parties are, in fact, full of salutes to them as the "instruments" or "fa-
cilitators" of democracy.

At the most fundamental level the American parties, and those of the
other democracies, serve the democratic ethos by reaffirming and promoting its basic values. The very activities of the two gigantic and diversified
American parties promote a commitment to the democratic values of compromise, moderation, and the pursuit of limited goals. They also encourage the political activity and participation a democracy depends on. And
they reinforce the basic democratic "rules of the game" — the methods and
procedures of orderly criticism and opposition, change by the regular
electoral processes, and deference to the will of the majority. These reaf-
firmations of the democratic fundamentals the parties achieve in part by
the example of their operations, in part by the values they promote among
their followers, and in part by their clarification and simplification of political choices.

Aside from the values and attitudes they encourage, the parties offer an operating mechanism for the processes of democracy. By organizing aggregates of voters, the major American parties enable the demands and wishes of countless Americans to be transmitted with meaningful political power to the seats of governmental authority. They are mobilizers of both democratic consent and democratic dissent. By channelling choices into a few realistic alternatives, they organize the majorities by which we govern. Through their "reductionism" the average citizen, distracted often by his personal worries and limited in his background and information, can participate more meaningfully in the affairs of politics. The party is, moreover, the instrument of compromise among competing claims on public policy. While interest groups generally represent a specific, comparatively narrow interest, the party must moderate among the wide range of interests it embraces if it is not to be split and torn by the diversity of those interests.

To put the matter very briefly, the political parties have helped fashion a workable system of representation for the mass democracies of the 20th century. They have mobilized an increasingly large and diversified political citizenry into potent aggregates of consent. And after the making of public policy, they and their candidates have stood as one important focal point for the fixing of ultimate political responsibility — for the making of those *post hoc* judgments which voters make of their elected representatives in office. Indeed, the whole nature of modern democracy has been transformed by bringing representatives closer to the people and constituencies they represent, and the parties have provided a major bond in that alliance. The resulting enhancement of the power of the electorate — and the decline of the unfettered representative acting on his own values and better judgment — has helped mightily to meet the democratic expectations of this century. The parties have offered the "many" a vehicle for mobilizing their major political asset, their sheer numbers, and thereby permitted them to counter the social and economic advantages of small groups and powerful individuals. The party is above all the political organization of the "many" operating through elections, the point in the political process at which numbers are most telling.

Nothing better illustrates the relationship of the political party to a democratic polity than its very origin. The major political parties of the United States and the other Western democracies arose in the late 18th and 19th centuries as a concomitant of the spread of democratic ideologies and democratic electorates. What had been largely legislative parties expanded shortly after the beginning of the 19th century into constituency-based parties as the states expanded the male suffrage by wiping out property-owning and tax-paying qualifications for the vote. Between 1800 and 1850 the mass convention as a way of selecting party candidates replaced the legislative caucus, and state and local party organizations blossomed.

One of the leading scholars of the origins of the American parties has summarized their genesis very well: [7]

> Parties proper are, apparently, the products of certain types of social-structural conditions and ideological configurations which have come to characterize political modernization as it has taken place in western societies. The relevant social conditions appear to be those which are related to the absence or dissolution of closed, traditionalistic, and hierarchical social structures and modes of conducting politics. The relevant ideologies appear to be those which point to mass or democratic involvement or participation in the political process. In short, parties proper appear to be products of the process of modernization and the emergence of mass or democratic politics, and of democratic or plebicitarian ideologies — and at the same time to be themselves steps toward political modernization.

Thus, the political party has been the effect as well as the cause of the political participation of the great number of adults. Its rise and growth directly parallel the development of popular democracy not only in the United States, but in Great Britain as well. Shortly after the Reform Act of 1832 had added some 250,000 voters to the British electorate and eliminated some of the unrepresentative parliamentary constituencies (the "pocket" and "rotten" boroughs), the parties in the Parliament immediately set up registration associations in the constituencies to give a popular base to parliamentary campaigns for election and re-election. Those constituency associations slowly increased their ties and loyalties to the parliamentary parties to create the party structures of contemporary Britain.[8]

As the parties were being formed and shaped in the emerging democratic forces, they also helped democratize the institutions within which they worked. As agencies of the newly expanded electorate they transformed the legislature into a truly representative assembly, and at the local level they became the first public instruments for mass political participation. Even though they are nowhere mentioned in the elegant brevity of the American Constitution, the democratization of the document was in part achieved by the power of the parties to organize and effectuate the political power of the newly political and newly enfranchised electorates.

---

[7] William N. Chambers, "Party Development and Party Action: The American Origins," *History and Theory*, Vol. III (1963), p. 117. See also his book on the beginning of the American parties, *Political Parties in a New Nation* (New York: Oxford Univ. Press, 1963).

[8] For an excellent brief summary of the development of political parties, see Austin Ranney and Willmoore Kendall, *Democracy and the American Party System* (New York: Harcourt, Brace, 1956), Chapter 5. For one of the classic histories of the development of parties in Britain and the United States there is a new abridgement of M. Ostrogorski's *Democracy and the Organization of Political Parties* (New York: Anchor, 1964) edited by Seymour M. Lipset.

For an example one has only to look at the transformation of the Electoral College which party voting wrought. What began as a meeting of notables to pick a leading notable for the Presidency soon became merely the instrument for recording the presidential preferences of party-organized majorities for a party-sponsored candidate.

.   .   .

These, then, are the American political parties — immense, conglomerate, semi-public political structures in which three greatly disparate elements are bound up in the common pursuit of electoral victory. Comprised both of hyper-political activists and far less involved political clienteles, they are both conventional political organizations and cue-giving "labels" or symbols. They are not vastly different, in structure or activities, from other political organizations, and yet an aggregate of specific and peculiar characteristics sets them well apart. As pervasive as their mobilizing influence is in American politics, they remain ambiguous and almost intangible political structures. Their contradictions and even their insubstantiality in the face of their major organizing role remains one of the great anomalies of American politics.

Chapter Two

THE AMERICAN
TWO-PARTY SYSTEM

After the humiliating Republican loss in the elections of 1964 Richard Rovere, one of America's most perceptive political reporters, noted at least partly in jest the emergence of a "one-and-a-half party system." "Today, by most of the accepted standards, the Republican Party is to the Democratic Party as one is to two," he wrote.

There are now, and will be next year, two Democratic governors for every Republican governor. In the Senate, when it meets in January, the ratio will be the same. In the House, it will be slightly more favorable to the Democrats, who will outnumber the Republicans two to one with about fifteen votes to spare, which may come in handy when the weather is bad or the golfing is good. And just this morning Dr. Gallup has announced that there are two Americans who regard themselves as Democrats for every one who regards himself as a Republican — or, to be a bit more precise, fifty-three Democrats for every twenty-five Republicans.[1]

The years since 1964 have brought a rapid Republican recovery, but the observation is no less important for its relevance to a passing point in time.

Whether fully in jest or not, the Rovere observation fairly questions the meaning of the easy and customary references to the American "two-party" system. Like the deceptively simple references to "political parties," those to "party systems" flow conveniently and a bit vaguely from common political usage. But it is by no means self-evident why we acknowledge only two parties and cavalierly disregard the whole array of smaller ones. Nor is it clear what we mean by the reference to a "system" — is it merely the simultaneous presence of two parties?

[1] "Letter from Washington," *The New Yorker* (November 14, 1964), p. 235.

26

The conventional terminology of party systems is erected on two major, related premises — that parties are primarily electoral organizations, and that their electoral activities are carried out in a direct competition with other electoral parties. The designation of a one-party, two-party, five-party, or multi-party system simply indicates the number of political parties able to compete for office with some prospects of success. Its terminology rests on a distinction between the competitive "major" parties and the non-competitive "minor" parties. The party system is composed, therefore, only of the electorally competitive parties. Minor (or "third") parties such as the Vegetarians and the Socialist Workers must be excluded from it.

For all of its elegant simplicity (and, to some extent, because of it) the conventional classification of party systems has a number of significant shortcomings.

It focuses solely on one dimension of the competition among political organizations. Consequently it overlooks the possibility that the major parties may compete ideologically or programmatically with the minor parties.

By focusing only on the political parties it blocks off an artificial segment of the total range of competition among all the kinds of political organization. Even in the business of nominating and electing candidates for public office a party may face prime competition from a local interest group or political elite.

By dealing exclusively with electoral competition, it ignores any differences in organization the parties may have and centers only on the size of the party's electorate.

Finally, it tends to ignore the very implications of the word "system." It overlooks the relationships and interactions one might expect in a system and settles instead merely for the presence of competitive parties and for their presumed electoral competings.

But so ingrained in both everyday use and in the scholarly literature is this concept of the party system that one has little choice but to work within its terms.

All is not clear and unequivocal, however, even if one takes the present terminology of party system on its own terms. How is one to define the "competitive" political party? That is to some extent the issue in the Rovere sally on the emerging American one-and-one-half party system. And how are we to reconcile the obvious fact of the overall two-party competitiveness of the American party system with the equally obvious facts of substantial one-party strength in districts and constituencies within the system? Is it possible that the American two-party system is merely an artificial summation of the equal and countervailing dominance of various parts of the country by each of two powerful political parties? Unhappily, even so circumscribed an approach to the description of party systems has its serious limitations.

THE NATIONAL PARTY SYSTEM

Since the Civil War only two political parties, the Democratic and the Republican, have maintained a competitive position for control of the American Presidency and the American Congress. That fact, exceptional in itself, is, however, overshadowed by the closeness of their competition. Of the twenty presidential elections from 1888 through 1964, the two major parties each won ten.[2] Of those twenty elections only four were decided by a spread of more than 20 per cent between the popular vote of the two major parties; that is, a shift of 10 per cent of the vote would have given the other party's candidate the lead in the popular vote. And in only three of those twenty presidential elections did the winners get more than 60 per cent of the popular vote: Warren G. Harding in 1920, Franklin Roosevelt in 1936, and Lyndon Johnson in 1964. Eight of the twenty were decided by a spread of less than 7 per cent of the popular vote, and in John F. Kennedy's victory in 1960 he polled only two-tenths of one per cent of the popular vote more than did Richard M. Nixon. So close have the American presidential elections been, in fact, that Dwight D. Eisenhower's 57.4 per cent of the popular vote in 1956 was widely called a "landslide." The shade over 61 per cent with which Lyndon Johnson won in 1964 set a new record for the size of the percentage of the winning presidential candidate's popular vote.[3]

As close as the results of the presidential elections have been, those of the elections to Congress have been even closer. If we move to percentages of the two-party vote for ease of comparison (and ease of collecting data), we quickly note the remarkable balance between the aggregate votes cast for Democratic and Republican candidates for the House of Representatives from all over the United States during this century (Table 1). From 1900 through 1966 only one of the biennial elections to the House of Representatives, that of 1920, saw a difference greater than 20 percentage points in the Democratic-Republican two-party vote. Even in the years of 1936 and 1964, years of historic presidential losses, the Republican candidates for the House around the country polled more than 40 per cent of the votes for candidates for the House. The median per-

[2] However, the Democrats led the popular vote in 11 elections, losing the election of 1888 in the Electoral College despite Grover Cleveland's lead in the popular vote.

[3] The reader may note some confusion here in "political record-keeping." Note that this 61.1 per cent figure for President Johnson refers to the percentage of the total popular vote and not to the percentage of the two-party vote. Other relevant "Presidential records":

a) greatest Electoral College vote: Franklin Roosevelt in 1936: 523 electoral votes
b) greatest percentage of two-party vote: Calvin Coolidge in 1924: 65.2 per cent

Table 1

PERCENTAGE OF TWO-PARTY VOTE WON BY REPUBLICAN CANDIDATES FOR
THE PRESIDENCY AND THE HOUSE OF REPRESENTATIVES: 1900 TO 1966 *

Year	Presidential Election		House Election	
	% Republican	% Spread between R. and D. Cands.	% Republican	% Spread between R. and D. Cands.
1900	53.1%	6.2%	52.7%	5.4%
1902			51.3	2.6
1904	60.0	20.0	56.3	12.6
1906			53.5	7.0
1908	54.5	9.0	51.9	3.8
1910			50.5	1.0
1912	35.6	−28.8	42.9	−14.2
1914			49.7	− .6
1916	48.3	− 3.4	51.1	2.2
1918			54.9	9.8
1920	63.8	27.6	62.3	24.6
1922			53.6	7.2
1924	65.2	30.4	57.9	15.8
1926			58.4	16.8
1928	58.8	17.6	57.2	14.4
1930			54.1	8.2
1932	40.9	−18.2	43.1	−13.8
1934			43.8	−12.4
1936	37.5	−25.0	41.5	−17.0
1938			49.2	− 1.6
1940	45.0	−10.0	47.0	− 6.0
1942			52.3	4.6
1944	46.2	− 7.6	48.3	− 3.4
1946			54.7	9.4
1948	47.7	− 4.6	46.8	− 6.4
1950			49.9	− .2
1952	55.4	10.8	50.1	.2
1954			47.5	− 5.0
1956	57.8	15.6	49.0	− 2.0
1958			43.9	−12.2
1960	49.9	− .2	45.0	−10.0
1962			47.4	− 5.2
1964	38.7	−22.6	42.5	−15.0
1966			48.7	− 2.6

* Sources: For the data from 1900 through 1960: Donald E. Stokes and Gudmund R. Iversen, "On the Existence of Forces Restoring Party Competition," Public Opinion Quarterly, Vol. XXVI (Summer, 1962), p. 162. For the data of 1962 through 1964, the Statistical Abstract of 1965. The data for 1966 come from the Congressional Quarterly Report for May 12, 1967.

centage spread between the candidates of the two parties for the House
from 1900 through 1966 was 6.7; it was 15.6 for the presidential candidates in the same period. Perhaps even more telling, in every year except
1948 and 1960 the margin of difference between congressional candidates
was smaller than that between the presidential aspirants.

The fineness and persistence of party competition in national politics is,
therefore, apparent in even the quickest survey of recent American political history. Even more impressive, perhaps, is the resilience of the major
parties. While the parties have lapsed from closely-matched competitiveness from time to time, they have in the long run shown a remarkable
facility for setting aright those brief competitive imbalances. The Democrats recovered quickly from the disasters of the 1920's, and the Republicans confounded the pessimists by springing back from the Roosevelt
victories of the 1930's. And despite the catastrophes of 1964 the Republicans picked up 47 seats in the House in the off-year elections of 1966.

But is this aggregate record of winning and losing in national elections
what we mean by a "two-party system"? There is ample reason for doubt-
ing that it is, for in reality there are no actual national parties and national constituencies in American politics. The American national parties,
to the extent that they exist, are really loose coalitions of variously organized and virtually autonomous state parties. The national party organs
exercise almost no authority or discipline over them. Furthermore, American politics lacks a national constituency. The congressional seats are
chosen from local constituencies in elections contested by local parties on
what are frequently local issues. The President, the one apparently national official, is elected from a constituency which, as it is defined by the
procedures of the Electoral College, is really a weighted sum of the state
constituencies. And it will remain so until the President is selected by a
national popular vote.

So, in American national politics it is difficult to locate a national party
system in the strictest sense of the term. There are no national constituencies, and more importantly, there are no unified, integrated national
party organizations competing and reacting against each other. The term
"American party system" must, therefore, be used in only its broadest,
almost figurative sense. It is best thought of, in the words of its chief
critics, as "a shorthand expression for the totality of party conflict in the
United States."

The Fifty American Party Systems

Beneath the cumulative totals that express a nationwide party conflict,
however, lie the considerable differences in competitiveness from state to

---

[4] Austin Ranney and Willmoore Kendall, *Democracy and the American Party
System* (New York: Harcourt, Brace, 1956), p. 161.

state. All but obscured in the incredible closeness of the presidential elections and the aggregate vote for congressmen is the range of competitiveness in the states and localities, a range that extends from long-run,
two-party parity to traditional one-partyism and stifled competition. Especially evident is a one-partyism not apparent when one examines only
national totals. In 1964, for example, Georgia cast its electoral votes for a
Republican presidential candidate for the first time since the Civil War,
and Vermont voted for its first Democratic presidential contender in the
same 100-year span. And although one may talk of the aggregate closeness of the biennial elections to the House of Representatives, the aura of
competitiveness vanishes in part if one looks at the individual races. In
1964, for example, 51.5 per cent of the congressmen won their seats with
more than 60 per cent of the total vote; the comparable percentage in
1966 was 65.7.

If we are to speak of the varying degrees of competitiveness of the fifty
state party systems, the practical and operational problem of defining competitiveness can be postponed no longer. Logically "competitiveness" may
at any moment reflect either an assessment of the quality of past competition or a prediction of the possibilities of competitiveness in the near future. Whichever alternative one follows, the methodological problems are
considerable. One first of all must decide whether to count vote totals and
percentages or simply the offices won. Does one consider a party which
systematically garners 40 or 45 per cent of the vote, but which never wins
office, any differently from one which hovers around the 20 to 25 per cent
mark? If one is to make distinctions between parties such as these, then
where does he draw the fine line between competitiveness and non-competitiveness? At 25, 30, 35, or 40 per cent? Without settling the intellectual
merits of the dispute, one can say that as a fact an impressive number of
scholars settle for the 40 per cent figure. Then, too, one must decide
whether and how to discriminate between the party which averages 45
per cent of the vote and wins office occasionally from the party which
averages the same 45 per cent and never wins. Finally, the classifier of
parties and party systems must determine which offices to consult — the
vote for presidential candidates, for governors and senators, for the statewide officials (such as the attorney general), or for the state legislature. A
state may show strikingly different competitive patterns in its national
and its state and local politics. Arizona in the 1950's, for example, voted
twice for Eisenhower, elected a Republican governor in three of the five
elections, and twice voted for a Republican senator, Barry Goldwater.
Yet, during those years the Arizona state Senate ranged from 79 to 100
per cent Democratic, and the lower house varied from 63 to 90 per cent
Democratic.[5]

[5] These data were drawn from the *Book of the States* (Chicago: Council of State
Governments) for the years of the 1950's and 1960's.

If one shifts to estimating the present nature of party competitiveness in any state, he takes up of necessity the even more fragile skills of prediction. Any statement that Alaska, Wisconsin, Oregon, or any other state has a two-party system today may imply a prediction that in the short-run future both parties are capable of a serious bid for public office — a prediction that each party's chances of winning are substantial enough to force each to "run" against the other and thus take each other's candidates and issues seriously. The easiest way to predict the immediate future, of course, is to extrapolate from the past, but it is a dangerous game. Even a long-run plotting of the Republican vote in the Southern states would have scarcely prepared one for the presidential results of 1964. The trends of the 1940's and 1950's indicated that Tennessee or Florida, rather than Alabama or Georgia, might have gone Republican in a presidential year. Issues shift rapidly and often deceptively, and the determinants of past trends may suddenly lose their force.

Despite all of these reasons for caution and timidity, some attempt to categorize the party systems of the states is imperative. At the outset it is impossible to dismiss the possibility of multi-party systems among the American fifty. To be sure, one can find examples of them in the American experience. In Minnesota, Wisconsin, and North Dakota in the 1930's and 1940's remnants of the Progressive movement — the Progressive party in Wisconsin, the Farmer-Labor party in Minnesota, and the Non-Partisan League in North Dakota — competed with some success against the Democrats and Republicans. But in all three cases the heavy pressures of the national two-party system forced them to disband and send their loyalists into the two major parties. In these and the few other instances of statewide tri-partyism which one can cull from the recent American past, the period of tri-partyism was brief and ended with an adjustment back into two-partyism.

The range of party systems among the fifty states, then, extends only the short way from the one-party system to the competitive two-party systems. But along this brief continuum it is still difficult to discern the point at which the one variety shades into the other. Drawing on the work of two other scholars, Austin Ranney recently divided the fifty state party systems into four categories: one-party Democratic, modified one-party Democratic, modified one-party Republican, and two-party (Table 2). (No states fell into the one-party Republican groups.) The Ranney rankings are based on a composite index of the popular vote for Democratic gubernatorial candidates, the percentages of seats held by the Democrats in both houses of the state legislature, and the percentages of all the gubernatorial and state legislative terms the Democrats controlled. The data cover the years 1946 to 1963. The resulting averages of those percentages yielded scores from 1.000 (complete Democratic success) to .000 (total Republican success); the scores are reported with the rankings in Table 2. The reader should note that the rankings do not take into account the state's vote in presi-

Table 2

THE FIFTY STATES CLASSIFIED ACCORDING TO
DEGREE OF INTER-PARTY COMPETITION *

One-Party Democratic	Modified One-Party Democratic	Two-Party		Modified One-Party Republican
South Carolina (1.0000)	Virginia (.8795)	Alaska (.6767)	Pennsylvania (.4050)	Wisconsin (.2997)
Georgia (.9915)	North Carolina (.8793)	Missouri (.6603)	California (.3930)	New Hampshire (.2680)
Louisiana (.9867)	Tennessee (.8715)	Rhode Island (.6327)	Nebraska (.3875)	Iowa (.2495)
Mississippi (.9805)	Oklahoma (.8193)	Washington (.5647)	Illinois (.3847)	Kansas (.2415)
Texas (.9590)	Kentucky (.7650)	Delaware (.5420)	Idaho (.3780)	Maine (.2405)
Alabama (.9565)	Arizona (.7490)	Nevada (.5263)	Michigan (.3770)	South Dakota (.2320)
Arkansas (.9427)	West Virginia (.7223)	Massachusetts (.5227)	New Jersey (.3605)	North Dakota (.1860)
Florida (.9220)	Maryland (.7137)	Hawaii (.4897)	Indiana (.3545)	Vermont (.1760)
	New Mexico (.7023)	Colorado (.4827)	Oregon (.3545)	
		Montana (.4695)	Ohio (.3523)	
		Minnesota (.4610)	Wyoming (.3470)	
		Utah (.4605)	New York (.3173)	
		Connecticut (.4420)		

* Source: Herbert Jacob and Kenneth N. Vines, Politics in the American States (Boston: Little, Brown, 1965), p. 65.

dential elections. Inclusion of those results would, as we suggested several paragraphs ago, alter the position of states such as Arizona which have mixed patterns of competitiveness.[6]

[6] Austin Ranney, "Parties in State Politics" (chapter 3) in Herbert Jacob and Kenneth Vines (ed.), Politics in the American States (Boston: Little, Brown, 1965), pp. 63–67. The data for Alaska and Hawaii are, of course, only from 1958–1963; the rankings of Minnesota and Nebraska are based only on the results of the gubernatorial elections, since their state legislatures are chosen on a non-partisan ballot. The Ranney categories are based on those of Richard Dawson and James Robinson, "Inter-Party Competition, Economic Variables, and Welfare Policies in the American States," Journal of Politics, Vol. XXV (1963), pp. 265–289. For other measures see V. O. Key, American State Politics (New York: Knopf, 1956), pp. 97–104, and Joseph A. Schlesinger, "A Two-Dimensional Scheme for Classifying the States According to Degree of Inter-Party Competition," American Political Science Review, Vol. XLIX (1955), pp. 1120–1128.

The complexities of party competition, however, are vastly greater than such indices, useful as they are, would suggest. An even spread of competitiveness rarely characterizes the politics of a state all the way from the election of presidential electors down to local officials. For example, Illinois in 1960 gave a bare .2 per cent more of its popular vote to Kennedy than Nixon, and yet 52 per cent of its congressmen were elected in that same year by 60 per cent or more of the vote. Or to concentrate on variations within state politics, gubernatorial elections generally reflect a higher measure of two-party competition than do the elections to the state legislature. Some 64 governors were elected or re-elected in the years 1960–62, and 86 per cent of them were elected with less than 60 per cent of the vote. Yet in early 1963 the state legislatures elected in the same period revealed a partisan composition that belied the implications of competitiveness one might draw from the elections of governors. In less than one-quarter of both the upper and the lower houses of the state legislatures did the percentage of Democratic legislators fall between 40 and 59 per cent (Table 3).[7] To be sure, some of the lack of partisan balance in the American legislatures can be explained by malapportionment, and some is doubtless the product of masterful gerrymandering. Yet with all allowances made, the patterns of competitiveness these data suggest are not those suggested by the data from the gubernatorial elections of the same time.

Table 3

Size of Democratic Contingent in 48 American
State Legislatures: 1963

Percentage Democratic	Upper House	Lower House
0– 20%	1	1
20– 39	10	11
40– 59	10	11
60– 79	13	12
80–100	14	13
	48*	48*

* *The total is only 48 because the states of Minnesota and Nebraska have non-partisan state legislatures.*

Thus, it is difficult to speak even of a state party system. Each one is, on closer inspection, an aggregate of different competitive patterns. It is not at all unusual for a party which wins most of the statewide elections to

[7] The data on the governors were drawn from Richard M. Scammon (ed.), *America Votes 5* (Pittsburgh: Univ. of Pittsburgh Press, 1964); those on the legislatures were taken from the *Book of the States* for 1964–1965.

have trouble filling its party ticket in some local elections. Those pockets of one-partyism may reflect any number of causes: local traditions, powerful local personages, gerrymandered pockets of party strength, local homogeneity of the electorate, or variations in party organization and resources. Powerful office-holders such as incumbent senators can use a long term and the advantage of office (e.g., status, publicity, office staff, and campaign funds) to build a personal following independent of party strength. They may and often do for the rest of their careers fend off competition and insulate themselves from the patterns of normally competitive politics in their states. In fact, nothing dampens two-party competition more effectively than the power of incumbency, especially when it is exercised in a small and homogeneous constituency.

THE CAUSES AND CONDITIONS OF TWO-PARTY SYSTEMS

Despite deviations to one-partyism, the American party system has been and is in its broad outlines a two-party system. For beyond all subtle variations in competition and despite instances of local one-partyism, there is the inescapable and crucial fact that almost all partisan political conflict in the United States has been channelled, however unevenly, through two great and enduring political parties. They rise and fall, they establish their own seats of strength, they endure their local weaknesses — but no political party since the Civil War has challenged their dualism. Perhaps even more remarkable is the fact that one does not easily find another democracy in which two parties have for so long contained the competitive politics of the country. Even in Great Britain, arch-progenitor of dual parties, the Conservatives, Liberals, and Labourites have remained in competition since the turn of the century. Despite its present greatly weakened position, the Liberal party refuses to die, winning twelve Parliamentary seats as recently as 1966 on 8 per cent of the popular vote.

The rareness of the two-party system and its dominance in American politics have together attracted a remarkable expenditure of scholarly effort. The problem is the obvious one: why should this one political system among so many others develop the two-party system? In the interests of an orderly attack on the problem one may place the most important explanations into four chief groups: the institutional, the dualist, the cultural, and the consensual.

INSTITUTIONAL THEORIES

By far the most widespread of the explanations of the two-party system is the one which associates it with electoral and governmental institutions. In part it argues that single member, plurality electoral systems are related to party dualism and that multi-member constituencies and proportional representation accompany multi-party systems. Plurality election in a single-member district means simply that the one candidate with the largest number of votes wins the seat. There is no second, third, or fourth prize for the trailing parties. In a system of proportional representation a party polling 20 per cent or so of a nation's votes may capture close to 20 per cent of the legislative seats; the main purpose of proportional representation is to guarantee minorities a measure of representation roughly equivalent to their strength. The same 20 per cent would win far fewer seats than that in the American plurality electoral system. It might in fact carry none.[8] The American election system offers no reward of office for losing parties, and so the theory goes, the discouragements of repeated inabilities to gain pluralities weed out the chronic minority parties.

Many of the institutional theorists, furthermore, concentrate their argument on the importance of the single, national executive. The American Presidency and the governorships, the main prizes of American politics, fall only to parties that can win pluralities. On the contrary, a Cabinet in a European nation may be formed by a coalition which includes the representatives of minority parties. In the palmiest days of multi-partyism in the French Third and Fourth Republics, for example, a party winning 10 or 15 per cent of the national vote could and did at times capture the premiership. Again, in countries with the single national executive the nature of the reward favors the strongest competitors. But beyond the loss of the executive office, the minor party is denied the national leadership, the focus of the national campaign, the national spokesmen which so increasingly dominate the politics of the democracies. The necessity to contend for a national executive, in other words, works against the local or regional party that may even elect candidates in its own bailiwick.[9]

DUALIST THEORIES

The dualists maintain that an underlying duality of interests in the American society has sustained the American two-party system. V. O. Key suggests that the initial sectional tension between the Eastern financial and commercial interests and the interests of the Western frontiersmen stamped itself on the parties and fostered a two-party competition in the incipient stages of the American parties. Later the early dualism shifted to the North-South conflict over the issue of slavery and the Civil War, and then

[8] Large numbers of states do have multi-member districts for one or both houses of the state legislature; see Maurice Klain, "A New Look at the Constituencies: The Need for a Recount and a Reappraisal," *American Political Science Review*, Vol. XLIX (1955), pp. 1105–1119. The fact that these districts have not altered the two-party system suggests that the principle of plurality election (rather than multi-member districting) is the operative one.

[9] The institutional theorists are best represented by Maurice Duverger, *Political Parties* (New York: Wiley, 1954) and by E. E. Schattschneider, *Party Government* (New York: Rinehart, 1942).

to the present urban-rural or socio-economic status divisions.[10] A related line of argument points to a "natural dualism" within democratic institutions: party in power versus party out of power, government versus opposition, pro and anti the status quo, and even the ideological dualism of liberal and conservative. Social and economic interests or the very processes of a democratic politics — or both — thus reduce the political contestants to two great camps and that resulting dualism gives rise to two political parties.

CULTURAL THEORIES

This school of explanation in many ways smacks of the older, largely discredited "national character" theories. Most simply, it maintains that the United States or Britain have nurtured two-party systems because of their "political maturity" or their "genius for government." More modestly, it attributes the two-party systems to the development of a political culture which accepts the necessity of compromise, the wisdom of short-term pragmatism, and the avoidance of unyielding dogmatism. The Americans and Britons are, in other words, willing to make the kinds of accommodations necessary to bring their extensive and varied citizenries into two commodious and omnibus political parties. Then as they develop the dual parties, their political cultures also develop the favorable attitudes and norms which endorse the two-party system as a most desirable end in itself.

SOCIAL CONSENSUS THEORIES

Finally, the American party system has been explained in terms of a wide-sweeping American social consensus. Despite a heterogeneous cultural heritage and society, Americans achieve a notable degree of consensus on the fundamentals which divide other societies. Virtually all Americans accept the prevailing social, economic, and political institutions; they accept the Constitution and its governmental apparatus, the regulated, free enterprise economy, and (perhaps to a lesser extent) current American patterns of social status and class. In the traditional multi-party countries such as France and Italy substantial chunks of political opinion favor radical changes in those and other basic institutions — with programs that support fundamental constitutional changes, the nationalization of the economy, or the disestablishment of the Church. Whether because they were spared feudalism and its class rigidities or because of a fortuitously expanding economic and geographic frontier, Americans have escaped the division on fundamentals that racks the other democracies and gives rise

[10] See, for example, V. O. Key, *Politics, Parties, and Pressure Groups,* 5th ed. (New York: Crowell, 1964), pp. 229ff, and James C. Charlesworth, "Is Our Two-Party System Natural?" *Annals,* American Academy of Political and Social Science, Vol. CCLIX (1948), pp. 1–9.

to large numbers of irreconcilable political divisions. Since the matters which divide Americans are of secondary concern — often they involve means to agreed-on ends or goals — the compromises necessary to bring them into one of the two major parties are easier to make.[11]

In appraising these explanations of two-partyism — and of the American two-party system in particular — one has to ask some searching questions. Are the factors proposed in these explanations *causes* or are they, indeed, results or effects of the two-party system? The chances are considerable that they are, at least in part, results. Certainly two competitive parties will choose and perpetuate electoral systems that do not offer entree to minor parties. So will they also channel opinion into alternatives, reducing and forcing the system's complexities into their dual channels. The two-party system will also create, foster and perpetuate the political values and attitudes which justify and protect itself. It will even foster some measure of social consensus by denying political voice to dissident movements which challenge the great consensus of the status quo.

Although they may be results or effects of the two-party system, these related phenomena are also likely to be causal. But if they are, why has the two-party system been such a comparatively rare phenomenon? If single-member constituencies and plurality elections explain American two-partyism, why did they not produce a similar outcome in Third Republic France? Certainly, too, the American society is not the first to have an overriding duality of interests in its politics. The socio-economic class divisions between "haves" and "have-nots" have plagued no small number of democracies. The implication seems clear that no single one of these "theories" can by itself explain the virtual uniqueness of the American party system.

At the risk of a fence-straddling electicism one may venture that all four categories of explanation can illuminate the development of the American party system. No one of them need exclude the impact of any other. Their special and unique combination has produced the special and unique American two-party system. At the root of the explanation lies the basic, long-run American consensus on basic beliefs and attitudes. No deep rifts over the kind of economy, society, or government we are to have have marked our politics; more than one European observer has remarked on the resulting curiously non-ideological character of American politics. Consensus, too, has been the result of American education and social assimilation, aided, of course, by two majoritarian parties inhospitable to challenges to that consensus.

Lacking cause or reason for profoundly ideological divisions and disagreeing on few fundamentals, Americans were easily formed into two con-

[11] See Leslie Lipson, "The Two-Party System in British Politics," *American Political Science Review*, Vol. XLVII (1953), pp. 337–358, and Frank J. Sorauf, *Political Parties in the American System* (Boston: Little, Brown, 1964), Chapter 2.

glomerate, majority-seeking political parties. The institutions of American
government — single-member constituencies, plurality elections, and the
single, national executive, especially — were free to exert their power to
limit the parties to two without having to repulse the countervailing
pressures from ideological conviction or social division. So, too, were the
dualisms of "ins" and "outs," for in the absence of deeply-felt ideologies, a
pragmatic, heterogeneous opposition to the party in power could develop.
And the very existence — and successful operation — of the American
party system fostered the values of moderation, compromise, and political
pragmatism which ensure its perpetuation. It created deep loyalties within
the American public to one party or the other, and deep loyalties to the
genius of the two-party system itself. Small wonder, then, that the force
of an entrenched, on-going, two-party system has been able to override
challenges to its dominating dualism.

Excursions into One-Partyism

The closeness of national, cumulative two-party competition often dazzles
the beholder and obscures the statewide and local pockets of one-partyism
in the United States. The states of the Deep South until recently spent
very close to their own "four score and seven" years as the country's most
celebrated and most taken-for-granted area of one-party domination. Much
the same could be said for the rock-like and rock-ribbed Republicanism
of Maine, New Hampshire, and Vermont. And scattered throughout the
country are the thousands of one-party cities, towns, and counties in
which City Hall or the County Court House comes perilously close to being the property of one party or the other. Just as important as the question of the causes of the two-party system is the question of the occasions
of one-partyism within it.

One-partyism in the context of broader two-party competitiveness normally reflects a "fault" in the distribution of loyalties which characterize
the electorates of the two national, competitive parties. Since the 1930's
the American parties have, especially in national elections, divided the
American electorate roughly along lines of socio-economic status — a point
that will be developed later at some length. Suffice it here to note that
Democratic loyalties have been far more common among ethnic, racial, and
religious minority groups, the urban workers, and lower socio-economic
status (SES) groups in general. The Republicans have on the other hand
drawn a disproportionate number of loyalists from higher status and rural
groups. One partyism may, first of all, result from some potent local basis
of party loyalty which overrides the SES dualism. In the classic one-
partyism of the American South, traditional regional loyalties long over-
rode the factors that were dividing Americans into two parties in most of
the rest of the country. Reaction to the Republican party as the party of

abolition, of Lincoln, of the Civil War, and of the hated Reconstruction was so pervasive, even three generations after the fact, that the impact of the SES division was precluded. Even today, there are those who wonder if the South may be in the process of trading-in a one-partyism based on the events of the 19th century for a new one-partyism based on more recent racial antagonism. In either event, it would be a one-partyism based on isolation from the factors which normally underlie the national two-party competitiveness. On a similar but smaller scale, the last Republican machine in Philadelphia maintained control of the city through the 1930's and 1940's with a politics of patronage and reward that stopped SES competitiveness at the city line. Other local one-party domination reflects the influences of local personages and purely local issues.

One-partyism may result, secondly, from a maldistribution of the SES characteristics. The local constituency especially may be too small to afford a "perfect sample" of nationally competitive politics. Hence the non-competitiveness of congressional districts such as the "safe" Democratic districts of the older, lower-middle-class neighborhoods of the metropolitan centers and the "safe" Republican districts of the more fashionable and spacious suburbs. In other words, the more heterogeneous a representation of the characteristics that go to make up socio-economic status, the more likely the district is to foster competitiveness. By and large it is the homogeneous districts that are the one-party districts, and it is apt to be the smaller sets of districts which are the least competitive, since by reason of their size they are likely to be inaccurate, homogeneous "samples" of the total electorate.

Empirical studies of the incidence of one-partyism suggest, however, that its causes are more complex than these generalizations would indicate. Competitiveness is associated with general socio-economic diversity in the constituency — especially to urbanism and its concomitants (industrialization, higher income levels, and ethnic and religious diversity). Yet the relationships are not always strong or dramatic.[12] For one thing, a homogeneous district cut, so to speak, from the middle range of SES fac-

[12] For an introduction to the study of the correlates of competitiveness in the American party system see: the Ranney chapter in Jacob and Vines, *Politics in the American States*, pp. 67–70; V. O. Key, *American State Politics* (New York: Knopf, 1956), pp. 227–246; Heinz Eulau, "The Ecological Basis of Party Systems: The Case of Ohio," *Midwest Journal of Political Science*, Vol. I (1957), pp. 125–135; David Gold and John R. Schmidhauser, "Urbanization and Party Competition: The Case of Iowa," *Ibid.*, Vol. IV (1960), pp. 62–75; Phillips Cutright, "Urbanization and Competitive Party Politics," *Journal of Politics*, Vol. XXV (1963), pp. 552–564; Thomas W. Casstevens and Charles O. Press, "The Context of Democratic Competition in American State Politics," *American Journal of Sociology*, Vol. LXVIII (1963), pp. 536–543; and Robert Golembiewski, "A Taxonomic Approach to State Political Party Strength," *Western Political Quarterly*, Vol. XI (1958), pp. 494–513. The reader who explores this literature should be aware of the shifting definitions of both competition and urbanness and of the difference between competitiveness of the states and competitiveness of units (e.g., counties) within a single state.

tors is apt to be more competitive than an equally homogeneous district at either the top or the bottom of the SES spectrum. Then, too, in counties and localities within states the patterns of competitiveness may have little to do with the patterns of national SES politics; they may instead reflect the influences of local personages, of local traditions, of local political conflict such as that between a dominant local industry and its disgruntled employees.

Those empirical studies suggest, furthermore, that one-partyism in a two-party system may be related to factors other than the distribution and loyalties of parties in the electorate. A single dominant party may shore up its supremacy, for instance, by carefully calculated legislative apportionment and gerrymanders. In the past the Southern Democrats stifled potential competitiveness by artificially restricting the electorate. In other cases majority parties have supported non-partisanship in local elections as a way of drawing on their one-party consensus. Even by separating state and national elections a dominant state party may deny a futile opponent the aid of its national candidate's coattails. In addition to these institutional buttresses to one-partyism, of course, there are the normal processes of education and social conformity which work against the development of two-party competition. That force of conformity, a number of observers have argued, works especially against competitiveness in the closely-knit, socially sensitive world of American suburbia.

The American party system, therefore, is made up of two electorally competitive parties, which is really to say that it is formed by two parties with stable, fairly equal parties in the electorate. The active, initiating sectors of the party, the party organization and the party in government, recruit and enlist the support of those electorates with assorted appeals — with programs, issues, candidates, personalities, traditional ties, records of past performance, and a generalized "image." But these party sectors compete within restricting limits and conditions, and frequently in some area or locality one party works at considerable competitive disadvantage which it never manages to overcome. Then one-party domination results or persists.

The competitive disadvantages a party faces may begin with immobile electorates. Voters may not be easily moved from their attachments to a party, even though the reasons for the original attachment have long passed. A party trying to pull itself into competitiveness may also find itself caught organizationally in a vicious circle of impotence. Its inability to win elections limits its ability to recruit organizational resources, including manpower, because as a chronic loser it offers so little chance for the achievement of political goals. It may also find that the majority party has used its power to create disadvantages by altering the rules of the electoral contest; it may have gerrymandered legislative districts, for example. But above all it may find itself without an effective appeal to the electorate. The Republican party in the South, for example, found for many years that the Democrats had pre-empted the viable political issues in that region.

Today the would-be competitive party finds the competitive disadvantage taking another form: the formation of party loyalties in the electorate along lines that are determined by national or state-wide political debate. A national politics of class or socio-economic status, for instance, may offer the local Democratic party little competitive opportunity in an affluent, upper-class suburb. Increasingly national or state-wide politics thus may rob the local party organization of the chance to establish its own competitiveness based on its own issues, personalities, and traditions. To the extent that political debate, political loyalties, and political party identifications are centered on and grow out of national politics, patterns of competitiveness and lack of it may in part be determined for the local party organizations.

THE "ALSO-RANS" — THIRD OR MINOR PARTIES

The colorful personalities and the often eccentric issues of the American minor parties have surrounded them with an endlessly diverting political lore. In the often portentous seriousness of American politics it may reassure us to think of a political party devoted to the moral superiority of the vegetable. It may even amuse us that Bishop Bill Rogers of the Theocratic Party sounds Jerico's trump of doom at the walls of courthouses all over Mid-America. And in a politics almost completely divorced from ideologies and systematic public philosophy, serious students have understandably been attracted by the political conscience of parties such as the Progressives or the American Socialists. While the decline of the third parties may occasion no disruption — and maybe even no notice — in the American party system, there is no doubt that our political literature will be considerably less lively without them.[13]

The minor or third parties — the terms are used interchangeably — are in many ways the rejects of an electorally oriented two-party system. The very looseness with which we customarily use the term "third" party to designate all minor parties may indicate that third place is as good (or bad)

[13] The literature on American third parties is rich and varied. Among the best are: Murray S. Stedman and S. W. Stedman, *Discontent at the Polls* (New York: Columbia Univ. Press, 1950); John D. Hicks, *The Populist Revolt* (Minneapolis: Univ. of Minnesota Press, 1931); Richard Hofstadter, *The Age of Reform* (New York: Knopf, 1955); David A. Shannon, *The Socialist Party of America* (New York: Macmillan, 1955); Robert L. Morlan, *Political Prairie Fire: The Non-Partisan League, 1915–1922* (Minneapolis: Univ. of Minnesota Press, 1955); K. M. Schmidt, *Henry A. Wallace: Quixotic Crusade 1948* (Syracuse: Syracuse Univ. Press, 1960); and H. P. Nash, *Third Parties in American Politics* (Washington: Public Affairs Press, 1959).

as last place in a two-party system. The minor parties freely accept their electoral failures, for they have by their very nature chosen ideological principle over electoral success. They have refused to make the pragmatic compromises and accommodations which working within a major party would entail. They know they have in most cases renounced the rewards of victory, for not even in their moments of wildest fantasy can the Prohibitionists or Socialist Workers hope for success at the polls. By choice and by consequence of that choice they are pre-eminently ideological parties in a party system ruled and dominated by the desire to win public office. Their commitment to program and interest, and the consequent narrowing of their popular appeal, often gives them more in common with interest groups than with the Democratic and Republican parties.

Table 4

POPULAR VOTES CAST FOR MINOR PARTIES AND UNPLEDGED SLATES IN 1960 AND 1964 PRESIDENTIAL ELECTIONS *

Parties: 1960	Vote: 1960	Parties: 1964	Vote: 1964
Socialist Labor	47,522	Socialist Labor	45,186
Prohibition	46,203	Prohibition	23,267
National States Rights	44,977	Socialist Worker	32,705
Socialist Workers	40,165	Constitution	5,060
Constitution	18,162	National States Rights	6,953
Conservative	8,708	Universal	19
Conservative	4,204		
Tax Cut	1,767		
Independent Afro-Amer.	1,485		
Constitution	1,401		
Scattered	2,377	Scattered	12,743
Minor Party Total	216,978	Minor Party Total	125,933
Unpledged slates	286,359	Unpledged slates	210,732
Total Minor-Unpledged	503,337	Total Minor-Unpledged	336,665

* Sources: for 1960, America Votes 5; for 1964, Congressional Quarterly Weekly Report (Number 13, part 1, March 26, 1965). The counting and collection of votes other than those for the major party candidates leaves a great deal to be desired; especially difficult to explain is the large number of "scattered votes." In 1960, also, the Conservative and Constitution parties are listed twice because two separate sets of candidates ran under that name in different states.

A brief glance at the presidential election data of 1960 and 1964 suggests the range and impact of minor party activity these days in American national politics (Table 4). While the 1960 vote for identifiable minor parties was small (216,978), it did add up to more than the 118,550 separating the two major party candidates, thus denying Kennedy a majority of the total popular vote. And in two states (Illinois and New Jersey) the total minor party vote was greater than the Kennedy margin over Nixon. That was the electoral impact of the minor parties in an extraordinarily close presidential election in which only .2 of one per cent separated the popular vote totals of the two major party candidates. But the fact remains that of all the minor parties competing in 1960, the most successful, the Socialist Labor party, polled only 47,522 votes, or a miniscule .07 per cent (7 of 10,000). In a city of 500,000 such as Cincinnati, Ohio, that would mean an average of 350 people. In 1964 the minor parties reached something of a nadir, accounting by themselves for only 125,933 of the 70,642,497 votes cast — less than .2 of one per cent. In the Johnson landslide it made no perceptible difference.

It would be a mistake to treat the minor parties as if they were indistinguishable except for their particular program or ideology. They differ as well in origin, in purpose, and in function, and American political history of the past 100 years affords a rich variety of their activity with which to illustrate these differences.

While it is true, first of all, that the minor parties are parties of ideology and issue, they differ in the scope of that commitment. The narrow, highly specific commitment of the Prohibitionist and Vegetarian parties is apparent in their names. In the 1840's, too, the Liberty party and its successor, the Free Soil party, campaigned largely on the single issue of the abolition of slavery. At the other extremes one finds the parties of the broadest ideological commitments — the Marxist parties and the recent profusion of Conservative parties, for example — whose program is one of major reconstruction of social, economic, and political institutions; so total in fact, is their ideology that they do not recognize the separability or autonomy of those institutions. In the middle ground between specific issues and total ideologies, the examples are infinitely varied. The farmer-labor parties of economic protest — Greenback, Populist, and Progressive parties — ran on an extensive program of government regulation of the economy (especially of economic "bigness") and government social welfare legislation. The Progressive party of 1948 — at least that part of it separate from the Communist party — combined a program of social reform and civil liberties with a foreign policy of friendship with the Soviet Union and reduction of Cold War tensions.

The minor parties differ, too, in their origin. Some were literally imported into the United States. Much of the early Socialist party strength in the United States came from the freethinkers and radicals who fled Europe after the failures of the Revolutions of 1848. Socialist strength in cities such as Milwaukee, New York, and Cincinnati reflected the concentrations of liberal German immigrants there. Other parties — especially the Granger and Populist parties and their successors — were parties of indigenous social protest, born of social inequality and economic hardship on the marginal farmlands of Middle America. Others among the minor parties began as splinters or factions of one of the major parties. The Gold

Democrats of 1896, the Progressives of 1912, and the Dixiecrats of 1948 come to mind. So great were their objections to the platform and candidate of their parent parties that the Progressives and Dixiecrats contested the presidential elections of 1912 and 1948 with their own slates and programs.

Finally, the third parties differ in their tactics and their *raison d'être*. For some their mere existence stands as a protest against what they believe is the limited choice and unqualified support of the status quo which the major parties afford. Operating as a political party offers a reasonably effective educational opportunity — the publicity of the ballot is good, and with it often goes mass-media attention the party could not otherwise hope for. But others among the minor parties have serious electoral ambitions. Often their goal is local, although the day seems long past when a minor party might control an American city, as the Socialists did, or entire state, as the Progressives did. More realistically today, they may hope to hold a balance of power between the major parties in the manner of the Liberals in New York. In the 1965 mayoral election, for instance, John Lindsay's vote on the Republican ticket was less than that of his Democratic opponent; his vote reached the necessary plurality only with the addition of the votes he won in the Liberal party column. Or a party may, as did the Dixiecrats of 1948, play for the biggest stakes of all — the Presidency. The Dixiecrats hoped that by carrying a number of Southern states they might prevent both the Truman and Dewey tickets from winning the necessary majority of votes in the Electoral College and thus throw the stalemated election into the House of Representatives. Only President Truman's surprising strength in the farm states offset his loss of New York (caused by the Wallace Progressives) and thwarted their plans.

Recent presidential elections have seen the entry of a new variety of minor party: the "non-party" minor parties. Found chiefly in the southern states, they have been dissident movements within the Democratic party which have, however, refused to run as separate parties on the ballot. They have instead exploited two other strategies. In some instances they have attempted to run their candidates (rather than those chosen by the party's national convention) as the official presidential candidates of the Democratic party. The only four states which J. Strom Thurmond carried in 1948 for the Dixiecrats were those (Alabama, Louisiana, Mississippi, and South Carolina) in which he, rather than Truman, ran on the ballot as the official candidate of the Democratic party. In other cases these party movements have run unpledged slates of presidential electors. In 1960 unpledged slates ran in Louisiana as a States Rights party and in Mississippi as the Democratic party (although there was another Democratic party ticket pledged to Kennedy). In 1964 another unpledged Democratic slate of electors ran in Alabama and successfully prevented the Johnson-Humphrey forces from appearing on the Alabama ballot!

These are essentially splinter movements of the major parties which seek temporary tactical advantage in three facts of American political institutions: the inability of the national parties to control the use of their name and symbols in the states, the freedom of presidential electors to support whomever they wish in the formal balloting in the Electoral College, and the requirement that the presidential winner get a majority of the votes in the Electoral College.

The variety is endless, and the details are colorful. But what have the minor parties contributed to the American political processes? The answer, to be candid, is that they have not assumed the importance which the attention lavished on them might suggest. "More interesting than influential" must be the verdict.

One line of argument has persistently maintained that the minor parties' early adoption of unpopular programs and innovations has ultimately forced the major parties to adopt them. Its proponents point, in illustration, to the platforms of the Socialist party in the years before the 1930's. The major point at issue is whether or not the Socialists' advocacy of the measures for twenty or thirty years had anything to do with their enactment in the New Deal years of the 1930's. There is unfortunately no way of testing or proving what might have been the case had there been no Socialist party. But the evidence suggests that the major parties grasp new programs and proposals in their "time of ripeness" — when large numbers of Americans have, and when grasping them, therefore, becomes politically useful to the parties. In their prior "maturing" time new issues need not depend on minor parties for their advocacy. Interest groups, the mass media, influential individuals, and currents or factions within the major parties may perform the propagandizing role, often more effectively than a minor party. More than one commentator has in this regard noted that the cause of prohibition in the United States was far more effectively served by interest groups such as the Anti-Saloon League than by the Prohibition party.

There remains, however, the impact the minor parties have had on elections. Increasingly that impact depends both on the nature of major party competition and the distribution of strength of the minor party. Magnitude of strength alone is beyond them; since the Civil War only three minor party candidates for the Presidency have polled more than 10 per cent of the popular vote.[14] We have already mentioned the strategic facts which maximized the opportunities of the Dixiecrats in 1948: regional concentration in the South, the close competition of the two major parties, and the complicating presence (especially in New York) of the Wallace Progressives. In 1912 the impact of the Bull Moose Progressives was sufficient to cut sharply into regular Republican (Taft) strength and permit

---

[14] They were James B. Weaver (1892: Populist), Theodore Roosevelt (1912: Progressive), and Robert M. La Follette (1924: Progressive).

Woodrow Wilson to enter the White House with less than 40 per cent of the popular vote. In national elections, in fact, significant impact has been largely limited to minor parties which were a splinter of a major party. Increasingly, too, the electoral power of the minor party in the states and localities depends on these special strategic cases in which the minor party can make itself a shifting weight between two massive, finely balanced major parties.

WHITHER THE AMERICAN TWO-PARTY SYSTEM?

In 1960, at the urging of its seven-time candidate for the Presidency, Norman Thomas, the Socialist party of the United States decided not to enter the presidential election race. It chose instead to concentrate its work on less expensive and more promising ways of popularizing its programs. Just four years later in the middle of a national presidential sweep by Lyndon B. Johnson, Alabama delivered its electoral votes to Barry Goldwater (with 69.5 per cent of the state's popular vote), elected Republicans in five of the state's eight congressional districts, and even sent a handful of Republicans to the state legislature. Clearly, important changes are afoot in the American party system when Republicans flourish in Alabama and when this century's most venerable and persistent minor party withdraws from the presidential sweepstakes.

To begin, the minor parties are clearly in a state of advanced decline. Perhaps at no time in all of American history have they been of less influence than they are now. Since 1924 no organized third party has carried a single state in a presidential election.[15] And in the states and the localities the minor parties continue to dwindle in strength. In the post-war period not a single minor party has threatened to carry a major state office in the United States, and third party mayors such as Socialists Frank Zeidler of Milwaukee and Jasper McLevy of Bridgeport, Connecticut, have found no successors.[16]

In part the decline of the minor parties reflects the higher hurdles they now face as electoral parties. A number of states — often to discourage the Communist party in the post-war years — have made it more difficult for minor parties to get on the ballot. Some have raised the minimum number of votes a party must poll in order to qualify automatically for ballot space at the next election, or they have raised the number of signatures a party must collect as the alternative way of staying on the ballot. Campaigning, too, has become more expensive, especially in those campaigns using appeals carried through the mass media. Faced with greater costs,

---

[15] In 1948 J. Strom Thurmond carried four states, but he won them as the officially listed candidate of the state's Democratic parties; in 1960 the major parties failed to carry some electors from Alabama and Mississippi, but the winners in all cases ran on unpledged slates.

[16] Both, it should be noted, ran officially in non-partisan municipal elections.

the minor parties find it harder and harder to raise money. Finally, amid these discouragements the spread of the direct primary in this century has given political dissidents the alternative of capturing a state or local organization of a major party rather than striking out on their own. The La Follette Progressives from about 1910 to 1930 in Wisconsin controlled the Republican primary most of the time and never had to set up their own political party until the 1930's. The Non-Partisan League of North Dakota worked within the Republican party of that state for the full span of its influence.

But more fundamentally the minor party has been the inevitable victim of gross and important changes in the American society. Almost all of the effective minor party activity of the past century has been intensely "provincial." The minor parties have each been concentrated in one section or region, in a city or two, of the country. Restrictions on immigration, however, have spelled the end of imported centers of minor partyism, such as the Socialist enclaves of New York, Milwaukee, and Cincinnati. And the growing nationalization of life in the United States has obliterated those regional identifications and conditions that underlay most of the third parties of economic protest. Local, provincial loyalties, interests and appeals have lost out in a mobile, migrating society and in a society which receives the same political messages via the same radio and television networks, the same magazines, and the same press services and syndicated columnists. And in this nationalization of American life a party's national image and national leaders increasingly dominate the responses of voters — to the obvious disadvantage of the locally-rooted minor party which has no national "presence" and no candidates with national visibility.

The second obvious trend in the American party system has been its increasing competitiveness. It is probably safe to say that in national and state-wide politics we are in the time of the most intense, evenly-spread, two-party competitiveness of the last 100 years. There are no regions of the country, and very few individual states, that can, in terms of the short-run electoral future, be thought of as one-party areas. Even the once-solid Democratic South is solid no more. In 1964 the Republicans carried Alabama, Georgia, Louisiana, Mississippi, and South Carolina, won seven congressional seats in those states, and offered substantial competition in a number of other districts. To take the longer view, Presidents have been winning increasingly with popular vote percentages that vary less and less from one state to another. Table 5 indicates that the standard deviations of the President's popular vote in the states from his national average have been diminishing in this century.[17] In other words, Presidents are no

---

[17] The standard deviation is a measure of the distance of the dispersal of items around the average. It discriminates, therefore, among the dispersals of the following three series: 3, 6, 9; 4, 6, 8; and 5, 6, 7. Even though the means and the medians of the three series would be identical (6), the standard deviations would decline in the order in which the three series are listed.

longer carrying some states by fat margins while losing others in a similarly lopsided way. As the overwhelming votes of the one-party states are
eliminated, they tend instead to pull more nearly uniform vote percentages all across the country.

Table 5

STANDARD DEVIATIONS OF PRESIDENTIAL PERCENTAGES OF THE
POPULAR VOTE IN THE STATES: 1896 THROUGH 1964

Year	Standard Deviation	Year	Standard Deviation
1896	17.5%	1932	14.0%
1900	14.0	1936	12.6
1904	18.8	1940	13.4
1908	14.9	1944	12.3
1912	15.8	1948	9.8
1916	13.4	1952	8.5
1920	16.1	1956	8.3
1924	16.0	1960	5.8
1928	13.5	1964	10.3

The reasons for this spread of major party competitiveness are not un-
related to those for the decline of minor parties. The same nationalization
of life and politics in the United States which threatens locally-based
minor parties also makes it difficult for one major party to maintain its
dominance — as did the Democrats in the South — on appeals and traditions different from the two-party battle in the rest of the country. Furthermore, the social and economic conditions for one-partyism (chiefly
SES homogeneity at present) are also disappearing. Fading especially are
the political monopolies of powerful groups which once dominated the
politics of a single state from a base in cotton, copper, oil, silver, or
organized labor. As Americans move about the country, as industry comes
to formerly agrarian states, as affluence softens the homogeneity of the
metropolitan centers, each state becomes a better sample of the diversity
of life and interests which undergirds the competition between the two
major parties. A combination of national mass media and national political
leaders also brings the symbols and dialectics of Democratic-Republican
conflict to all corners of the country.

Thus the party electorates are increasingly recruited to the parties by
the appeals of national candidates and issues — and regardless of whatever
special appeals the local party organization may make. State party organizations and their leaders cannot hold out against the political issues and
images which engulf the rest of the country; they cannot set up an independent, competitive sub-system. As a result of that fact a "creeping
competitiveness" accompanies the end of one-partyism at the state level.
First the states become competitive in national elections, and then the old

one-party ties and fears slowly break down and competition seeps down to local elections. Pennsylvania, for example, became competitive in presidential politics in the 1930's after forty years of domination by the GOP; by the 1950's and 1960's the state was competitive in state and local politics. In the 1960's the process of competitive infiltration seems to be underway in a number of the southern states. Local patterns of competitiveness increasingly reflect not so much what local party organizations and candidates do, but what the national fortunes of the parties are.

Yet, to say that we increasingly have a spreading of two-party competitiveness is not to say that we have had a regular alternation of power between the two major parties. A party may remain a competitive party and still be a losing party; competitiveness may begin at 35 or 40 per cent of the vote, but victory ordinarily does not. The long- or short-run dominance of one party remains, therefore, a distinct possibility within a competitive politics, leaving the other major party to win occasionally and come close frequently.

Ironically, however, the increasing degree of two-party competition has begun to create a set of vexing problems for the American parties. By eliminating pockets of one-party strength the new competitiveness eliminates a source of stability in the party system. When a party holds noncompetitive strongholds of its own, it can survive even a catastrophic national loss with victories and continued office-holding in its own areas of strength. Without those one-party strongholds to fall back on, a losing party may in the future find it more difficult to begin its comeback. Secondly, the spread of two-party competitiveness expands the scope of party competition and, thus, makes extra demands for the resources the parties must employ. When one-party areas could be "written off" in a presidential campaign and election, it reduced the effective area of political combat for the parties and the presidential contenders. Now they must mobilize and organize more men, more money, more energy than ever before, for a presidential campaign must now be fought in fifty rather than thirty states.

THE IMPORTANCE OF COMPETITION

The conventional typology of one, two, and multi-party systems does indeed deal with only one dimension of one activity of a political party — its ability to mobilize electorates in the contesting of elections. It measures only one of the competitions among parties, and it ignores their competition with non-party political organizations. But the typology conceals behind its simple summation of electoral relationships a good deal of information about the parties as structures and political actors. The parties are electoral political organizations, and their substance and their activities reflect their electoral capacities and their competitive statuses.

Their electoral competings are the chief activities through which each of the three sectors of the parties seeks its own particular political goals. Electoral success or failure determines whether they continue to invest their resources and/or support in the party. Understandably, therefore, the form of the party organization reflects the pattern of competitiveness. The organization of a non-competitive party cannot offer the activist or contributor the incentives which depend on electoral victory — whether they be patronage jobs or the legislative enactment of a program — and consequently it is forever undermanned. The party which remains competitive generally maintains more organizational vitality, more appeal for would-be candidates, a greater ability to recruit resources, and a greater general attractiveness to the electorate. Furthermore, the degree of electoral competitiveness is related to most of the party's activities. It affects its ability to control nominations and to minimize the impact of the direct primary, for example, and competitive patterns seem also related to the ability of the party in the legislature to maintain cohesion in roll calls.

Finally, the presence or absence of competition shapes all of the ways in which the political parties organize (as the unintended consequences of their activities) the democratic political processes. Two competitive parties provide the alternatives in candidates and issues on which a meaningful democratic choice depends. Parties contending for public office may indeed provide the only set of clear, dramatic political alternatives which the less sophisticated voter can grasp and on the basis of which he can act. Similarly, the party-organized alternatives in Congress and the state legislatures provide the chief institutionalized sources of opposition, dissent, and policy alternatives we have. Furthermore, the presence of one competitive party imposes limits on the other; each must then so tailor its candidates and its programs to minimize the defections of its workers and its voters to the other party. The presence of the real alternative is as sharp a limitation, as sure a guarantor of responsibility, in the political system as it is in the economic marketplace. The party that does not have to reckon with the responsiveness of the other is less compelled to consider the reactions of its democratic "customers." Briefly put, the *quality* of the competition in the American party system depends on its quantity.

One-partyism on the other hand, shifts the organization of political conflict and the sponsorship of alternatives to factions within the dominant party. That factionalism, too, is usually transferred to the conflict of the one-party state legislatures. The dominant party for its part suffers the torments of factionalism. Classic parties of this type, such as the Southern Democratic parties until recently, lose whatever cohesion they might have had and become instead collections of factions and followings based on personalities, regions of the state, the rewards of patronage, or specific coalitions of interests. Their organization is transient and shifting, and they cannot identify over time with issues or interests; what emerges in fact is a caricature of the political party. The subordinate party lapses into a torpid state, maintained by a few militants hoping for national party patronage or a voice in national party affairs. One-partyism also transforms the electoral processes. The meaningful choice can be made only in the primary election of the dominant party, and with primaries thus serving as quasi-general elections, the business of nominating must be done earlier and informally by party factions and personages. The full patterns of political conflict, thus managed within one party rather than between two, are inevitably altered, and the structures and activities of both parties undergo the severest dislocations.[18]

Yet, for all of its importance, competition is no more natural, inherent, or inevitable in politics than it is in the economy. Competition may break down simply as a result of the collapse of capacity: the atrophy of organization, the loss of electorates, the loss of face and status. Or it may break down because men choose not to compete. Throughout the years of Democratic domination of the South the Republican parties there became merely small circles of seekers after national patronage who could achieve their goals without contesting a local election. In a few other localities elsewhere in the country, parties have been known to enter a kind of political "restraint of trade" whereby they share or split offices. And in 1964 some observers were convinced that the Republican national convention was far more concerned with the triumph of an ideology within the party than with victory in the presidential election. Suffice it to say for the moment that if one American major party ever is permanently convinced that electoral victory is the prime goal only under certain circumstances, the competitive assumption on which the two-party system rests will have been mightily shaken.

Despite the occasional flagging of their competitive urges, the American parties have largely been driven by the need to compete for the support of electorates — and to do so they have not hesitated to make those frequent pragmatic shifts in appeal and image calculated to improve their attractiveness and thus their competitiveness. To be sure, they have not been able to bring an even two-party competitiveness to every ward, city, and county of the country, for their competition has been limited, and often frustrated by immobile electorates, intractable institutions, and uncontrollable events. It has been limited as well by the failings and incapacities of the party organizations and candidates themselves. But ironically, these very restraints on a "perfect" political competition have also worked to preserve the competitive two-party system. For the very

---

[18] See V. O. Key's magistral work, *Southern Politics* (New York: Knopf, 1949) for a picture of the classic one-partyism of recent American political history. See also, Allan Sindler, "Bifactional Rivalry as an Alternative to Two-Party Competition in Louisiana," *American Political Science Review*, Vol. XLIX (1955), pp. 641–662.

rigidities in party competition which permit a party to dominate both the loyalties of certain groups in the electorate and the elective politics of certain areas also protect that party from annihilation, give it a foothold for competitive recovery, and shield it from challenges from new parties seeking to break into the circle of competitiveness.

.   .   .

The two chapters of Part I have each centered on a very basic topic: the political party and the party system. It is electoral competitiveness which characterizes both. It sets the party apart from the other political organizations, and it is the touchstone to the very concept of a party system. Unquestionably it is a mistake to restrict one's view of the political party and of inter-party relationships to that single dimension of competitiveness, but it is equally unquestionable that electoral competitiveness offers the most important key to understanding them.

The competitive relationship of the major American parties has been amazingly even and stable, and very probably they can continue to monopolize the American party system. It is by no means as clear, however, that they can continue to dominate the broader competitions of all the political organizations. All of our attention to the complexities and niceties of the party system may blind us to changes in the more extensive competitive system of all the political mobilizers. Descriptions of state party systems, for example, tell us little or nothing about how successfully the parties compete with other political organizations for scarce political resources or for control of the local nomination process. The future of the major American parties — and to a considerable extent, the future of the American political system — depends on the parties' continued monopoly of the competition for public office as well as on the persistence of the two-party system. For once the parties cease to control that competition, and thus the access to public office, they cease to be political parties as we have known them.

PART TWO

The Political Party as an Organization

It is often easier to see the activity than the actor. The tense excitement of a bitterly-fought election, the carnival antics and revival meeting fervor of national conventions, the wrangling between partisan blocs in a state legislature — these and the other activities of the political parties could not be more obvious. But there is a very palpable political "actor" behind the activity — a political party with structural characteristics not greatly unlike those of large national corporations, trade unions, or fraternal societies. The political party is no mere bundle of activities, no ghostly presence or "unseen hand" in the political process. It is a definable, observable social structure which, in order to organize political interests, must itself be organized.

Within that structure we call the political party, all three sectors — the party organization, the party in office, the party in the electorate — exhibit some stability of relationships and some rough division of effort and responsibility. But only one of the three, the party organization, appears to have the characteristics we associate with an "organization" — the identifiable members, the common pursuit of goals, the systems of authority and labor. If the party as a whole can be thought of as a "political actor," it is only the party organization which has the organizational capacity to plan and initiate the major share of its actions. It is the sector of the party which initiates most of its electoral activities and which sets major party goals and the strategies by which to reach them. It is the part of the party which the laws of the states create and recognize as the political party. It is also the sector in which one finds the most active partisans and those whose loyalty and commitment to the party is the deepest.

The party organization is the formal apparatus of the precincts, wards, cities, counties, and states that results from the legislation of the states. It is also the national committees which the parties themselves erect and the legislative parties which their symbol-bearers in Congress and the state legislatures set up. It is the totality of the machinery operated by party officials, leaders, members, and activists — what popular usage has come to call (with considerable shrewdness) simply "the organization." It is true that in the American political system the party as an organization does not control all of the activity done in the name of the party. Unwelcome candidates may capture the party symbols through the avenue of the direct primary. And office-holders in legislatures and executives may employ the party name and symbols free from the discipline of the party "organization." Yet the parties do exist as organizations, and they do attempt to control actions done in their name. And they often succeed, for political success, like success in the other pursuits of American life, is the reward of organization.

All three of the components of the party struggle for control of the party and its political capabilities. All three of them have goals, at times competing goals, and each seeks control of the party as a goal-achieving "means" to its particular ends. In fact, it is one of the prime characteristics of the major American parties that the three components of the party are so poorly integrated and that the party organizations must, as a consequence, be ever protective of its position in the party. By contrast the parties of Western Europe often bring the party electorates (or part of them) into the party organization as dues-paying members or as participants in its year-around social activities. They may also permit greater control by the party organization over the legislative wings. The organizational "hard core" of these parties, in other words, by integrating electorates and office-holders into the party organization manages to control a higher percentage of the activities that go on in the name of the party. But in the loose, semi-public American parties the party organization carries the extra burden of greater dependence on and submission to both the party in government and its fellow partisans in the electorate.

In addition to their strained and often dependent relations with the other sectors of the party, the party organizations also confront formidable internal problems. Contrary to popular misimpression, they are not unified and omnipotent monoliths. They have within them men of differing values and goals, and they have always been plagued with dissidents and competing factions. They, or parts of them, may and do display amazing degrees of organizational apathy, inefficiency, ineptness, and even organizational disintegration. More than that, they are organizations of a special semi-private, semi-public sort. They must share the business of selecting their own candidates with the voters who for various, often casual, reasons decide to vote in their primaries. Moreover, the statutory regulations of the states often control their internal finances, the selection of their leaders, the conduct of their meetings and conventions. Very few of their organizational affairs, indeed, are truly under their own control.

Even compared by the standards of parties in general, the organizations of the two American major parties show few signs of strength. Their shapelessness, and even their disorganization and disintegration, sets them apart from the party organizations of many other Western democracies. It is not unusual, for example, to find entire county organizations of the Democratic or Republican party in total desuetude. Furthermore, their decentralization is the despair of politicians as well as scholars. The national committees of the parties are almost without power over state and local party organizations. And at all levels American party organizations have been run by small groups ("cadres") of activists. Often they must struggle just to maintain the party organization at a level of vitality sufficient to fight off their chief non-party competitors. In short, these organizations do not generally possess the vaunted organizational power they are widely imagined to. The thoughts of their leaders more often turn to begging a loyalist to accept appointment to a party committee than to the maneuvering of organizational steamrollers.

The public life and activities of the political party is the one characteristic we know best — the espousal of ideas, the contesting of elections, the organizing of government. But the parties have as well a "private life" which involves the kind of internal relationships and behavior not unlike that which one might find in any complex organization. A systematic survey of any party organization might reasonably include a checklist of these dimensions:

the formal structure of the organization: the definition of its units, the selection of its personnel and officials.

the locus of power: the relative centralization or decentralization of power within the organization, and the identification of final, effective authority within it.

the patterns of decision-making: the degree of intra-organizational democracy, and in general the processes for setting organizational goals and strategies.

the development of cohesion: the maintenance of consent, discipline, and unity within the organization.

the recruitment of resources: the ability of the organization to attract men, money, and skills, and the incentives it uses to do so.

the personnel: the divisions of labor and the various roles within the organization; the characteristics and the values and goals of the individuals within the organization.

While we may separate these aspects of the "private life" of a political party organization from its public activities, its public and private lives are obviously related. To a considerable extent the internal, organizational aspect of the party shapes its potential or capacity for the external, public political activities we see in the political system.

To bring these necessary organizational resources together — the man-power, knowledge, and money — and to maintain the divisions of labor and authority within itself, the party organization must offer appropriate rewards and incentives. The organizations are competitive mobilizers of political resources, and they must compete against the powerful induce-ments of the other political organizations. They are also brokers of politi-cal rewards who exchange or convert the resources or "inputs" of their partisans for the rewards of partisan success and its advantages. In other words, they organize varied groups of men and women who seek their special, and often differing, goals through the medium of party action. The rewards and incentives from the "mobilizing" viewpoint of the party organizations are merely the goals and ends their activists and loyalists seek and for which they have come together in the party. Many of the party organizations' activities, therefore, may be viewed in terms of their attempts to win those goals and thereby reward the faithful for their investment of resources, loyalties, and support.

But for all of the palpable organizational activity and "private life," it is difficult to escape the overriding weaknesses and problems of American party organization. It is even difficult to take it seriously in an analytical or scholarly enterprise. The party organization is in many ways, however, the core of the party; it is certainly its most tangible, responsible, and stable part. Any study of the American parties slights it at a very great peril. This entire book, as well as the approaching chapters, represents an understanding of the parties as very concrete and specific structures which mobilize political resources in the pursuit of political goals and rewards.

Such an approach is hardly a novel one. It has been the dominant scholarly point of vantage of three of the greatest scholars of political parties in the Western democracies: Roberto Michels, Moisei Ostrogorski, and Maurice Duverger.[1] All three centered their attention not so much on what the parties do but on the "doers" themselves and their organizational forms and activities. The organizational approach has not been totally foreign to the study of the American parties by American scholars, how-ever. The chronicling of the American city "machines" certainly reflects a

---

[1] For the chief works of these three pioneering scholars of parties as organizations, see: Roberto Michels, *Political Parties* (Glencoe: The Free Press, 1949, first published in 1915); Moisei Ostrogorski, *Democracy and the Organization of Political Parties*, first published in 1902 and now available in an edition of two volumes edited and abridged by Seymour M. Lipset (New York: Anchor, 1964); and Maurice Duverger, *Political Parties* (New York: Wiley, 1954).

concern with organizational matters.[2] But those machines have always been something of a genetic "sport" among American party organizations; the rest of the organizations have presented a less obvious, less compelling, and less prepossessing organizational edifice. Largely for that reason, probably, the great classics on party organization were written in Western Europe rather than the United States.

[2] Much of the American literature on parties as organizations is noted and summarized in the three chapters of this section. Joseph A. Schlesinger in his chapter, "Political Party Organization" in James G. March (ed.), *Handbook of Organizations* (Chicago: Rand McNally, 1965), has recently essayed an organizational approach to the parties. His notes and bibliography are also especially useful.

Chapter Three

THE PARTY ORGANIZATION:
STATE AND LOCAL

The semantics of American politics often reflect its most tenacious myths. The entire popular vocabulary touching party organization suggests and reinforces an impression of almost menacing strength. "Machines," headed by "bosses," keep the local "captains" toeing a "party line." Their power or strength, in a lately fashionable idiom, has become their "clout." And yet, even the most cursory experience with American party organization suggests that all the semantic puffery only hides a vastly less imposing organizational reality.

In many ways the myth of monolithic party organization — and its re-lated vocabulary and idiom — is in itself a part of the greater American fear of politics and politicians. In what has become virtually a conspira-torial theory of American politics, the party organization or "machine" is only the prime conspirator or corruptor in a wider net of political intrigue. The truth about American party organization is, therefore, difficult for many Americans to accept, for it involves not only a recognition of reality about the parties but the modification of preconceptions about American politics and the unwholesome role of the parties in general. Perhaps for precisely the reason that they carry no such preconceptions, foreign ob-servers have found it easier to see American party organization as it really is. Recognition of the truth may surprise them, but it forces no major reorientation of political values or perceptions.

One of the latest in a long series of distinguished foreign commentators on the American polity, H. G. Nicholas, cut quickly through the major myth of party organization in the early 1950's: [1]

[1] H. G. Nicholas, "A Briton Considers Our Bewildering Party Apparatus," *The Reporter* (November 25, 1952), pp. 28–29.

Englishmen who have viewed American elections from three thousand miles across the Atlantic have generally been impressed by the elaborateness of the organizations involved as well as by the magnitude and professionalism of it all. The very language of American politics suggests a planned, powerful, smooth-running, and disciplined instrument. Surely, these Englishmen have decided, an American party is the counterpart in the field of politics of the corporation in the field of American business — a great, synthetic, efficient, productive mechanism, smoothly controlled from above and ordering the movement of millions below.

I have discovered in the last few weeks that such an image quickly vanishes when confronted with reality. Even a cursory inspection of the American political scene at election time reveals a wholly different condition of affairs. Far from order, there is a rich and riotous confusion; in place of impersonal "machines," there is every kind of spontaneous organism. The disciplined ward heelers turn out to be an unseemingly scramble of enthusiastic volunteers; the symmetrical pyramid we have heard about — from precinct to ward to county to state to nation — is an untidy cairn composed of stones of every conceivable size, with mortar either inadequate or nonexistent, and with an apex whose location shifts according to wherever you happen to be standing at the moment.

. . .

The American party organization is a phoenix, burning itself out after each election, soaring with a new (or at least a rewelded) pair of wings after each primary. The effort this must involve for all concerned is something that appalls the visitor; the energy that is given to it excites his admiration; the complexities that result therefrom befuddle his poor comprehension.

So it is that things are seldom what they seem in American political organization. Our main problem may be that we are always shifting among three levels of political reality: the party organizations as they are stipulated in state legislation, the party organizations as they are in fact, and the party organizations as large numbers of Americans imagine them to be.

THE FORMS AND OUTLINES OF ORGANIZATION

While the United States Constitution makes no mention of or even oblique reference to political parties, the constitutions and statutes of the fifty states literally bulge with the most detailed prescriptions defining the nature of party organizations and the duties they are to perform. The statutes of Oregon, for example, consume more than 5,000 words simply in outlining and creating the structure the parties must assume in that state. Only South Carolina of all the states remains mute, a result of its futile attempt in the 1940's to make the party primaries completely private affairs and thus free them from the scrutiny of the Federal courts.[2] A few

[2] The entire controversy over the "white primary," of which this incident is a part, will be taken up in Chapter 8.

other states, generally those of the South, deal only in the briefest terms
with the parties, again a result of the historical fact of decades of one-
partyism.

The rest of the states, well over forty of them, have enacted a kaleido-
scopic variety of legislation on the parties which literally defies summary
or classification. In scope and extent they range from detailed and full-
blown provisions such as those of the Oregon statutes to those of Georgia
which dispose of the parties in a grand total of two extended sentences.
And in between are all grades and degrees of statutory specificity — those
which permit the parties to determine the composition of the state central
committee and those which not only specify it but set the dates and
places of its meetings, those which spell out legislative district organization and those which don't, those which leave the running of the parties
to the parties and those which even set the agendas of their periodic
meetings. And yet, despite the variety of state approaches, the cardinal
fact remains that the definition and regulation of political party organization in the United States has been left entirely to the states.

The great mass of state legislation on the parties covers an extensive
range of subjects. Virtually every state has attempted to define the ways
in which parties and their candidates will be admitted to the ballot in the
state. They usually set vote minima — 5 or 10 per cent of the vote cast at
the last gubernatorial election, perhaps — or alternatively, prescribe the
number of signatures required on petitions for access to the ballot.[3] Additionally, the states may prohibit some political parties, particularly those
which urge or teach the overthrow of the United States or the particular
state in question. And they inevitably assign specific tasks to the parties —
the replacement of candidates who die during the campaign or the selection of presidential electors, for instance. Yet in many ways the central
and most pressing of the statutory provisions are those which outline the
organizational form which the parties must assume and the procedures
they must observe as they organize or reorganize. Often the parties in
practice modify or embellish that statutory structure, but they never fully
escape its imperatives. The examination of the political parties as organizations must begin with it.

The party organizations created by the states have in common one
dominant characteristic: they match the voting districts and constituencies
of the state. They form great step pyramids as they reflect the myriad,
overlapping constituencies of a democracy committed to the election of
vast numbers of office-holders (Figure 1). At the bottom they are built on
the smallest voting districts of the state. The basic functionary in the

[3] See Joseph Starr, "The Legal Status of American Political Parties," *American
Political Science Review* (1940), Vol. XXXIV, pp. 439–455, 685–699, on the scope
and constitutionality of state legislation on the legal rights and status of the parties
under state law.

party organization is the local committeeman, be he from a ward, a precinct, or a township. Then in a confusion of layers one finds ward and city committees, county committees, and sometimes even state legislative and congressional districts piled on top of each other.[4]

Figure 1
TYPICAL PYRAMID OF PARTY ORGANIZATION IN A STATE

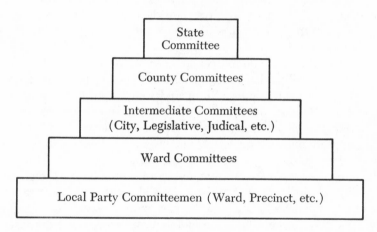

At the apex of the pyramid there is invariably a state committee, usually called a "state central committee" in the idiom of these statutes. The degree to which this entire structure is actually specified by the statutes differs from state to state. State statutes generally ordain the county and the state committees; some then mandate the other levels, while others leave the full articulation of the organizational hierarchy to the parties themselves.

THE ELECTED COMMITTEEMAN

Most frequently the committeeman is chosen from the local precinct — the smallest voting district in the states — but occasionally he may be chosen from the ward (especially in larger cities) or from the township (in rural areas). Since there are by conventional agreement more than 100,000 precincts in the United States, a fully-manned, two-party system would assume the organizational participation of at least some 200,000 men and women. In truth, of course, many of the local committee positions are either vacant or else only nominally occupied.

The local committeemen are generally selected in one of two ways:

[4] Within the same state, of course, the various intermediate committees may cover geographical areas of varying sizes, and thus they may occupy different positions in the organizational pyramid. Congressional districts, for example, may be smaller than a city or larger than a county, depending on population concentrations.

either at local party caucuses or at the primary elections of the party. In those states choosing committeemen at the primaries, any voter may generally place his name in nomination for the party position with a petition signed by a handful of local voters. If, as it often happens, there are no nominees, he may be elected by an even smaller handful of write-in votes. In other states the statutes direct or permit the party to hold local caucuses in the wards and precincts to which any voters of the area who declare themselves attached to the principles (always unspecified) of the party may come. These party loyalists then elect the precinct and/or ward committeemen in the caucus; they also generally elect delegates to county and/or state conventions.

The duties of the local committeeman are not often fully spelled out in the statutes. Naturally, where local parties are active, the committeemen develop organizational responsibilities and functions which the statutes never mention. They are the fabled local committeemen or "ward heelers" of the American political "machine." They know the local voters, shape their voting preferences, cater to their needs and problems, introduce the party candidates to them, propagandize the parties' causes and issues — all with the ultimate purpose of "turning out" a bloc of votes for the party on election day. If the committeeman is elected from a ward in a large American city such as Philadelphia, he may indeed preside over a group of precinct workers whom he has appointed and whom he supervises in the shepherding of the local electorate. Alternatively in less active local parties the committeeman may do little more than occasional campaigning or meeting going.

THE LOCAL COMMITTEES

A welter of local committees springs from the elected committeemen. Most commonly the committeemen either collectively make up the city, town, village, legislative, county, and congressional district committees — or they elect the delegates who do. In a few cases, however, these committees or some of them are to be chosen at county conventions or by the party's candidates for public office. Regardless of this profusion of committees and the various mechanics of their formation, the chief active committee is generally the county committee, although in some states the congressional district committees assume a comparable importance. Organizations in state legislative districts, for example, generally exist solely for the purpose of performing party activities directly related to elections for those offices.

In some metropolitan areas, however, the local party structure may be both more complex and more diverse. In the Bronx in New York the Democratic county committee is composed of some 3,750 local committeemen. The committeemen in each state legislative district (for the state Assembly) elect district leaders who in turn elect the county leaders. Typi-

cally, the Democrats of neighboring Brooklyn and Queens have somewhat differing organizational structures. In other metropolitan centers the
city committees of the large, central city assume an unusual importance.

The dominance of the county committee in most parts of the country is
not difficult to explain. The county as a political division elects not one
but a considerable number of public officials. And those officials often
control the one major remaining source of political patronage: the county
court house. Furthermore, many other constituencies — such as congressional districts, state legislative districts, and judicial districts — are defined
largely in terms of counties. Then, too, in much of America, life and trade
are drawn to the local county seat from the surrounding area of the
county. Finally, the statutes of most states recognize the key position of
the county committees. Often their members form other parallel committees, and often, too, they send their chairmen or delegates to form the
state central committee.

The states, however, do more than create the structure of a party organization. They regulate as well its activities and its internal processes. Something of the detailed nature of this kind of regulation may be seen in
Minnesota's strictures on the operation of its ward and precinct party
caucuses. Minnesota statutes specify, for example:

the full details of the public announcement of the caucus that must be
made at least twenty days before its convening.

its minimum length (one hour).

the length of time during which the caucus must receive nominations
(one-half hour).

the procedures for challenging the presence of any of the participants.

the use of the secret ballot in all caucus elections.

the use of Robert's Rules of Order (revised edition) in the caucus deliberations.

Other states spell out equally detailed standards for party operation of
one sort or another. They may require that local committees meet within
thirty or forty-five days after the primary elections, that they notify the
secretary of state or the county clerk of the election of officers within a set
period, that they not permit the voting of proxies, that they observe a
fixed order of business at their organizational meetings, or that they hold
their conventions in certain categories of public buildings. Again, the variety is endless, but the point is clear: the political parties are no mere
private political organizations under the laws of most states.

THE STATE CENTRAL COMMITTEES

The state central committees of the fifty states are created in almost as
many ways as human ingenuity can devise. In some states the lawmakers
have left the composition to the decision of the parties, but in most they

have decided the matter themselves. Basically, the range of difference concerns two variables: the lower party unit from which the state committeemen are chosen and the ways in which they are chosen. The unit represented may be the county, the congressional district, the state convention, cities, or a mixture of them. The methods of choice include election at the party's primaries, election by a lower committee, *ex officio* representation, or selection by a party convention. The possible number of combinations of the two factors is enormous, and state practice confirms that fact. Hence, for example, the following state committees:

Illinois: one representative from each congressional district chosen at the primary election.

South Carolina: one representative per county chosen at a convention.

California: the chairman of each county committee, plus each party candidate for congressional, statewide, and state legislative office, plus the appointed representatives of each party candidate and office-holder (for a grand total of about 700 citizens).

Oregon: the chairman and vice-chairman, *ex officio*, of each county committee.

New York: two representatives elected at the primary from each state Assembly district.

Wisconsin: at least two representatives from each congressional district chosen by the state convention, plus the chairman of the district committee *ex officio*.

The activities of these state committees (i.e., the "state central committee," as they tend to be called) often are set down in what must be for them a painful detail. (California statutes, for example, provide that the chairman of the state central committee shall serve a two-year term, that he cannot succeed himself, and that the office must be held alternately by residents of the northern and southern halves of the state.) It is common to assign them responsibility for calling and organizing party conventions, for drafting party platforms, for supervising the spending of party campaign funds, for the selection of the party's presidential electors, national committeemen, and national convention delegates and alternates. As for the main organizational business of running a party organization and supporting candidates in the primaries and general elections, state statutes are generally silent except to say occasionally that they may make whatever rules are necessary for the conduct of party business. Some do, however, forbid or permit the committees to endorse candidates in the primary. But on these "political" political activities, state statutes are more commonly silent.

A number of states, especially those endemically suspicious of party organization, set up statewide conventions in which they vest many of the powers and responsibilities that other states leave to the state central committees. They may ordain that the state convention write the platform, select the national committeemen from the state, nominate presidential electors, choose delegates and/or alternates to the party's national convention. Indeed, some provide that the state convention select the state committee itself. Furthermore, in a small number of states — which will be discussed more later — the state convention of the party actually nominates candidates for some statewide offices, a reminder of the power of conventions in the days before the direct primary.[5]

Such, then, are the formal organizational structures created for the parties in the states. Three general, over-all observations about them may be in order. First of all, one cannot help but notice that the men who pass the state statutes view the parties almost exclusively as electoral organizations. The organizational layers relate to voting districts and the constituencies in which public officials are chosen, and the duties assigned to them are almost exclusively concerned with the contesting of elections. The political party organization — as one views it in the statute books of the states — clearly serves as auxiliary machinery to the state's regulation of nominations and elections. Indeed, the dominant concern in its creation too often seems to be its usefulness in helping the state administer the electoral processes rather than its viability as a healthy and on-going political organization.

Secondly, it is perfectly clear from the statutes that state legislators have viewed the parties as skeletal organizations run by a small number of party officials. There is little evidence that they have entertained the possibility of membership parties, or even of parties attracting the concerns and labors of bands of activists. Indeed, they assume the contrary. By opening the election of local committeemen, and even of other party officials, to the electorate of the primary election, they have defined the parties' voters as a quasi-membership group. They have by legislative fiat tried to democratize, to "open," the parties to the ultimate participation and authority of all voters. The party which results is thus no closed association whose participating members choose its leaders and chart its affairs. It is the quasi-public, quasi-private hybrid of which we have already spoken.

Finally, while the formal organization of the parties within the state appears to be strictly hierarchical, it is not perfectly so. The state party hierarchies have more aptly been described by V. O. Key as "a system of layers of organization."[6] In some states, for example, the state central

---

[5] There is no genuinely comprehensive summary of the state statutory provisions on party organization readily available. Some summarization can be found in L. R. Gaitskill, *State Regulation of Political Parties* (Frankfort, Ky.: Kentucky Legislative Research Commission, 1962). The provisions of a specific state's law can be found easily in that state's codified statutes; the material on party organization can usually be found under the general heading of "elections," a revealing fact in itself.

[6] V. O. Key, *Politics, Parties, and Pressure Groups*, 5th ed. (New York: Crowell, 1964), p. 316.

committee's members are chosen directly by the voters; the committee, therefore, does not grow out of the committees below it. And even where the linkage is direct between the layers of organization, the links move from bottom to top. Such a system would hardly appear to be ideally designed to produce the centralization of power at the apex which the very concept of "hierarchy" presumes. Basically, this is a system of party committees close to and growing from the political "grass roots." The result is to build into the party organizational structure a great deal of local autonomy and freedom from statewide direction.

THE SUBSTANCE AND REALITIES OF PARTY ORGANIZATION

These elaborate statutory parties, with their many layers of committees and their armies of committeemen, conform to the mental images most Americans have of the party organizations. These are the "machines," the organizations, the bosses, the ward heelers, and the party cabals of which the great party juggernauts are said to be made. But in truth, political party organization in many states and localities is weak, undermanned, even torpid. Where statutes and public expectation see active legions of committeemen and layer on layer of virile organization, there is often only sporadic activity by a handful of dispirited party regulars.

Disciplined, effective party organization does exist, to be sure. The classic urban political machine is the best example. Its heyday was the turn of the 20th century, and its promised land was the burgeoning American city. Its annals are replete with the colorful histories of Tammany Hall in New York, the knaveries of the Prendergasts in Kansas City and Frank ("I am the law") Hague in Jersey City, the cheeky threats of Chicago's "Big Bill" Thompson to punch the King of England on the nose, and the genial rascality (and mail fraud conviction) of Mayor James Curley of Boston. The antics of Mayor Curley have in fact been immortalized — and somewhat romanticized — in the recent novel (and its movie version), *The Last Hurrah*.[7] Recently, however, the urban machine has fallen on bad days; the defeat of Carmine de Sapio and the other organization Democrats of New York by Mayor Wagner and the reformers in 1961 marks its most spectacular defeat. But the "machine" continues in a variety of forms in many of the Democratic cities of the northeastern quarter of the United States, and in some (such as Chicago, Philadelphia, and Pittsburgh) it continues in something approaching the classic, pristine form.

The big city "machine" — in the past and today — stands as the maximum in party organization. Its disciplined ward and precinct workers are expected to maintain the closest possible contact with the voters of their district. Frequent door-to-door canvassing of local political opinion often

[7] Edwin O'Connor, *The Last Hurrah* (Boston: Little, Brown, 1956).

is supplemented by interviews in a local office or contacts at the local
party headquarters. There, especially, the committeeman can hear the
problems of his constituents; often they are personal — unemployment or a
delinquent son — as well as public or governmental. His stock in trade is
his ability, and the party's ability, to find a social welfare agency for the
troubled, jobs (often on the public payrolls) for the jobless, political "pull"
for the uninfluential, contracts for the loyal merchant, or even the much
storied Christmas basket or delivery of coal for the needy. From his own
personal ties of friendship, his concern for the needs of "his people," and
his ability to do something tangible for them, he creates the web of loyalties and gratitude which enable him to "deliver the vote" at the primary
or general election. It is a political relationship close to the immediate
needs of urban populations. The party organization meets those needs
and wins political allegiance in return. And the critical link in this relationship — personal and compassionate, but disciplined and purposeful
— is the committeeman. His ability to control the local vote may reach as-
tounding levels. Stories are told, for example, of Philadelphia Republican
ward leaders who, sensing that the GOP was dead in that city after the
loss of 1951, switched to the Democratic party and carried "their" voters
with them into Democratic columns.

Within the organization of the classic urban machine, a tight hierarchy
of authority exists. Precinct workers work under the direction of ward or
district leaders, and they in turn labor under the vigilance of a powerful
city leader or "boss." For able and faithful workers in the organization,
the rewards are attractive. They enjoy the social and psychological rewards of the acquaintanceship of the great and near great. Their political
positions bring them into contact with social circles and economic opportunity otherwise denied them. They often win employment through the
party; as recently as 1960 "nearly three out of four Democratic committeemen and one out of three Democratic committeewomen [in Pittsburgh]
held public jobs, chiefly with the Pittsburgh city government and the
Allegheny county government." [8] For other party workers the opportunity
comes to run for public office, since the machine often chooses its candidates from among the active faithful. And since the party leadership can
control these rewards, they have in their hands an important rein on the
local independence of party committeemen.

These city or county "machine" organizations are no mere electoral parties. Their services to their voters continue the year round, for the problems of their urban clienteles know no season. Their activity is, in the
classic form, virtually continuous; the fellowship of the local party club or
headquarters is unceasingly convivial. At election time their control is

---

[8] William J. Keefe and William C. Seyler, "Precinct Politicians in Pittsburgh,"
Social Science, Vol. XXXV (January, 1960), p. 28.

almost total; the American urban machines have, in fact, often been able literally to hand-pick candidates because their disciplined armies of voters enabled them to control the party's primary. The winners of the primary win the general election because these are one-party cities; by their very nature there is not room in any metropolitan center for two such leviathans. Their entire system of rewards depends on the continuous holding of public office. And the role that party has had in nominating and electing public officials makes them sufficiently beholden to the "machine" to assure an easy hearing for party wishes in city hall or the county court house. In sum, the classic urban political machine was and is part electoral organization, part "informal government," part social welfare and social service agency, and part self-improvement association. Its politics are those of the immediate needs of its participants and its supporting clienteles; conversely, its disinterest in national issues and ideologies is monumental.[9]

Yet, the big city machines have never been and are not now typical of party organization in the United States. Awesome as they are, they represent only one extreme in the many varieties of party organization. Very likely, too, their reality never matched the myth of their monolithic power. The other extreme — quite unrepresented in the scholarly literature because it offers so little to study — is one of virtual disorganization. In these cases, most of the committee positions in the party's county unit are unfilled or held by completely inactive incumbents (who may, indeed, have been elected without their consent by four or five write-in votes). A chairman and a handful of loyal party officials may meet occasionally to carry out only the most essential affairs of the party, or the affairs that state statutes require of them. Their main activity occurs shortly before the primary elections as they plead with members of the party to offer themselves as candidates in order to "fill the party ticket." They are largely without influence or following, for often their party is a chronic minority party. They meet infrequently, raise little money for election campaigns, and in general create little or no public attention. The extent of such organizational weakness is difficult to estimate, although it is often the rule rather than the exception in much of rural America. A recent survey found that more than one-fifth of the party committee positions in Kansas, South Dakota, North Dakota, and Iowa remained unfilled after the 1962 primaries at which they were to have been filled.[10]

Most of American party organization lies between these two extremes. But "between" encompasses a broad organizational distance. It might be

[9] The literature on the American urban machine is staggering in its size. For example, see Edward Banfield and James Q. Wilson, *City Politics* (Cambridge: Harvard Univ. Press, 1963) and Harold Gosnell, *Machine Politics: Chicago Model* (Chicago: Univ. of Chicago Press, 1937).

[10] Marvin Harder and Thomas Ungs, paper delivered at the meetings of the Midwest Conference of Political Scientists in May, 1963.

accurate, however, to say that the average or median local party organization comes closer 'o the pole of disorganization than to the pole of maximum organization. In some instances, in fact, local party leaders will fight the strengthening of party organization, lest new party activists challenge their little arena of power and claim their patronage rewards. And even where the recruitment of party activists and leaders is relatively open, popular apathy works toward a "middling" party organization. In 1960, for example, only 1,154 men and women attended the open, biennial precinct caucuses of the Democratic party in Minneapolis. The median turnout per precinct was four people. On such levels of involvement great organizational strength is not easily erected.

One may construct an imaginary city or county organization close to the average or median American local party with these characteristics:

An active chairman and executive committee, plus a few associated activists, who in effect make most of the decisions in the name of the party, who raise funds, who seek out and screen candidates (or approve the candidates who select themselves), and who speak locally for the party.

A ward and precinct organization in which only a minimum of local committeemen are active and in which there is little door-to-door canvassing or other direct voter contact.

The active participation in organizational matters of some of the party's elected public officials who may often share effective control of the organization with the official party leadership.

A distinctly periodic calendar of activities marked by a watchful waiting and planning at any other than election times.

Nowhere here does one find the serried ranks of party foot soldiers. The active minority operates not with threats and iron discipline but with pleading and cajoling. There are few incentives and rewards left in the hands of these parties with which they might recruit all of the effort and manpower the statutory structures would seem to require.

Such a model of the "average" local party organization cannot begin to suggest the multitude of forms which local parties take in the United States. It takes no account, for instance, of the oligarchic rural or small town machines in which a few local notables (who may or may not hold party or public office) dominate a political organization with a variable combination of patronage, local prestige and status, friendship and kinship, and private economic power. (It is one of the most durable and romantic myths of American politics that political "muscle," and even corruption, must of necessity be urban; it is also one of the least supportable myths.) The "average" takes no account either of urban party organizations operating at a level of considerable effectiveness, albeit a level below that of the prototypic "machine." A recent study of parties in the Detroit area defined the precinct committeeman's three "critical" tasks to be the registration of new voters, the canvassing of the already registered (by phone or personal visits), and the roundup of voters on election day. Only 17 per cent of the Democratic precinct leaders and 25 per cent of the Republican leaders performed all three; another 38 per cent of the Democrats and 22 per cent of the Republicans carried out any two of the three.[11]

THE EXTRA-LEGAL ORGANIZATION

These forms and types of party organization occur largely within the formal outlines set down in state statutes. But the parties have additionally made organizational embellishments which go beyond the words, sometimes the clear expectations, of many state statutes. Women's organizations have sprung up in a number of states, more commonly in the Republican than the Democratic party. And a good many parties have also experimented with youth organizations; in fact, both parties have national federations of these youth organizations, the Young Democrats and the Young Republicans. In general the ladies' groups have been more closely integrated into state and local party organizations, helping the regular organization in fund-raising and in unglamorous organizational work. But more than one state or local party organization has felt itself embarrassed — rightly or wrongly — by the exuberant and independent actions of a youth organization in a county, in a state, or at some college or university. Either as a cause or a result of being cut off from the central electoral business of the parent political party organizations, the Young Democrats and Young Republicans have developed a heavily ideological orientation. It is this orientation, and their often independent exposition of it, that causes the frequent frictions between them and the senior party organizations.

However, partisans in a number of states have effected greater transformations in party organization than the mere addition of auxiliaries. Examples from around the country would include the following.

THE NEW YORK DEMOCRATIC REFORM CLUBS

Formed largely to break the old-style machine power of Tammany Hall, these clubs draw an educated, upper-middle and upper-class avocational party activist. In organization they have attempted to substitute a membership, "club" style for the conventional cadre organization of the regular party. Within the party they seek to replace the traditional ethos and coin of patronage and to replace the centralized, hierarchical authority of the leader ("boss") with a measure of intra-party democracy. They were and are deeply committed to a set of "liberal" policy goals and to a reorientation

[11] Samuel J. Eldersveld, *Political Parties: A Behavioral Analysis* (Chicago: Rand, McNally, 1964), pp. 349–350.

of organization politics to ideological issues; in part they began in dissatisfaction over the failure of the party regulars to support Adlai Stevenson actively in the 1950's. More than anything else theirs is a rebellion against the essentially issueless politics of personal reward and ethnicity that has for so long typified urban party organization.[12]

THE WISCONSIN VOLUNTARY ORGANIZATIONS

In the 1920's the conservative wing of the Wisconsin Republicans, repeatedly the losers in primaries to the La Follette Progressive wing, formed a separate, extra-legal party organization to represent its ideology and support its candidates in the GOP primary. When the Progressives left the cover of the party in the 1930's and formed their own state party, the "regular" Republicans found it easier to operate through their voluntary party organization than through the carefully regulated statutory organization. The Democrats, casting about for a more effective party organization, followed suit in the 1940's and 50's. At present, therefore, both parties operate through these duplicating but separate voluntary organizations which parallel — county organization for county organization — the statutory organizational structure. Secure in their power by now, both control the statutory organizations, keeping them docile and using them only to perform the mandated statutory activities. The voluntary organizations, bolstered by membership organizations in many counties of the state, retain and exercise the substance of party power. By the late 1950's the two parties' voluntary organizations had enrolled some 20,000 dues-paying members, most of them in urban areas.[13]

THE CALIFORNIA CLUBS

The splendid profusion of club-style party organizations in California all began in the 1930's when liberal Republicans founded the California Republican Assembly to revivify the faltering Republican party. A conservative competitor, the United Republicans of California, sprang up in the early 1960's to oppose the liberals of the CRA, but conservatives captured the CRA just a short time later. In 1965 the liberal Republicans repaired to a new set of organizations, the California Republican League. On the Democratic side, the older of the organizations, the liberal California Democratic Clubs, was founded in 1953 with the remnants of the Stevenson supporters of 1952. It has alternately fought against Republicans entered in the Democratic primaries and against the more traditional Democrats led by Assembly Speaker Jesse Unruh. In 1964 Unruh organized his forces into the Democratic Volunteers Committee. In both parties these club organi-

---

[12] The reform clubs have not been limited to New York; see James Q. Wilson, *The Amateur Democrat* (Chicago: Univ. of Chicago Press, 1962).

[13] Leon D. Epstein, *Politics in Wisconsin* (Madison: Univ. of Wisconsin Press, 1958), pp. 80–81.

zations have featured some separate local organization, a hard core of dues-paying members, and a series of tumultuous conventions at which the clubs' ideologists have endorsed candidates to support at their party's primary. Although their approximately 80,000 total members constitute a notable roll of activists, in neither party have the organizations been able to develop the scope or unity to match Wisconsin's control of the statutory organization.[14]

Finally, it should be added that while other states have not matched this degree of extra-legal party organization, parties in some have in a limited way grafted membership organizations onto the regular statutory organization. In others they have begun to hold special endorsing conventions apart from the formal conventions they are required to hold. In other states, too, the outlines of the party's statutory organization is sufficiently loose to permit the parties to shape an organization as they please.

The development of these voluntary organizations speaks volumes about the inadequacy of the conventional statutory party organization within which the parties must operate. They have arisen in part because the inflexible statutory organization could not accommodate the new middle-class style of organization with its emphasis on ideological and avocational activists and greater participation by dues-paying members. Furthermore, most reflect the problems that statutory party organizations have in controlling their party's primary. In Wisconsin the statutory party conventions must convene *after* the primary, and in California the statutory party organizations are forbidden to make endorsements in the primary. In other ways, too, the voluntary organization may be a release from state regulation of parties; in Wisconsin the voluntary structure enables the parties to elude the state's severe restrictions on electoral spending by statutory organizations. Finally, the voluntary organizations have often been instruments of factional warfare that has almost always been ideological in nature. Fervent ideologists have used them to combat other ideologists or non-ideologists within the party.

THE LOCUS OF POWER

Finally, it remains to ask what in reality is the locus of power within these state party organizations. Is the hierarchical chain of authority maintained in reality? Most scholars feel that in most states the major locus of organizational vitality, and thus of organizational authority is the county com-

[14] The figure of 80,000 members comes from a series of reports on the California voluntary organizations in *The New York Times* of early 1966. The specific membership figures are these: 50,000 in the CDC; 7,000 in the DVC; 11,500 in the CRA; 7,500 in the URC; and 4,000 in the CRL. For the general literature on the California clubs, see Wilson, *The Amateur Democrat;* Francis Carney, *The Rise of the Democratic Clubs in California* (New York: Holt, 1958); Currin V. Shields, "A Note on Party Organization: The Democrats in California," *Western Political Quarterly,* Vol. VII (1954), pp. 673–683; and Joseph P. Harris, *California Politics,* 3rd ed. (Stanford: Stanford Univ. Press, 1961).

mittee. Most state party organizations are merely federations — and loose confederations at that — of semi-autonomous or autonomous local political baronies and baronial county chairmen. The Democratic party of Ohio may exemplify these loosely-knit, decentralized state party organizations. Writing of it in the early 1960's, one observer noted that "there was, in fact, no statewide Democratic party in Ohio. The state's Democratic party was an aggregation of city machines which had little or no interest in statewide elections unless the candidate was from their city. Ray Miller, the Cuyahoga County (Cleveland) Democratic boss, explicitly maintained that his organization was an independent entity with neither legal nor moral ties with a state Democratic party." [15] Its weakness was amply displayed in the 1958 Democratic gubernatorial primary. Among the seven candidates for the nomination were the mayors of Youngstown, Cleveland, and Columbus, and the former mayor of Toledo; each carried his home county and ran well in neighboring counties. Often, too, this decentralization is accentuated by intra-party factionalism — regional factions, urban-rural factions, factions centering around powerful personages, liberal-conservative factions, or a mixture of factional lines. Every state party has it; its effect is only a matter of its relative strength.

There are, of course, always those few exceptional state organizations that do manage to dominate the city and county organizations. Ohio Republicans achieved it to some extent in the 1950's and 1960's as a result of ideological unity and centralized control of party finance. Furthermore, for a part of that period they were aided by the organizational skills and efficiency of Ray Bliss, a pragmatic, publicity-shy organizational technician and a professional's professional among state party chairmen. In an entirely different, lord-in-the-manor style was the Virginia fiefdom of former Democratic Senator, Harry F. Byrd. Long a rebel against the national Democratic party and its presidential candidates (Harry S. Truman in 1948 was the last one to merit the Senator's support), he nonetheless forged a potent state organization from central control of county patronage and the fees and salaries of county officials. (The salaries of six officials in each Virginia county depended on the decisions of a single state board appointed by the Governor.) A limited suffrage, a prevailing homogeneous rural conservatism, and the active support of a social and economic oligarchy supported Byrd as well. The Byrd organization was finally crippled in the 1966 elections by an electorate swelled by new Negro voters and a new urban electorate.

Specific consequences in party activities and roles follow from various modes of state party organization. The centralized state party organization has a vastly greater power over the nomination of statewide candidates for office and a greater capacity for enforcing party discipline over its partisans in the state legislature. Duane Lockard has offered a useful

[15] John H. Fenton, *Midwest Politics* (New York: Holt, Rinehart, Winston, 1966), p. 137.

outline of the varieties of state party organization and their chief characteristics: [16]

I. THE TWO-PARTY STATES
  A. *Cohesive, strong organizations*
    1. Clearly identified and continuous leadership
    2. Considerable leadership control over ascent up the ladder of political promotion (i.e., considerable control over nominations in the hands of the leadership)
    3. Centralization of party finances and relatively centralized conduct of election campaigns
    4. Great party influence in the making of legislative policy decisions (e.g., an influential role for the state party chairman in working out policy in the legislature)
  B. *Splintered, weak organizations*
    1. Factional cleavage extensive (e.g., sectional or urban-rural)
    2. Personality battles for statewide nominations common; little leadership control over nominations
    3. Relatively little leadership influence on legislative policy formation

II. THE ONE-PARTY STATES
  A. *Machine-led; one faction predominant*
    1. Clear, continuous leadership
    2. Control over nominations and advancement in the hands of organization leaders
    3. Considerable influence over legislative policy in the hands of the organization
      a. Dominated by one or two powerful interests (such as those based on a natural resource or an important farm crop), or
      b. A more confusing array of economic powers controlling decision-making
  B. *Bifactional party structure*
    1. Two contesting factions with relatively continuous and identifiable leaderships
    2. In varying degree some questions of policy transferred to primary contests
    3. Moderate to minor legislative policy identification of factions
  C. *Multifactional party structure*
    1. Party organizations as holding companies — virtual non-participants in policy-making
    2. Factions and their leaderships ever shifting and non-continuous and without clear identification
    3. Personality conflicts dominate in primaries
    4. Policy formation a lottery in which the "haves" use the disorganization of politics to achieve their conservative ends

[16] Duane Lockard, *New England State Politics* (Princeton: Princeton Univ. Press, 1959), pp. 325–326.

Whether or not a state committee, state chairman, or governor can weld the city and county committees into a reasonably coherent state organization depends on a matching of wits, influence, resources, and informal political power. A state committee or governor supported by a large reservoir of state appointments (patronage) may force recalcitrant county chairmen into line if they are to receive state jobs for themselves and their legions. Conversely, a county or city committee with patronage or other resources of its own may hold out against state centralization. Alternately, the personal prestige and electoral following of a governor or senator, or the dominance of state or national issues or ideologies, may be thrown on the side of domination by the state organization. Conversely, local issues and the prestige of a local official may thwart it. But if all of these factors are held equal, the advantage rests with the county or city organization. It alone in American party politics is an on-going political organization with grass roots political support. It alone can develop a base of power directly in the electorate.

TRENDS AND CHANGES

The classic forms and statutory models of American party organization have declined markedly in the last several generations. The effect and meaning of that decline, however, are less than clear. Our traditional image of the well-oiled party machine and the monolithic party organization is in many ways a 19th century norm, a reflection of the politics, the social needs and structure, the educational levels, and the communication patterns of that distant time. Today it becomes increasingly obvious that it may not be a sign of organizational weakness if a party does not have an active committeeman or captain in every precinct. New methods of media-centered campaigning, indeed, suggest that the traditional form of local party organization may be evolving the way of the human vermiform appendix.

Party organization must and will reflect the political culture and the socio-economic conditions of the time. As they change, the parties also do. No case better illustrates that fact than the decline of the city machine in American politics. Civil service and merit systems have gradually robbed it of the patronage jobs with which it rewarded its workers and officers. The ethnic minorities who supported it in its palmiest days have been largely integrated into American life. Increased education and literacy have created a political awareness and sophistication which rebels at being led, sheeplike and docile, to the polls in a "delivered" vote. The growth of the welfare state, too, has provided freely and openly the relief and welfare services which the urban machine "gave" only to its deserving patrons. The growth of suburbia has sapped the center, core cities of their population concentrations. And the growth of national, ideologized poli-

tics and national candidates has helped to break down the isolated political community and the essentially issueless politics of the machine.

Small wonder, then, that the old-style machine organization has fallen
on bad days. One increasingly hears its style and ethics condemned. Its
military discipline and its central authority — its "bossism" — do not sit
well with middle-class Americans in the 1960's. Nor do its issueless politics or its patronage ethic. But all of this is, perhaps, only to say that as an
organizational mode and style the urban machine has outlived its appointed time. And in our tendency to dismiss it we too often forget that
the urban machine was once one of the few agencies integrating the
newly arrived city dwellers into American life and softening their often
desperate condition in strange surroundings. It was also the instrument of
popular democracy, the means by which the popular majorities of the
cities first won control of their cities from old aristocratic and largely
Anglo-Saxon elites.[17]

Indeed, where something approaching the old-style urban machine persists today, it is in circumstances not unlike those the new immigrant
faced in American cities at the turn of the century. The Negro and Puerto
Rican newcomers to the northern cities, for example, face the same (or
more severe) problems of poverty, discrimination, political powerlessness,
ethnic isolation, and inability to cope with the life of the city. Many of the
older political incentives and organizational styles "work" in their neighborhoods. Where lack of education and opportunity restrict job possibilities, the power of the patronage job or political "pull" increases. The new
middle-class politics of affluence has little to offer the citizens of the new
ghettoes, and its middle-class styles and values are those of an America
into which they have not yet been integrated.

It is not easy to measure the decline of the urban machine or the decline of the full range of conventional American party organization. Louis
Harris reported a 1961 study, for example, in which only 4 per cent of
people who had voted in the previous six years had been contacted by
personal canvassing and only 24 per cent of the same group had been
contacted in a campaign by person, mail, or phone. Three-fourths of the
voting electorate, in other words, were reached exclusively, if at all, by
the mass media. While we have no comparable data from earlier periods
of time, it is likely that the Harris data reflect the advent of media campaigning and candidate-centered politics. The candidate projecting his
image and message through the media and personal appearances can replace the political party as the chief organizer and persuader of voters.
And it is unquestionably exactly this revolution in campaigning that has
undermined the power of the conventional party organizations. They are
no longer the indispensable instrument for election to office. The candi-

[17] See M. Ostrogorski, *Democracy and the Organization of Political Parties* (New
York: Anchor, 1964).

date may now purchase the information and skills necessary for the campaign from the pollster and the public relations specialist. Several generations ago he would have had no alternative but to get them from the party organization — at the party's "price."

Contemporary developments in party organization, therefore, feature the sporadic development of both of these candidate-centered campaign organizations and of a club-style, membership organization to accommodate the avocational, middle-class ideologists. What we have today in American party organization is far removed from the *a priori* organizational hierarchies that state legislators have stipulated. They, or something close to them, do exist here and there across the United States, but they are not (and probably never were) the norm in American party organization. Today the state and local party organizations are looser and more flexible. They can more accurately be seen as coalitions of political groupings and a "pool" or reservoir of party-oriented personnel. The county organization may, in other words, be a loose coalition of:

the statutory organization (or that part of it actually manned);

a cluster of related, satellite organizations (the women's and youth auxiliaries, the clubs, and the personal followings of candidates and office-holders);

allied, non-party political organizations (the chamber of commerce, trade unions, other local interest groups, civic organizations, or non-party liberal and conservative groups); and

active and might-be-active individuals.

From this pool of possible activists, groups and individuals are activated differently — and usually only for the short run — by different candidates, different issues, different elections. A hotly contested election of county officials (often dispensers of the local patronage) will activate one cluster of support within the party, and an ideological crusade by the local congressional candidate will activate quite another. What we have usually thought of as "the party organization" is really a nucleus of organization, a continuing "hard core" of organization and activists around which collect the shifting organizational coalitions that speak and act in the name of the party.

In searching for change in American party organization, it is easy to lose sight of what does not change. Despite recent trends the American parties remain largely skeletal, "cadre" party organizations, manned generally by small numbers of activists and involving the great masses of their supporters scarcely at all. The shift away from the hierarchical organizational forms inherent in the statutes of the states has largely been a shift from one tighter, hierarchical kind of cadre organization to newer, looser cadre organizations. For, despite the brave appearance of some membership clubs, the American parties are still a long way away from the mass membership parties of the European democracies. And they are still some distance from the continuously active, year-around tempos of those parties. By the standards of the parties of much of the rest of the world, American party organization continues to be characterized by its unusual fluidity and evanescence, by its failure to generate activity at non-election times, and by the ease with which a handful of activists and public office-holders dominate it.

Chapter Four

THE POLITICAL PARTY
OF THE ACTIVISTS

Behind the imposing facades of the hierarchical structures the states create are the living, organizational realities of the political parties. For the statutes do not reckon with the men and women of the party, their goals and motives, their interactions and relationships, the contributions they make to the party, the price they exact for those contributions. The statutes do indeed set limits and suggest outlines for party organization, but the questions of who staff the party, why and how they do, and how they act in the party's name are closer to the real world of political parties than all the statutory paragraphs put together. Where there is a gap between the reality of party organization and the mandates of a state law on party organization, it is because party organization is far more likely to reflect the goal-seeking behavior of men than even the most determined legislative plans.

While it may not always appear so to the politically cynical, the American major parties are purposive, goal-seeking organizations. As the most completely electoral parties in the democracies of the world, they are preeminently committed to the winning of elections and the capture of public office. Indeed, as we have already commented, the very notion of an American competitive two-party system presumes that electoral victory is their major goal and their highest priority. Additionally, the parties may choose to seek any number of short- and long-run goals — the spread of an ideology, the enactment of a set of public policies, or the easing of state regulation of political finance. But whatever the goal or goals, the political party must select means and strategies for their achievement, always choosing in the knowledge that the other major party and other political organizations are very likely trying similarly to achieve competing goals of their own.

The major political party as an organization, therefore, is a mechanism for uniting adherents in the pursuit of general goals or hierarchies (priorities) of goals. It recruits and mobilizes the resources and skills for political action. In the employment of those resources it works out a division of labor and a hierarchy of authority. Like any other complex organization it, too, has its leaders and followers, its own specialization of role and function, its own internal system of communication. And it is a decision-making apparatus in which choices must repeatedly be made about the mobilization of resources, the setting of strategies, and the deployment of assets. All of these internal processes are what the "private life" of the political party is all about. They are the processes by which the party organization converts "inputs," the raw materials of men, resources, and expertise, into "outputs," the goal-oriented activities of the parties.

Goal-seeking, however, goes on within the party organization on a personal, individual level as well. Individual party leaders, workers, and members are in the party organization for some identifiable, if covert or implicit, set of reasons or motives. There must, in other words, be rewards or incentives — "payoffs" in the very broadest, non-literal sense of the word — for devoting one's leisure time to party activity rather than the service of Kiwanis or Rotary or the improvement of one's golf game. And the recruitment of the right individuals with the right political skills remains the chief organizational problem of the parties.[1]

THE SYSTEM OF INCENTIVES

The American political parties have never operated primarily in a cash economy. They have rarely bought or hired the millions of man-hours of labor they need; even today paid staffs are small or non-existent in most party organizations, and it is a rare party chairman who draws even a pittance of a salary from the organization he serves. The great number of Americans active in the parties receive no cash in return for their often considerable time and skills. Even the earthy old custom of paying precinct workers on election day is vanishing. What is it, then, that induces party workers to lavish their hours and efforts on the affairs of the parties? If the parties' rewards and "payments" are not made in cash, in what coin are they made?

PATRONAGE

Patronage, the use of appointive governmental positions to reward past party work and induce future labors, is hardly unique to the American political parties. Even today the municipal services of the Italian cities swarm with the partisans of the party or parties in political power. But

---

[1] A similar "economizing" model of the American parties is developed in Anthony Downs, *An Economic Theory of Democracy* (New York: Harper, 1957).

very probably no other party system has over its history relied as systematically on it as the American. The easy confidence of the Jacksonians
that no public task was so complex that it demanded experience, and
their matching conviction that "to the victors go the spoils," set its tone
and ethic early in the 19th century. From then to the present a vast array
of public job-holders — from elevator operators and charwomen in city
hall to American ambassadors in foreign capitals — have owed their appointment to political worthiness and the right political sponsorship.

Even with the explosive growth of government bureaucracy in this
century the amount of patronage available to the parties has declined
precipitously. The expansion of civil service and merit systems has been
the chief reason. What was once a flourishing federal patronage — his-
torians write of the hordes of ill-mannered job-seekers overrunning presidential inaugurations — has by now dwindled to something less than 1
per cent of the Federal establishment.[2] There still remain the U.S. mar-
shals, the collectors of customs, and the rural mail carriers, to mention a
few of the classic federal patronage posts, but theirs is a shrinking roster.
Similar declines have come, albeit more slowly, to the states and localities. While any number of states, counties, and cities have virtually
abolished patronage (at least one governor of Wisconsin has estimated his
available patronage positions at about a baker's dozen), it flourishes in
others. Pennsylvania, for example, still has about 50,000 jobs available
for reward, and a number of localities in that state have until very recently included jobs as teachers, police, and firemen within the local
patronage. In fact, the county and city remain the chief centers of patronage. For example:

A recent survey of Democratic party members in St. Louis indicates
that more than 40 per cent hold or have held patronage jobs.[3]

Almost three-fourths of the Democratic committeemen in Pittsburgh
in the late 1950's held public jobs.[4]

And yet for every such example there are many others in which only a
small fraction of party leadership is on the public payrolls.

The reasons for the decline of patronage as an incentive for party work
go beyond the encroachments of civil service reform. The increasing
complexities and importance of many appointive positions forces chief
executives to seek skills as well as political merit. It is difficult enough to
find ambassadors and heavy equipment operators with the desirable

[2] On the federal patronage see Harvey C. Mansfield, "Political Parties, Patronage,
and the Federal Government Service" in *The Federal Government Service* (New York:
The American Assembly, 1954).

[3] Robert H. Salisbury, "The Urban Party Organization Member," *Public Opinion
Quarterly*, XXIX (Winter, 1965–66), p. 558.

[4] William J. Keefe and William C. Seyler, "Precinct Politicians in Pittsburgh,"
Social Science, XXXV (1960), p. 28.

occupational skills without adding a set of political credentials. Also, at a time of relatively full employment the usually poorly paid patronage appointments seem greatly less attractive; the politics of patronage have always worked best among the depressed and disadvantaged. Most patronage positions do not tempt the educated, "successful," "respected" middle-class leadership the parties would like to attract. Furthermore, elected executives may use patronage to build their own political followings rather than the party apparatus; a sizeable percentage of the patronage of the Kennedy administration, for example, went to Democrats "for Kennedy before West Virginia." [5] Finally, the parties may not be able to use the patronage available to them. Especially when they win power after years of failure, they do not have the necessary administrative machinery, the list of job-seekers, or even the will to fire ruthlessly the opposing partisans and replace them with loyal followers.[6]

Perhaps in response both to the shrinking availability of patronage and to the party's shrinking need for it, recent years have seen the development of a new patronage variant: the "political non-job." One writer has recently summarized the development with equal parts of wit and insight: [7]

The members of the new elite corps of American politics — the fund raisers, the intellectual counselors, "media coordinators," and leaders of the growing citizens' movements — are profitably employed already, with better pay and working conditions than government can offer. To them, the most appealing aspect of a public job is the prestige which sometimes accompanies it.

Happily, political leaders have devised ways to bestow the status symbols of high office without the job itself. At Democratic national headquarters in Washington, where many such split-level appointments are routinely requisitioned and cleared, the new institution is known as "the honorary." Elsewhere it has been dubbed the patronage non-job, and it can range from nomination to a White House advisory committee to an invitation to be an honored member of an Air Force civic-inspection tour of California, arranged at the behest of your local Congressman.

So, while by 1961 count there were only 133 full-time appointive jobs available for patronage use in the Interior Department (many of them carrying, moreover, skill and experience qualifications), the Department had 49 advisory committees and commissions with a total membership of about 800, 52 of them presidential appointments (with which the recipient

[5] The phrase refers to those early Kennedy supporters who made a commitment to him before he won the important West Virginia presidential primary in May of 1960. It was an attempt to bypass those johnny-come-latelies who rushed to the Kennedy bandwagon after West Virginia.

[6] On patronage see Daniel P. Moynihan and James Q. Wilson, "Patronage in New York State, 1955–1959," *American Political Science Review,* LVIII (1964), pp. 286–301; James Q. Wilson, "The Economy of Patronage," *Journal of Political Economy,* LXIX (1961), pp. 369–380; and Frank J. Sorauf, "State Patronage in a Rural County," *American Political Science Review,* L (1956), pp. 1046–1056.

[7] Don Oberdorfer, "The New Political Non-Job," *Harpers* (October, 1965), p. 108ff.

receives a parchment certificate signed by the President). The development, one should be clear, is not a novel one. The King or Queen's Honors List has in part served the same function for some time in Britain, and Kentucky has been appointing Colonels for almost as long.

POLITICAL CAREER

Elective political office has for many Americans all of the income, the responsibility, the prestige, and the excitement — not to mention the power — that most patronage positions do not. And since the political party offers an efficient, and in some cases the only, avenue to elective office, it was inevitable that the search for an elective political career would recruit new party activists or sustain that activity after other incentives had "worn off." In the middle 1950's, for instance, about half of a group of Wisconsin party officials from both parties said they either had been elected or defeated in a past try for elective office; 21 per cent declared that they "intended" to run, and 35 per cent "desired" to make a race for office.[8]

There exist those party organizations with such disciplined control over their primaries that they can and do "give" public office, especially at the state and local level, to loyal party workers. If the party dominates the politics of the area, control of the primaries makes public offices into an "elective patronage." The candidate is offered the chance to run and then does little more as the party organization runs up the necessary majorities. More commonly, party endorsements elsewhere carry enough weight and money to make running against the party's choice hazardous or difficult at the least. But regardless of party control over the primary, the party's ability to select its candidates from among its loyal workers depends on the degree of two-party competitiveness in the constituency. The greater the competitiveness the less the possibility of electing any "warm body" and the greater, therefore, the necessity of considering candidate appeal in addition to political worthiness.

But the would-be candidate needs more than the "nod," approval or selection by the party. He needs advice, know-how, manpower, and money — and in most parts of the country the party still remains a likely source of them. Service in the party, then, yields the skill, the experience, the connections, the approval, and the resources that any candidate needs. It is, of course, possible for the candidate without party ties to seek election, but for every one who does, there are hundreds or thousands of successful office-seekers who have party ties. And for the partisan who already holds office there is no easier way to assure reelection or to move to a more attractive office than by work in the party. So sedulous

[8] Leon D. Epstein, *Politics in Wisconsin* (Madison: Univ. of Wisconsin Press, 1958), pp. 91, 187.

are the party's office-holders in currying the support of the party organizations that speculation over their aspirations and "moves" remains one of the most enduring intra-party recreations.

PREFERMENTS

The tangible, material rewards of politics may take, especially in the states and localities, a series of forms other than appointive or elective office. The active partisan or the financial "fat cat" may, for example, seek preference in the awarding of public contracts. In this respect, it is not accidental that the leaders of the construction industry should be so active politically in the states and localities which spend millions every year on roads and public buildings. Preference may take other forms: a tolerant or haphazard application of regulatory or inspection policies, the provision of unusually prompt or efficient public services (premiere snow and garbage removal, for example), a forgiving instrument of the law (e.g., the "fixed" traffic ticket), or the granting of a scarce public service (admission to crowded mental hospitals, for instance). It may also involve the granting of scarce "opportunities," such as liquor licenses or franchises. By "preferment," in other words, one means the gaining of special treatment or advantage, and it is dependent usually on the party's holding the administrative decision-making positions of government. It is partly in this sense that parties talk of "controlling" city hall, the county court-house, or the state capitol.

One particularly unappealing form of political "preferment" is that given activities which operate on the shady side of the law. It may involve a calculated ignoring of prostitution, bookmaking, the numbers game, or traffic in drugs in return for some form of political support; in other forms it has involved the parties' taking a share of protection money or the proceeds from crime, vice, or the rackets. The link between crime and politics in New York, write Glazer and Moynihan, was "complex." [9]

The politicians of course needed money; and political protection was on the whole more important to illegitimate than to legitimate businessmen. Other elements were mixed in. There was ethnic pride, which motivated a Frank Costello as much as it did a businessman who had not become rich as a bootlegger. There was a desire to help out relatives and friends. There was the fact that bootleggers, politicians, lawyers, judges, and policemen had all grown up on the block together, and had never lost touch. How was one to sort out the influences, and decide the significance of the fact that judges and ex-bootleggers and gamblers all sat around the same table to raise money for an orphan's home?

The prevalence of such an incentive to party effort is understandably difficult to estimate. Perhaps it suffices to say that it is probably less vital than the political cynics think and more important than the Pollyannas admit.

[9] Nathan Glazer and Daniel P. Moynihan, *Beyond the Melting Pot* (Cambridge: MIT Press, 1963), pp. 210–212.

SOCIO-ECONOMIC MOBILITY

Political activity offers easy publicity (or notoriety) and contacts for those who seek them — young lawyers trying to build a practice, owners of food and watering spots, insurance and real estate brokers, storekeepers, and the socially ambitious. Party activity often opens up the contacts within the party and public life, and the easy publicity outside, that lead to prosperity in business or profession, to a new job or business opportunity, even to raised social status. It is a generally accepted form of self-advertisement. Writes one observer of the Philadelphia organization men: [10]

One explanation of their motivation would locate the "boys'" essential urge in the factor known as "prestige." The truth is, many intellectuals and many members of the upper class who have come in contact with politicians argue that, for the Irish, Jewish, Italian bright boys who pursue it, politics is a "status-conferring" occupation. The Bill Greens and the Victor Blancs and the Aus Meehans, they point out, could no doubt have earned wealth and even the respect of their fellow-men by selling insurance, practicing law, and the like. But the one thing that they could not earn in these ways is "place" in the community. Politics gives them that.

In the tired American phrase, some people join the active ranks in the parties to "get ahead," whether they define getting ahead in terms of social or economic upward mobility.

SOCIAL AND PSYCHOLOGICAL SATISFACTIONS

The personal, non-material rewards of party activity are not easy to identify, and certainly they are not easy to measure. But one can sense the social rewards of politics in the camaraderie of the "gang" at party headquarters or the court house, and he can see it at a party dinner as the workers press around the great and near great of the party, hoping for a word of greeting or a nod of recognition. In the new style political clubs the attractiveness of the social life and friendship circle is explicit. "Many volunteers are rootless, transient newcomers searching the city for a means of associating with like-minded people." [11] The party organization offers an open and hospitable occasion for meeting people. But while the parties' clubs rely on the social incentives, those incentives are probably either secondary or they attract large numbers of low-activity partisans:

Although many clubs in various cities offer their members reduced air fares to Europe on charter flights, a full schedule of social events, forums featuring prestigious speakers, and the opportunity to play the political game, and although some members join simply to find a mate quickly or get to Paris inex-

[10] James Reichley, *The Art of Government: Reform and Organization Politics in Philadelphia* (New York: Fund for the Republic, 1959), p. 104.
[11] James Q. Wilson, *The Amateur Democrat* (Chicago: Univ. of Chicago Press, 1962), p. 165.

pensively, if the clubs should cease to define themselves as organizations devoted to liberalism or reformism or similar worthy causes, they could not for long sustain the interest of any but the handful who simply enjoy the company of others or like being district leader.[12]

At a more general level, almost all of the reported research on the motivations of party activists finds that large numbers of them reply that they "like people" or that they "like politics."

Social satisfactions merge almost imperceptibly with the psychological. Political activity may bolster the sagging ego or sustain the demanding one.

Like the theater, politics is a great nourisher of egos. It attracts men who are hungry for attention, for assurance that somebody loves them, for the soul-stirring music of their own voices. . . . A main ingredient in the make-up of every successful politician is a thick slice of ham.[13]

Party work may offer the individual a cause or an enterprise with which to identify, a charismatic leader to follow, a round of activities which can lift him above the personally unrewarding tasks of the workaday world. The party may be a small island of excitement in a sea of routine. It may even offer an occasion for the manipulation or domination of others — a chance to decide or command, even an avenue for the projection of aggressions and hostilities.

IDEOLOGY AND POLICY ISSUES

Even the most casual soundings of party rhetoric these days indicate an increasing identification of partisans within the major parties as "liberals" and "conservatives." Behind these phrases lies a potent motivation to party activity: a commitment to clusters and patterns of related attitudes about government and politics — especially about the proper and desirable role of government in contemporary society. Other patterns of attitudes may be wrapped up in commitments to "good government" or "reform." On a more modest and limited scale the spur to activity may be concern for a single issue or interest (tax cuts, the war in Vietnam, the maintenance of local schools, the well-being of a neighborhood or a racial or ethnic group) or a single area of policy concern (foreign policy, civil rights, local planning and development). The "cause" may, indeed, be the reform or rehabilitation of the political party itself.

Just as the importance of the immediate, material, personal rewards of politics have recently declined, those of issue and ideology have increased. Even in Manhattan, long the fief of Tammany Hall, the trend is evident:

[12] *Ibid.*
[13] John Fischer, "Please Don't Bite the Politicians," *Harper's* (November, 1960), p. 16.

. . . there is a "new look" among today's political activists. They are "respectable," solid middle-class citizens. The party "hack" of fiction, films, and the traditional literature is hard to find among the young, well-educated, affluent, and
socially acceptable committeemen — and women — of the nineteen-sixties. Con-
comitantly, both the nature of political motivation and the character of political
activity have changed. The contemporary politician considers his party organization an instrument for effectuating policy rather than a haven of personal
security. He tends to be more interested in social reform than in catering to
individual constituents.[14]

In national politics the country in 1964 witnessed the capture of the Republican national party by partisans whose chief criterion for candidate
and platform was frankly ideological.[15]

The activist may also be drawn to the party by a more general civic
ideology. A sense of political responsibility and obligation, a concept of
the duty of a citizen, may impel him. Scholars who have questioned party
officials and workers about their reasons or motives for working in the
parties know the familiar answers. They were "asked" to serve, and they
acceded out of a personal view of good citizenship. Often that response,
in whatever words it may be couched, merely masks what the respondent
feels are less acceptable motives. Often, however, it is an honest testa-
ment to the power of deeply-ingrained civic values. Those values rarely
operate alone, but they do reinforce and provide important rationaliza-
tion for other goals and motives.

THE PARTY ITSELF

Two final varieties of incentive, both essentially related to the party *per
se*, must be mentioned. First of all, as a party activist works within the
party, the health and well-being of the party itself become an incentive
for work; the party becomes an end in itself. It retains its capacity for
achieving the goals and rewards of politics, but at the same time its
workers attach many of their loyalties and aspirations to it. The party's
wins and losses become issues in and of themselves, and attacks on it are
far more than attacks on its policies and activities. Secondly, it may be,
as Robert Salisbury suggests in his study of St. Louis politicians, that
large numbers of party activists participate "because they were brought
up in a highly politicized atmosphere." [16] The party

participant *per* family socialization was probably not exposed to involvement
in other kinds of organizations, any more than a devout young communicant of
the church would necessarily be taught to carry his devotion into other organizational settings.

[14] Robert S. Hirschfield, Bert E. Swanson, and Blanche D. Blank, "A Profile of
Political Activists in Manhattan," *Western Political Quarterly*, XV (1962), p. 505.
[15] Party ideology will be considered more fully in Chapter 16.
[16] Robert H. Salisbury, *op. cit.*, pp. 562, 564.

Our findings suggest that much political behavior is to be explained as habitual. It is not directly derived from the intellectual, economic, social, or characterological features of the actors. It is an aspect of a life style that has been accepted uncritically since childhood by a relatively small number of people in the society.

Party workers may gravitate to the party because they are accustomed to it and because through years of socialization they have invested loyalties in it.

No party organization depends on a single incentive, and very few individual partisans labor in the party for only one. The party organization relies on a varied series or "system" of incentives. That incentive system differs from organization to organization, and it differs within a single organization as well. One set of incentives may recruit the precinct workers while another lures the party leadership. Eldersveld reports that in Wayne County, Michigan, precinct chairmen depend heavily on the rewards of social contacts and associations, but party leadership in the county and congressional districts seeks immediate economic gain and ideological-philosophical rewards.[17] The individual worker for his part is recruited by a congeries of incentives. He may, furthermore, shift his motivations in the course of party work. Part of the socialization process within the party organization may be to make the worker aware of the range of incentives open to him.

THE PROCESSES OF RECRUITMENT

The mere existence of the incentives for work in the party organization will not automatically produce a full roster of active workers. In the political party, as in any other large organization, the organization itself may want to limit or control recruitment in order to assure itself useful and compatible recruits. It has a "shopping list" of qualities it would like its activists to have. And the potential activist may lack both the knowledge of the opportunity or the stimulus to act. There must, therefore, be some process of recruitment which will join "opportunity" and "stimulus" to the incentives in order to attract the activist.

The parties, however, find it especially difficult to undertake this recruitment and, thus, to undertake their own continuing renewal. Frequently their incentives are not attractive enough to compete even with the modest pleasures of activity in the PTA. They lack any effective mechanism for recruiting new personnel, and they may even lack the awareness of the necessity. Furthermore, state statutes often take at least part of the recruitment process out of their hands; open party caucuses and the election of party officials at primaries tend to encourage self-

[17] Samuel J. Eldersveld, *Political Parties: A Behavioral Analysis* (Chicago: Rand McNally, 1964), p. 278; see also all of Chapter 11.

recruitment at the expense of party initiatives and control. Above all, the generally low level of organizational vitality, and the chronic need for personnel of any kind, disposes the parties to laxness in recruitment. Even in patronage-rich organizations in job-poor communities the parties tend not to be rigorous in recruiting new activists. Friendship and contacts within the party organization may speed the entry of the new activist more effectively than political skills or promise of performance.

In the absence of regular, rigorous party recruitment procedures, opportunities and occasions for party work come in a haphazard way. Initially, a certain degree of awareness of and information about the parties is necessary. A significant percentage of partisans acquire them at home; large numbers of American politicians have had at least one politically active parent. The later, immediate stimulus for the initial involvement in party work will be one of two kinds:

1. *self-starting:* these stimuli originate within the activist himself and are a direct result of the rewards and incentives he perceives in partisan politics.
2. *external:* these originate outside of the potential activist; most commonly they involve the persuasiveness of party leaders, friends, relatives, and occupational and social contacts.

Activists tend to ascribe their initial recruitment largely to external stimuli; two recent studies of local party workers set the self-starters at 10 and 29 per cent of the group interviewed.[18] In view of popular disapproval of the man aggressively seeking the office, however, the party workers may well protest too much.

The explicit recruitment activities of party organizations, party leaders, or outsiders, however, do not adequately explain why specific men and women have entered the active corps of the parties. In a broader sense we have an extensive, informal "recruitment system" — a complex of interrelated factors which selects out of the American population a particular group of men and women. Among its elements one would have to include:

the motives and goals of the men and women with the kinds of skills and assets the parties want to recruit.

the incentives to party activity which the party can offer.

the external factors which alter the value of the incentive (e.g., the impact of employment levels on the value of patronage) or the ability of the individual to accept it (e.g., laws such as the Hatch Acts which forbid active party work by U.S. civil servants).

[18] Phillip Althoff and Samuel C. Patterson, "Political Activism in a Rural County," *Midwest Journal of Political Science,* X (1966), pp. 39–51, and Lewis Bowman and G. R. Boynton, "Recruitment Patterns Among Local Party Officials," *American Political Science Review,* LX (1966), pp. 667–676. Generally, on the initial recruitment to party work, see also Eldersveld, Chapter 6.

the factors which limit the party's recruitment role (e.g., the election of precinct workers at primaries).

the contacts, overtures, opportunities, and persuasions that are the immediate, proximate occasions of recruitment.[19]

The components of this system change constantly, and as they do they affect the supply of personnel entering the organization and, thus, the organization itself. Recruitment in whatever form, though, is a matching of the motives and goals of the individual with the incentives and expectations of the party organization. The immediate act of recruitment is either the catalyst or the occasion for the matching.

An auxiliary recruitment system may also work within the organization to promote especially successful party workers to new positions of higher party responsibility. What data we have on the political careers of party activists, however, do not suggest that party workers uniformly inch, position by position, up a career ladder in the party. For example, only about one-third of a recent group of county chairmen and co-chairmen in Oklahoma had ever held any other party office, and half of them had never held any public or party office at all.[20] But on the other hand, Detroit area party leadership tends to rise almost exclusively through the avenues of party and public office; one group comes up through the precinct positions, another through the auxiliary organizations (i.e., the women's groups, youth organizations, political clubs), and a third and smaller group moves from the race for public office to a career within the party.[21] In general the way stations of a political career vary with and reflect the nature of the political organization. In those party organizations of relatively open and free access and easy mobility, political careers are easily, almost spontaneously, developed. In the disciplined, hierarchical party organization, the party activist works up the hierarchy in carefully graded steps and expectations.

THE PARTIES' RECRUITS

Since recruitment patterns both change over time and differ from locality to locality, it is difficult to generalize about the activists they recruit into the party organization. Note, for example, the differences between the local committeemen and committeewomen of the Democratic parties of Pittsburgh and Manhattan that are related to fundamental differences in the incentive and recruitment systems: [22]

[19] For an alternate, but similar, recruitment model, see the Bowman and Boynton article cited in footnote 18.

[20] Samuel C. Patterson, "Characteristics of Party Leaders," *Western Political Quarterly*, XVI (1963), pp. 343–344.

[21] Eldersveld, *op. cit.*, pp. 142–143.

[22] Taken from Keefe and Seyler, *op. cit.*, and Hirschfield, Swanson, and Blank, *op. cit.*

	Pittsburgh (1954)	*Manhattan (1959–60)*
Patronage holders:	¾ of men, ⅓ of women	Approximately 5% "on public payroll"
Education:	18% attended or graduated from college	67% attended or graduated from college
Age:	20% under 40	28% under 35
Occupations:	Overwhelmingly governmental	19% business executives and professional; 24% small businessmen

This is not to suggest that any single factor in the recruitment (in this case the presence or absence of the patronage incentive) fully explains the differences between the Democratic activists of these two city organizations. Here and in other instances the differences may also reflect the kinds of personnel the organization wants and needs, differences in organizational roles and tasks (as between dominant and minority parties or "machine" and club-style parties), or even differences in what the local community considers acceptable motives and incentives. And since most of these differences are not primarily differences between the two major parties, the differences among party activists are frequently greater from region to region in the country, or from urban to rural area, than they are between Democrats and Republicans.[23]

American party activists, despite all of the variations in recruitment systems, do have in common two characteristics which set them apart from the general population of adults. First, they tend rather uniformly to come from families with a history of party activity. Study after study indicates that large numbers of party activists had in their immediate family an adult party activist as they were growing up. Secondly, they are marked by their relatively high socio-economic status (SES), whether one measures SES by income, by years of formal education completed, or by occupation. The highest SES among the active partisans can be found, as one might expect, in the top leadership ranks of the parties. Close to two-thirds of the membership of the national party committees from 1948 to 1963 had at least one college degree, and virtually all of them (except women with no occupations) fell into professional, official, and managerial occupations.[24] Every study of county and congressional district leadership indicates that those activists, too, are far above the national population in SES. Only some local organizations, and especially their precinct workers, have been exceptions; in general only in patronage-

[23] For a comparison of the differences in incentives and recruitment between dominant and minority parties, see Peter H. Rossi and Phillips Cutright, "The Impact of Party Organization in an Industrial Setting," in Morris Janowitz (ed.), *Community Political Systems* (Glencoe: Free Press, 1961), pp. 81–116.

[24] Cornelius P. Cotter and Bernard C. Hennessy, *Politics Without Power* (New York: Atherton, 1964), pp. 47–52.

oriented, favor-dispensing machines in the center cities are the party workers at all representative of the populations in which they work. The effect, then, is for the parties to attract men and women with the time and financial resources to be able to "afford" politics, with the information and knowledge to understand it, and with the skills to be useful in it.

Table 1
INCOME, OCCUPATION, AND EDUCATION FOR MIDDLE AND
LOWER-LEVEL PARTY LEADERS:
WAYNE COUNTY (MICH.) STUDY

	Republicans		Democrats	
	Executive Board	Precinct Leaders	Executive Board	Precinct Leaders
Income				
Under $4,000	0%	15%	0%	7%
$4,000–$5,000	10	10	0	16
$5,000–$10,000	52	35	100	53
Over $10,000	38	35	0	17
Not ascertainable	0	5	0	6
Education				
Only elementary	9	11	0	14
High school	30	38	75	60
College (other than business college)	61	51	25	26
Completed college	52	22	18	14
Occupation (of head of household)				
Professionals	43	19	18	16
Managers, proprietors	17	36	29	10
Clerical and sales	9	14	6	17
Blue collar (craftsmen, foremen)	30	16	41	35
Blue collar (semi- and unskilled)	0	15	6	22
Number of cases	23	143	18	138

In most parts of the country, however, Republican activists come from higher SES groups than do their Democratic counterparts. One table (Table 1) in the Eldersveld study of the Detroit area parties illustrates economically this SES difference between the two parties (and also between their middle leadership and precinct workers as well).[25] The higher SES of Republican workers and leaders is also generally matched by the similar characteristic of voters who vote habitually for Republican candidates or identify with the Republican party. Their higher SES in turn reflects the policy and ideological sympathies of the Republicans for

[25] Eldersveld, op. cit., p. 52.

higher income and status groups over the last generation or more.[26] One exception to the SES ascendancy of the Republicans does, however, appear. In one-party Democratic areas the dominant Democratic party attracts high-status leadership, probably because it is both "respectable" as the party of power and inviting as the party of opportunity.[27]

Within this overloading of high-status activists one special dominance — that of lawyers — is both too obvious to be overlooked and too well known to bear much more elaboration. In all of American politics, including the political parties, the lawyers are the high priests of the cult. Over 40 per cent of national committeemen (as distinguished from the national committeewomen) from 1948 to 1963 were lawyers.[28] Recent studies of county chairmen in Oklahoma, Kansas, and Wisconsin show a median percentage of attorneys among the county chairmen somewhat above 20 per cent.[29] To an extent unduplicated in other democracies the lawyer is in the American society the professional political careerist. He has cultivated skills of oratory and debate, and he is occupationally concerned with laws and the actions of governments. He is also schooled in public issues and practiced in parliamentary procedures. Naturally he appears to many Americans ideally prepared and suited to assume political leadership. He generally also has the necessary community contacts and flexible time schedules for party activity; his professional income and stature also stand to gain from political activity. The major parties even reserve for him a special type of attractive political reward — the elective and politically appointive judgeship.[30]

Workers in the two parties tend also to vary in religion and ethnic background. In a significant number of localities across the country the Democratic party organizations have larger percentages of Catholics and Jews, those of the Republican party larger percentages of Protestants. Similarly (and very much relatedly), Democratic workers more frequently than Republicans come from Irish and Southern and Eastern European national and ethnic stock. Republicans come more frequently from North and Western European backgrounds and from "old Yankee" families.[31] These inter-party differences again reflect the basic voter coalitions of the two parties, and ultimately they mirror the SES divisions between them,

[26] The nature of the parties' electoral coalitions will be discussed more fully in Chapter 6.

[27] See Samuel C. Patterson, "Characteristics of Party Leaders," *Western Political Quarterly*, XVI (1963), pp. 332–352. It is also interesting to note that while the party leaders do come from upper SES groups, they do not, by and large, come from the true community elites or "establishments."

[28] Cotter and Hennessy, *op. cit.*, p. 50.

[29] Patterson, *op. cit.*, p. 339.

[30] One cannot list, or even summarize, the literature dealing with lawyers in American politics. For example, see Heinz Eulau and John D. Sprague, *Lawyers in Politics* (Indianapolis: Bobbs-Merrill, 1964).

[31] For example, see Keefe and Seyler, *op. cit.*

for it is by now no secret that the ethnic groups of the Republican electorate rank higher in SES than do those of the Democrats. Of course,
there is an equal tendency for the party activists of both parties to reflect
the ethnic, racial, national, and religious composition of a homogeneous
area. They are the sons and daughters of the locally dominant or prominent groups. While they are thoroughly "representative" of these groups,
their education, income, and occupation (especially of the Republicans)
may still be well above the SES average for the area.

So much for the social characteristics of the organizational activists.
There remains the tantalizing and elusive question of their personalities
and their psyches. On a common sense level, one can say without fear of
contradiction that party activists are often gregarious and extroverted.
Yet, that observation is almost true by definition alone, for party activity
is not apt to appeal to the introvert or the misanthrope. But Harold Lasswell and others have argued that there is a special "political personality,"
that political life attracts men and women with personal tensions that can
be easily projected on public objects or personal needs that can be sub-
limated or satisfied in political activity.[32] No convincing evidence exists,
however, that the parties attract activists with any different or more
pressing personality needs than the American population as a whole. One
study does find, in fact, that the incidence of "authoritarian personalities"
is not high in party work. (The few authoritarians do tend to favor both
disciplined, hierarchical party organizations and non-ideological party
goals and activities.) [33]

It goes without saying that "people" are the parties' chief resource, its
major organizational input. But different people bring different expectations, different goals, different skills to the party. To a considerable extent
the style of party organization, and its goals and activities, will reflect the
men and women its incentives are able to recruit into party activity. The
differences in organizational characteristics between Democrats and Republicans in any locality — or between reformers and regulars within a
party — begin with differences in the party workers themselves, their
backgrounds and skills, their personal goals and motives, their perception
of their rights and roles as party activists, and their understanding of the
ultimate goals and priorities of the party and its representatives.

LIFE WITHIN THE PARTY ORGANIZATION

It may be unnecessary to suggest that the party organization *is* an organization. It is more than the sum of the resources it has recruited and the
aggregate of the activity of its activists. Its very nature and usefulness

---

[32] Harold Lasswell, *Psychopathology and Politics* (Chicago: Univ. of Chicago Press,
1931) and his *Power and Personality* (New York: Norton, 1948).
[33] Louise Harned, "Authoritarian Attitudes and Party Activity," *Public Opinion
Quarterly*, XXV (1961), pp. 393–399.

arises from the fact that groups of political activists can, through its mobilizations and its divisions of labor, gain in concert a measure of political power they could not amass as individuals. The party organization is an efficient apparatus for recruiting political resources and expending them in the pursuit of political goals. And its vast network of roles, relationships, and activities are essential to that apparatus. Its very organizational capacity results from its stable patterns of authority, decision-making, and responsibility — from the specialization of role and skills employed in the achievement of common political objectives.

There is no single form of American party organization. There is only diversity of organizational form and, therefore, diversity of organizational goals, styles, and resources. For decades the American model or ideal in party organization has been the form of local organization typified by the classic urban "machine." Its organizational hierarchy, its full range of year-around services and activities, and its army of eager workers in the wards and precincts have represented organizational perfection to many party leaders. It is an organizational form in which the personal attention, service, friendship, and persuasiveness of the local party worker is directed at the local electorate. All of its activities through the year are geared to earn the support of that electorate (i.e., to "deliver" its vote) and thus enable the activists and office-seekers of the party to achieve their political goals through victory at the polls.

As the last chapter suggested, the ideal has never been the norm. The classic machine organization was never widespread in either of the two major parties in the United States. Its chief and indispensable ingredient, the local ward or precinct worker, has too often been inactive or completely absent. The recent evidence, even in the American cities, has begun to mount:

> Of party activists in St. Louis, some 27 per cent do not perform "any significant amount of political or electioneering tasks." [34]

> Only about one-fourth of a group of workers in Massachusetts and North Carolina performed all four "critical" campaign tasks (door-to-door canvassing, telephone campaigning, transporting people to the polls, and talking to voters about the election); only one-half of them performed any three.[35]

> In the Detroit area only 13 per cent of the Democratic precinct workers and 3 per cent of the Republicans met criteria of organizational efficiency close to the model of the well-organized political machine.[36]

Were there comparable data on rural and small-town party organization, it would surely suggest further disorganization.

[34] Salisbury, op. cit., p. 557.
[35] Lewis Bowman and G. R. Boynton, "Activities and Role Definitions of Grassroots Party Officials," Journal of Politics, XXVIII (1966), pp. 132–134.
[36] Eldersveld, op. cit., p. 348.

However, the organizational problem extends beyond inert or "under-active" committeemen. The parties do not easily maintain the nexus of roles and relationships on which the organizational paragon depends. Eldersveld's study of the Detroit parties offers the fullest analysis. Communication lines in the parties, he found,[37]

were not a perfect pyramid; communication was highly voluntaristic and non-coercive. From one-fourth to two-fifths of the precinct leaders did not have contacts with their district leaders, and from 10 to 15 per cent seemed almost completely isolated. Further, the content of communication in the party seemed highly preoccupied with "vote getting" and campaign tactics.

Nor were authority relationships pyramided.

. . . the vast majority of precinct leaders were "little oligarchs," running their operations alone or with "friends and neighbors," with limited contact and involvement in district-level operations, and with limited reasons for self-consciously adjusting their work patterns and plans to perceive district-level demands.[38]

Throughout the Detroit parties, in fact, there is only diversity where the ideal would assume monolithic homogeneity. Local workers enter and remain in party service for a splendid variety of motives. They carry out different tasks, even within the same party, and they have differing political values and differing perceptions of political reality — even different views of their own and the opposing party. And they differ greatly in the way they perceive their roles as precinct leaders. The parties "did not communicate one particular role conception to rank-and-file leaders. The party line, if there was one, was confused and poorly communicated." As a result, some 45 per cent saw themselves chiefly as vote mobilizers, 24 per cent as ideological leaders, 18 per cent as welfare promoters for local residents, and 10 per cent appeared to have formulated no role at all.[39]

Yet, the ideal and the myth of American party organization remains strong. Party organizations across the country are judged against it, and hopeful party leaders aspire to it. Almost every concept of organizational strength or vitality employs it. Yet, it is in many ways a late 19th century ideal; it reflected the methods of campaigning and the nature of the American electorate in that era. Perhaps as an organizational type it is either not necessary in view of today's campaigns and elections or not feasible in view of today's political resources. Very possibly voters can be reached — or will have to be reached — by means other than the ubiquitous precinct worker. Certainly no one form or style of party organiza-

---

[37] *Ibid.*, p. 377.
[38] *Ibid.*, p. 408.
[39] *Ibid.*, p. 254, 270. For 3 per cent of the leaders the roles were not ascertained. On organizational relationships in general, see also the Rossi and Cutright study cited in footnote 23.

tion (and no one kind of organizational incentive or activist) is best or optimal; different political traditions, resources, and styles demand different kinds of party organization.

Leaving judgments of strength and weakness aside, American party organizations do differ in their distance from the classic organizational type. And it is possible to generalize roughly about the conditions under which they will or will not approach it.

URBAN-RURAL DIFFERENCES

The close proximity of people in residential neighborhoods makes possible the intense political activity, the intricate organizational life, and the stable political loyalties of the highly developed political machines. So, too, do the problems of the cities and the presence of the unassimilated minorities there. Door-to-door campaigning, election rallies, party headquarters, even regular contact with the voters — all the signs of strong and vigorous party organization make far less sense in rural America. Party nominating and electioneering differ there, and so do the incentives for and the total amount of party activity. Not surprisingly, then, the acmes of party organization have been reached in the urban, and especially in the metropolitan, centers.[40]

DIFFERENCES IN POLITICAL CULTURES

The expectations citizens have about political party organization may and do differ. The persistent canvassing by committeemen and their frank questions about voter preferences may be taken as a matter of course in some quarters, but not in others. Similarly, patronage and the political organization founded on it may be respectable in some states or localities but not in others. What may seem a benevolent party organization to one set of voters may appear equally malevolent to others. These differences in political culture tend to follow urban-rural lines, thus reinforcing those differences in party organization, but there are as well regional and social-class differences in norms and expectations for the parties.[41]

DIFFERENCES IN TWO-PARTY COMPETITIVENESS

Unquestionably the great number of defunct — or extinct — party organizations occur in the long-term minority parties. The Republican parties of the Deep South until the 1950's served for a long time as their classic illustration. Badly demoralized, only scarcely respectable, and shorn of both influence and hope, the minority party easily lapses into organizational feebleness. It can provide none of the rewards, tangible or intan-

[40] See Frank J. Sorauf, *Party and Representation* (New York: Atherton, 1963), especially Chapter 3.

[41] The problem of the impact of the political culture on the political parties will be taken up more fully in Chapter 17.

gible, that induce men to give their time, skills, or money to a party organization.[42]

DIFFERENCES IN STATE STATUTES

Within a single state the inflexible statutory forms can usually be adapted more comfortably to urban than rural areas. Attempts to impose the neighborhood organization and the full-blown party hierarchy on the small town or rural area work to their disadvantage simply by forcing them into uncongenial molds. Among and between the states, the statutory forms and regulations of some states are simply more burdensome and cumbersome than those of others. All other things being equal, for example, a party is handicapped by a state requirement that all party functionaries be chosen at the primary.

DIFFERENCES IN PRIMARY LAWS

In a number of states with a high order of efficient party organization — Indiana, Connecticut, and Rhode Island come to mind — the organizations still nominate candidates for statewide offices and some local ones at conventions. That is, the direct primaries of those states are among the least comprehensive in the country, and in the case of Connecticut the primary did not come until 1955. Consequently the party still has a vital and important nominating role left to it — a purpose for which to maintain organizational capacity. Lockard has written of the Connecticut parties: [43]

In the absence of a primary the opportunity for political advancement lay with the organization, not through independent appeals to the electorate in a primary election. Local organizations had reason to exist even where there was little hope of winning an election for their party, for there were state conventions biennially in which important decisions were made. In contrast to many states in which the primary has been employed, there has been no appreciable withering away of the party organization in local areas.

V. O. Key, in fact, has argued that the introduction of the direct primary into American politics in this century is primarily responsible for the "atrophy" of local party organization throughout the country.[44]

Such a list of explanations is not intended to be comprehensive. The availability of patronage or other rewards of preference explain the development of some powerful local or statewide organizations. In other instances one may simply have to introduce the explanation of the effort and skill of a particular party leader or group of leaders. Hard work and

[42] V. O. Key, *Southern Politics* (New York: Knopf, 1949), Chapter 13.
[43] Lockard, *New England State Politics*, p. 255.
[44] V. O. Key, *American State Politics* (New York: Knopf, 1956), Chapter 6.

organizational ability are as easily felt in the parties as they are in any
other large social group.

POWER AND DISCIPLINE IN THE ORGANIZATION

Organization implies discipline — at least enough discipline to maintain
the coordination of its parts and the implementation of its decisions. It
also implies some well-established system of power or authority for making those decisions. The organizational myths of American politics have,
if anything, overreacted to these implications and posited the necessity
and the presence of centralized and virtually authoritarian control within
the party organization. Some leader generally identified as the "boss" has
widely been thought to wield absolute power over its minions. Much as a
Renaissance despot, he was said to rule by reason of his cunning, knav-
ery, and sheer force of will. The "boss," in fact, became something of an
American folk hero, feared for his ruthlessness and admired for his rascality and intrepid daring. He has been celebrated in the public arts,[45]
and if he had not existed, it might have been necessary to create him, if
only to justify the political cynicism of generations of Americans.

Very few organizational leaders ruled or now rule absolutely by personal magnetism, tactical adroitness, or the use of sanctions. Even in the
era of boss rule his power was shared with influential underlings, and the
terms of that sharing were deeply rooted in all of the hierarchical traditions of the organization.

. . . the persistent attacks on "Boss rule" have misrepresented the nature of
power in the old machine system. Power was hierarchical in the party, diffused
in the way it is diffused in an army. Because the commanding general was
powerful, it did not follow that the division generals were powerless. Tammany
district leaders were important men, and, right down to the block captain, all
had rights.[46]

Yet it does remain true that in many of the classic political organizations
power and discipline was greatly centralized and largely removed from
the control of workers and activists in the wards and precincts. The local
leader had his rights, but they were bounded by the greater rights and
authority of his superiors.

Much of that centralization was possible because the foot soldier in the
ranks of the machine accepted its hierarchical system of authority. If he
was a Catholic, and many were, the party's hierarchy may have seemed
as natural and inevitable as that of the Church. Furthermore, his goals
were clear and simple; if he received his patronage job, he cared little

---

[45] For example, note Edwin O'Connor, *The Last Hurrah* (Boston: Little, Brown,
1956); Garson Kanin, *Born Yesterday* (New York: Viking, 1946); and Robert Penn
Warren, *All the King's Men* (New York: Harcourt Brace, 1946).

[46] Glazer and Moynihan, *op. cit.*, p. 227.

about what the party did or did not do. More recently, however, the party activist demands a voice in the affairs of the party. He brings to his work a fuller set of expectations about the party itself and about his role and responsibility within it. He comes to the party more to "participate" than to "work." He is an ideologist, and a goodly portion of his ideological fervor may be directed at reforming the party's authoritarianism and bossism.[47] He is committed to the norms and imperatives of democracy, at least in part because of his rising level of education and political information. His commitment to intra-party democracy also follows logically from his desire to move the party to ideology, for the achievement of his own political goals hinges directly on the party's achieving congruent ones. So, he must reform the American parties if he is to reform American society.

The maintenance of discipline within the organization depends largely on the control of sanctions. Sanctions in turn depend on the ability of the organization to withdraw or withhold its incentives. Much of the discipline of the classic machine resulted from the willingness and ability of party leaders to manipulate the material rewards of patronage and preferment. The recalcitrant, rebellious, or inefficient committeeman sacrificed his public job or his hope for it. The party controlled — even monopolized — these rewards; what it had given it could take away. The newer incentives, however, cannot be as easily given or revoked. The party is only one among many organizations pursuing policy or ideological goals; and given the party's very imperfect control of its legislators, it may not even be the most efficient means to these issue ends. The ideologically-oriented activist may find substitute outlets for his activities in interest groups or non-party political associations like neighborhood associations, the Americans for Democratic Action, or the John Birch Society. As for the partisans pursuing social rewards, there is no way the party can deny these to them short of expulsion or ostracism. The least satisfactory incentives for the parties are exactly these non-manipulable, non-political incentives. They do not in themselves spur political activity, and they cannot be used as sanctions.[48]

Whether or not concentrated, irresponsible power has been a fact within the party organizations, it is just as important that large numbers of Americans have thought it to be. The American political culture is almost haunted by the fear that a few men, responsible to no one, will (in "smoke-filled rooms") control the selection of public officials and set the agendas of political debate and policy-making. Understandably, the search for mechanisms with which to control that power has been a long and diligent one.

[47] Wilson, *The Amateur Democrat,* Chapter 5.
[48] I have dealt in greater length with the organizational uses of incentives in *Political Parties in the American System* (Boston: Little, Brown, 1964).

EXTERNAL CONTROLS

"Political laissez-faire" suggests that two competitive parties will set limits to each other's exercise of organizational power by their very competitive presence. The argument is, of course, directly parallel to the argument of the self-regulating effects of economic competition in the free market-place. If one party offers the electorate a shoddy political product or if it "overprices" its political goods, it will lose its political consumers to its competitor. But one-partyism — the "monopoly" of the political system — negates the argument; and some of the very centers of greatest organizational power are without serious two-party competition. The spread of two-party competitiveness and the expansion of the electorate in some areas of the country may, however, spur the development of watchfully competitive parties in what had been areas of one-party domination.

Additionally, the states have imposed statutory controls on party power. Their successes have, however, not matched their disappointments. In those states in which voters at the primary pick precinct committeemen and other party officials, there are rarely contests for the offices; frequently, indeed, there is not even a single candidate. And in other states the attempts to regulate the holding of party caucuses and conventions may not effectively guarantee access to all qualified comers. The members of the Mississippi Freedom Democratic party charged at the 1964 Democratic national convention that they were not admitted to the regular party meetings which elected county convention delegates; when they were elected delegates, they were not seated at the conventions. Or, statutory access may merely facilitate the alternation of oligarchies. Of the capture of the Republican party in the state of Washington by the Goldwater forces in early 1964, Theodore White writes: [49]

> Precinct caucuses are held in Washington every two years — in homes, in apartments, in libraries, some attended by a few hundred people, some by only three or four. A good guess is that only some 60,000 Washington Republicans turn out for their precinct caucuses. Of these, 15,000 get elected to county conventions; of these, 877 go on to the state convention, which chooses national delegates. It does not take too much money to dominate the system, and the Goldwater Republicans in Washington did the entire job on $35,000 — "not a nickel from out of state," says Luke Williams. . . . In February the precinct groups caucused, and the Goldwater people were all these; the delegates they elected met in county committees in March and April; by June 11th to 13th, when the counties had sent their delegates to the state convention to choose 24 national delegates, the Goldwater people, under Luke Williams, controlled the state convention lock, stock and barrel.

The effect of these external controls is extremely difficult to gauge. Competitiveness does make a difference, however — even if it is only the

[49] *The Making of the President—1964* (New York: Atheneum, 1965), pp. 140–141.

limited competitiveness of factionalism. The major outrageous and blatant uses of party power in the United States have indeed occurred in the one-party cities or regions. Statutorily protected access has in many states opened the party both to the competitions of other factions or oligarchies and to reinvigoration by new party personnel. And in all of the states the direct primary has at least forced the parties to face the scrutiny of voters on one very key decision: the nomination of candidates for office. Beyond these two mechanisms, the mass communications media and the other political organizations do, by their watchfulness and readiness to criticize, set other limits to organizational power. But realistically, the major sources of control remain within the party itself.

INTERNAL CONTROLS

In his sweeping "iron law of oligarchy" Roberto Michels declared without reservation or qualification some sixty years ago that majorities within organizations were incapable of governing themselves. Organizations were by their nature oligarchic or "minoritarian," for only the active minority had the experience, the interest, and the involvement necessary to manage the affairs of complex organizations.

Organization implies the tendency to oligarchy. In every organization, whether it be a political party, a professional union, or any other association of the kind, the aristocratic tendency manifests itself very clearly. The mechanism of the organization, while conferring a solidity of structure, induces serious changes in the organized mass, completely inverting the respective position of the leaders and the led. As a result of organization, every party or professional union becomes divided into a minority of directors and a majority of directed.[50]

To the extent that we are all "believers" in the myths of the bosses, the smoke-filled rooms, and the "deals" between oligarchs, we are all in one sense children of Michels.

The kind of intra-party democracy that Michels lamented has, however, little relevance to the non-membership, cadre organizations of the American major parties. For, who are the participating members, the ineffective "majorities" here? The party in the electorate which the state statutes permit to choose some party leaders are "members" in only the loosest sense. Only in isolated parts of the country have the parties developed bona fide membership organizations. American parties are largely made up of "chiefs" of varying degrees of importance; there are relatively few "indians." Or to return to Michels, there is really no inactive majority within the American parties. The party is the cadre, and it is made up of activists — active in varying degrees, of course — who are reckoned as being "of" the party simply because they *are* active as work-

[50] Roberto Michels, *Political Parties* (Glencoe: Free Press, 1949; originally published in 1915), p. 32.

ers, officers, leaders, or even hangers-on. Control of party power must, therefore, come largely from within the party cadre. The relevant question is really not so much one of "control" as it is of the distribution of power within the organizational leadership.

The distribution of power within most American party organizations can be described in Samuel Eldersveld's apt term: stratarchy. It is "the enlargement of the ruling group of an organization, its power stratification, the involvement of large numbers of people in group decision-making, and, thus, the diffusion and proliferation of control throughout the structure."[51] Various levels of party organization operate at least semi-independently of other, even superordinate, levels. Precinct committeemen, district leaders, even county officials freely define their own political roles and nourish their separate bases of party power. So, "although authority to speak for the organization may remain in the hands of the top elite nucleus, there is great autonomy in operations at the lower 'strata' or echelons of the hierarchy, and . . . control from the top is minimal and formal."[52]

What accounts for stratarchy and the failure of top party leaders to centralize organizational power in the hierarchy? One might suppose, given the relatively low levels of activity at the lowest party levels, that they would pose no barrier to that centralization. Indeed, significant numbers of precinct leaders may not even want or expect a voice in party affairs. Experience and expertise are surely on the side of the top party leadership, and so is the need for tactical flexibility. So, too, is the power to manipulate some of the party's incentives for the purposes of centralizing power.[53]

Yet, weighing in against the centralization of authority and power, against the development of a centralized party oligarchy, are these factors:

1. *Participatory expectations.* Larger percentages of the new party activists — accustomed to being beneficiaries of the democratic ethos in the PTA or their fraternal clubs — expect also to find it in the political party in which they have chosen to work. The party may, therefore, have to tolerate or even "create" intra-party democracy (or consultation) to maintain organizational vitality, lift morale, and achieve cohesion.

2. *Controls of lower party levels over the higher.* Most notably the chieftains of the lower party organizations collectively make up the conventions or consultative bodies that select or form the levels of party officialdom above them. Patterson, for example, brings together data on the percentages of county chairmen from Oklahoma, Kansas, and Wiscon-

---

[51] Eldersveld, *op. cit.*, p. 99. The term "stratarchy" comes from Harold Lasswell and Abraham Kaplan, *Power and Society* (New Haven: Yale Univ. Press, 1950).

[52] Eldersveld, *op. cit.*, pp. 99–100.

[53] See Moynihan and Wilson, *op. cit.*, on Averill Harriman's gubernatorial use of patronage in the state of New York.

sin who were delegates to state conventions (Table 2).[54] Clearly, the county chairmen in these states are forces to be reckoned with in the state party organizations.

Table 2
PERCENTAGES OF COUNTY CHAIRMEN SERVING AS
DELEGATES TO STATE CONVENTIONS

	Okla.	Kansas	Wisconsin
Delegates to state convention (Democrat)	89.8%	71.2%	95.3%
Delegates to state convention (Republican)	86.7	84.3	100.0

3. *Internal competition.* Party organizations rarely are unified monoliths; they engender competing organizations or factions within the organization. Differences in goals and political styles produce continuing competitions in the selecting of party officials and the mapping of party activities. In 1956 and 1957 in Wisconsin, at least some county party offices were contested in 39 per cent of the Republican organizations and 59 per cent of the Democratic.[55]

4. *Organizational insufficiencies.* This theme is sounded repeatedly in the study of the Wayne County, Michigan, party organizations. The mutual role perceptions of various party leadership levels do not "square"; there is no "neat overlap . . . between role perceptions. This divergence and lack of unanimity suggests no clear understanding or expectation in the party hierarchy as to specific tasks of those in precinct and executive board positions, either as perceptions by others or among themselves." [56] Communication among levels of the hierarchy is sporadic and discontinuous. Motivational and ideological structures differ widely and even conflict, both among levels in the hierarchy and from area to area in the organization.

Diffusion of power marks all but the exceptional party organizations. Top party leaders engage in much mobilizing and wooing of support within the organization; their consultations with middle-level leadership are endless. Even the ward or precinct leader with a small electoral following and a single vote at an important convention must be cultivated. And above all, party leaders in the eras "after patronage and preferment" no longer command, for their commands no longer carry potent sanctions. They plead, they bargain, they cajole, and they reason — and they even learn to lose gracefully on occasion. And they mobilize party power not as much by threats as by the solidarity of common goals and interests.

[54] Patterson, *op. cit.*, p. 346.
[55] Epstein, *op. cit.*, p. 90.
[56] Eldersveld, *op. cit.*, p. 111.

American party organizations have by any standards been "under-financed." They have probably never commanded incentives and rewards at all equal to their organizational goals and ambitions. Certainly they do not now. They never have been able to induce or recruit the kinds of resources they would have to have in order to "flesh out" the organizational forms and expectations of the state statutes on party organization. The thousands of inactive precinct workers and unfilled precinct positions testify to that poverty of incentive. The parties have, therefore, had no alternative but to establish *de facto* organizational forms within their "means" and within the limits of local political need and expectation.

Chapter Five

NATIONAL ORGANIZATIONS:
THE UNCERTAIN SUMMIT

So extreme are the usual observations on the decentralization of the
American parties that one is tempted to dismiss them as empty rhetoric
or pure hyperbole. One noted scholar of the American parties writes: [1]

> Decentralization of power is by all odds the most important single charac-
> teristic of the American major party; more than anything else this trait dis-
> tinguishes it from all others. Indeed, once this truth is understood, nearly
> everything else about American parties is greatly illuminated. . . . The Ameri-
> can major party is, to repeat the definition, a loose confederation of state and
> local bosses for limited purposes.

Is it possible, one wonders, that these disparate, often disorganized, local
party organizations are not subordinated to or coordinated by some
higher party unit? Are the local or state organizations free to use the
name and traditions of a nation-wide political party for their own local,
parochial interests without any fear of control by a spokesman for that
national party? Closer examination of the American parties reveals that
what seems to be hyperbole is merely bald statement of reality, for power
and authority in the party organizations is precisely that diffuse and it
does color virtually every aspect of party activity.

Despite all of the appearances of hierarchy in the American party organization, there are no signs of hierarchical authority and control. In
absolutely no important way does any national party unit limit the autonomy of the state and local party organizations; with virtually no exceptions they pick their own officers, nominate their candidates, take their
own stands on issues, raise and spend their own funds. Every four years

[1] E. E. Schattschneider, *Party Government* (New York: Rinehart, 1942), pp. 129,
132–133; emphasis omitted.

they come together as a national party to select a presidential candidate and write a platform, careful always to leave none of the trappings or structure of national organization behind as they break camp. It has, indeed, often been said that in reality there are no national parties, that what we blithely call the national parties are merely hydra-headed coalitions of jealous and wary — and very diverse — state and local party organizations.

No firmer proof of the decentralization of party organization in the United States exists than the basic weakness — if not fecklessness — of their national committees. What appears to be a pyramiding of state party committees into a single, integrating national party authority is in reality nothing of the kind. At best the national committees serve as arenas for the bargaining and jockeying for influence among the powerful organizations and currents within the party. At worst, the important jockeyings and strivings within the parties pass them by. Indeed, the authors of the leading study of the national committees chose pointedly to title it *Politics Without Power*.[2]

"Decentralization" and "weakness" are hardly precise terms. They are, furthermore, highly relative ones, for one party system's decentralization may be another's centralization. What standards we have can only be found in looking at the party systems of the other democracies. A few illustrative items should suffice to document the status of national committees elsewhere:

The national executive committee of the Italian Christian Democratic party suspended two members of Parliament from party membership in late 1964 for organizing opposition in the Italian presidential election to the candidate of the majority of the party's electors.

The national executive committee of the Congress party of India in 1957 refused to renominate almost one-third of the party's incumbent members of Parliament because it preferred instead to recruit new and younger candidates.

The British Labor party's national executive committee in 1967 was composed of 28 members; 18 of them were members of the House of Commons, and 13 of that 18 were serving as members of the government of Harold Wilson.[3]

[2] Cornelius P. Cotter and Bernard C. Hennessy, *Politics Without Power: The National Party Committees* (New York: Atherton, 1964). The following discussion of the national party organs relies heavily on this work and on Hugh A. Bone, *Party Committees and National Politics* (Seattle: Univ. of Washington Press, 1958).

[3] It should be clear, however, that the overlap between the Parliamentary party and the national executive does not lead necessarily to domination by the Parliamentary party or the Government; the Parliamentarians on the NEC may be dissidents who, having lost their fight in the parliamentary party, have carried it to the national executive.

Clearly the Democratic and Republican national committees have no such disciplinary powers, no such powers to control nominations of congressmen, no similar overlap with the party's legislative leadership. Who and what, then, are they?

THE NATIONAL COMMITTEES AND NATIONAL OFFICERS

Technically, the nominating conventions which each party holds midway in the years of presidential elections are their supreme national authorities. But the conventions' constructive role rarely goes beyond the selection of presidential and vice-presidential candidates and the formulation of party platforms. They do ratify the selection of national committeemen, and they do specify the structure and powers of the national committees. The Republican convention of 1952, for instance, expanded the size of the Republican national committee. But since the convention adjourns *sine die* (i.e., without setting a time for a future meeting) until four years later, it can exercise no continuing supervision over the national organizational apparatus of the party.

The national committees of the two major parties are similarly composed. In each of the parties a national committeeman and committeewoman is selected from each state, the District of Columbia, Puerto Rico, and the Virgin Islands. The Democratic national committee, in addition, adds two from the Canal Zone. And within the Republican party the state party chairman joins the Republican national committee if:

1. the governor of the state is a Republican, or
2. the majority of the state's senators and representatives (taken as a group) are Republicans, or
3. the state delivered its electoral votes to the Republican candidate at the last presidential election.

As of late 1966, then, the Democratic national committee had a fixed membership of 108, and the Republican committee was at a strength of 131 (106 regular members and 25 state chairmen).

As in so many aspects of party organization, there is a gulf between the form and the substance of the selection of the members of the national committees. Formally, the national conventions select them, but that action merely ratifies decisions made within the states and state parties. The state parties, however, make their decisions in a number of ways; in nineteen states, in fact, the two parties choose their national committeemen differently. Among the four main methods — selection by state party convention, by the party delegation to the national convention, by the state central committee, and by election at a primary — the first, selection by state convention, is the most popular in both parties (Table 1). In this welter of selection processes, one point is worth noting. While the parties'

Table 1

METHODS OF SELECTING NATIONAL COMMITTEEMEN
IN THE 50 STATES *

Method of Selection	Democratic Parties		Republican Parties	
State convention	20	(40%)	24	(48%)
Delegates to nat'l convention	14	(28%)	16	(32%)
State central committee	12	(24%)	7	(14%)
Primary election	4	(8%)	3	(6%)
	50	(100%)	50	(100%)

* *These data came from Cotter and Hennessy,* Politics Without Power *(New York: Atherton, 1964), pp. 25–31.*

organizations in the states can control the selection of committeemen by the state committee and (usually) by the state conventions, the selection in primaries and by convention delegates may be less controllable. Especially in states which choose convention delegations in presidential primaries, the delegation may represent voter support of a momentarily popular candidate more than it represents the leadership of the state party. A number of Democratic state delegations in 1956, for example, were composed of party mavericks who ran pledged to Estes Kefauver while the leadership of the state party supported Adlai Stevenson.

The roughly equal representation of each state and territory indicates the confederational nature of the national committees. It suggests in form what is true in fact: that each state organization, regardless of its efficacy or the size of its electorate, is represented as an autonomous equal. As the United States and Tanzania have equal representation in the United Nations, so do New York and Alaska in the Democratic national committee. The size or regularity of the state's vote for the party has nothing to do with the matter. With their third, "bonus" seat for state support of Republican candidates, the Republicans since 1952 have moved away from the principle of full equality; by late 1966, 25 of the states qualified for the additional representative. But the heavy loss in the 1964 elections did strange things in the name of a more "representative" national committee. South Carolina, hardly a bastion of Republican strength yet, went for Goldwater and earned the third seat; its three votes on the national committee then represented one for each 103,000 votes cast for Barry Goldwater. California, still a competitive state, failed to qualify on any count for the extra representative; its two members on the national committee each represented some 1,950,000 votes for Goldwater.[4]

So, it remains true that the national committees overrepresent the parties

[4] California, of course, picked up the bonus seat on the Republican National Committee in 1967 after the election of Governor Ronald Reagan.

of the smaller states and non-competitive areas. The practical, effective consequence of that overrepresentation is to strengthen the conservative wings of each party on the committees. Especially within the Republican party in recent years it has meant an overrepresentation of Taft, and then Goldwater sentiment. The chief effect of the "bonus" representative has been instead to bring into the committee a group of men who, as the chairmen of their state parties, come more uniformly from the top rung of active, experienced party leadership than do the national committeemen and committeewomen. They bring new ideas, authoritative information, and organization experience, as well as "ambassadorial rank," to the committee.

The chairmen and other officers of the national committees do not have to be — and often are not — members of the committees. They are elected and removed by the committees. Immediately after the conventions, however, tradition recognizes the right of the parties' presidential candidates to name the national chairmen for the course of the presidential campaign. The committees ratify their choices without question. And since the party of the President will continue to respect his choice of a national party chairman after the election, only the committee of the "out" party in effect selects its own national chairman. The committees generally have much greater freedom to select other committee officials — vice-chairmen, secretaries, and treasurers — many of whom come from the committee itself. In addition, both of the national committees select executive committees which include the officers and from ten to fifteen other members of the committee.

Within this apparatus — supplemented, of course, by the permanent committee staffs — it is the chairmen who dominate. The full committees meet only two or three times a year, and occasionally even less than that. As Cotter and Hennessy report: [5]

Collectively the national committee is not much more than a categorical group. . . . The national committee members have very little collective identity, little patterned interaction, and only rudimentary common values and goals.

Except for occasional meetings — largely for show and newsmaking purposes — the national committees may be thought of not so much as groups, but as lists of people who have obtained their national committee memberships through organizational processes wholly separate in each state.

The other officers of the party are not especially influential, and the executive committees meet only somewhat more frequently than the full committees. Like the full committees, they are men and women whose concern and attention is in state (and even local) organizational work and who may scarcely know their fellow members.

So, the chairman, with the permanent staff, directs the work of the na-

[5] Cotter and Hennessy, *op. cit.*, p. 39.

tional party organization. If his is the party of the President, he enjoys the support but suffers the dominance of the President. He must be a man congenial to the President, representative of his ideological stance, and willing to be the President's man or willing to be subordinate to the men of the President. If he represents the opposition party, he will be a man congenial to the various factions or segments within the party; often he is chosen for his lack of identification with any of the party factions or any of the men seeking the party's presidential nomination for the next election. Most frequently he comes to the position with experience in a state party organization, although the parties lately have shown some inclination to pick members of Congress. The appointment of Ray Bliss by the Republicans in January, 1965, is illustrative. Widely characterized as a tactician and organizer, and as a man without strong ideological attachments, he was acceptable to both the conservative Goldwater Republicans (who were reconciling themselves with some difficulty to the departure of Dean Burch as chairman) and to the moderates and liberals of the party.

What one might call the functions or roles of the national committee are, then, largely those of the chairman and the committee staff. The chairman as an individual, especially in the party out of power, can assume an important role as a spokesman of the party. For the committed workers and loyalists of his party he is the essence of partisanship and a reinforcer of their commitments. He and the committee staff also play a role in the organizing of campaigns, although they may be overshadowed by the personal organization of the presidential candidate or the congressional campaign committees (of which more later). They circulate organizational wisdom and information and "new ideas" to the state and local parties, and they provide some speech-writing and public relations advice to those in the party who seek it. Depending on the taste of the President, they may, if they are of his party, help him with the distribution of the Federal patronage; President Eisenhower was especially relieved to shift that burden, but his successors have preferred to retain greater personal control of it. Finally, the national chairmen and their staffs must plan the quadrennial national party conventions, all the way from selecting the host city to distributing spectator tickets for the galleries.[6]

COMPETITORS FOR NATIONAL POWER

THE CONGRESSIONAL CAMPAIGN COMMITTEES

Through the years the parties have developed an almost tropical overgrowth of organization in the two houses of Congress. In each house both parties organize themselves for the legislative work of the chamber. From

[6] For a good brief section on the Republican national committee and its operations, see Charles O. Jones, *The Republican Party in American Politics* (New York: Macmillan, 1965).

that organizational structure develop the party caucuses, the policy committees, whips, and floor leaders. This is the organizational complex that
culminates in the Speaker of the House, and the majority and minority
leaders of both the Senate and the House. In addition to this partisan organization of the two chambers, however, each party in both houses has
created campaign committees for the single purpose of electing their
partisans. They are called the Republican and Democratic Congressional
Campaign Committees and the Republican and Democratic Senate Campaign Committees.

The two sets of campaign committees are similar in composition. The
Republican Congressional Campaign Committee includes one member
from each state with even a single Republican congressman. The entire
state delegation from the party chooses its representative. The Democrats
in the House follow the same practice, with the addition that the chairman may appoint representatives from states not having any Democratic
congressmen. That option is, however, rarely exercised. The Senatorial
Campaign Committees include up to ten or so members, usually drawn
from those senators not up for reelection at the coming election. The Republican committee is chosen by the Republican party caucus, and the
Democratic floor leader selects his party's. For the 90th Congress, 1967–
68, the chairmen and sizes of the committees were:

> Democratic Congressional Campaign Committee: Rep. Michael Kirwan
> (Ohio) – 48 members plus the Speaker, and the floor leader, and whip
> *ex officio.*
>
> Republican Congressional Campaign Committee: Rep. Robert Wilson
> (California) – 39 members.
>
> Democratic Senate Campaign Committee: Sen. Edmund S. Muskie
> (Maine) – 10 members.
>
> Republican Senate Campaign Committee: Sen. George Murphy (Cali-
> fornia) – 7 members.

It might also be noted in conclusion that Senator Barry Goldwater chaired
the Republican Senate committee until his presidential nomination in
1964 and in that capacity won considerable gratitude from other Republican senators and from Republican organizations around the country for
his tireless work in their behalf.

As their name suggests, these campaign committees exist for one chief
purpose: the election of the parties' candidates to the Congress. They assist their incumbent senators and representatives by providing speech
preparation, TV and radio tapes and scripts, press releases, legislative histories and roll-call research, photographic services, and campaign literature. For non-incumbent candidates – especially those in closely competitive districts – they provide campaign assistance that ranges from money
and research on the record of the incumbent opponent to organizational
help in the district and advice on the skillful use of press, radio, and tele-

vision. Furthermore, the most helpful and thorough of the four, the Republican Congressional Campaign Committee, has recently developed a field staff which can work with the inexperienced candidate and his constituency party organization. The field staff is also an effective source of information for the committee and its staff as they make the difficult decisions on the allocation of campaign funds to candidates (non-incumbents).

The campaign committees in both chambers share one important characteristic with the regular legislative committees of the Congress: they, too, tend to be dominated by their chairmen.

He, along with the top staff people, makes not only the day-to-day decisions but most of the policy decisions also. Both committees are large, unwieldy bodies that seldom meet. When they do meet, the sessions are largely perfunctory. Since the primary concern of most congressmen is re-election, some who serve on the campaign committees are occasionally puzzled and disturbed by the fact that little attention is given to getting their committees together for discussions of how best to grapple with the problem of making the group a more effective instrument of assistance to members of Congress. Although there is little evidence of widespread House dissatisfaction with the way the committees function, it is generally recognized that membership carries with it little power and few responsibilities.[7]

While these comments were intended to apply only to the two campaign committees of the House of Representatives, they are appropriate as well for their senatorial counterparts.

The "Hill committees," as they are colloquially known, compete in a number of important ways with the national committees of their respective parties. While the national committee deals with national politics and the party's national candidates, national image, and national issues, the Hill committees may minimize national issues and candidates if it is prudent to do so in the essentially local elections with which they are entirely concerned. And always there is competition for money. Even though the Republicans have created a supra-organizational Finance Committee to coordinate the fund-raising of the national committee and the two Hill committees, it has not succeeded in imposing its budgetary control over the Hill committees. The Republican Congressional Campaign Committee continues, for example, to maintain its Boosters Club in which a membership "fee" of $1,000 or more entitles one to the occasional company and camaraderie of the House Republicans. Competition among the Democratic organizations may not be as intense simply because their Hill committees are on the whole less imposing organizations.[8]

[7] Charles L. Clapp, *The Congressman: His Work as He Sees It* (New York: Doubleday Anchor, 1964), p. 408.

[8] On the Hill committees, see Guy B. Hathorn, "Congressional and Senatorial Campaign Committees in the Mid-term Election Year 1954," *Southwestern Social Science Quarterly*, XXXVII (1956), pp. 207–221.

SATELLITES AND SUBORDINATES

The national committees are more or less obliged to deal with the Senate and Congressional campaign committees as equals. Their age and influence command respect if not affection. At the same time the committees must juggle a set of vague relationships with another set of less imposing national or multi-state organizations: the regional organizations and the women's and youth groups.

Within recent years both parties have made tentative beginnings in developing regional party organizations. Democrats in fourteen midwest states have begun to hold periodic conferences of party leaders and officeholders; so, too, have Republicans in thirteen western states and Democrats in eleven. Their three-day meetings have offered a platform for national party leaders and personages, an occasion for swapping organizational wisdom and tips, and an opportunity for passing resolutions, especially on issues of especial importance to the region. Thus, the Republican Western States Conference of November, 1965, tackled the problem of extremists, especially members of the John Birch Society, within the party and heard speeches from National Chairman Ray Bliss and past presidential candidates, Richard Nixon and Barry Goldwater. Others in the past have struggled with issues of water resources and land use. As of the present these regional conferences have developed no permanent organization and are, therefore, a long way from becoming an intermediate organizational level between the states and the national committee. For the moment they are handy forums for the parties' interests and points of view on special regional issues. They also serve as instruments for solving common state organizational problems and for maintaining united relationships with the national committees and officers of the parties.

The national headquarters of each party has a feminine division. The Office of Women's Activities within the Democratic party serves the Democratic women's clubs chartered by the various state committees; there is, however, no national women's organization as such. The Republicans, on the other hand, have both a Women's Division within the national office and (in the same building) the national offices of the National Federation of Republican Women, whose officers are elected by the Federation's own convention. So, only one of the parties really has a possibly competitive organization of women partisans, and that one is "competitive" only in the sense that its officials and convention pronouncements add another voice to the chorus speaking for the party. The very fact of the separateness of women's divisions and organizations in the two parties — including the self-conscious requirement of a national committee-woman — serves as a reminder that women have yet to achieve even a rough measure of equality of influence within the parties. The doctrine of "separate but equal," now banned in education and public facilities, still flourishes in the major American parties.

The Young Republican National Federation and the Young Democratic Clubs of America represent the local city, county, and college clubs of the young people of the party. But as in the case of the women's organizations, the Democratic party has integrated the Young Democratic bureaucracy into the national organization. The executive secretary of the Young Democratic Clubs serves also as the director of the national committee's youth division. The Young Republicans enjoy a greater independence and a therefore greater potential for embarrassment to the senior party. The chairmanship of the Federation was won in 1965 by Tom R. Van Sickle, a state senator from Kansas who had been a staff worker for the Goldwater Citizen's Committee in 1964; the Committee reportedly contributed some of its surplus funds to aid his campaign for the chairmanship. The politics of the Young Republican Federation have, in other words, afforded one more sounding board for the divisions within the Republican party. Even as late as 1966 the Federation had twice taken action against two of its state organizations — those in California and New Jersey — for extremist conservative views and, in the case of New Jersey, anti-semitic songs and jokes at informal gatherings.

THE PARTY'S GOVERNORS

The governors of a party will inevitably speak with authority in the councils of the national party. They have the prestige both of high office and of electoral success, and many additionally command the support of state party organizations. Many will also head state delegations to the party's next national convention, and a few of those will contend for the party's presidential and vice-presidential nominations. Only in the Republican party, however, has the gubernatorial presence been recently organized. Led chiefly by liberal governors such as Smylie of Idaho (since defeated in 1966), Love of Colorado, and Chafee of Rhode Island, the GOP governors sought immediately after the Goldwater defeat of 1964 to create a counterweight to the party's conservative ideologists. Buoyed later by the party's successes in 1966, they agreed to meet twice a year in 1967 and after. During 1967 they also established a full-time Washington office with financial help from the Republican national committee. So recent is the development that it remains to be seen how forceful a competitor for national Republican power the governors will be.[9]

[9] It should also be noted that the Republican party and its national committee was plagued increasingly in the 1960's by less formal, less national, and less purely partisan groups (i.e., the Ripon Society, Republicans for Progress, United Republicans of America). They were formed mainly to represent various ideological currents in the party. They will be discussed briefly in Chapter 16.

WHO SPEAKS FOR THE PARTY?

In the often nebulous verbiage of its platform a party's national convention establishes a party "policy" every four years. But who is to interpret it and enforce it, and who is to formulate the party's position in the long intervals between conventions? And just as importantly in the non-ideological American politics, who is to comment on public events and issues, who is to comment on the other party and its partisans, to mediate differences within the party, to keep the party name before the public eye and ear, to defend the records and actions of the party's leaders?

When the party holds the presidential office, the matter is easily settled. The President's policy and program — and his record of decisions — become the party's. It is the President who interprets the party's platform and its voters' mandate. His preferences, whether embodied in the formal measures of the State of the Union address or tossed off casually at a press conference, put a policy orientation on his party. He may consult the chairman or other party worthies, but no one mistakes the presidential initiative. His control over the national chairman and through him the national committee staff insures at the very least the tacit support of the national party headquarters. What opposition develops within the party ranks will almost surely come from disaffected state or local organizations or from dissident partisans in Congress.

Presidential relations with the national committee and its chairman, of course, differ with the experience and inclinations of the President. President Eisenhower, totally without experience in party politics, preferred to leave the national committee considerable latitude and a free hand with patronage and organizational matters. Under John F. Kennedy the Democratic national committee and its officers declined in importance as the President, his brother Robert, Lawrence O'Brien, and other Kennedy aides centralized in the White House many contacts with state party leaders, the mapping of electoral strategy, the raising of party funds, and the issuing of party pronunciamentos. In the same period an old Kennedy friend and Boston lawyer, Richard Maguire, became the treasurer of the national committee.

The recent presidential years of Lyndon B. Johnson illustrate fully the difficult, ambiguous, and shifting relationships between the White House and the national committee. The approach of the President toward the committee and its chairman, John Bailey of Connecticut, seems to have gone through three periods after the 1964 presidential victory:

> Initially there was a period of dominance of the national committee by Johnson men, many of them old Texas associates. Clifton C. Carter, long a member of the Johnson entourage, was the committee's executive director, and with the President's support he took charge of both organization and finance. Within the year of 1965, however, programs

and staff were cut back sharply because of the debts remaining from 1964; in December of that year the national committee's staff was cut by one-third.

Late in 1965 and in 1966 President Johnson began to replace committee operations with those of his own White House advisors (chief among them: Marvin Watson, formerly a chairman of the Texas Democratic party) and the Postmaster-General, Lawrence O'Brien. He relied on them increasingly for political counsel and for contacts with state and local party organizations. Carter resigned from the national committee post in August of 1966.

After the party's losses in 1966 many Democratic governors and state leaders complained increasingly of the national committee's torpor. It functioned, they claimed, neither as a liaison with the Johnson administration nor as a source of campaign and organizational assistance. But signs of a revitalization of the national committee appeared in 1967; the debt of 1964 was under control and a program expansion was planned. In March of 1967 the national committee met for the first time in more than a year, and later in the month the chairmen and vice-chairmen of the state organizations came to Washington for one of their rare conferences.

These events invite an observation. The organizational and activity level of the national committee is, like other American party committees, definitely periodic; it comes to life for elections and then sinks back into inactivity. Presidents and other party leaders tend to view the national committee as one more party campaign organization, this one for the presidential conventions and campaigns every four years. Clearly they do not see it as a continuous, coordinating unit at the peak of a party hierarchy.

The events of the Kennedy and Johnson years do not please the leaders of state and local organizations who, while they want a weak national headquarters, want one which will also offer them the campaign help, patronage, and services to which they have become accustomed. A vigorously political President, on the other hand, wants the national apparatus to serve *his* interests — he will want its organizational skills to serve his political future, its pronouncements to assist his program, its dealings with Congress to help his dealings with Congress. The limited Federal patronage he will see as an opportunity to achieve the goals of his administration or his political career rather than as a set of rewards for workers in the state and local organizations. Quite simply, if the President permits the national committee apparatus to go its way, it will attend to the decentralized power of local candidates and organizations. If he wants to use it to support his presidential power, he must dominate its outlook and decisions.

By contrast, in those long four years after presidential defeat a national party suffers an almost incessant jockeying for the right to define its position. The defeated candidate, the party's legislative leadership, the national chairman, and other party notables may all purport at once to be the voice of the party. This contention, furthermore, is over much more than the narrow issue of policy positions and initiatives. It is as well a part of the continuing struggle to define the party's strategies and pick its next presidential candidate.

The formal traditions of American politics rather sententiously label the defeated presidential candidate the "titular head" of his party. Whatever the term may mean, a losing presidential candidate usually must fight to maintain even a precarious influence in his party. Almost never does he monopolize the tribune of leadership. How effective a voice he has in party policy depends on his own base of power within the party. All other things being equal, a candidate who lost by a few hundred thousand votes will maintain it better than one who lost by several million. His political skills, his policy orientations, his control of a state party, his taste for party conflict, even his own ambitions, also affect his power. Indeed, by 1967 Richard Nixon, a Republican loser "once removed," probably came closer to being a spokesman for the Republican party than did its more recent loser, Barry Goldwater.

Most generally, however, the leadership of the "out" party falls to its leadership in Congress. The congressional leadership, simply because its legislative responsibilities force it to take policy stands, formulates the party position and challenges the program of the President. Indeed in the early 1960's the periodic television appearances of the Republican congressional leaders, Senator Everett M. Dirksen and Representative Charles Halleck — the programs were jocularly called the "Ev and Charlie Show" — came to symbolize the organized Republican opposition. The series continued in a slightly changed format after Representative Gerald Ford replaced Halleck as the Republican floor leader in the House in early 1965. While the two leaders tend naturally to be its congressional spokesmen, other legislators of the party do not hesitate to speak out. The policy committees, especially in the Senate, may formulate positions as a semi-official representative of the party's full contingent in the chamber.[10]

This congressional domination of the opposition party rarely pleases all groups within the party. The congressional wings of both the Republican and Democratic parties were until 1964 appreciably more conservative than the coalitions in the parties which nominated the presidential candidates. Thus, the Stevenson Democrats from 1952 to 1960 and the Eisenhower-Nixon Republicans after 1960 tried to stake out for themselves a greater voice in opposition. In both cases they created special national

---

[10] On the Senate policy committees, see Bone, *Party Committees and National Politics.*

party organizations as their vehicles: the Democratic Advisory Council and the All-Republican Conference. One might also note that they ignored the national committees for at least two reasons: the general ideological conservatism and endemic ineffectiveness of the committees.

The Democratic Advisory Council was born of the Democratic defeat of 1956. A group of Stevenson friends and admirers took the initiative and, supported by national chairman Paul Butler, launched the Council. It was intended, in its own words, "to provide a collective voice for the Democratic Party, representing on a year-round basis the millions of Democrats who may or may not be represented in either House of Congress." [11] In original plans the DAC was to include ten congressional leaders, five governors and mayors, five national leaders of the party at large, and the fourteen members of the national committee's executive committee. But congressional leaders and most Southerners — well aware of the thrust and purpose of the Council — boycotted it.

Meeting two or three times a year, the Democratic Advisory Council created a number of advisory committees headed by newsworthy names such as Dean Acheson and Mrs. Eleanor Roosevelt. The DAC and its committees emitted more than sixty assorted policy statements before June of 1960. They not only excoriated the Eisenhower administration but struck a liberal posture for fellow Democrats, for the absence of the conservative boycotters freed it to proclaim an uninhibited liberalism. Its last months of life were spent working on the drafts of the Democratic platform of 1960, and it went out of existence with the convening of the party's national convention in July of 1960.

The liberal Republican search for a forum within the party actually began before the defeat of 1960. The failure of the party at the 1958 congressional elections stirred the President and the liberals of the party to take stock. After a White House meeting the national chairman, Meade Alcorn, with the approval of the national committee, appointed a Republican Committee on Program and Progress. Soon it became known as the "Percy Committee" after its chairman and chief founder, Charles Percy of Illinois. The committee, broadly representative of the party, did not suffer the indignities the Democratic Advisory Council did; Senator Dirksen and Representative Halleck accepted membership with good grace if not with enthusiasm. After a year of meetings and task-force activity, the final set of reports came out of a July, 1959, meeting.[12] Like the DAC, it too

---

[11] Quoted in Cotter and Hennessy, *op. cit.*, p. 215.

[12] The reports later appeared in a commercial edition: *Decisions for a Better America* (New York: Doubleday, 1960). It might also be noted that the relationship between congressional leadership and these forms of national coordinating conferences may be affected by the legislative responsibilities of the party's congressional leadership; that is, the fact that the Dirksen-Halleck duo were in the minority may have made cooperation less difficult than it would have been for Johnson and Rayburn, who were majority leaders at the time.

left the public stage in time for the approaching national convention of 1960.

In the Kennedy and Johnson years the moderates within the GOP gravitated both literally and figuratively to Gettysburg for leadership. General Eisenhower in the summer of 1962 convened an All-Republican Conference at his Gettysburg farm, and the Conference formed the National Republican Citizens Committee as its organizational arm. The former President was chosen as its honorary chairman. The Citizens Committee in turn spawned a policy-making body, the Critical Issues Council, headed by Milton Eisenhower and replete with former members of the Eisenhower administration. Again, the congressional leadership adopted a "cool but correct" attitude. Senator Barry Goldwater, speaking as a Republican conservative, criticized it as a splinter group and as an untimely reincarnation of the citizens groups that had led the Eisenhower draft of 1952.

After the loss of 1964, and again at the suggestion of former President Eisenhower, the party set up a similar Republican Co-ordinating Committee composed of the party's congressional leadership, five Republican governors, and the party's five living presidential candidates.[13] The Committee has issued some studies, but little else seems to have been heard from it.

In this travail of the party of opposition, then, the national committees play no preeminent role. Leaders of the party define the national committee's role chiefly as an organizational coordinator and campaign manager. They do not concede it any great role as a policy enunciator. The events of recent years suggest that if the committee (and its chairman) of the "out" party is to influence the policy image of the party, it must find allies in the task. It may ally itself with the congressional party, an alliance which may be perfectly natural if the chairman is a senator or representative. It may join the defeated candidate, or it may "go along" with *ad hoc* organs like the Democratic Advisory Council or the All-Republican Conference. But it cannot speak alone with important effect.

THE NATIONAL PARTIES: TROUBLES ON THE SUMMIT

Like so many groups in American life — the American Bar Association, the American Medical Association, the United States Chamber of Commerce, the large, international trade unions, to mention only a few examples — the organizational structure of the Democratic and Republican parties follows the lines of American federalism. Above the state organizational units they have erected a single national committee. But unlike so many federated organizations, the parties' national committees have

13 At that time they were: Herbert Hoover, Alfred Landon, Thomas Dewey, Richard Nixon, and Barry Goldwater.

never surmounted the autonomous power of the state and local organizations. They remain relatively powerless victims of the decentralization of American politics.

The apparently hierarchical form of party organization deceives again. The causes of national committee weakness are many. Like all American parties it is a skeletal organization without any base of mass membership; but unlike state and local organizations, it is even without the circles of workers and loyalists that sustain even the cadre parties. It furthermore must depend on financial levies on the state parties ("quotas") to help pay its staff and expenses, and experience has shown it that state organizations may fall quickly into arrears on their payments when miffed or disappointed. Furthermore, the national committees lack the full-time attention of their members whose main concern is with state and local politics. Even the chairman may be preoccupied with his own business or profession, with his role in state party affairs, or with a governmental office such as the Postmastership-General or a seat in Congress. Even if he devotes full time to the job, the chairman rarely stays long enough to master the complexities of the national committee operations; from 1940 to 1966 the Republican chairmen averaged about one and three-quarter years on the job, and the Democrats a shade over two years. Finally, the national committees just do not have any sanctions over state or local organizations or over rebel congressmen and senators. They cannot control or even greatly influence nominations in the states. Even if the traditions and mores of political localism would not prevent such interventions, the direct primary would. Nor can the national committee control the selection of local party officials; custom and state law prevent it again. And so far it has not been able to develop the power of the purse as a weapon of party authority.

Yet, decentralization of power in the American parties explains only part of the problems of the national committees. Beyond being plagued by federalism, they are cursed by the separation of powers. Incumbent Presidents may dominate them and turn them into little more than auxiliary personal organizations. Congressional party organs at best concede them only a co-ordinate status. The Senate and House campaign committees compete with them in the waging of campaigns, and party leadership in Congress competes in formulating party policy and shaping the party image. In this variant of separation of powers it is clear that the national committee represents the "presidential party" — it is chosen to nominate and elect him and to create an image and organization useful to him; it is his ally against the locally rooted, decentralizing power of Congress. And ironically, it is the national committee's victory in the presidential election that signals its own temporary demise as the submissive handmaiden of presidential power.

The congressional parties have an easier time in setting a role for themselves. To be sure, they are something of an anomaly in American politics — neither fully national nor fully local in their outlook. They have obvious ties to the national party, and its image and popularity, but they are also products of state and local politics, of local influence and local electorates. The congressional parties, furthermore, have interests different from both the national and local parties. They are concerned with legislative power, with the status and prestige of Congress, and with the group life and patterns of influence within Congress. The rewards, the advancement, and the esteem a congressman seeks come from the congressional party; the reelection he seeks comes from the state or locality. Few of his accustomed blessings come in any way from the national committee or its staff. His party in Congress even recognizes his special political problem with its congressional campaign committees:

. . . the congressman finds himself a party orphan, with these [state and county] committees giving him a minimum of attention. His district generally does not coincide with county lines, and comparatively few areas have a full-fledged congressional district organization. Unlike state, county, or municipal officers, the congressman is away from his district more than half the time, and he cannot hope to maintain as close contact with the local organization as can, for example, a state legislator or a county commissioner. The congressional committee is a device for catering to certain of the congressman's needs in campaigning, in his constituent relationships, and in his work at the Capitol. These needs are not fully met by either the national or the local committees.[14]

Both the peculiar legislative and political needs of Congress, therefore, spawn special party structures. They speak for the policies and programs of the congressional party, and they fight the individual, localized political campaigns of the congressmen. They reflect the separate, specific interests of the party's men in Congress.

In summarizing the dilemmas of national party organization it may be useful for analytical purposes to divide the operations (however artificially) into two main categories: those directed to party organizational matters and those concerned with developing a party position on issues and programs. Table 2 summarizes the chief national competitors of the national party committees, both when their party holds the Presidency and when it does not. The table illustrates two main generalizations. First, the incumbent President has at his command the power and resources to dominate his party's national party apparatus in both sets of operations. Secondly, the national committees have a better chance of carving out an organizational role for themselves than they do in becoming a party spokesman on issues and programs. Even though they do not control the personnel and decisions of state committees, they can in the less dramatic, day-to-day business of organizational politics influence

[14] Bone, *op. cit.*, p. 154.

Table 2

CHIEF PARTY COMPETITORS OF THE NATIONAL COMMITTEES

Types of Activities	Party in Power	Party out of Power
Organizational	1. Congressional campaign committees 2. Presidential political organization	1. Congressional campaign committees
Issue-program	1. The President and his administration	1. Party's congressional leadership 2. Other party notables (defeated candidate, etc.)

them by the myriad organizational services local organizations need: conferences on organization, research and expertise, contacts with other party organizations, help and encouragement. And that, of course, is what the state party organizations, the king-pins of the organization, expect of them — assistance without control.

Changes are in progress in the American political system, however, which would seem ultimately to promise an increased nationalization of American politics. The centralization of governmental power in the American federal system focuses attention on national politics, national candidates, and national issues. Men and women are increasingly brought to political activity by a concern for issues and ideology, and these days issues and ideology are increasingly national in scope. Furthermore, political coverage by television and the mass media generally means attention on national conventions, national campaigns, and national personalities. Presidents capture staggering amounts of media attention with even an uneventful news conference, and on every weekend national political figures star in the news summaries and TV question-and-answer shows. Presidents increasingly attract the national coverage and stamp their program and accomplishments on their party. And it appears more and more difficult for any state party to isolate itself from the currents of national politics and to base its electoral appeals solely on local issues and local personalities.

What seems less clear, however, is whether the shift to a more nationalized politics will mean an enhanced role for the parties' national committees. In the case of the President's party the growth in national power will primarily be a growth in the power of the President in the party. He will very likely continue to define the role and power of the national committee. Within the opposition party the search goes on for a satisfactory instrument or combination of instruments for the exercise of national power, whether it is the national committee, the congressional leaders, old party warriors, Republican governors, or special party organs. At the moment it does not appear that any single unit of party organization will easily outstrip its competitors and thus end the present pragmatic and diffuse mixture of national party organizations.

And so the paradox persists. There are presently no signs of the growth of any national organizational power that would diminish the organizational autonomy of the state parties. Decentralization of party organization persists despite the centralization of governmental power and the nationalization of American politics. The future of the national committee appears to be linked to the future of presidential power. As the representative of the presidential constituency and party, it confronts two dangers. On the one hand, it invites the resistance of the party's congressional leaders and organizations. On the other, it risks being diverted from its party tasks and position and to a cultivation of presidential power. The way between the dangers is very narrow indeed.

To put the matter in purely organizational terms, the national committees of the two parties do not control many of the rewards and incentives of partisan politics and, therefore, they do not control the recruitment of resources into political activity. They are thus unable to exert any substantial control over the state and local organizations which do. If the national committees were to begin to control the recruitment of resources (such as, for example, campaign funds), the present distribution of power within the party hierarchy would be sharply altered.[15] But until they do, decentralization will continue to be the key to party organization in the United States.

· · ·

We have come to accept large-scale organization as an important social reality in this century. In business, government, universities, and voluntary organizations it is a time of complex social structures and of their men, the bureaucrats and "organization men" who (along with the miles of "red tape") have become their symbols. We have every right to call the party "organizations" by that name, but it is an inescapable and central fact that the parties, chief among our social institutions, have resisted the development of "big," efficient, centralized organization.

Even by the standards of the parties of the other democracies, the American party organizations cut an unimpressive figure. They lack the hierarchical control and efficiency, the unified setting of priorities and strategy, and the central responsibility we associate with contemporary large organizations. Instead of a stable set of relationships, continuity of

[15] The abortive attempt of 1966 and 1967 to permit taxpayers to turn over a dollar of their federal income tax payment to a fund be divided equally between the parties for their national campaigns raised precisely this issue. The fund would undoubtedly have strengthened the presidential wing of the party and the national committee; that may have been the chief reason for Congress's decision to repeal the plan before it had a chance to go into operation.

form, and continuousness of operation, the American party organization features only improvisatory, elusive, and sporadic structure and activities. And where the party organizations of the rest of the Western democracies have had an almost permanent, highly professional leadership and large party bureaucracies, the American organizations have generally done without a professional bureaucracy or leadership cadre.[16] The business of American party organization is largely in the hands of part-time activists, which is perhaps to say that its business and organizational relationships require no specialists and no full-time professional care.

One is tempted to wonder at the reasons for the stunting of American party organization. In part it results from statutory limits and prescriptions. And traditional fears of political parties and party strength have certainly contributed as well. (There is little in American political values which would welcome an "efficient" or "business-like" operation of the parties.) In large part, however, the "under-organization" of the American parties results from their fundamental character as parties. They have been pragmatic electoral parties, involved chiefly in supporting candidates for public office and active mainly during campaigns. As such they have long been led and dominated, not by career bureaucrats, but by public office seekers and holders. To many of these campaigners and their followers, a routinized and fully staffed party organization would represent a major intra-party threat. Perhaps, too, the degree of pragmatic flexibility to which Americans have carried their party politics rules out the routine and fixity of a large organization. Organization is to some extent routine and unchanging, and it is therefore more compatible with the party pursuing unchanging ideology or principle than with one committed to the shifts and adjustments necessary for electoral success.

[16] On party bureaucracy, see the perceptive article by Charles E. Schutz, "Bureaucratic Party Organization Through Professional Political Staffing," *Midwest Journal of Political Science*, VIII (1964), pp. 127–142.

PART THREE

The Political Party
as an Electorate

In very few party systems is the gulf between the party organization and the "party in the electorate"[1] as great as it is in the American system. Unlike most of the parties of the European democracies, the small bands of workers and leaders who are the American party organizations have not been able to integrate the party's most loyal supporters into the party organization. Substantial membership groups within the organizations have always been and still remain comparatively rare in the American parties. Nor have these party organizations even mounted any systematic attempts to introduce their loyal electorates into the positions and traditions of the party. The organization remains apart from even its most loyal sector of the electorate. It initiates the activities by which the party sets goals and mobilizes support, and it views even the most sympathetic voters as a clientele to be wooed and reinforced anew at each election. Those sympathetic voters, for all of their protestations of loyalty to the party, also stand apart. They consider their obligations to the party amply filled if they support its candidates in a substantial majority of instances.

This "party in the electorate" is, unlike the party organization, largely a categorical group. There is no interaction within it, no structured or stable set of relationships, no organizational or "group" life. And as any categorical group, it is an artifact of the way we choose to define it.

[1] The term has been popularized by V. O. Key, Jr., in his *Politics, Parties, and Pressure Groups,* fifth edition (New York: Crowell, 1964), p. 164. Key, however, attributes the term to Ralph M. Goldman.

There is common scholarly agreement, however, that the "party in the electorate" is characterized by its feelings of loyalty to or identification with the party. In the American political context its people are the men and women who consider themselves Democrats and Republicans — they may even, in the loose usages of American politics, consider themselves "members" of one political party or the other. In practical, operational terms they are the partisans who respond to survey questions such as, "Generally speaking, do you usually think of yourself as a Republican, a Democrat, an Independent, or what?" [2]

The size of the American parties in the electorate depends, of course, on the measures of them we employ. The 1964 data of the Survey Research Center, for example, indicate the following breakdowns of party identifications within the American electorate: [3]

Strong Democrats	26.5%
Weak Democrats	24.5%
Independents	22.5%
Weak Republicans	13.4%
Strong Republicans	10.9%
Others (no answer, apolitical, other party, etc.)	2.2%
	100.0%

If one groups all of the partisan identifiers together, he defines two party electorates which account for three of every four American adults (75.3%). On the face of it a more reasonable alternative would be to accept the "strong" identifiers, totalling 37.4% of the American adults, as more reasonable approximations of the two parties in the electorate.

Furthermore, that latter percentage should probably also be reduced by some figure less than 5 per cent to subtract the personnel of the party organizations. At the same 1964 survey of the SRC 5 per cent of the respondents claimed to have worked for one of the parties or presidential candidates in the 1964 campaign. That percentage, by including work for a candidate alone and probably by including also some self-flattering, over-estimates of activity, very likely inflates the percentage of activists

[2] The question is the chief one the Survey Research Center uses to determine party identification. The Gallup Poll (American Institute of Public Opinion) has recently been using the following similar question: "In politics, as of today, do you consider yourself a Republican, Democrat, or Independent?"

[3] The identifications here were developed in responses to the question above and several follow-up questions on the basis of which the Independents were broken into the following sub-groups: Independent Democrats, 9.2%; Independents, 7.7%; Independent Republicans, 5.6%. In 1964 the Gallup Poll found a similar distribution of loyalties within the American electorate:

Democrats	53%
Independents	22%
Republicans	25%

in or associated with the party organizations *per se*.[4] If one, therefore, arbitrarily scales the 5 per cent down to 3, he then places just a shade more than one-third (34.4%) of the American adults in the two parties in the electorate. Such estimates of magnitude, it should be repeated, are exceptionally arbitrary. (What is clearly more important than the matter of sheer size, however, is the issue of the division of the group between the two parties.)

Despite their expressions of party loyalty the members of the parties in the electorate are fickle and sometimes waiver in the support of the party of their choice. The party organizations and candidates know that even their electoral support cannot be taken for granted; other political appeals and loyalties may on occasion override even the staunchest party loyalties. And some of them — probably a minority — express a loyalty that is little more than an empty formula; they may be Democrats or Republicans in the same sense as they may be "members" of a religious denomination who have not stepped inside a church for years. And yet for all of this, the members of the party electorates do vote for the candidates of "their" party and support its public positions with a faithfulness far beyond that of the rest of the total electorate. They tend, in other words, to be the party "regulars" and straight-ticket voters. They are the men and women who, in the argot of Madison Avenue, display the greatest partisan "product loyalty."

For all of its uncertainties the party in the electorate does provide the party organization and candidates with a stable, hard core of electoral support. Its existence and relative reliability release the organization and its standard bearers from the intolerable burden of convincing and mobilizing a full majority of the electorate in every campaign. But the party in the electorate performs additional services for the party. It is a reservoir of potential activists for the organization. Its members may also make financial contributions to the party, or they may be sometime workers in a specific campaign. Those people who attend party rallies, who talk about politics and persuade friends, or who express any form of political enthusiasm in the community very probably come from its ranks. Its members are most active in perpetuating the party by socializing their children into loyalty to it and, possibly, activity in it. In sum, they give the party a substance, an image, a presence in the community, and the most involved among them may constitute something of an auxiliary

[4] The data on participation in the 1964 campaign comes from the Survey Research Center of the University of Michigan. The 5 per cent positive response was to this question: "Did you do any work for one of the parties or candidates?" Two prior questions brought positive responses from 4 and 9 per cent, respectively; the questions were: "Do you belong to any political club or organization?" and "Did you go to any political meetings, rallies, dinner, or things like that?"

"semi-organization" which supports the exertions of the local party organization.

The party in the electorate is an alarmingly diverse group largely because the kind of simple gesture of loyalty which defines it — a word or two in response to a stranger asking questions — means so many different things to so many different people. (Note that we include people in the party electorate because of their own attribution of attachment, and not because of any actual voting, or activity, or contribution to the life of the political party.) Understandably, the boundaries of the party electorate are indistinct and imprecise. Individuals also move freely in and out of it, either to or from the more active circles of the party organization or the less committed ones of the electorate at large (or even rarely into the electorate of the other party). A compelling, charismatic candidate, for example, may move adults across the group lines. Adlai Stevenson drew a large number of young adults into the membership clubs of the Democratic party organization.

But a party in the electorate is more than a categorical group or even a quasi-organization. It is an aggregate of cognitive images; it is, in other words, a system of impressions, or an object of opinion and judgment, "within" large numbers of individual voters. It is a loyalty or identification ordinarily so strong that it assumes a dominant position in the individual's political cosmos. It is the "party *in* the elector." It acts as a reference symbol, a political cue-giver, and a perceptual screen through which he sees and evaluates candidates and issues. Loyalty to a political party is, therefore, often a dominant (though not invariably dominating) factor in the subtle calculus by which the American political man sees, reacts, decides, and acts. And for that political man the political party of his cognitions may be far more real and tangible than any overt political activity or any observable political organization. For he reacts to what he perceives, and the political party of his perceptions may be a loosely codified set of judgments and impressions of men, issues, and events, both of the past and the present. He may be completely unaware of the party of leaders, platforms, even organizations and their many committeemen.

Since the American parties are still cadre parties without important membership contingents, the party in the electorate gives the party its mass, popular character. It is to the party in the electorate that popular usage generally refers when it speaks of "Democrats" and "Republicans." It is certainly to the party in the electorate that the casual observer refers when he says, for example, that the Democratic party is the party of "the little man" or that the Republican party is the party of the small towns. Many of the differences in the programs and the public images of the major parties spring from differences in the segments of the American electorate they are most successful in enlisting. In fact, the interplay between the appeals of the party (i.e., its candidates, issues, and traditions) and its loyal electoral clienteles — each one shaping and reinforcing the other — comes very close to determining who and what the parties are. Thus, we think of the loyal electorate as a loosely associated sector of the party — as something more than a detached and passive consumer of party appeals.

All of this is not to suggest that the rest of the American electorate is of any less concern to the American parties. It is not, for at no time can a party or its candidates find within its party electorate the majorities they need for election to office. Even though the voters outside of the loyal party electorates have lighter commitments to party and issue and lower levels of political involvement and information, competition for their support is keen, for the two American parties are ever aware of the need for majority support. They cannot, as can some of the parties of the parliamentary democracies, fall back on a safely committed and heavily ideological 15 or 25 per cent of the electorate. So, despite the limited capacity of a minimal party organization with a negligible membership corps, they must mobilize majorities from vast, fluid, heterogeneous, often disinterested electorates.

The individuals of the American electorate, therefore, range along a continuum from heavy, almost blind commitment to a political party to total lack of commitment, not only to a political party but to any other political cause or object. The competitive American parties do not ignore or take for granted any segment of that continuum. The three chapters of Part III examine its variety and importance. The first deals with the amorphous parties in the electorate, especially to ask who are the Democrats and who are the Republicans. It is, as we earlier suggested, concerned with the party electorate as a categorical group. The second takes up the party "within" the elector, the party as a set of cognitive images. It deals above all with the impact of party loyalty or identification on the political behavior of the individual. The third chapter focuses on the legal and self-imposed restrictions on the total electorate which limit the parties' attempts to activate their loyalists and recruit new supporters. It suggests also the possibilities and advantages the parties see in extending their loyal electorates to newly eligible groups in the electorate.

Chapter Six

THE LOYAL ELECTORATES

For millions of Americans, unconcerned with the intricacies of party life and organization, the group of party loyalists we call the "party in the electorate" *is* the political party. Much of the written history of the American parties and politics has reinforced that impression. It has concentrated on the wins and losses of the parties in their competitions for the Presidency and the Congress. It has recorded the successes of the parties, not in terms of party organization, strategy, or activity, but rather in terms of the enduring blocs of voters supporting them. Thus the parties have been defined at various moments in time as parties of the East or West, the North or the South, the city or the country, the rich or the poor, the white or the Negro. Their loyal electorates are their most apparent and visible components to the less concerned and involved segments of the electorate.

This salience of the party in the electorate, even though it is a loosely defined categorical group, is one of the major sources of its importance. Its interests and involvements contribute significantly to the public image of the party, and its life styles and political values will inevitably be impressed on it. The importance of that impact is, however, matched by a second. Within the cognitive mechanism of the individual American voter, loyalty to or identification with a political party is the single most important influence on his political behavior. It colors his judgments of candidates and issues, and it guides his decisions on how to cast his vote.

Two-Party Divisions in the Electorate

In the period since 1860 the two major parties have each enjoyed a time of long-run ascendancy. From 1860 through the presidential election of 1928 Republican presidential candidates won fourteen of eighteen times.

Their supremacy was broken only by the two victories of Grover Cleveland, each won by an eyelash margin, and by the two of Woodrow Wilson. Moreover, Wilson's initial victory in 1912 was built on less than 40 per cent of the popular vote, a result of the fact that Teddy Roosevelt's Bull Moose candidacy split off a sizable chunk of Republican votes from the regular Republican candidate, William Howard Taft. Furthermore, in the period the Democrats managed to set one record in futility; in the election of 1924 they won only 34.8 per cent of the two-party popular vote for President.

Since the 1930's the Democrats have enjoyed a period of similar dominance. Of the nine presidential elections from 1932 through 1964 the Democrats won seven, losing only two to Dwight D. Eisenhower. Their 78 per cent victory in the period matches exactly that of the Republicans from 1860 to 1928. Furthermore, in this latter period the Republicans set two records of their own in futility. In 1936 they won only eight electoral votes, the smallest number for a major party in modern times, and in 1964 Lyndon Johnson rolled up a record 61.1 per cent of the total popular vote at their expense.

The same two periods of dominance or ascendancy are reflected in party control of the two houses of Congress (Table 1). The very fact that the cycles of control of Congress follow those of the Presidency so closely lends further support to the conclusion that these are cycles of *party* ascendancy. Since the Civil War, in fact, only twice (1956) did a winning and President see the opposing party carry both houses of Congress in a year *1968* of his election.

Table 1

PARTISAN CONTROL OF THE HOUSES OF CONGRESS,
1861–1931 AND 1931–1967

	House of Representatives		Senate	
	Dems.	Repubs.	Dems.	Repubs.
1861–1931 (37th–71st Congress)	12	23	5	30
1931–1967 (72nd–90th Congress)	17	2	16	3

Behind the striking dominance of the Republicans from 1861 to 1930 and the Democrats from 1930 to the present lies the great probability that each party was in the time of its ascendancy the "majority party." During the period of its successes, that is, the dominant party commanded the partisan loyalties of a majority of Americans. Its loyal, supportive party in the electorate was large enough to guarantee it victory in the great percentage of elections. The minority party could win only sporadically by nullifying the dominant party loyalties with an uncommonly attractive candidate or an especially pressing issue. That the Republicans were such a majority party before 1930 we must take more or less on faith; more precisely, we make that assumption in a projection backward of what we have learned about the American electorate and the power of party loyalty through public opinion surveys since the 1940's.

With an amazing regularity the American adult population has been preferring, identifying with, or expressing loyalty to the Democratic party for the past generation.[1] Table 2 indicates the persistence of the

Table 2

PARTY IDENTIFICATION OF AMERICAN ADULTS:
1952 TO 1964 [2]

Identification	Oct. 1952	Oct. 1956	Oct. 1960	Oct. 1964
Strong Democrats	22%	21%	21%	24%
Weak Democrats	25	23	25	22
Independent Democrats	10	7	8	7
Independents	5	9	8	10
Independent Republicans	7	8	7	5
Weak Republicans	14	14	13	17
Strong Republicans	13	15	14	11
Apoliticals	4	3	4	4

Democratic party's superiority among the party identifiers. It also illustrates the remarkable stability of party identifications in the United States — a stability so great in recent years that not even a popular President of the minority party, General Eisenhower, could jar it. Finally, it should be clear that such data on party identification assesses not patterns of voting, but rather the fundamental loyalties to or preferences for party ab-

---

[1] Among the questions asked of American adults to determine their party identification is this one of the Survey Research Center: "Generally speaking, do you think of yourself as a Republican, a Democrat, an Independent, or what?" Then this follow-up question is asked of the Independents: "Do you think of yourself as closer to the Republican or Democratic party?" Angus Campbell, Philip E. Converse, Warren E. Miller, and Donald E. Stokes, *The American Voter* (New York: Wiley, 1960), p. 122.

[2] The data of Table 2 come from the Survey Research Center of the University of Michigan. The data of the Gallup Poll (American Institute of Public Opinion) are very similar, even though the categories are different. For example (*Minneapolis Tribune* of November 8, 1964):

	1960	1964
Democrats	47%	53%
Independents	23	22
Republicans	30	25

stracted from momentary candidates and issues in an election campaign.

But more important than the question of how many Democratic and Republican identifiers there are is the question of who they are. From what educational backgrounds, what regions, what occupations, what religions, what social groups come the Democrats and the Republicans? On what bases of loyalty do the parties attract supporters and voters? Or conversely, what experiences and values shape the decisions of Americans to align themselves with one party rather than the other? Why do some Americans identify with one party and others with another?

THE ACQUISITION OF PARTY LOYALTIES

It is a commonplace among Americans to say that one is a Democrat or a Republican because he was "born" one, just as he was "born" a Methodist, *Buddhist,* a Catholic, or a Christian Scientist. The processes of political socialization *Mos lem* begin early in life as the child begins to be aware of political parties and *atheist* absorb judgments about them. He soon begins to realize that one of the parties is the family's party, that it is "good," that it is "our" party. Even in later life many Americans recognize the early origins of their party loyalties:

I'm a borned Republican, sister. We're Republicans from start to finish, clear back on the family tree. Hot Republicans all along. I'm not so much in favor of Eisenhower as the party he is on. I won't weaken my party by voting for a Democrat.

I was just raised to believe in the Democrats and they have been good for the working man — that's good enough for me. The Republicans are a cheap outfit all the way around. I just don't like the Republicans, my past experience with them has been all bad.[3]

Even though they do not often engage in overt indoctrination of their children into loyalty to a political party, parents nonetheless are the prime agents of political socialization in the American culture. Their casual conversations, their references to political events, and the example of their political activity are sufficient to convey their identifications to their children. And so stable are the resulting party loyalties that the intergenerational similarities in party loyalty persist even when the children reach adulthood (Table 3).[4] Furthermore, as Table 3 suggests, the intensity and consistency of parental influences affect the socialization. Politically active parents and parents with consistent, reinforcing party loyalties are more likely to produce "strong" party identifiers among their

[3] Angus Campbell, Gerald Gurin, Warren Miller, *The Voter Decides* (Evanston: Row, Peterson, 1954), p. 92.

[4] Angus Campbell, Philip E. Converse, Warren E. Miller, and Donald E. Stokes, *The American Voter* (New York: Wiley, 1960), p. 147.

Table 3
INTERGENERATIONAL RESEMBLANCE IN PARTISAN ORIENTATION, POLITICALLY ACTIVE AND INACTIVE HOMES, 1958

Party Identification of Offspring	One or Both Parents Were Politically Active			Neither Parent Was Politically Active		
	Both Parents Were Dems.	Both Parents Were Reps.	Parents Had No Consistent Partisanship	Both Parents Were Dems.	Both Parents Were Reps.	Parents Had No Consistent Partisanship
Strong Dem.	50%	5%	21%	40%	6%	20%
Weak Dem.	29	9	26	36	11	15
Independent	12	13	26	19	16	26
Weak Rep.	6	34	16	3	42	20
Strong Rep.	2	37	10	1	24	12
Apolitical	1	2	1	1	1	7
	100%	100%	100%	100%	100%	100%
Number of cases	333	194	135	308	187	199

children. Interestingly, too, a number of studies have found that the relationship in party preferences between generations is greater than the relationship in political attitudes. Thus, as one writer has put it, "we have suggestive evidence that the socialization of the individual into a *party* is a much more direct process than the socialization of the logically congruent area of ideology." [5]

That the acquisition of party loyalties comes surprisingly early and easily is also one of the conclusions of a recent study of school children in New Haven, Connecticut.[6] More than 60 per cent of the fourth-grade children were able to state a party preference — a percentage, the author notes, roughly the same as the SRC data show for the 21–24 year-old segment of its national adult sample. At this age, however, few of the children can support their identification with much information about party leaders, issues, or traditions. Not until they are eighth graders do they develop the supportive knowledge which permits party identification to become fully operative in the political world. Every indication, therefore, points to the family as the chief socializer; at least the party loyalties are present so early as to rule out virtually all other possibilities. And every indication, too, suggests that an abstract, unsupported party loyalty

[5] Herbert Hyman, *Political Socialization* (Glencoe: Free Press, 1959), p. 74. Hyman summarizes a good deal of the data and literature on intergenerational relationships in party loyalties from pp. 74–84. For a more recent report in the literature, see Roberta Sigel (ed.), *Political Socialization: Its Role in the Political Process*, Annals of the American Academy of Political and Social Science, Vol. 361 (1965).

[6] Fred I. Greenstein, *Children and Politics* (New Haven: Yale Univ. Press, 1965).

is much more easily and directly acquired than information about political issues and ideology. Party identification, in fact, seems possible regardless of differences in social class and background of the family; lower SES children identified with a party just as frequently as children from higher SES backgrounds.

The process of socialization, including the development of a party identification, need not be a single, "one-shot" influence. At the least it involves a life-long series of refinements and reinforcements of the initial socialization. The loyalty to a political party may even, despite its usual durability, change in time. Although the duration of the initial party loyalty will be greater the greater is the strength of the identification, it may be weakened or altered during adulthood by social issues and events such as the Civil War or the Great Depression of the 1930's. While changes in occupation alone seem not to affect party identification, a general change in life-style and peer groups — such as those changes associated with drastic upward social mobility — often does.[7]

In part the stability of these party loyalties results from the relative absence in the American political system of other agencies of political socialization that might challenge the early influences of the family. To see that that is the case one has only to compare political socialization in the United States and Europe. American schools and churches generally steer very clear of partisan commitments, contrary, for example, to the willingness of many European churches to support the various Christian Democratic parties of Europe. The American parties themselves engage in very little direct socialization; they do not maintain the youth groups, the flourishing University branches (which may have offices, lounges, and eating facilities), the social or recreational activities, or the occupational organizations that their European counterparts do. Business and worker groups — especially trade unions — do engage in this kind of socialization, but often with a gingerliness one would not find as often in their European counterparts. Indeed, it is a maxim of American middle-class gentility that one does not discuss either religion or politics in polite social circles.

Thus, the adolescent and young adult finds that his party loyalty is supported by a homogeneous political environment of family, friends, and secondary groups into which no new political socializers threaten to intrude. Even as a young adult his friends, associates, and relatives will largely have the same partisan loyalties that he does. And the chances are close to ten-to-one that his spouse, too, will share his party identification. In short, most individuals are "anchored in a matrix of politically harmonious primary associations — a result, to some extent, of conscious

---

[7] Campbell, Converse, Miller, and Stokes, *The American Voter,* p. 459 and Chapter 7.

selection and of the tendency for the social environment to bring together people of like views." [8]

Party identification, therefore, is acquired early, and it lingers late. It often remains far past the stimulus or stimuli for its formation; it may even survive significant changes in socio-economic status. Conventional wisdom assumes to the contrary, for example, that the upward mobility represented by the first move to the suburbs from the center city makes Republicans out of many Democrats and fashions a ring of solidly Republican suburbs around the Democratic city. New perceptions of a new social status, plus the influences of new primary groups, are said to bring about the change in party identification. There are, however, a number of things wrong with the assumption that party "conversion" accompanies the escape to the suburbs. The suburbs are by no means uniformly Republican. Furthermore, survey data seem to suggest that no great changes in party identification follow emigration from the city. Very probably the more plausible explanation of the party complexion of the suburbs is one of "transplantation" or selective migration.

Given the strength of partisan identifications, it seems possible that former city Democrats and Republicans carried their affiliations with them as they fled the city. Some sought suburbs of like-minded and like-situated people, and thus there developed working-class as well as elegant suburbs, each homogeneous in its distinctive party and economic contours. Other movers, with different partisan and economic backgrounds, came together in the same place to form a "mixed salad" suburb. From such combinations we can postulate a continuum of suburbs, ranged in terms of those factors here termed "life-style." Each life-style with its distinctive socio-economic syndrome is accompanied by a special partisan cast.[9]

Many of the same considerations that determine the selection of a party loyalty may, in other words, determine the selection of a suburb. In any event, party loyalties are not necessarily changed even by changes in residence and life-style. An attachment so deep and enduring as a party identification does not merely follow and reflect other personal decisions. It may often even fail to reflect the important changes and milestones of life.

[8] Herbert McClosky and Harold E. Dahlgren, "Primary Group Influence on Party Loyalty," *American Political Science Review*, Vol. LIII (1959), p. 775. On the homogeneity of primary group influences, see also Bernard R. Berelson, Paul F. Lazarsfeld, and William N. McPhee, *Voting* (Chicago: Univ. of Chicago Press, 1954), Chapter 6.

[9] Frederick M. Wirt, "The Political Sociology of American Suburbia: A Reinterpretation," *Journal of Politics*, Vol. XXVII (1965), pp. 664–665. See also Campbell, *et al., The American Voter*, pp. 455–460; G. Edward Janosik, "The New Suburbia," *Current History* (August, 1965), pp. 91–95; and Fred I. Greenstein and Raymond E. Wolfinger, "The Suburbs and Shifting Party Loyalties," *Public Opinion Quarterly*, Vol. XXII (Winter, 1958–59), pp. 473–482.

SOCIAL CLASS AND PARTY IDENTIFICATION

The processes of political socialization do not, however, explain the distribution of party loyalties in the United States. They describe "how," rather than "why," the individual acquires his particular party loyalty. At best the explanations of socialization, resting as they do on parental influences, merely push the question back a generation in most instances. The search for an explanation of these party loyalties should very likely begin with social class, for it is probably true, as Seymour Lipset has asserted, that the principal generalization one can make about the democratic parties of the world is that they are primarily based on social classes.[10]

We have referred before to social class and to socio-economic status, and a longer explanation of the terms is probably overdue. Much of the literature uses them interchangeably (or almost interchangeably), but the preference here is for the latter term and its conventional abbreviation, SES. It refers simply to the relative ranking of the economic and/or social deference the individual can command. Social and economic status generally accompany each other, but not always. The exceptions may be important — the wealthy member of a minority group whose economic status far outruns his social acceptability, or the genteelly impoverished scion of a still-prestigous old and good family. But regardless of the rubric one chooses, status differences underlie the party electorates of the mature, industrial democracies with which one can most reasonably compare the United States. The very nature of economic and political development seems to transcend the older party lines based on ethnic, racial, religious, or regional differences.

The signs and marks of SES conflict are scattered throughout all of American history. James Madison, one of the most knowing observers of human nature among the Founding Fathers, observed in his famous tenth paper of *The Federalist* that economic differences were the most common source of faction.[11] Social and economic status differences clearly underlie the battle between the wealthy, aristocratic Federalists and the less privileged Jeffersonian Democrats. And almost a century later William Jennings Bryan made the Democratic party the vehicle for the protests of the Grangers, the emerging Socialists, the Greenbackers, the Knights of Labor, and the Populists — all of them composed largely of the discontented and disadvantaged. Bryan ("The Great Commoner") had come to the Democratic convention of 1896 as the voice of prairie Populism, and

---

[10] *Political Man* (New York: Anchor, 1963), p. 230.
[11] See Madison's tenth paper, *The Federalist* (New York: Modern Library, 1937), p. 56: ". . . the most common and durable source of factions has been the various and unequal distribution of property."

there he challenged the conservatism of Grover Cleveland in his celebrated attack on the gold standard and hard money. ("You shall not press
down upon the brow of labor this crown of thorns. You shall not crucify
mankind upon this cross of gold.") Stirred by the Nebraska prophet, the
convention repudiated its conservative leadership and picked Bryan himself as its candidate. Despite his defeat, the Democrats twice (1900 and
1908) returned to him as their presidential candidate. For his part, Bryan
never appeared to tire of his crusade against corporate wealth, Eastern
banking interests, and what he liked to call the "plutocracy."

In many ways Bryan and the Democrats of 1896 appear to be the har-
bingers of modern American SES politics. Their political "causes" reflect
the new problems, conflicts, and classes which develop with industrialism.
And throughout this century one can perceive long-run SES differences
between the two major American parties. The Republican party has been
identified with higher status groups, with wealth and business, with high
tariffs and hard money, and with the world of finance. The Democrats
have drawn on lower SES groups, on immigrants and first-generation
Americans, on racial and ethnic minorities, and they have supported the
use of governmental power for social and economic reform. Obviously,
the relationship has not been perfect; the Democrats reverted to genuine
conservatism with Judge Alton B. Parker in 1904, and in some of the states
of the Midwest the Republicans, infused by the Progressive movement,
became the party of social and economic reform through the 1930's. In
the suffusing prosperity of the 1920's, moreover, most of the class differences between the two parties were greatly muted. Yet, in the broadest
terms party loyalties appear in this century to have broken at least in part
along SES lines.

Even their candidates have suggested something of the SES images the
parties projected to the American electorate. Among the Republicans
there was Calvin Coolidge, son of a great Boston Brahmin family and
virtually an incarnation of the "Wasp" (White, Anglo-Saxon, Protestant)
domination of American life. Dignified and withdrawn, always the sober
Puritan, he seemed the essence of the Protestant ethic and sober fiscal
conservatism. When he affirmed that "the business of America is business," the observation sounded with a ring of profundity and sincerity.
For the nation that had kept "cool with Coolidge" in 1924, the Democrats
proposed in 1928 a boisterous "Happy Warrior," Alfred Smith, the Governor of New York. No Puritan or Brahmin he, Smith was a "wet," a
jubilant, cigar-smoking son of New York's lower East Side. The son of
immigrant parents and the first Roman Catholic nominated for the Presidency, he sprang from industrialism's working class. Although he was
born only 200 miles from Calvin Coolidge's Boston, the distances in social
status and style of life were virtually immeasurable.

By the 1930's the SES stamp of the parties became even more apparent.

The migration to the cities and the crushing impoverishments of the Great Depression were the events out of which Franklin Roosevelt built a Democratic party, more firmly than ever a party of social and economic reform. This intensification of the SES lines between the two parties was his "revolution" in party politics. His New Deal programs — labor legislation, social security, wages and hours laws — solidified the Democratic party's image as the party of the relative "have-nots." Even groups such as the Negroes, long allied with the Republicans as the party of Lincoln, were lured to the Democratic banner; the strength of SES issues even kept them as allies of southern whites in the Roosevelt coalition. In brief, Franklin Roosevelt buttressed the class divisions of industrialism by adding to its conflicts the consequent response of government; the Welfare State. Its programs and expenditures heightened the stakes, and thus the commitments, of socio-economic status politics.[12]

All of this is not to argue that only socio-economic status differences divided the major American parties in this century. But the evidence is strong that it did constitute a very important, and possibly even overriding, dimension of difference between them. Only since the 1940's and the advent of public opinion polling, however, has it been possible to make more precise and confident statements about the attitudes, the SES, the party identifications, and the votes of individual Americans. Within the past twenty-five years, therefore, we have moved to a new precision in describing the composition of the parties in the electorate.

The contemporary relationships between party and SES are clear in the nature of the two party electorates in 1964 (Table 4). The relationship lurks even where it is not obvious. The partisan differences in educational levels cannot, for example, be taken at face value. Generally it seems reasonable to suppose that the positive relationship between years of education and Republicanism results from the intermediating SES variable (i.e., a higher percentage of upper SES parents send their sons and daughters to college, and the college degree leads to higher SES jobs.) There seems little reason to suspect that the intellectually liberating experiences of formal education lead young men and women overwhelmingly to the true path of Republicanism. Also, given the fact of the higher SES of Protestants in the United States, their relationship with Republicanism unquestionably reflects those status differences in part. And there certainly is no need at this late date to elaborate the enormous SES differences between whites and non-whites in the United States.

---

[12] Among the histories of the American parties, see Wilfred Binkley, *American Political Parties* (New York: Knopf, 1962); Herbert Agar, *The Price of Union* (Boston: Houghton Mifflin, 1950); George H. Mayer, *The Republican Party: 1854–1964* (New York: Oxford Univ. Press, 1964); Malcolm C. Moos, *The Republicans: A History of Their Party* (New York: Random House, 1956); and William N. Chambers, *The Democrats: 1789–1964* (Princeton: Van Nostrand, 1964).

Table 4
SOCIAL CHARACTERISTICS OF PARTY IDENTIFIERS: 1964 *

	Strong Dem.	Weak Dem.	Independent	Weak Rep.	Strong Rep.	Apolitical, etc.
Race:						
White	80%	90%	92%	96%	98%	66%
Non-white	20	10	8	4	2	34
Total	100%	100%	100%	100%	100%	100%
Occupation:						
Professional	8%	10%	12%	10%	12%	6%
Business, mgrs., official	13	15	20	20	22	13
Farmers	5	7	3	6	5	6
Clerical, sales	10	11	11	10	14	13
Skilled, semi-skilled, protective service	34	34	36	28	18	31
Unskilled, service	13	10	8	6	2	9
Retired	15	12	8	19	25	16
Unemployed	2	2	1		1	6
Total	100%	101%	99%	99%	99%	100%
Income:						
$0–$1,999	12%	11%	9%	10%	10%	44%
$2,000–$3,999	23	19	14	12	14	16
$4,000–$5,999	22	23	19	16	21	16
$6,000–$9,999	28	31	34	34	25	9
$10,000–$14,999	10	13	16	19	16	9
$15,000 and over	5	4	8	9	13	6
Total	100%	101%	100%	100%	99%	100%
Education:						
None through 8 grades	35%	26%	18%	19%	15%	44%
9 through 12 grades	48	54	54	53	47	41
Some college	9	10	16	14	18	9
Baccalaureate degree	6	8	9	11	16	3
Advanced degree	1	2	3	3	4	3
Total	99%	100%	100%	100%	100%	100%
Religion:						
Catholics	26%	26%	27%	14%	18%	16%
Jews	3	3	5	1	1	
Protestants	71	71	67	84	82	84
Total	100%	100%	99%	99%	101%	100%

* Source: The Survey Research Center of the University of Michigan, made available through the Inter-University Consortium for Political Research.

The strongest evidence of the SES or class basis to party identifications in contemporary American politics is that of the differences between the two party electorates in income, education, and occupation. And significantly, students of class and stratification in American society are well agreed that income, education, and occupation are three of the most reliable indexes to the socio-economic status of an individual.[13] Refinements within these gross education, income, and occupation categories bring even clearer differences between party identifiers. For example, the likelihood of corporation executives identifying with the Republican party increases as the size of their firm increases (Table 5). Finally, the

Table 5

RELATIONSHIP BETWEEN SIZE OF FIRM AND PARTY IDENTIFICATION
OF CORPORATION EXECUTIVES IN 1955 [14]

Size of Firm	Republican	Democratic	Independent
100 to 999 workers	69%	12%	19%
1,000 to 9,999 workers	80	8	12
10,000 and over workers	84	6	10

relationship of the objectively measured SES characteristics with party identification increases if it is reinforced by the class perceptions of the individual. If, for instance, the prosperous businessman sees himself as a member of the upper class rather than the ubiquitous middle class, he is more likely to adhere to the GOP.[15]

Yet, the lines of SES difference between the American parties are less distinct than their rhetoric and campaigns might lead one to expect. Just as certainly, those lines are less clear than comparable ones in European party systems. In a comparison of party identifiers in the United States and Norway, Campbell and Valen report: [16]

In both countries the occupational distribution of identifiers differs among the parties. In the United States, the differences are rather small. The Democratic Party draws 30 per cent of its adherents from the white-collar occupations, 46 per cent from the blue-collar. The Republicans come 36 per cent from the white-collar occupations and 39 per cent from the blue-collar. The occupational differences are very much greater among the various Norwegian parties. Of the

[13] See Milton Gordon, *Social Class in American Sociology* (Durham: Duke Univ. Press, 1958) for a full discussion of indices and measures of class and status.

[14] Lipset, *Political Man*, p. 305. The data are from the Center for International Studies of MIT.

[15] For the effect of subjective class perceptions see Heinz Eulau, *Class and Party in the Eisenhower Years* (Glencoe: Free Press, 1962).

[16] Angus Campbell and Henry Valen, "Party Identification in Norway and the United States," *Public Opinion Quarterly*, Vol. XXV (1961), pp. 514–515.

Labor Party identifiers 79 per cent are blue-collar workers, 17 per cent are white-collar; among the Conservatives the proportions are 19 per cent and 76 per cent.

Even the two Norwegian parties of the center, whose ideologies are not primarily economic, are more distinctive in their division of occupational groups than are the American parties.

So, we approach the conclusion of most observers of the American parties — that socio-economic status and party loyalty are not as closely associated in the United States as they are in a number of the other Western democracies.[17] Both American parties have within their loyal electorates an important number of representatives from upper, middle, and lower status groups. Consequently, they find it difficult to formulate overt class appeals or to enunciate ideologies which reflect class or status differences. The heterogeneous nature of their loyalists is perfectly consistent with their pragmatic, relatively non-ideological tone, and their mission as brokers among diverse social groupings. And so is the heterogeneity of their office-holders. It is not uncommon for U.S. senators of different parties — e.g., Democratic Senator Joseph Clark of Pennsylvania and Republican Senator Jacob Javits of New York — to have a larger area of issue agreement with each other than with some senators of their own parties. The lines of SES division between the major American parties are, therefore, indistinct and overlapping, and while SES is one explanation of inter-party differences, it is by no means the only one.[18]

In part the weakness of SES differences between the two party electorates may result from the imperfect and inefficient translation of general status differences into differences in party identification. Among the influences muting the translation of status differences into political ones the following may be the most important:

1. *The shifting SES lines of American federalism.* SES lines differ from state to state, and it is difficult and somewhat misleading to make aggregate, national comparisons using identical categories. The distribution of SES groups in Montana, for example, differs greatly from that in New York. Some large and powerful groups in New York — Negroes, Jews, and urban laborers come to mind — are considerably less important and numerous in Montana. The Republican parties of the two states, therefore, recruit electorates of greatly different SES compositions. By the sheer necessity of remaining competitive the Republicans of New York will amass a more heterogeneous electorate than the Republicans of Montana may feel compelled to.

2. *The suppression of SES differences.* Some state and local party lead-

---

[17] See, *inter alia,* Robert R. Alford, *Party and Society* (Chicago: Rand McNally, 1963), Chapter 8.

[18] See *The American Voter,* Chapter 13, for a discussion of the problem of "social status polarization."

ers may (with decreasing success, probably) obliterate SES lines by fostering an issueless politics of localism and loyalty to personalities. For years the Democratic parties of the Southern states were classic examples of that kind of determinedly non-SES politics. In great part their successes sprang from their ability to disenfranchise large segments of the lower SES groups, both white and Negro.

3. *Diffidence about class politics.* American mores do not encourage a politics of class or socio-economic status. Many Americans do not see class divisions or conflict in the American society, nor do they see themselves in any but a broadly inclusive, "classless" middle class. Explicit class appeals would probably antagonize one group of Americans and pass by another "classless" group. Furthermore, American uncertainty and naivete about class leads some voters to perceive their class differently than the objective indicators might suggest. The owner of a modest home may, because of that ownership, identify with SES groups somewhat above the one to which all educational, occupational, and income indicators might point. Finally, even as measured by social scientists, SES differences are not so great in the American society to begin with.

4. *The slowness of SES translation into politics.* So persistent are the loyalties of party identification that they tend to respond only very slowly to changes in SES. Many party loyalties formed early as a result of family influences, in fact, are responses to SES one or two generations "late." The young man raised and socialized into the Democratic party by a working-class father may cling to that party identification long after graduating from college, entering the business world, and reaching the country club. Also, party loyalties shaped as SES responses to depressions, recessions, or prosperity may remain long after the event.

ALTERNATIVES TO THE SES BASIS OF LOYALTIES

In view of the relatively weak SES divisions between the Democratic and Republican electorates, there must clearly be additional explanations for the distribution of party loyalties in the United States.

SECTIONALISM

The greatest challenge to the SES interpretations of American politics has come from the school which ascribes the primary differences between the parties, not to SES differences, but to sectional differences.[19] The sectional theories hold that the varying geographic areas or sections of the country have separate, identifiable, and deeply-felt political interests which, when honored and favored by a political party, unite large num-

[19] For example, Arthur N. Holcombe, *The Political Parties of Today* (New York: Harper, 1924) and *Our More Perfect Union* (Cambridge: Harvard Univ. Press, 1950).

bers of otherwise differing voters behind its standard.[20] Thus, in the sectional explanations one speaks of the Republicans and the Democrats building national coalitions behind presidential candidates by joining the votes of one section to those of another or of parties' dominating the loyalties of this or that section.

Unquestionably the most enduring sectionalism in American party history was that of the Democratic party in the South. Even before the Civil War the sectional interests of the South in slavery and in an agriculture geared to export markets had unified it as a political section. The searing experience of that war and the Reconstruction which followed made the South into the Solid South and delivered it to the Democrats. United by historical experience and by a desperate defense of a way of life, the eleven states of the Confederacy cast their electoral votes for Democratic presidential candidates in every election from 1880 through 1924, except for Tennessee's defection in 1920. Al Smith's Catholicism frightened four of them into the Republican column in 1928, but the Roosevelt economic programs reinforced the region's economic interests — and in no way greatly challenged its way of life — and brought the South back to the Democratic party for the four Roosevelt elections. Only with the successes of the Dixiecrat ticket in 1948 did the South begin to move away again from its traditional party loyalties.

Similarly, strong East-West differences have periodically marked American party conflict. In the early years of the Republic the fading Federalists held to an ever-narrowing base of Eastern seaport and financial interests while the Jeffersonians expanded westward with the new settlers. Jackson, too, pointed his party appeals to the men of the frontier, and the protest movements that thrust William Jennings Bryan into the 1896 campaign sprang from the agrarian discontent of the Western prairies. Indeed, the geographical distribution of the presidential vote of 1896 is striking affirmation of sectional voting (Figure 1). Many of the Populists' loudest complaints were, indeed, directed at Eastern capitalism, Eastern bankers, and Eastern trusts.

Sectionalism can most easily be identified by its most obvious characteristic: sectional one-partyism. When sectional loyalties were strong enough to override all of the other sources of party loyalty, they unified the section behind a single party. When the sectionalism endured, it reinforced the one-partyism both socially and psychologically. Young voters learned that the dominant party was the party of the section in that it was the defender of the style and quality of its life.

The pull of sectionalism has declined steadily within the past several generations. The sectional homogeneity of life, and the resulting common-

[20] For a somewhat different and excellent essay on the nature of sectionalism, see V. O. Key, *Politics, Parties, and Pressure Groups*, 5th ed. (New York: Crowell, 1964), pp. 232–233.

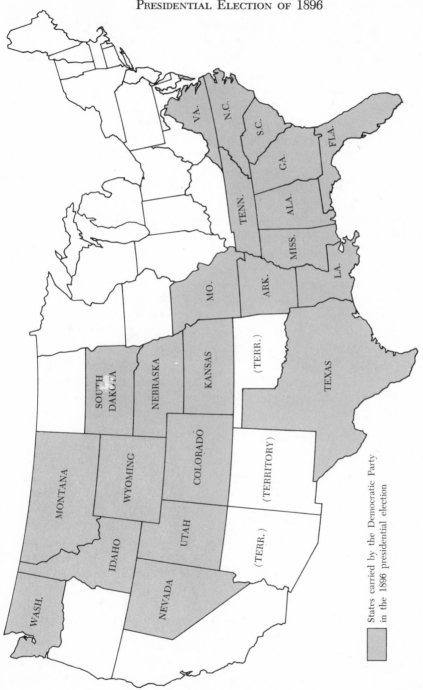

Figure 1
STATES CARRIED BY THE DEMOCRATIC PARTY IN THE
PRESIDENTIAL ELECTION OF 1896

States carried by the Democratic Party
in the 1896 presidential election

ality of interests, yields now to diversity and a nationalization of life throughout the country. One-party areas or sections are breaking down into two-party competitiveness, and that in itself is the best clue that sectional loyalties no longer have the power they once did. Sectional loyalties, of course, have not completely disappeared. Southern sectionalism awakened in a new guise in 1964 as five deep Southern states supported Barry Goldwater, the Republican presidential candidate. The five states — Alabama, Georgia, Louisiana, Mississippi, and South Carolina — were among the states with the smallest percentages of pupils in integrated schools and the smallest percentages of adult Negroes registered to vote. But elsewhere sectionalism now appears to have receded into a secondary position in the development of political party loyalties.

In retrospect it is difficult to say what force sectionalism had even at its zenith. The great difficulty with the sectional explanations is that the "section" may simply be an obscuring short-hand for a geographical concentration of other, identifiable interests — ethnic, racial, or possibly SES. Much sectional voting in the past, for instance, reflected conflicts among crop economies in the various agricultural sections. Thus the central question: Are the "sections" the source of motivating sectional interests, or are they merely categories or concentrations of voters who identify with a party for SES or other reasons? It contributes little of explanatory value to say that the Midwest supported FDR in 1936 or that the West backed Eisenhower. To be sure, the South has been more than a descriptive category; its political behavior has been "sectional" in the sense of unified interests and an awareness of the region and its distinctiveness. But the case for sectional explanations weakens perceptibly as soon as one looks beyond the South, its greatest piece of evidence.[21]

URBAN-RURAL DIFFERENCES

So many of the present differences between the party electorates fall along urban-rural lines that one is tempted to entertain the urban-rural explanations of the party electorates. But like the sectional explanations, these deal with aggregates of individuals in geographical areas — with groups of people categorized by where they live rather than by who they are. And like the sectional theories they seem to suggest that urban or rural one-partyism is produced by the unified interest of city or country and by a consequent conformity to the party of that interest and the social reinforcement behind it.

Especially if one separates the South from the rest of the country, it is clear that the Democratic identifier is more apt to live in a city, the Re-

---

[21] It may well be that the sectional interpretations were in fact a reflection of the fact that before the late 1940's the only electoral data for analysis were the gross, aggregate totals in which the units were geographical areas of some sort. Since then the data of the sample surveys have made the individual the unit of analysis.

Table 6

PLACE OF RESIDENCE OF NON-SOUTHERN PARTY IDENTIFIERS: 1964 *

	Strong Dem.	Weak Dem.	Inde- pendent	Weak Rep.	Strong Rep.
1. Central cities of 12 largest SMSA's [1]	24.9%	14.9%	15.0%	11.0%	11.9%
2. Cities of 50,000 and over (not included in 1)	21.7	14.5	19.8	17.3	16.3
3. Urban places, 10,000–49,999	20.5	22.4	24.2	21.4	28.1
4. Urban places, 2,500–9,999 and urbanized areas	13.7	19.1	17.6	13.3	17.8
5. Rural areas in SMSA's	6.0	10.4	11.4	12.7	10.4
6. Rural areas not in SMSA's	13.3	18.7	12.1	24.3	15.6
Total	100.1%	100.0%	100.1%	100.0%	100.1%

* *Source: the Survey Research Center of the University of Michigan, made available through the Inter-University Consortium for Political Research.*

[1] *Standard Metropolitan Statistical Area.*

publican more likely to reside in a rural area or small town (Table 6). But again we confront the central question: do the urban-rural differences have an explanatory power of their own? Within the cities SES differences clearly affect party identifications and voting patterns. One can break down most urban centers by value of housing and find the expected correlation between lower-cost rental housing and the Democratic vote. And in the suburbs similar distinctions prevail. Democratic vote percentages are higher in the new tract suburbs of low-cost and virtually identical homes; Republican percentages rise in those suburbs of rolling lawns, expansive vistas, and spacious mortgages. And within rural areas the Democrats poll most heavily in the marginal, less prosperous farming areas in which National Farmers Union membership is greatest; the Republicans dominate the more successful, large crop areas in which the American Farm Bureau Federation has its greatest strength. There are also ethnic, racial, and religious differences; rural America largely remains a bastion of white, Anglo-Saxon, Protestant America, the very groups that have been fleeing the cities in recent decades. The cities increasingly are left to the racial and ethnic minorities which identify with the Democratic party.

All of this notwithstanding, it is also undoubtedly true that important urban-rural interests do exist. The very nature of the city — crowded, interdependent, and complex — creates social problems and dislocations for which there may be no practical solution except through government action. Crime, unemployment, poverty, traffic snarls, and the other ills of the city cry out for public solutions, and the Democratic party, more the advocate of positive government, is ideologically better able to advocate them. Furthermore, many Democratic cities, confident that they can expect little help from Republican-dominated state legislatures, have made alliance with the national government for the attack on civic problems. On the other hand, the smaller towns and cities and the rural areas cling to a simpler world — a world of voluntary action by friends and neighbors and of community self-help, in which the interventions of government seem less important and vital. Their political ethos is more in the spirit of the Republican credos of limited government (whenever possible) and dependence on local government (whenever necessary).

As the United States becomes an increasingly urban and metropolitan nation — almost 62 per cent of the American population in 1960 lived in 212 standard metropolitan areas the Census Bureau defines — the question ceases to be one of urban versus rural America. It becomes instead one of distinction within the urban sector. Selective migration out of the old, center or core cities promises to leave them ethnic, racial, and lower SES enclaves (if not ghettos) and thus more solidly Democratic. Urban diversity, therefore, is moving to the suburbs and urban fringe areas, and their diversity reflects the continuing SES differences between the parties (Table 7). The new suburbs and suburban cities may soon, therefore, be-

Table 7

PARTY COMPETITIVENESS AND MEDIAN INCOMES
OF 19 MINNEAPOLIS (MINN.) SUBURBS

I. SUBURBS DIVIDED BY MEDIAN INCOMES (1960 CENSUS)

	Percentage Vote for Democratic Gubernatorial Candidate: 1962 [*]
Ten Suburbs with Highest Median Incomes	42.0%
Nine Suburbs with Lowest Median Incomes	52.9%

II. PERCENTAGE DEMOCRATIC: 1962 GUBERNATORIAL VOTE ([*])

	Number of Suburbs
0–39.9%	3
40–49.9%	6
50–59.9%	8
60–69.9%	2
	19

(Median: 50.5%)
(Statewide Democratic Percentage: 50.0)

[*] *The 1962 gubernatorial election between Elmer L. Andersen (Rep.) and Karl Rolvaag (Dem.) ended in a virtual tie; after a lengthy recount, Rolvaag was declared the winner by 91 votes.*

come the major sites of two-party competitiveness. But to be a "site" of competition is not necessarily to be its explanation.

RELIGION

Even when income, education, and occupation are held constant, Catholics and Jews tend to support the Democratic party, and non-Southern Protestants the Republican party. Again, however, the statistical relationships are exactly and only that; they do not answer the questions of cause or explanation. Very possibly these relationships between religion and party mask differences that are primarily urban and rural. Perhaps, too, despite the holding of SES factors constant, there remains an SES factor; a Jew of high income, lengthy formal education, and professional occupation (with, that is, the usual formal characteristics of high SES) is often denied by prejudice the status he might otherwise expect. The same illustration could still apply to some Catholics, but presently not with the force it would have had a generation or two ago when anti-Catholic bias was greater and when Catholic identification with the Democratic party was at its strongest.

Yet, it does appear that religion — both as theology and as group identification — is involved here. A Jewish internationalism and concern for social justice, rooted in the religious and ethnic traditions of Judaism, disposes many Jews to the Democratic party as the party of international concern, support for the state of Israel, and social and economic equality.[22] In the case of American Catholics, the tie to the Democratic party is in great part a tie of personalities and political organization. The political machines of the cities were traditionally led by Catholics, and their patronage and largesse often went to the newly immigrated Catholics from Europe. The roll call of Catholics in Democratic leadership, furthermore, extends beyond the local bosses. All but one of the national chairmen of the Democratic party since the late 1920's have been Roman Catholics, and it has also been the party of the two Catholic candidates for the Presidency: Al Smith and John F. Kennedy. The ties of Protestantism to Republicanism are less obvious, probably in part because of the enormous diversity of the sects which it embraces. Very possibly, however, the theological individualism of more conservative Protestantism disposes individuals to Republicanism; there has at least been a clear relationship in recent years between Protestant fundamentalism and political conservatism.[23]

[22] Lawrence Fuchs, *The Political Behavior of the American Jews* (Glencoe: Free Press, 1956).

[23] The 1960 presidential election occasioned a reexamination of the religious factor in American party loyalties and voting behavior. See Scott Greer, "Catholic Voters and the Democratic Party," *Public Opinion Quarterly*, Vol. XXV (1961), pp. 611–625; and Philip E. Converse, "Religion and Politics: The 1960 Election," in Campbell, *et al.*, *Elections and the Political Order* (New York: Wiley, 1966), pp. 96–124.

RACE

Not too long ago the Republican party, as the party of Lincoln, the Civil War, and the hated Reconstruction, was associated with Negro equality in the minds of both American Negroes and whites. In the generation between 1930 and 1960, however, the wheels of racial politics turned 180 degrees. It is now the Democratic party and the Kennedy and Johnson administrations which Southerners see as the threat to Southern traditions. Negroes identify with the Democratic party in overwhelming numbers, and quite regardless of any other set of social characteristics. And clearly, these deeply-felt issues often override SES issues and differences, both for whites and for Negroes. The virtually overnight growth of Republicanism in the South is in part based on that single, overpowering issue, and some Northern Republican parties have also profitted from the white "backlash." Finally, whites with a belief in the necessity and/or morality of racial equality may choose the Democratic party wholly or partly for that reason.

TRADITIONALISM

Attachments to a political party need not be associated with an interest, a set of goals, or a group need. It is sufficient for some Americans that their party is the party of their parents, their friends, or their locale. Or that it is the party of their fellow workers or worshipers. For these identifiers it suffices to say, for example, that "everyone around here is a Democrat (or a Republican)." In some sections of the country the prevailing homogeneity of party identification may still reflect the loyalties of the original migrants into the area. Southern Illinois, settled by Democrats from the South, maintains an inclination to the Democratic party even today.[24]

PARTY LEADERSHIP AND PERSONALITIES

The individual may very well identify the political party with a particular leader or group of leaders within it. He may attach himself to the Democratic party as the party of Franklin Roosevelt or John F. Kennedy, or to the Republican party as the party of Dwight D. Eisenhower or Barry Goldwater. For him the party is little more than an extension of an attractive, compelling personality, and his loyalty to it in great part reflects confidence in and affection for those personalities. Such an explanation for party identification is, however, probably easily overestimated; President Eisenhower, despite the magnitude of his victories and personal popularity, clearly made little dent on long-run loyalties, even of the Democrats who voted for him.

[24] For a discussion of these traditional loyalties resulting from patterns of migration, see V. O. Key, *American State Politics* (New York: Knopf, 1956), Chapter 8.

NON-SES ISSUE INVOLVEMENT

Those well-informed citizens who are involved in political issues and ideologies will possibly identify with a political party chiefly out of approval
of the policy positions it takes. For most of this century, for example, the
Democratic party has been more willing than the Republican to espouse
American commitments abroad — beginning with entry into the League
of Nations and continuing today over questions of foreign aid. Republicans have on the whole been more chary of foreign involvement, more
nationalistic, and more prone to isolationism in foreign policy. Naturally,
the two parties should attract their respective shares of partisans for
whom foreign policy issues are especially important.

These foreign policy differences have been fairly enduring over the past
fifty years. Other short- run policy differences may have had an equal, if less
lasting, impact. The issues of Prohibition and the Noble Experiment of
the 18th Amendment have by now receded into the mists of American
history. But in the 1920's and 1930's the question divided the two parties
and, very probably, some of their identifiers. The "dry's" who supported
the Experiment were largely in the Republican party, and most of its
"wet" opponents worked within the Democratic party. One could find
more contemporary examples, too, of non-SES issues on the basis of
which some parts of the electorate may be prepared to "swear loyalty" to
a political party. The issue of national moral rectitude and its converse,
"crime in the streets" — an issue developed by Barry Goldwater in 1964 —
may be an illustration.[25]

COMPLEXITY AND CHANGE IN PARTY IDENTIFICATION

The puzzle remains. By all measures of socio-economic status (such as
income, education, and occupation) the relationship of SES to party identification in the American party system, while clearly apparent, is not
great. And yet, much of the partisan rhetoric and combat between the parties appears to run along SES lines — whether it is a congressional debate
over the poverty program or medicare, presidential campaign centering
on labor-management relations, or a state or local clash over sales and
income taxes.

The puzzle becomes even knottier on examination of the relationship
between party identifications and attitudes on what appear to be SES-
related issues. As Table 8 indicates, the relationship of party identifications to attitudes on the recent question of medicare is far greater than
the earlier reported relationship between party identification and the

---

[25] Undoubtedly this issue had racial overtones for many voters in that they identified the "crime in the streets" with Negro demonstrations and rioting; however, for
many other voters it was probably perceived and reacted to "at face value."

kinds of personal characteristics usually denoting SES. So, SES-related attitudes appear to be far more related to party identification than are the objective indicators of SES. Examination of recent data of the SRC will also show that these attitudes are more directly related to party identification than are the status perceptions of the voters themselves.

Table 8

OPINIONS OF PARTY IDENTIFIERS ON MEDICARE: 1964 *

	Strong Dem.	Weak Dem.	Inde-pendent	Weak Rep.	Strong Rep.
1. Favors Medicare	66.3%	54.0%	47.2%	35.4%	21.3%
2. Uncertain	6.5	4.4	6.0	7.2	8.3
3. Opposes Medicare	12.0	24.4	29.5	38.3	62.1
4. No interest, don't know, etc.	15.2	17.1	17.3	19.1	8.3
Total	100.0%	99.9%	100.0%	100.0%	100.0%

* Source: The Survey Research Center of the University of Michigan, made available through the Inter-University Consortium for Political Research.

Several solutions to the paradox of the different issue positions of Democratic and Republican identifiers are self-evident.

1. It may well be that Americans develop what appear to be SES sympathies and goals which are not congruent with their own SES positions. There may be at work some feeling for the SES "underdog" or some deference to the SES "overdog," or some residual loyalties to a status or class of some years before. We may be looking, in other words, for simplistic explanations when we seek a one-to-one relationship between SES characteristics and SES loyalties. In politics, after all, it is the operational attitudes, not the SES itself, which are important.

2. It may also be that the SES division of party loyalties is being absorbed in the broader "liberal" and "conservative" ideologies about the proper and useful role of government. These ideologies may, indeed, be more sophisticated formulations which set SES issues in the context of broader social problems, which see the implications that SES problems have for all status groups, and yet which recognize that it will be lower-SES groups who seek the help of governmental action and the upper-SES groups which need it less. For some partisans, in other words, the liberal and conservative ideologies come between SES conflict and their loyalties to the parties; the new ideologies subsume old SES lines and restate them in broader, abstract, non-SES terms.[26]

Very likely both explanations have some force. As an illustration one

[26] A third possible explanation — that the party identification produces the attitudes on public issues such as these — will be examined in the next chapter.

might take the much-commented upon alliance of some high-status "intellectuals" with the Democratic party. Without getting mired in the definitional bogs which surround intellectualism, it need only be said that the identification is clear between the Democratic party and some Americans who pursue (or who are at least thought to pursue) the life of the intellect. Why the relationship? Democrats have flattered intellectuals by calling college professors, writers, and even poets to Washington and by offering a presidential candidate in the 1950's who was an unashamed "egg head." The tie probably also springs in part from the alienation of these groups from the values and styles of life — the Babbittry and anti-intellectualism — they associate with a predominantly business culture of middle- and upper-class America. In part, too, it results from their acceptance of the values of equality and social progress and their confidence in the efficacy of governmental solutions, all of which comport more easily with the "welfare state" reformism of the Democratic party and its New Deal and Great Society. And if it is the case with these Americans that political attitudes need not reflect directly the individual's personal SES, it may be the case for others.

Thus, the influences underlying the division of American party loyalties at present is complex. Among them are important, though not dominant, SES influences and potent non-SES influences. But whatever their configuration there is no reason to assume that any axis or axes of division of the party electorates will persist for all time. It is thoroughly possible that a stunning American military loss, a major defeat in the space race, or a series of grave diplomatic miscalculations might elevate defense or foreign policy issues to a new dominance in determining party loyalties. It is equally possible that a serious depression or a galloping inflation might drastically sharpen and polarize the SES division. The determinants of party loyalties are themselves shifting, dynamic, and vulnerable to change. Historically such shifts have been triggered by the conjunction of presidential elections and cataclysmic events — the Civil War, panics, depressions, and foreign wars. The resulting changes in the bases of the division of party loyalties crystallize at the election and persist for a period thereafter.[27] Most recently the events of 1932 renewed and reaffirmed the SES divisions that had been dulled during the 1920's.

Not all of the changes in the parties in the electorate, however, are in the nature of these sharp, fundamental, long-term realignments. In the shorter run the parties struggle to hold the loyalties of their electorates in the face of shifts within the range of the current divisions between them. The American population ages, and the parties must appeal to a new group, the nation's "senior citizens." Another group, the Roman Catholics,

[27] See V. O. Key, "A Theory of Critical Elections," *Journal of Politics*, Vol. XVII (1955), pp. 3–18; Angus Campbell, "A Classification of Presidential Elections," in Campbell, Converse, Miller, and Stokes, *Elections and the Political Order*, pp. 63–77.

emerges from three generations as a discriminated-against minority, and its ties to the Democratic party are possibly weakened. Migrations to the West and the cities alter the distribution of the electorate, and automation and mechanization (and their educational demands) threaten to shift patterns of unemployment and occupational status. And a nagging war in Vietnam raises foreign policy issues and differences to a new salience.

The American party electorates are, very clearly, less homogeneous — especially in SES — than those of the party systems of many comparable democracies. They are bound together, not by SES-related programs or ideologies, but by loyalty to the political party *per se*. The American party electorate is distinctive, therefore, in that it is a group defined primarily by that loyalty and not by loyalty to an ideology or a class position (and in which the party is merely a means to those ends). This very "partisan-ness" and heterogeneity of the American party electorates make them staunch allies of the two-party system. As Campbell and Valen have observed: [28]

The strength of these party attachments and the general weakness in the American electorate of ideological interest both serve to maintain the two-party system. The failure of various attempts to launch third parties appealing to the special interests of the farmers or the urban working class reflects the conserving force of these two attributes of the American party system. Deriving from the two-party system, they have become important factors in its preservation.

[28] Campbell and Valen, *op. cit.*, p. 524.

Chapter Seven

THE PARTY WITHIN
THE ELECTOR

The hyperactive world of American politics is at best difficult to understand. The periodic contentions of parties and candidates, the overlapping layers of party organization, the stylized hyperbole of political charge and countercharge may baffle even the highly politicized and active party workers. The confusion is more widespread among the somewhat less experienced and involved members of the party electorate. Their best guide to the trackless political world is their party identification. As Donald Stokes has written: [1]

In view of the fact that very few Americans have any deep interest in politics, it is a mild paradox that party loyalties should be so widespread. A partial key to this puzzle is that these identifications perform for the citizen an exceedingly useful evaluative function. To the average person the affairs of government are remote and complex, and yet the average citizen is asked periodically to formulate opinions about those affairs. At the very least, he has to decide how he will vote, what choice he will make between candidates offering different programs and very different versions of contemporary political events. In this dilemma, having the party symbol stamped on certain candidates, certain issue positions, certain interpretations of political reality is of great psychological convenience.

The political party, therefore, exists in two forms for the individual. Obviously he can see the party of the real world — the party of conventions, candidates, campaigns, and organization. But he comes also to depend on a cognitive party — the party of his attitudes, goals, and loyalties — which

[1] Donald E. Stokes, "Party Loyalty and the Likehood of Deviating Elections," in Angus Campbell, Philip E. Converse, Warren E. Miller, and Donald E. Stokes, *Elections and the Political Order* (New York: Wiley), pp. 126–127.

is a party "within the elector." It is an organizing point of view, a screen or framework through which he sees political reality and in terms of which he organizes it in his own mind. We all perceive the world about us selectively, and for the committed partisan, the member of the party electorate, it is the party loyalty which is the key to the selectivity. Because this party identification will very likely be the most enduring of his political attachments, it serves as something of a "political gyroscope," stabilizing his political outlooks against the buffetings of changing political currents and appeals.

Before undertaking a discussion of the impact or influence of the party identification, two points ought to be reiterated about the party identification itself. It is, first of all, remarkably unchanging, despite all the flux of American politics. Not only is the national distribution of the identifications between the two parties relatively unchanging, but the identifications of individual Americans do not change easily. In the mid-1950's, for example, at a time during which voters were closer to the shifts in party lines of the 1930's, only 10 to 20 per cent of the party identifiers of the two parties indicated they had ever been independents or identifiers of the other party; in 1956, in fact, 93 per cent of the "strong" Democrats professed to have been life-long Democrats.[2] The data of that and more recent surveys also indicates, not surprisingly, that party identification endures more surely the greater its strength.

Secondly, the sheer descriptive and predictive power of the party identification can scarcely be overstated. Knowing that one fact about a group of people tells us more about their political perceptions and political activities than will any other fact about them. It is very clearly the single most important influence on the political behavior of the American adult.[3]

PARTY IDENTIFICATION, POLITICAL ACTIVITY, AND THE PARTY

The stronger the party identification, the greater is the probability that the individual will be active in politics generally and active in the political party in particular. In general political interest and activity, the individuals with the strongest party identifications are more likely:

> to evince an interest in coming elections and to express a concern about their outcome. They attend to the events of the campaign, and they think it definitely makes a difference who wins.

> to expose themselves to the newspaper, magazine, television, and radio

[2] Angus Campbell, Philip E. Converse, Warren E. Miller, and Donald E. Stokes, *The American Voter* (New York: Wiley, 1960), p. 148.

[3] It should be clearly understood that this chapter will be concerned only with party identification and its influences and impacts. The chapter is by no means an attempt to deal with the entire range of American political or voting behavior.

reports about politics or a campaign, or indeed, to the events of the campaign themselves.

to talk with their friends about the election and to try to persuade them to support this or that candidate. They are also more apt to work in a party or a campaign.

To put these relationships in more general terms, the men and women whose political interest and activity would place them within or very close to the activists of the party organization come in disproportionate numbers from these identifiers.[4]

Short of activity in the parties, the strong party identifiers also see the parties in a clearer focus than the weak identifiers and independents. They are more confident that there are important policy differences between the two parties than are the other identifiers and independents (Table 1). They are also more able to identify the two parties with liberal and conservative ideologies and with differing dispositions to support governmental action as the proper course for the solution of public problems. They themselves also have, as a group, more fully developed and more cohesive stands on the political issues of the day.[5]

Table 1

OPINIONS OF PARTY IDENTIFIERS ON PARTY MORE LIKELY TO FAVOR STRONGER GOVERNMENT IN WASHINGTON: 1964 *

Choice of Party More Likely to Favor Stronger Government in Washington	Strong Dem.	Weak Dem.	Inde- pendent	Weak Rep.	Strong Rep.
Democrats	64.8%	44.2%	52.1%	55.8%	75.2%
No Difference	26.6	46.4	32.4	27.9	7.5
Republicans	8.6	9.4	15.5	16.3	17.3
	100.0%	100.0%	100.0%	100.0%	100.0%

* Source: The Survey Research Center of the University of Michigan, made available through the Inter-University Consortium for Political Research. This table also eliminates the respondents who had no interest or opinion on the question; of the total original group they accounted for the following percentages: Strong Dem. (38.6), Weak Dem. (41.8), Independent (39.7), Weak Republican (38.6), and Strong Republican (22.2).

[4] Data on the political activity and involvement of party identifiers can be found in virtually all of the studies of American voting behavior. See The American Voter, especially Chapter 6; see also Bernard Berelson, et al., Voting (Chicago: Univ. of Chicago Press, 1956) on the "opinion leader."

[5] The same is apparently true of party identifiers in Norway. See Angus Campbell and Henry Valen, "Party Identification in Norway and the United States," Public Opinion Quarterly, Vol. XXV (1961), pp. 505–525. It is also reprinted in Elections and the Political Order (see footnote 1).

Such relationships by themselves offer no reasons for a leap to the conclusion that party identification somehow causes or "produces" the greater party activity or the sharper issue image of the party. Party activity — or any political activity, for that matter — appears to be the result of a complicated set of recruitment, access, incentive, and availability factors.[6] That one of these factors is very probably loyalty and commitment to a party would seem to be clear. Positive party identification thus appears to be a necessary, but hardly sufficient, condition for party activity.

IDENTIFICATION AND THE JUDGMENT OF CANDIDATES AND ISSUES

The party identification, and the loyalty and commitment it represents, operates as a screen with which the individual selects his political information from the welter of political messages which assail him. It also serves as a judgmental aid which assists him in the evaluation of the information he receives. The communications to which he is subjected can be conveniently grouped into three different categories: those concerned with party, with candidates, and with issues. The effect of party identification on judgments of party can easily be surmised. But the effect of that identification on the individual's perceptions of candidates and political issues is less obvious.

In the assessment of partisan candidates the "perceptual predisposition" of a party identification is clearly present. "The stronger the voter's party bias, the more likely he is to see the candidate of his own party as hero, the candidate of the other party as villain."[7] In the 1960 presidential election, a powerful set of competing perceptual predispositions was also at work. Catholics tended to perceive John F. Kennedy more favorably than did Protestants. Nonetheless, party identification kept its organizing power. When religious loyalties were held constant, the party identification had its effect on the perception of Kennedy. And when party identifications were held constant, the religious loyalty had *its* effect. When one says, therefore, that a candidate is "attractive" or compelling, he is saying something about the electorate as well as about the candidate.

The control that party identification exercises over the perception of candidates may, however, be somewhat selective. That, in any event, is the conclusion of a recent study of a sample of Detroit voters.[8] The partisan perception appears to extend to the candidates' political traits but not to such purely personal matters as his personality, his appearance,

---

[6] Chapter four offers a fuller discussion of this point.

[7] Donald E. Stokes, "Some Dynamic Elements of Contests for the Presidency," *American Political Science Review*, Vol. LX (1966), p, 23. All of the material of this paragraph is drawn from this article.

[8] Roberta A. Sigel, "Effect of Partisanship on the Perception of Political Candidates," *Public Opinion Quarterly*, Vol. XXVIII (1964), pp. 483–496.

or his social characteristics (e.g., his religion). However, since it is the political traits that voters indicate as more frequently governing their voting decision, even the selective impact of party identification on the perception of candidates remains important.

The impact of party identification on political issues is not so easy to determine. For one thing, it is not a completely parallel case to the impact on candidate perception. The candidate is a tangible person, but an issue is an abstraction with far more subtle symbolic components. It is easy to show that party identifiers of the two parties take more sharply defined positions on public policies than the non-identifiers (Table 2).

Table 2

RELATIONSHIP BETWEEN ATTITUDE ON FEDERAL AID
TO EDUCATION AND PARTY IDENTIFICATION: 1964 *

Issue Position	Strong Dem.	Weak Dem.	Inde- pendent	Weak Rep.	Strong Rep.
Favors Federal aid	34.1%	27.5%	27.4%	14.2%	12.3%
Uncertain, doubtful	18.6	19.9	19.1	19.0	10.5
Opposed; prefer local program	27.6	31.9	33.7	50.4	70.5
No interest, no answer, don't know, etc.	19.4	21.4	19.4	16.1	6.3

* Source: *The Survey Research Center of the University of Michigan, made available through the Inter-University Consortium for Political Research.*

They are also more apt to have an issue or ideological position congruent with the one generally associated with the party of their choice. There is also evidence to suggest, however tentatively, that party identification encourages that congruence in the first place by guiding the party loyalist to his party's position on issues. Party identification is simply so stable and fundamental a loyalty that it is likely, when coupled with the necessary information, to affect shorter-run judgments. The likelihood is all the greater when it is linked — as it is for many strong party identifiers — with a liberal or conservative political ideology. Any belief system must guide the formation of judgments about issues involving its application to concrete and specific policy issues. In any event, it is difficult to dismiss the relationship between party identification and issue position. William Flanigan, for example, finds that the relationship between party identification and stands on medicare and federal aid to education is three times stronger than the relationship between social class and those stands.[9] The values and outlooks, even the ideologies, associated with party loyalty appear to be a powerful guide to the complexities of political issues.

[9] William H. Flanigan, *Political Behavior of the American Electorate* (Boston: Allyn and Bacon, 1968), Chapter 3.

PARTY IDENTIFICATION AND VOTING

So powerful and stable is party identification in the voting behavior of the American adults that the Survey Research Center organizes its main typology of American presidential elections around the question of the part party loyalties played in them. Thus, the SRC describes three chief election types: [10]

> the *maintaining* election in which the party attachments of the recent past prevail without any great change; the elections of 1948 and 1960 would appear to be examples.

> the *deviating* election in which the basic distribution of party loyalties is not changed but in which short-run forces (such as an attractive candidate or an issue of great salience) cause the defeat of the majority party; the Eisenhower and Republican successes of 1952 and 1956 are examples.

> the *realigning* election in which a new distribution of party loyalties emerges and governs the outcome; the elections of 1928 and 1932 offer the most recent examples.

These latter realigning elections are those which are distinguished by "the presence of a great national crisis, leading to a conflict regarding governmental policies and the association of the two major parties with relatively clearly contrasting programs for its solution." [11]

Implicit in this typology is another useful trichotomy to which we have already referred. Scholars of voting behavior find it useful to break the influences on the voting decision into three main categories: party identification, candidate, and issues. And of the three, party identification dominates, not only because of its depth and endurance, but also because it affects perceptions and judgments of the other two. Only very appealing candidates and issues can overturn the power of the long-run party identification (in what would be a "deviating" election.) The case of the 1952 presidential election is a classic recent example in this respect. A national hero, General Eisenhower, combined with the issues of domestic Communism, ethical lapses among Truman appointees, and the war in Korea, overcame the Democratic majority in party identifications.

The stronger the party identification, however, the less likely it is that the voter will be deflected from support of his party by the short-run appeals of candidates or issues (Table 3). And the stronger the identification, the more likely it is that the voter will make that most tangible gesture of party solidarity — vote the straight ticket (Table 3). This evi-

[10] See Angus Campbell, "A Classification of the Presidential Elections," in *Elections and the Political Order*, pp. 63–77.
[11] *Ibid.*, p. 76.

Table 3

VOTE DECISION AND INCIDENCE OF TICKET-SPLITTING
AMONG PARTY IDENTIFIERS:1964 *

	Strong Dem.	Weak Dem.	Inde- pendent	Weak Rep.	Strong Rep.
I. Vote for Presidential Candidate: 1964					
Democratic	77.2%	59.1%	46.2%	35.9%	8.9%
Republican	3.8	12.9	23.6	47.2	82.8
Other, no answer, etc.	.5	.8	1.6	1.5	.0
Didn't vote	18.5	27.2	28.7	15.4	8.3
	100.0	100.0	100.0	100.0	100.0
II. Percentage voting straight ticket in 1964 elections	44.9%	23.1%	17.8%	23.1%	47.8%

* Source: *Survey Research Center of the University of Michigan, made available through the Inter-University Consortium for Political Research.*

dence for 1964, clear and dramatic as it is, could be duplicated for earlier presidential years.

The 1960 presidential race between Richard M. Nixon and John F. Kennedy affords a fascinating instance of the clash of party loyalties and another potent set of social loyalties — those of religion. Kennedy's Catholicism was in this sense more than an "issue" or a "candidate"; it was the stimulus for another, largely non-political "perceptual predisposition." The effect of those loyalties on the perceptions of Kennedy himself we have already assessed. But despite the strength of the religious loyalties, Philip Converse concludes after an examination of attitudes and voting in the 1960 election that in casting their votes "Protestant Democrats were more likely to behave as Democrats than as Protestants, and Catholic Republicans were more likely to behave as Republicans than as Catholics." [12]

These observations on the impact of party identification on the voter largely reflect decisions in national or state-wide elections. Party identification may have either more or less impact in local elections. Where the voter has personal, face-to-face contact with the candidates in a rural county, candidate information and judgment may be so strong as to override party loyalties. Or some voters may find the application of party loyalties inappropriate to the less partisan campaigns for local office, especially where the office appears to have little policy-making responsibility (e.g., the local clerk of the court or the registrar of deeds.) Furthermore,

[12] Philip E. Converse, "Religion and Politics: The 1960 Election," in *Elections and the Political Order*, p. 123.

local issues may cut across the lines of the local party electorates; a local school bond election or open housing referendum will very possibly be no respecter of party lines. On the other hand, voters may in local elections have to rely even more than in national elections on the guidance of party. In a large city, the voter facing a long ballot and having to make choices on a long ballot of city, county, state, and other offices may have no alternative to reliance on the party label. In these elections his information on issues and candidates may be only a fraction of what it is in a presidential election.

THE MYTHS OF THE INDEPENDENT

That party loyalties should govern so much political behavior in a political culture that so warmly celebrates the political "independent" — the voter who "votes for the best man rather than the party" — is too striking a paradox to have escaped attention. It has been easy on the basis of the data of the SRC to puncture the myth of the American political independent. But before the myth is finally put to rest, we ought, perhaps, to be clear what myth we are interring.

If by "independent" we mean those Americans who refuse to identify with one or the other political party, then the myth *is* a casualty of survey research. While it is true that the self-styled independent does split his ticket more frequently, does wait longer in the campaign to make his voting decision, and does show a moderate level of interest in government generally, he falls short of the picture of the independent in most other respects. He is less concerned about specific elections than identifiers, less well-informed and less active politically than they are. And he is more apt than they not to vote at a given election. He is, in short, less politically active and involved than the party identifier and, in many respects, less the "good citizen."

There is no reason, however, why we cannot define the political independents in terms of their behavior or activity. In his last work, published posthumously,[13] V. O. Key attempted to reclaim the independents from their current obloquy by dealing not with the self-styled independents but with voters who switched their party allegiance in a consecutive pair of presidential elections. The picture of the American voter which emerges from American political folklore and the new electoral studies, Key noted, is not a pretty one: it is one of an electorate whose voting decision is determined by deeply-ingrained attitudes, perceptions, and loyalties and without its having grasped the major political issues and alternatives.

Key's search for electoral "rationality" centers, therefore, on the "switch-

---

[13] V. O. Key (with the assistance of Milton C. Cummings, Jr.), *The Responsible Electorate* (Cambridge: Harvard Univ. Press, 1966).

ers," the voters who do *not* keep voting for the same party in consecutive elections. Key's switchers, by the usual criteria, come much closer to the image of the independent than do the self-described independents. He finds their levels of political interest no lower than those of the "stand-patters" who remain firm in their voting allegiances. By definition, of course, the switchers are not non-voters. Above all, they are marked by an issue-related "rationality" that fits the usual picture of the independent well. They agree in policy issues with the standpatters toward whom they shift and disagree with the policies of the party from which they defect.

THE CONTRIBUTIONS OF LOYAL ELECTORATES

The party identification, therefore, is a commitment so strong that it affects other commitments and so pervasive that it colors and codifies the perceptions of reality. It organizes the political struggle within the individual as it organizes it in the political system.

These political characteristics of the American party electorates — their size, their disposition to vote, the nature of the parties in the electorate, the strengths of their party identifications — define them as arenas for the electoral contests of the Democrats and the Republicans. Parties and their candidates in their campaigns play on these party loyalties and party-screened perceptions. Their over-all strategy often is to stimulate and reinforce the party loyalties of one's own partisans while making candidate and issue appeals to the independents and partisans of the other party.

Furthermore, the political outlines of an electorate set more specific strategies. The present pattern of party loyalty in the United States, for example, suggests that the Republicans must minimize party-stimulating issues, party identifications, and SES issues. Its hope rests, at least in the short run, with attractive candidates and non-class issues. It is surely not coincidental that the Barry Goldwater campaign of 1964 emphasized a large number of issues that were not directly SES in character: crime and morality, local responsibility for civil rights and racial equality, and defense and foreign policy. Yet at the same time the sheer diversity of the parties in the electorate force campaign strategists to mute any kind of appeal that will divide the heterogeneous loyalists of a party. That very heterogeneity is, therefore, a powerful influence in reducing the disposition of party leaders or candidates toward ideological emphases.

The sheer power and durability of the party identifications of large numbers of Americans — and thus of the party electorates they form — contribute a tremendous stability to American politics and the American party system. A comparative study of French and American political socialization notes the relative absence of party loyalties in France. The authors link that fact to French political instability, noting that in France there is available "a mass base for flash party movements. . . ."[14] The fact that the American parties, in contrast, have associated with them these durable party electorates enables them both to recover from defeats in two-party competition and to fend off challenges from political currents who might aspire to form their own political party.

In a subject (and chapter) filled with paradoxes, it might be fitting to conclude with one more. It has often been said that the very source of the weakness of the American parties is their refusal to make commitments to ideology, their inability to take distinctive policy stands. They have been pragmatic, brokerage parties without the programs that might attract mass followings to them. Yet, it is precisely this relative absence of political ideology in American politics that makes the parties in the electorate as strong as they are. In the United States it is the political party and loyalty to it which guides the individual. The party itself, not a class-based ideology or some other social loyalty, structures political reality and decisions. The political party in the American context is, therefore, closer to the cognitive and behavioral "center" of the American voter and his judgments. It has many organizational competitors in the recruitment of resources and clienteles — but the major American party is without serious competition in the organization of the worlds "within" the American voters. It is that fact above all which underlies the stability of the American two-party system.

[14] Philip E. Converse and Georges Dupeux, "Politicization of the Electorate in France and the United States," in *Elections and the Political Order*, p. 291.

Chapter Eight

THE AMERICAN
ELECTORATE

Much of the history of the political parties in the last century can be written in terms of their responses to the expansion of the suffrage. They began in the Western democracies as essentially aristocratic instruments mobilizing very homogeneous and limited electorates, and they have had to alter their organizations and their appeals as the electorates expanded to include virtually all adults. And on no established parties has that impact been greater than on the major American parties. In multi-party systems new parties often rose to represent new groups admitted to the suffrage; one need only point to the European Socialist and Labor parties that developed to cater to the newly enfranchised industrial workers. The stability of the American two-party system has, however, ruled out such an accommodation of new electorates. The major American parties themselves have had to expand their hospitality progressively to the new groups winning the vote.

Since the American parties are overwhelmingly electoral parties, any changes in the size, the composition, or the activity level of the American electorate affect all of their aspects. From its total dimensions they recruit and establish their own, especially loyal, party electorates. They must also recruit from it the men, the skills, and the money for the party organizations and for their candidates and campaigns. And above all, they seek in it the majorities they most mobilize if they are to win elections. For the fact that the American parties are largely electoral parties puts a heavy premium on electoral success, and the fact that there are only two of them forces them to mobilize majorities in order to enjoy that success.

Unfortunately, just who constitutes the American electorate is not entirely clear. Obviously it is something less than the total number of

American adults, its dimensions sketched by two kinds of factors: the restrictions placed on it (or, if one prefers, definitions of it) by the states, and the unwillingness of the eligibles either to register or to vote. Just how and why these limitations operate, on whom they fall, and the numbers they disenfranchise are not at all easy matters to settle. It is, for example, impossible to give anything more than an educated guess about the number of Americans who actually meet the legal requirements for voting in presidential elections in the fifty states. That "guess" is made especially difficult by the fact that the requirements differ from state to state; the task is really the definition of fifty electorates.

If the American electorate — either in its legal or its self-defining ("turn-out") dimension — were a good sample of the adult American population, the issue of its exact composition would be settled (i.e., it would be a sample) and that of its dimensions would be far less important. But the effective electorate is nothing of the sort. It overrepresents some groups in the American society and underrepresents others. Given the preference of various groups in the American society for one party or the other, the composition and possible enlargement of the electorate are matters of important implications for the parties. If it is true, as we have indicated earlier, that American Negroes identify largely with the Democratic party at present, various attempts to bring Negroes into the American electorate will affect the nature of the parties' appeals and loyal electorates and the patterns of their competition.

THE ELECTORATE: THE PROBLEM OF MEASUREMENT

After every presidential election commentators on American civic values don sack cloth and ashes to note that, as usual, a relatively small percentage of American adults stirred themselves to vote. In 1964, for instance, a campaign of unparalleled cost and scope (up to 40,000,000 Americans at a time were watching the nominating conventions on television) attracted only 62 per cent of the "potential electorate" to the polls. In Mississippi, Alabama, and South Carolina the turnout percentages were 32.9, 36.0, and 38.0, respectively; by most authorities' reckoning Utah (76.9), Minnesota (76.8), and Idaho (75.8) led the states.[1]

These and similar "turnout" percentages, regardless of what election happens to be involved, depend on two categories of data, one fairly reliable and the other highly suspect. Given the generally accurate counting and reporting of vote totals which prevail in most localities, the figures on actual turnout (the numbers of voters voting) are fairly reliable. However, the base figures of total possible voters (on the basis of which the turnout percentages are calculated) are questionable. Whether the

[1] These data come from the World Almanac for 1966.

base is called "total voters," "potential voters," or the "potential electorate," it usually turns out to be a simple total of all citizens of voting
age in the states (by the count of the U.S. Census Bureau). Thus, the
widely quoted 62 per cent turnout for the 1964 presidential election was
computed on such a base of some 113,900,000 "potential voters."

Such reckonings of "potential voters" are essentially misleading because
they fail to take into account the restrictions on the suffrage other than
that of age and citizenship. Nor do they consider the number of voters
made ineligible to vote by their failure (where required) to go through
the administrative processes of registration. The most reasonable remedy,
therefore, would be to substitute for the concept of "potential voters"
some measure of "eligible voters," but it is precisely that total which is so
hard to come by. So, the outer limits to the American electorate are not
hard to determine; it can be no larger than the number of adults of age in
the country and no smaller than the number of actual voters (categories
one and three in Table 1). But the intermediate estimate of the eligible
electorate (category two on Table 1), the one so badly needed for accurate estimates of turnout percentages, is the puzzle. Until we have that
figure, the easy availability of the larger number of total adults (the "potential electorate") will dictate its use, and we will continue to manufac-
ture inaccurately low (and even more unflattering) turnout percentages.

Table 1

CATEGORIES OF POTENTIAL, ELIGIBLE, AND ACTUAL VOTERS:
PRESIDENTIAL ELECTIONS OF 1960 AND 1964

	1960 Presidential Election	1964 Presidential Election
1. Individuals meeting the minimum age requirement for voting; the so-called "potential electorate"	108,459,000	113,900,000
2. The eligible electorate: individuals meeting state requirements and who have registered (where required)	?	?
3. Individuals actually voting in election (the turnout)	68,839,000	70,642,000

The size of the effective American electorate (whether one defines it as
either the eligible or the actual electorate; categories two or three in
Table 1) results from the impacts of forces internal and external to the
individual. The external influences include the legal restrictions of the

states, their application by the administrative machinery of the state, and the informal restrictions of force, or economic and social sanction. The internal influences refer to the values and goals, the motivational levels, the role perceptions, the sense of civic responsibility within the individual. The external definitions of the American electorate are the clearer for being the more tangible, and we turn to them first.

THE LEGAL DEFINITION OF THE ELECTORATE

The decentralizing influences of the American federalism touch almost every important aspect of American electoral politics, and the electorate itself is no exception. The definition of the American electorate over the past 150 years has expanded through the curiously and uniquely American interlacing of national and state action. Thus:

> In the early 19th century the states themselves gradually repealed the property and tax-paying qualifications for voting by which they had so severely restricted the male suffrage. By 1860 there remained no states which required property-holding and only four which required tax-paying as a requisite for voting.

> By the mid-1870's women began to work through the states for their right to vote, and in 1890 Wyoming became the first state to grant the full franchise to women. Progress slowly bogged down, especially in the Eastern states, and the ladies shifted their hopes to the U.S. Constitution. The 19th Amendment, forbidding states to deny the vote on grounds of sex, was finally ratified in 1920.

> The expansion of the Negro suffrage began by state action in some of the states of New England before the Civil War, but it culminated after the War with the passage of the 15th Amendment; Congress and the federal courts from that time to the present have periodically attempted to enforce its limitations on some reluctant states.

The major expansions in the American electorate have, therefore, been three, and only one of them has been accomplished without national intervention limiting the power of the states to define the electorate. But despite these and other limitations on their power, the fifty states continue to hold the major initiating control in its definition.[2]

Undoubtedly it was the intention of the Founding Fathers to vest that major control in the states. At least that outcome was assured by writing in Article I, section 2, that for elections to the House ". . . the electors in each state shall have the qualifications requisite for electors of the most numerous branch of the state legislature." And that was as much as they

---

[2] For background on the early development of the American electorate, see Kirk H. Porter, *A History of Suffrage in the United States* (Chicago: Univ. of Chicago Press, 1918).

said on the suffrage in the entire constitutional document. No more was necessary, for senators were to be elected indirectly by state legislatures, and the President and Vice-President by a genuinely deliberative Electoral College. As for the electors to the Electoral College, section 4 of Article I stipulated that each state was to "appoint in such manner as the legislature thereof may direct, a number of electors. . . ." When the Congress and the states converted the election of senators to a direct and popular election, they wrote into the 17th Amendment the same formula that applies to the House: "The electors in each state shall have the qualifications requisite for electors of the most numerous branch of the state legislature."

So, contrary to the traditions of other countries and even of other federal systems, initiative in formulating voting requirements was left to the states. The inevitable result has been the absence of a uniform national electorate even for national elections; 18-year-olds may vote in presidential elections in Georgia or Kentucky, for example, but not in any of the other forty-eight states. The constitutional authority of the United States government, therefore, has been limited to the relatively passive role of saying in three amendments that the states shall not deny citizens the vote solely and explicitly on grounds of race or color (15th), sex (19th), or failure to pay a tax (24th). Furthermore, the 14th Amendment's equal protection clause ("No state shall make or enforce any law which shall . . . deny to any person within its jurisdiction the equal protection of the laws.") has been interpreted by the Supreme Court to prevent a state from discriminating against Negroes in defining its electorate. Presumably that same clause would similarly protect ethnic, religious, occupational, regional, or other social groups in the unlikely possibility that a state should deny the suffrage to, say, Presbyterians, Italian-Americans, or government employees.

Between the constitutional territory of the states and that of the nation there is a tiny, "no man's land," the District of Columbia. For almost all of American history the citizens of the District have remained voteless, even in their own local affairs. Every President since World War II has pressed for "home rule" for the District, only to be frustrated by a coalition of interests in Congress opposed to it. In part the opposition springs from Southern opposition to local autonomy for the predominantly Negro District, in part it results from the desire of Congress to rule its own backyard, and in part it reflects some fears of a politically potent federal service. However, since the passage of the 23rd Amendment to the Constitution in 1961, the District of Columbia has had three votes (the minimum) in the Electoral College. The setting of the electorate in the District for presidential elections was left to the Congress, and that body created an electorate for the 1964 elections that was limited to persons of twenty-one years of age who had resided in the District for at least one year.

THE AMERICAN ELECTORATE TODAY

Despite the freedom accorded to them under the Constitution, the states have developed legal definitions of the suffrage that are surprisingly similar. In part, the negative controls of the Constitutional amendments have hemmed them in. So, too, have the political pressures for universal adult suffrage and the examples of the other states. In any event, it is thoroughly possible to deal with the state definitions of the suffrage in a small number of relevant categories.[3]

AGE

All of the states but four fix the minimum voting age at twenty-one. In Kentucky and Georgia it is eighteen; in Alaska, nineteen, and in Hawaii, twenty. During World War II and the Korean conflict there developed considerable support for lowering the age to eighteen, much of it embodied in the phrase "old enough to fight, old enough to vote." Indeed, President Dwight Eisenhower in his 1954 State of the Union message proposed a constitutional amendment to set a national minimum voting age of eighteen. Without strong presidential support and without appreciable party or organized group support in Congress, it came to naught.

CITIZENSHIP

All states now require that voters be citizens of the United States. As surprising as it may seem, there were still eleven states in 1900 which permitted aliens to vote, even though some required the individual to have begun to seek American citizenship. But in 1926 Arkansas, the last state to capitulate, closed off the alien suffrage. More than any other single factor the end of mass and open immigration into the United States signaled the end of the vote for non-citizens.

POLL TAXES

Until 1964 five states — Alabama, Mississippi, Texas, Vermont, and Virginia — continued to require the payment of a poll tax (i.e., a head tax or a per capita tax) as a qualification for voting.[4] The tax amounted only to one or two dollars a year, but its "nuisance" (and disenfranchising) effect was often increased by stipulations that it was cumulative, that it had to be paid well in advance of the election, or that the taxpayer had to keep the receipt and present it at the polling booth. The 24th Amendment to the Constitution, however, invalidated taxpaying as a condition for voting

---

[3] For a general survey of state laws defining the electorate, see Constance E. Smith, *Voting and Election Laws* (New York: Oceana, 1960).

[4] In Vermont's case the poll tax was a qualification only for voting in local town affairs; the state repealed it in early 1966.

in national elections in 1961. Four years later in the Civil Rights Act of 1965 Congress legislated a "finding" that poll taxes in *any* election were in fact discriminatory. It instructed the Attorney General to bring a test case in the federal courts challenging their constitutionality. In March of 1966 the Supreme Court declared the Virginia poll tax ($1.50) in violation of the equal protection clause of the 14th Amendment. In wording clearly broad enough to include the other state poll taxes, the Court noted that a state violates the Constitution "whenever it makes the affluence of the voter or payment of a fee an electoral standard." [5]

RESIDENCE

The states have generally devised three-layer residence requirements: a period of time in the state, a shorter period of time in the county, and an even shorter period in the local voting district. (The scope and range of these residence requirements are summarized in Table 2.) In general, one

Table 2

TABULATION OF STATE RESIDENCE REQUIREMENTS FOR VOTING [*]

	Residence in state	Residence in county	Residence in voting dist.
1. Number of states having requirement	50	36	40
2. Maximum requirement	2 years	1 year	1 year
3. Minimum requirement	6 months	1 month	10 days
4. Median among states with the requirement	1 year	3 months	1 month

* *Taken from the* Book of the States *for 1966–67. Note also that the 30-, 60-, and 90-day requirements were treated identically with one-, two-, and three-month requirements.*

can observe that the longest residence requirements are found in the Southern states where they tend to disenfranchise migrant and mobile Negro farm labor. The most demanding state is Mississippi which requires two years in the state and a minimum of one year in the voting district. At the other extreme, Minnesota, the state of the most modest residence requirement, specifies only a six-month residence in the state and no period in the county or district.

The trend in residence requirements has been steadily toward their

[5] The 1966 case was *Harper* v. *Virginia State Board of Elections*, 383 U.S. 663 (1966). It overruled *Breedlove* v. *Suttles*, 302 U.S. 277 (1937). On the poll tax generally, see Frederic D. Ogden, *The Poll Tax in the South* (University, Ala.: Univ. of Alabama Press, 1958).

liberalization. The states have increasingly tried to meet the needs and demands of a physically mobile society. Unlike the farmers of yesterday, the young executives of today move up the corporate ladder with frequent moves to new communities and often to new states. Within the last few years the states have concentrated their attention on the problem of this mobile electorate's disenfranchisement in presidential elections. More than a dozen states have set special lower residence requirements for newcomers wishing to vote in the presidential election. In 1964, in fact, fifteen of them waived all residence requirements for voting in the presidential contest. Another seven approached the problem as the responsibility of the "old" state of residence and extended an absentee ballot to former residents who could not meet the residence requirements of their new state.[6]

DISQUALIFICATIONS

Virtually all of the states restrict the suffrage for reasons of crime or mental incompetence. Institutionalization for insanity or severe mental illness temporarily removes an individual from the suffrage in all states, and in forty-three states so also do convictions for certain categories of crimes (the most common being felonies and electoral corruption). In a few states, such as South Carolina and Louisiana, one loses the vote in convictions for most misdemeanors as well. Arrest for trespassing in a "sit-in" or disturbing the peace in a "voting march" would be sufficient in Louisiana. Generally all of these disqualifications are temporary, and the vote is often restored when the individual regains mental health, finishes his jail or prison sentence, or is pardoned by gubernatorial or legislative action.

LITERACY TESTS

Twenty states in early 1965 — before the passage of the Civil Rights Act of that year — required that the applicant for the suffrage demonstrate his literacy. Often the test, especially when administered by an election clerk, constituted little more than a test of the ability to scrawl a signature. In other states one proved his literacy by the act of filling out application forms for registration. In a few states, such as New York, the test was more substantial; in New York a comprehensive test, drafted and administered by educational authorities, included questions to test the reader's understanding of brief expository paragraphs. In one of the twenty states, Alaska, the applicant could demonstrate his facility in English either by reading or speaking it. Furthermore, it had been customary for literacy to mean literacy in English; only Hawaii offered an alternative: Hawaiian.

---

[6] See Morris S. Ogul, "Residence Requirements as Barriers to Voting in Presidential Elections," *Midwest Journal of Political Science,* III (1959), pp. 254–262; and W. Ross Yates, "The Functions of Residence Requirements for Voting," *Western Political Quarterly,* XV (1962), pp. 469–488.

Associated with these literacy tests have been "understanding" or "interpretation" tests. Originally the states intended them as alternatives to literacy tests. If the individual could not read or write, he might qualify for the franchise by demonstrating his ability to explain some aspect of the governmental system or some section of the state constitution. In other states such as Louisiana and Georgia the local voting registrar could permit an illiterate person to register if he was convinced the individual was of "good character." Mississippi, home of the interpretation test, required it in addition to requiring literacy and good character. Local voting registrars in that state selected one of the 286 sections of the state constitution for the applicant to read and interpret; the registrar was, of course, the judge of the adequacy of the interpretation.[7]

While the literacy tests and their various accouterments remain on the state statute books, the effect of some of them was suspended by the Civil Rights Act of 1965. Under the "automatic trigger" of that law the literacy tests of any state or county were automatically suspended if less than 50 per cent of the voting age population was registered or voted in November of 1964. Immediately after the passage of the act the Attorney General moved to ban the use of the tests in Alabama, Georgia, Louisiana, Mississippi, South Carolina, and twenty-seven counties of North Carolina. The tests remain in effect in other states. A state affected may regain the use of its test only by showing it has not used the test as a discriminatory device for the preceding five years. The justification of the "automatic trigger" rests on the congressional judgment that in states with low turnout or registration percentages there exists a strong presumption that literacy tests have been used for discriminatory purposes. Furthermore, the Civil Rights Act of 1964 also created a presumption (rebuttable) that any individual with a sixth-grade education would meet literacy requirements. The 1965 Act was amended to include a sixth-grade education gotten in a U.S. territory, even if the language was not English; the effect was chiefly to enable Puerto Ricans to by-pass the New York requirement that literacy be in English.

FEDERAL RESERVATIONS

Traditionally, the states have refused to recognize citizens living on federal reservations — military posts, national parks, and veterans hospitals, for instance — as citizens of the state for the purpose of voting. Only three states — California, Utah, and West Virginia — consider those individuals residents of the state for the purposes of voting. Hence the great majority of Americans living on one or another of the 5,000 separate pieces of land over which the national government exercises exclusive jurisdiction are

[7] See *Time* of February 26, 1965, pp. 23–24, for a diverting exchange between a Mississippi voting registrar and a member of the U.S. Civil Rights Commission, Dean Erwin Griswold of the Harvard Law School.

effectively without a vote. The residents of the District of Columbia, of course, do now vote in presidential elections.

THE SPECIAL CASE OF THE NEGRO

Throughout these past paragraphs there runs a repeated theme: the special limits placed on the Negro suffrage. The American Negro, despite the protections of the 15th Amendment, would be at a disadvantage were it only for the preceding vote qualifications. Even were the literacy and interpretation tests administered with complete fairness, they would work against the Negro in the areas of the country (not only in the South) where his schools have been less than good. The residence requirements penalize him once more for his badly paid job as an itinerant farm laborer, a job which, parenthetically, may prevent him from educating his children. For it is hardly unfair to say that Negro disenfranchisement is a major reason why the poll tax persisted in the South, why residence requirements are more stringent in the South, why criminal disqualifications are broadest in the South, and why literacy, interpretation, and understanding tests are more common in the South.

But beyond all of these explicit limitations the Negro has traditionally found himself blocked by the administration of registration and election law. Endless delay, unavailable registrars, niggling technicalities, double standards — these have been his greatest barrier in recent years. The hearings of the United States Civil Rights Commission document his problem with ample detail.[8] Charles C. Humpstone, staff attorney of the Commission on Civil Rights, reporting on the leniency of registrars in Issaquena county, Mississippi, in evaluating the "interpretations" of white applicants:

A number of inadequate answers were accepted. For example, one white applicant asked to interpret section 35, which reads, "The senate shall consist of members chosen every 4 years by the qualified electors of the several districts," wrote only, "equible wrights" . . . and passed.

Mrs. Mary Oliver Welsh of Humphreys county, Mississippi, recounting her attempts to register to vote (Mrs. Welsh was on old-age assistance and receiving government surplus commodities):

Well, when I went to register, the registrar asked me what did I come down there for. I told him "to register." He said "Register? For what?" I told him, "To vote." He said, "Vote? For what?" And I told him I didn't know what I was coming to vote for. He hollered at me and scared me so, I told him I didn't know what I came to vote for. I was just going to vote. . . . He told me I was

[8] Hearings before the U.S. Civil Rights Commission, I (held in Jackson, Mississippi, on February 16–20, 1965), pp. 49, 53, 95–96, 131–132.

going to get in trouble, and he wasn't going to give me no commodities. That's what he said.

William B. Eskridge, Carroll county, Mississippi, school teacher explaining why his efforts to get his fellow teachers to register had not been successful:

My opinion is they were afraid of their job. In the first place some of the teachers in the school went to the courthouse and paid their poll tax. The superintendent got and heard of it and called them in and let them know if they are going to register for voting they wouldn't have a job, and consequently everybody had to back up. All the teachers at least. Now, that's the teachers told me that. I didn't hear the superintendent say that.

Jesse J. Brewer, Tallahatchie county, Mississippi, reporting on the events immediately after his registration:

After we got out, the sheriff told us to go on out of the courthouse, back out in the yard. So, we went back out in the yard there where the others were standing out there, and when we got back out there were about 65 gathered around there. Lot more white people drove up there in pickup trucks with gunracks on them. They had guns on them and one ranch wagon comes with three white men with guns and they told us, "You niggers get away from the courthouse. You don't have any business up here." They circled the courthouse about three or four times and when they registered all the people that went up there, the sheriff told us we did what we came up there to do and to get out of town and don't stop in town.

These extra-legal barriers are in many ways the highest; they are at least the most elusive, the most unpredictable, and ultimately the most demoralizing. Whether they are the physical intimidations of the Ku Klux Klan, the economic reprisals of the White Citizens Councils, or the closed doors and glacial speeds of the unwilling registrars, they are also the hardest to stop.

In the beginning the struggle for the Negro franchise began in the classic American way as a legal and constitutional issue. For years in fact the states and the United States Supreme Court played a grim game of constitutional "hide and seek" after the end of Reconstruction. The states would devise a scheme of disenfranchisement, the Court would strike it down, and the states would find another — ad infinitum. The states sometimes were careful not to disenfranchise poorer whites along with the Negroes — hence their devising of "grandfather clauses" which automatically registered all persons whose ancestors could vote at some specific date before the ratification of the 15th Amendment. The manic quality of this constitutional chase is perhaps best illustrated by the series of white primary cases. The "white primary" was an attempt to keep Negroes from voting in primary elections in the period during which victory in the Democratic primary, because of Republican feebleness in the South, was tantamount to election. The litigation went this way:

Texas passed a law stating that no Negro could vote in the Democratic primary in the state; the Supreme Court held that the law violated the 14th Amendment's "equal protection" clause.

Texas repealed its law and authorized the parties to control access to their own primaries, and the Democratic party then excluded Negroes; the Supreme Court declared the action unconstitutional since the party was acting at the behest of the state and since the state was therefore involved.

The state convention of the Democratic party in Texas closed the Democratic primary to Negroes; the Supreme Court held that the action was not state action and therefore did not violate the 14th Amendment.

After an intervening case on another aspect of electoral law, the Supreme Court reconsidered its recent "white primary" case and overruled it, holding that the totality of electoral law in Texas made the primary a part of the election machinery and thus an instrument of the state.

South Carolina next seized the initiative and repealed all of its laws on the primary, leaving their entire control and management to the parties; two federal courts held that the South Carolina primary was nonetheless an integral part of the process of choosing public officials and a responsibility of the state under the 14th Amendment; the Supreme Court refused to hear an appeal of their decisions.

The white primary, therefore, expired after five test cases and twenty-one years of litigation.[9]

Court action, however, is much less well adapted to dealing with informal administrative evasions. To be sure the Supreme Court did in the spring of 1965 invalidate the Louisiana interpretation test on the grounds that a persistent pattern of discriminatory enforcement made it clear that it existed solely as a device for keeping Negroes from voting.[10] But increasingly the most useful remedies are legislative and administrative, a fighting of fire with fire. The Civil Rights Acts of 1957, 1960, and 1964, and 1965 all manifest this kind of an attack on discrimination against the would-be Negro voter. For example:

---

[9] The cases in order are: *Nixon* v. *Herndon*, 273 U.S. 536 (1927); *Nixon* v. *Condon*, 286 U.S. 73 (1932); *Grovey* v. *Townsend*, 295 U.S. 54 (1935); *Smith* v. *Allwright*, 321 U.S. 649 (1944); and *Elmore* v. *Rice*, 72 F. Supp. 516 (1947); and 165 F. 2d 387 (1947).

[10] The 1965 Louisiana interpretation case was *Louisiana* v. *U.S.*, 380 U.S. 145.

The *Civil Rights Commission* is authorized to investigate and report discrimination against Negro voters (1957).

The *Attorney General* has been authorized to seek injunctions against individuals preventing Negroes from voting in primaries or general elections (1957). In those instances where he can convince a federal court that a "pattern or practice" of discrimination exists in a district, the court may order registration and send referees to the area (1960). Under later authority the Attorney General himself may send federal examiners to an area to register anyone who meets the state's qualifications (1965).

Local registrars have come under greater regulation and control. They must keep voting and registration records for 22 months (1960). And they must not apply voting requirements unequally (1964), nor are they permitted to seize on immaterial errors or omissions in the application process as a reason for refusing registration (1964). Any tests of the applicant's literacy must be in writing and kept as a part of the official records (1964).

In these four laws, by contrast, only one of the formal, legislated qualifications was challenged: the literacy test. The proof of a sixth-grade education was set up as a presumption of literacy (1964), and the force of literacy tests was automatically suspended in those districts in which less than 50 per cent of the adults of voting age voted or were registered (1965).

It is both inaccurate and unjust to treat all of the states of the South (however one defines the "South") as a single piece. They vary greatly in the formal requirements for registration, and they vary, too, in the extra-legal bars they raise. Those differences are reflected in the data of Table 3 which shows the percentages of voting-age Negroes registered in the South. There are, furthermore, substantial differences within different states, some of which may reflect different racial ratios, different socio-economic characteristics, and different political traditions.[11] Furthermore, it should be clear that Negro registration and voting percentages in the rest of the country are consistently below those of whites. The residence requirements and literacy tests of the northern states may also effectively disenfranchise groups of Negroes. What has set the South apart are the

---

[11] Donald R. Matthews and James W. Prothro articles on Negro voter registration in the South, *American Political Science Review*, LVII (1963), pp. 24–44, 355–367. See also, John H. Fenton and Kenneth N. Vines, "Negro Registration in Louisiana," *American Political Science Review*, LI (1957), pp. 704–713; Harry Holloway, "The Negro and the Vote: The Case of Texas," *Journal of Politics*, XXIII (1961), pp. 526–556; and H. Douglas Price, *The Negro and Southern Politics* (New York: New York Univ. Press, 1957).

repeated instances of systematic and explicit attempts to keep Negroes out of the electorate.

Table 3

PERCENTAGES OF VOTING-AGE NEGROES REGISTERED IN
11 SOUTHERN STATES: 1961, 1964, and 1966 *

	1961	1964	1966
Alabama	13.7%	19.2 (23.0)%	51.2%
Arkansas	37.7	40.3 (54.4)	59.7
Florida	39.0	51.2 (63.7)	60.9
Georgia	incomplete	27.4 (44.0)	47.2
Louisiana	30.9	32.0 (32.0)	47.1
Mississippi	6.1	6.7 (6.7)	32.9
North Carolina	38.2	46.8 (46.8)	51.0
South Carolina	incomplete	37.3 (38.8)	51.4
Tennessee	48.1	69.5 (69.4)	71.7
Texas	26.8	57.7 (57.7)	61.6
Virginia	23.0	34.2 (45.7)	46.9

* The data for 1961 and 1964 come from the reports of the U.S. Civil Rights Commission; the data for 1964 in parentheses and for 1966 are the estimates of the Southern Regional Council. The differences between the two sets of figures for 1964 illustrate the difficulties in acquiring data on Southern Negro registrations; they also exemplify the generally higher estimates of the Southern Regional Council.

THE CUMULATIVE EFFECT

The voting requirements of the fifty states whittled down the American electorate well below the 113,931,000 persons of voting age in 1964 (Table 1). Just what number of American adults they pared off that figure is a matter of informed estimate at best and pure conjecture at worst. Various estimates place the loss in residence requirements alone at close to 10,000,000. Very probably other disqualifications — lack of citizenship, illiteracy, residence on a federal reservation, and institutionalization, chiefly — account for another four million. That would bring a realistic total of eligible voters in 1964 to something close to 100,000,000. Additionally, the necessity to go through the formal, administrative processes of registration culled out additional voters (especially where those processes were geared to discouraging Negro voters). All but thirteen states have complete and comprehensive registration procedures for an individual to qualify to vote; no registration is required in Alaska and North Dakota, and in parts of another eleven states (generally the rural parts).[12]

[12] In these 11 states (and in Alaska and North Dakota) the individual merely presents himself at the polling place and his eligibility to vote is determined more or less "on the spot" by voting judges and inspectors. None of these 11 states is in the South.

In 1964 the states with full registration systems had registered 29,000,000 fewer than the total number of adults; a reasonable (if hazardous) estimate might deduct another 3,000,000 for those states with partial or no registration. Therefore, Table 1 might be reconstructed in this fashion:

1. Individuals meeting minimum age
   requirements for voting in 1964:   113,931,000
2. Individuals meeting all state
   requirements for voting (1964): . . . .   approx. 100,000,000
3. Individuals registered where
   required and eligible where
   registration not required: . . . .   approx. 82,000,000
4. Individuals voting in 1964
   presidential election: . . . .   70,642,000 [13]

Using the second and third figures as bases for a turnout percentage, therefore, we arrive at figures of 70.6 and 86.1 per cent, respectively. And yet the various restrictions of the states are only one limiting force to account for the comparatively low American voter turnout percentages. The fact is that in most non-presidential elections far greater numbers of Americans voluntarily disenfranchise themselves, either by failing to register or failing to vote, than do the voting laws of the states.

TURNOUT: THE SELF-DEFINING ELECTORATE

Turnout levels vary wildly among the states, even at presidential elections. In 1964 the turnout percentage (i.e., the number of voters taken as a percentage of the total adults of voting age) of Utah was considerably more than twice that of Mississippi. The greatest variations, however, occur between and among different kinds and types of elections. That fact itself suggests that there are important political limitations on turnout inherent in the American political system itself. Clearly, the attention and interest of the American voters flag as they face the four-year cycle of American politics, and many of them respond only to those elections of greatest salience or prominence. Probably no electorate in the democratic world is more frequently driven to the polls than is the American. Within a four-year cycle it confronts national, state, and local elections for legislative and executive office-holders (and for the judiciary in a majority of the states), not to mention school and park boards and assorted other local authorities. Most of these elections are also preceded by primaries, and initiatives, referenda, and even an occasional recall election further

---

[13] Two points about these data may be in order: (1) registration figures for some states are probably too high because registration authorities do not cull out the names of the dead and those who have left the state; and (2) the 70,642,000 figure is probably high relative to the total in category two because some states waive residence requirements for the Presidential election.

complicates the calendar. So, while the British voter in a four- or five-year cycle may go only twice to the polls — once for a parliamentary election and once for the election of local officials — civic obligation may call his beleaguered American counterpart to the polls for from six to ten primaries and general elections.

SIZE OF CONSTITUENCY

In the first place, voter participation varies substantially with the size of the constituency. It is generally greatest in presidential elections and smallest in local elections. While the voting percentage in presidential elections runs now between 60 and 70 per cent (of all the adults of voting age), it is less for gubernatorial elections which come in the non-presidential years. The congressional elections, too, draw considerably fewer voters in the years between the presidential elections (see Figure 1). Since, of course, most states choose more than one official at a given election, it is not often possible to attribute the turnouts to the attraction of the campaigns for specific offices. Many states, however, do have elections which mix national and state officials, those which choose only state

Figure 1

PERCENTAGE OF ADULT CITIZENS PARTICIPATING
IN PRESIDENTIAL AND CONGRESSIONAL ELECTIONS, 1920–1962

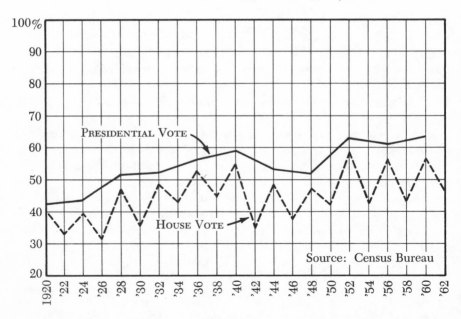

Source: Congressional Quarterly Weekly Report, *Vol. XXII (September 18, 1964),* p. 2179.

officials, and those electing purely local officials. The turnout rates among those three sets of elections drop in almost all cases with the size of the constituencies.

The reasons for this phenomenon are not hard to imagine. The greater intensity of the campaigns for the Presidency and the governorships unquestionably sparks greater voter interest and involvement. The personalities are famous or at least well-known, and the issues seem more momentous. Furthermore, party fortunes are involved and party loyalties are inflamed — contrary to the case in many non-partisan local and judicial elections. Then, too, the presidential elections in most states are really an aggregate of elections at which a President, a congressman, often a senator and governor, and perhaps local officials are on the ballot. On the other hand, the local election held in the odd-numbered year — and often so held purposely to isolate it from the currents of state or national politics — is local only. To simplify greatly, one should hardly be surprised that a presidential election in which two national political figures and two national parties engage in a three-month mass media campaign draws even three or four times the number of voters to the polls than does a non-partisan judicial campaign in which the candidates talk discreetly and a bit dully of the efficient administration of the courts. The wonder really is that it is not eight or ten times the number.

THE NEGLECTED PRIMARY

Generally throughout the United States voting in primary elections falls far short of that in general elections. It is not unusual for primary turnouts to be half or less of turnouts in general elections — more precisely, only 20 or 25 per cent of the adults of voting age (the so-called "potential electorate"). Key's work on gubernatorial primaries marks some of the dimensions of primary voting:[14]

In a sample of 15 nonsouthern states over the period 1926–1952, in three out of four primaries not more than 35 per cent of the potential electorate voted in the primaries of one or the other of the major parties. That is, the total Democratic primary vote plus the total Republican primary vote did not exceed 35 per cent of the number of citizens 21 years of age or over. In about one of six primaries the voters in Democratic and Republican gubernatorial primaries did not exceed 20 per cent of the number of citizens 21 and over. At the extreme of high participation in only one out of twelve primaries did more than 50 per cent of the potential vote turn up at the polls. Most often between 25 and 35 per cent of the potential electorate voted in the primaries.

Among primaries for the same office, turnout tends to increase under two circumstances. It increases with competition in the primary and the usually lively campaign which attends a contested primary. Secondly, it in-

14 V. O. Key, *American State Politics* (New York: Knopf, 1956), p. 134.

creases sharply within the dominant party of one-party states or states tending to a one-partyism. In the Southern one-party states voter turnout in the Democratic primary has historically even exceeded the voter turnout of the general election. In the gubernatorial elections held in 1962 and 1963, for example, seven states had more voters in the gubernatorial primary than in the general election: Alabama, Arkansas, Georgia, Mississippi, South Carolina, Tennessee, and Texas.

ISSUES AND REFERENDA

Elections on issues — referenda and constitutional amendments, chiefly — do not attract the same turnout as do ordinary elections. Even when these issues are on the ballot of regular elections, fewer voters choose to vote in them than for the candidates at the top of the ballot. Very possibly the absence of a personal clash in these questions reduces their interest and immediacy. Perhaps, too, their frequent complexity confuses many would-be voters. But having said this about issue elections on the over-all, it should be noted that voter turnout among referenda fluctuates greatly. An emotionally charged and relatively clear issue such as a referendum on nondiscriminatory housing, daylight saving time, or the sale of alcoholic beverages will attract more voters than esoteric questions of taxing bonds or reorganizing state administrative agencies.

All Americans are, however, more or less confronted by the same plethora of elections. The crucial point is that some of them show voter fatigue more quickly than others. It is also true that all American voters are subjected to the same immediate political "causes" of non-voting (the uninteresting campaign or the obscure issue, for example), and all face the same immediate personal ones (sickness, forgetfulness, bad weather). But again, these cumulative hardships or discouragements affect only some citizens' intentions to vote. Deeply involved in the explanations of non-voting, therefore, are the internal motivational systems of individual voters: their degrees of political involvement, their sense of political obligation, their levels of political information.

The non-voter in the United States is part of a broader group of political non-participants and apathetics. That is to say, he resembles the citizens who abstain from all forms of political activity — whether it be voting, discussing politics, working for a candidate, joining a political party or other political organization, or attending political speeches, rallies, or dinners. In terms of social or demographic characteristics, voter turnout is higher:

among men than women.

among higher income groups.

among the better educated.

among the middle-aged (than both the young and the older).

among city-dwellers, especially those in metropolitan centers.

among those with higher status occupations.

among Jews than Catholics, and among Jews and Catholics than among Protestants.

among whites.

Behind these group differences there appears once again the factor of socio-economic status (SES). To be sure it does not explain everything. The greater voting among men than women probably reflects both the greater difficulty many women have in freeing themselves from children and home responsibilities and the lingering feeling in some quarters that woman's political place is in the home. And non-voting in the. Southern rural areas undoubtedly contributes to the greater voting among urbanites and non-Protestants. Yet SES clearly explains many of the relationships, and the data of the Survey Research Center suggest that the most striking relationships with voter turnout are those of income and educational level, two of the surest indexes to socio-economic status.[15]

Furthermore, we can add other details to this portrait of the regular voter. He has higher levels of political interest and involvement than the non-voter; he knows who the candidates are, what the burning issues are. He is more apt to be a strong and loyal identifier of a political party, rather than a self-styled "independent" or half-hearted partisan. Furthermore, he believes that politics and elections touch important matters and that it really does matter which of the candidates is elected. He also has a strongly ingrained sense of his duty and obligation to vote. And according to the researches of Angus Campbell and his associates, he possesses a sense of "political efficacy." He believes his vote really does make a difference and that he and other voters can direct the decisions of the political community. His is a stance of political self-confidence and political power. One does not often hear from him the question, "What difference does my vote make?"[16] Similarly, another scholar suggests that

the non-voter actually views those with high status in his community, whether they be the editor of the local paper, a labor leader, or his job superior, as politically knowledgeable people with whom to identify himself and to follow. One might speculate . . . that, to the extent that the non-voter depends politically upon the local authority or leader symbols, he betrays a personal sense of inadequacy and insecurity.[17]

[15] See Angus Campbell, Gerald Gurin, and Warren E. Miller, *The Voter Decides* (Evanston: Row, Peterson, 1954). For general works on political participation, including voting, see Robert E. Lane, *Political Life* (Glencoe: Free Press, 1959) and Lester W. Milbrath, *Political Participation* (Chicago: Rand McNally, 1965).

[16] Angus Campbell, Philip E. Converse, Warren E. Miller, and Donald E. Stokes, *The American Voter* (New York: Wiley, 1960), pp. 96–110.

[17] Philip K. Hastings, "The Voter and the Non-Voter," *American Journal of Sociology*, LXII (1956), p. 307.

The decision to vote may also spring from reinforcing social experience and stimuli. The voter is far more apt than the non-voter to belong not only to parties and political organizations, but to other groups and associations as well. He more often engages in political discussions and debates, and he is a greater consumer of newspapers, magazines, and political programs on TV. In fact, by his SES, by his own perception of his place and value in society, by his sense of efficacy in it, by his acceptance into its group and associational life, the regular voter is preeminently a man or woman with a comfortable and comforting place in the life of his community. Conversely, the low-status, non-voter, poorly educated and economically disadvantaged — and possibly further handicapped by racial or ethnic prejudice — has feelings of powerlessness, alienation, and anomie. Rarely sharing in the prosperity or esteem of the community, he has not surprisingly concluded that he is not influential in it and that those who are care little what he may think or want.[18]

Indeed, if one seeks explanations of non-voting by focusing on the non-voters rather than the voters, another possibly important point stands out beyond the fact of alienation and low sense of political efficacy. Voting is often a threatening activity for the citizen who decides not to. In the case of the Southern Negro in some counties of the deep South it may be overtly threatening; he may face physical intimidation or economic reprisal should he decide to vote. But more commonly the threat is psychological. For the adult who knows little of politics, of the candidates, or of the issues, the act of voting exposes his own ignorance and threatens his own sense of confidence and self-esteem. For the citizen whose political "cues" are mixed — who was, for example, raised as a Democrat but has Republicanism urged on him by a persuasive spouse, or who favors the ideology of one party but the candidate of the other — the necessity of voting threatens decisional turmoil. Rather than resolve these conflicts he may "escape" from the difficulties of decision and not vote at all.[19]

Finally, voting or non-voting may reflect the passive political culture of a group or sub-group in American life. We have already referred to the case of "woman's place," a less-than-rare extension of the male political ego. Especially in some Eastern and Southern European and oriental ethnic groups in the United States the female role still shares something of the *"kinder, kirche, kuchen"* tradition. To take another example, Negro adults who have for years been taught their own political inferiority and "place" do not easily become active voters even if the opportunity presents itself. Conversely, most middle-class Americans — reinforced by the

[18] On the related subject of political cynicism see Robert E. Agger, Marshall N. Goldstein, and Stanley A. Pearl, "Political Cynicism: Measurement and Meaning," *Journal of Politics,* XXIII (1961), pp. 477–506.

[19] For example, Morris Rosenberg, "Some Determinants of Political Apathy," *Public Opinion Quarterly,* XVIII (1954), pp. 349–366.

persistent teachings of civics courses — have been taught since childhood that regular and thoughtful voting is a responsibility of citizenship and that the non-voter is a social shirker. Perhaps it is not an exaggeration to say that for these Americans it is non-voting, with its attendant feelings of guilt and irresponsibility, that is threatening.

CONSEQUENCES FOR THE POLITICAL PARTIES

The American parties must, therefore, operate within an American electorate which constantly shifts in size and composition — but which, regardless of its momentary size and composition is never a sample of either the full American adult population or that segment of it eligible to vote. Much of the strategy of the parties in pursuing their goals — especially the contesting of elections — must take account of those facts.

THE LONG-RANGE CONSEQUENCES

The long-run consequences of changes in the electorate spring from basic changes in its legal definitions. Since electorates in democracies expand rather than contract, the changes invariably result from the addition of new groups to the eligible electorate. At the moment the American parties are witnessing the addition of part of a major group to the electorate: the disenfranchised American Negro. Not only is Negro registration rising sharply in the South, but improved education and a new militancy — and its new political culture — will increase Negro registrations elsewhere in the country as well. Despite the earnest and increasingly competitive efforts of Republicans, the fact remains that this new electorate will be, at least in the short run, a Democratic one. All of its SES characteristics predispose it to the national Democratic party, and we know that more than 90 per cent of the Negroes who voted in 1964 voted for the Johnson-Humphrey ticket. By 1965, in fact, the Negroes had become one of the most overwhelmingly Democratic of all American social categories. While it is difficult to say exactly how many Negroes may be added to the American electorate in the next few years, modest estimates suggest that by 1968 they may account for between 5 and 7 per cent of the American electorate. In the Southern states alone close to 800,000 Negroes may be added to the voting rolls between 1965 and the presidential elections of 1968. That, in a party system in which elections are frequently decided by 1, 2, or 3 per cent of the vote, is obviously a significant addition.

The effects on the parties and their electoral competition of the expanding Negro electorate have already been felt in the South. In 1966 the primary defeats in Virginia of two Democratic incumbents, Representative Howard Smith and Senator Willis Robertson, by Democratic moderates were widely attributed in part to new Negro voters. In Arkansas, where Winthrop Rockefeller defeated a segregationist Democrat for the governorship by some 45,000 votes, the Southern Regional Council estimated that 75,000 or more Negroes (of the 115,000 registered) had voted for Rockefeller. At the same election of 1966 six Negroes were elected to the Tennessee legislature; only one had previously held a legislative seat. Three Negroes were also sent to the Texas legislature, the first in this century. Even in local elections the impact was felt; at least one Negro sheriff was elected in a Southern county, and in others Negro votes put moderate candidates in office over the opposition of die-hard segregationists.

Long-run consequences to the parties also result from changes in the "shape" or "distribution" (rather than the size) of the American electorate. Any electorate has importance only as it is divided and sub-divided into the constituencies in which the contests for public office take place. Political parties long ago discovered that the drawing of these district lines would inevitably have an impact on them, and they early resolved to try to make sure the impact was to their liking. Partisan advantage is, in fact, the express purpose of all "gerrymanders" and of many other districting decisions. Similarly, alterations in the counting of the votes of the electorate — and that is precisely what is at stake in proposals to reform the Electoral College — alter the electorate for all intents and purposes by giving differing weights to different votes. (These changes in the electoral rules of the game, however, will be explored more fully in the next four chapters.)

SHORT-RUN CONSEQUENCES

In addition to the changes in the basic structure of the eligible electorate, the political parties must react to short-run changes resulting from changes in turnout from election to election. And since these increases or decreases in turnout are unlikely to benefit all parties and candidates equally — because non-voters as a group have different political characteristics from voters (Table 4) — these matters too have potent political consequences for the party. The increasing or decreasing of voter turnout, or the exploiting of variations in turnout between and among elections, frequently become focal points in party strategy. The somewhat innocent campaigns of Boy Scouts and Leagues of Women Voters to "get out the vote" sometimes miss this point. "Getting out the vote" may be tantamount to "getting" one or the other party into office.

The conventional wisdom of American politics has it that big turnouts favor the Democrats. With the general truth of that maxim there is little room for quarrel. The greatest percentage of non-voters in the United States comes from the lower SES groups ordinarily disposed to the Democratic party. It is for this reason that effective registration or "get out the vote" campaigns help the Democrats more often than not. The

Table 4

COMPARISON OF STRONG PARTY IDENTIFIERS, VOTERS IN
PRESIDENTIAL ELECTION, AND NON-VOTERS IN PRESIDENTIAL
ELECTION: 1964 *

	Strong Party Identifiers	Presidential Voters	Presidential Non-Voters
Percentage male	46%	46%	39%
Percentage white	85%	91%	81%
Median age	49 yrs.	45 yrs.	40 yrs.
Median education	12th grade	12th grade	10th grade
Percentage who "care a lot" about the outcome of the election	45%	34%	21%
Percentage who are "very much interested" in the campaign	51%	43%	21%

* Source: Survey Research Center, University of Michigan; data made available through the Inter-University Consortium for Political Research.

truth of the maxim explains the money and manpower that organized labor spent in registration campaigns in 1960. It explains the ancillary maxim that rainy weather is Republican weather. And it also suggests why in some states Republicans prefer an electoral calendar in which the gubernatorial elections are held in the non-presidential years and, therefore, in a smaller electorate a bit more favorable to Republican candidates.

Despite the general truth of the maxim linking big turnouts with the Democrats, the relationship is a more subtle and complicated one. Dwight D. Eisenhower, for example, won the Presidency as a Republican in two high-turnout elections, and what's more, the non-voters those years were disposed also to the Republican candidate (Table 5).[20] The Eisenhower success seems to force a clarification. High turnout works to a Democratic advantage only in elections in which party loyalty is a chief or overriding factor. A heavy turnout may be spurred and stimulated by a candidate

Table 5

POST-ELECTION PREFERENCES OF NON-VOTERS: 1948–1964

	1948	1952	1956	1960	1964
Would have voted Democratic	82%	52%	28%	51%	80%
Would have voted Republican	18%	48%	72%	49%	20%
	100%	100%	100%	100%	100%

[20] See Campbell et al., The American Voter, pp. 110–115; Table 5 is from p. 111.

(Eisenhower) or an issue which works to Republican advantage. Especially since the non-voter is less partisan, he may be more responsive to the momentary, dramatic appeal of issue or candidate. Therefore, the maxim "works" best in elections or party systems in which the SES division underlies the division of party loyalties and in which party loyalties remain the chief key to the decisions of voters.

Party strategists cannot fail to consider the likely voting electorate as they prepare their campaigns. They nourish the often fragile hope that turnouts can be affected selectively and differentially, and they attempt, therefore, by the campaign to mold the size of the participating electorate itself. When they must contest a primary election, they may hope by discrete and selective campaigning to minimize the turnout, for (generally) the smaller the turnout the larger a share of it will be accounted for by the party's own loyal electorate. In general elections they may try to concentrate campaigns, and thus maximize turnout, in areas of known party strength. The especially effective party organizations can take registration lists or their own file of canvassed voters and stimulate only their own partisans to vote.

Nor can the campaign strategists overlook the turnout differences from election to election. For example, the differences in electorates threaten the parties with the possibility that the man able to appeal to the small, party-oriented electorate of the primary may not appeal to the larger, less-partisan, and less-informed electorate of the subsequent election. And the planning of a congressional career always confronts the fact that the congressman will seek reelection by different electorates in alternate elections — the large turnout of the presidential election followed by the smaller turnout of the mid-term elections two years later.

THE BROADER ISSUES

The democratic ethos presumes the desirability of full popular participation in the affairs of democratic self-government. All of the instructions of civics courses and all of the canons of "good citizenship" stress it. The very case for democracy itself rests on the wisdom of the widest possible sharing of political power and political decision-making within the society. And it is precisely this ethos which the relatively low voting percentages of American adults offends. The affront to the democratic ethos seems all the greater, moreover, in view of the fact that voting percentages are higher in countries which Americans would like to think have less stable and responsive democracies.

The widespread non-voting also casts some doubt on the effectiveness with which the political parties — the political organizations primarily concerned with contesting elections — manage to mobilize the support and involvement of the total eligible electorate. Presumably the parties,

heralded so often as the instruments of democratic politics, should maximize political participation in the American society. The political parties
themselves are, after all, the results of the expansions of democratic electorates; they are the political organizations which developed to mobilize
the new democratic masses and all of whose capabilities are directed to
recruiting large political aggregates. Much of the case for their superiority
as political organizations rests on that ability.

Related to all of these expectations is the additional one that a vigorous
two-party competition will result in the widest possible mobilization of
the American electorate. The two parties, ever alert to the competitive
advantage of new bodies of support, will gradually expand their appeals
to all corners of the potential electorate. Competition abhors a vacuum,
and the two major parties will rush to enlist the support of all possible
voters. It is unquestionably true, in fact, that political activity of any kind
is greater in the presence of party competition and widespread attitudes
of party identification and involvement. Drawing on that fact, a presidential commission, appointed by John F. Kennedy to ponder again the problem of American non-voting, reported in 1963 that: [21]

A great ally of education in the long-range fight against apathy is politics
itself — the two-party system. Effective two-party competition prompts political
involvement, spurs interest in politics and campaigns, and strengthens a person's feeling that his vote counts. We believe that two-party competition is
essential to build and maintain interest in public affairs, and consequently leads
to greater voter participation. It is no coincidence that the growth of the Republican party in the South has impelled many more voters of both parties
toward the polls.

And yet the fact remains that, making allowances for the relationship
between the two-party competitiveness and higher turnouts, many of the
turnout percentages that shock observers prevail in areas of considerable
competitiveness.

The record of the parties in mobilizing and involving the American
electorate is a mixed one. One can point to many examples of effective
competing for the support of new groups entering the electorate; the two
parties of the South in various areas, despite the strength of old racial
mores, have recently made room for Negro voices in party councils and
for more moderate appeals to the new Negro electorate. Furthermore, it
is clear that the parties' efforts to maximize electoral response confront
limitations not of their making. One can hardly blame the parties for all
of the legal and administrative restrictions on the suffrage, nor can they
be blamed for patterns of racial or ethnic discrimination, or for poverty,
illiteracy, and alienation in the American society.

[21] President's Commission on Registration and Voting Participation, *Report* (Washington: 1963), p. 24.

Even so, the hands of the parties are not completely clean. They often appear not to relish the challenges of new electors, especially those of low status. The experience of political power has made them (and especially their parties in government) sympathetic to the comfortable status quo of two-party competition. Party leadership and office-holders themselves have been largely recruited from high-status groups in American society and have little quarrel with prevailing norms and institutions. They do not welcome the uncertainties which a radical alteration in the electorate would bring. The party in government, which will have to make the changes in the formal definition of the electorate, has won office with the support of the electorate as it now exists, and it is understandably not anxious to alter it greatly. Furthermore, some state parties in one-party areas have entrenched themselves in power largely by restricting the electorate; in many Southern states the Democratic party until recently stayed in power with the aid of an artificially homogeneous suffrage. Not unexpectedly, then, the history of women's suffrage and the end of Negro disenfranchisement indicates that the parties were not in the vanguard of either movement to expand the electorate.

Do the parties also carry a share of the responsibility for the voluntary disenfranchisement of the American non-voter? To be sure, they do take tactical advantage of turnout differentials in campaigns. It would be hard to expect them not to, especially where they are competitive. But beyond that tactical exploitation of non-voting, they have been blamed for suppressing participation by their failure to interest large numbers of Americans in the dialectics and personalities of politics. E. E. Schattschneider, for example, has argued that to 35 million non-voters the rituals and choices of American politics are virtually meaningless.[22]

The danger with the Schattschneider thesis is in its implication that non-voters are "rational," informed, and careful surveyors of the political scene who decide they find it irrelevant to their goals. One might imagine that they are well-informed political non-consumers. All that we know about the American non-voters, of course, indicates quite the contrary. However, our data on the non-voter suggest only "what" he is, not how he happened to become what he is. It is thus possible to argue that the political parties are one of a number of important political and social institutions which fail to socialize and involve various sectors of the American society. If one talks about the alienation and low sense of political efficacy of non-voters, for instance, it is important to remember that these feelings are not developed in a social vacuum. They are, at least in part, responses to experiences in and perceptions of the real political world, and the political parties are among the major shapers of that world.

[22] E. E. Schattschneider, *The Semi-Sovereign People* (New York: Holt, Rinehart, and Winston, 1960), Chapter 6.

In the American society — for better or for worse — the disaffection, alienation, and low status we identify with political apathy find no outlet or encouragement. Unmobilized, these Americans tend to become apolitical and apathetic. The groups of the disaffected which in many other Western countries form the base of revolutionary or protest parties drift away into impotence and self-imposed political silence here. Not in the last fifty years has the United States seen a movement of mass political protest.[23] In part this is true because of the decline of third-party movements; in part, too, it results from the formal disenfranchisement of disadvantaged groups, such as the Negro. Furthermore, it appears that the major parties of a competitive two-party system cannot represent the groups they often describe as being "outside of the mainstream of American politics." And at the same time the two-party system works against the development of minor parties which might represent them.

The American parties, therefore, work within an artificially homogeneous "active" electorate. That electorate reduces the totality of political conflict and the range of political interests the parties must respond to. In every way their political job is easier for the cumulative restrictions (regardless of how they are imposed) on the American electorate. They find it easier to be moderate, pragmatic parties because the electorate to which they respond is largely settled in and committed to the present basic social arrangements. Compromise and tactical movement come more easily when the effective electorate is more homogeneous and in agreement on fundamentals. In brief — while it has been fashionable to say that the moderate, pragmatic, non-doctrinaire American parties are the result of an electorate itself agreed on the fundamental questions, it is probably also true that the pragmatic, majoritarian parties in a two-party system cannot easily draw into their ambit the low-status, alienated, dissident groups which are not a part of that moderate consensus.

What began as a problem in the democratic ethos and democratic expectations can only end in the same way. Even if the incidence of nonvoting were reduced and the parties succeeded in stimulating greater involvement and voting, there is little reason to think that the new voters would add greatly to the rationality of democratic debate or the wisdom of democratic decision. But on the other hand, democracy also involves a set of relationships whose stability and regularity we generally consider useful — the peaceful settlement of conflict, the processes of accommodation, the healthiness of the democratic "safety valve." When large numbers of Americans opt out of politics, they open the way for the well-organized, the interested, and the militant to rush in. They reduce their own effective political power, and their powerlessness and sense of power-

[23] The "New Left," that loose coalition of student groups, pacifists, civil rights organizations, and other militant leftists, presents in the 1960's a rather classic illustration of the alienation of the American radical.

lessness breeds greater powerlessness. A pluralistic democracy finds, as a result, that substantial segments of the society are not taking their place in the processes of accommodation, that they are not exerting their countervailing and controlling political influence, that they are in effect abdicating a role in the system. The effectiveness of democracy as a resolver of social conflict cannot help but be reduced.

PART FOUR

The Political Parties in the Electoral Process

The contesting of elections unites, however briefly, the disparate and fragmented American parties. The choice of a presidential candidate and the following campaign bind the state and local parties into a fleeting semblance of a national party. A statewide election similarly focuses the activities and energies of local organizations and leaders within the state. Furthermore, any election joins the three party sectors into a grand coalition of the party elites (the party organization and the party in government) and the party clienteles (the party in the electorate). The pursuit of electoral victory and public office is the one time in the life of the party at which all of its various sectors are united in the pursuit of their varied goals and incentives through the common means of winning office.

The pursuit of victory in the elections unites the party for a number of reasons. The election is the event which, above all, elevates the business of politics to a level of visibility and salience which stimulates even the less concerned members of the electorate. The contesting candidates personify and simplify the difficult choices of American politics. Furthermore, the recruitment of resources for the party organization (money, manpower, and skills) depends on the party's establishing the likelihood, or at least the possibility, of electoral victory. The incentives which lure resources to the party flow in the long run only to those parties which win. Only from electoral victory come the patronage job, the triumph of an interest or an ideology, or even the social and psychological rewards of politics. The American parties are electoral parties which must win

197

elections — and which must, therefore, be able to mobilize majorities in the electorate.

The conventional references to the American parties as "electoral parties" are, perhaps, a little too glib and hackneyed. The phrase suggests what the parties and their personnel "do," but it does not clarify how well they do it or what goals they achieve in doing it. At times, in fact, the reference to the electoral preoccupation of the American parties might appropriately be taken to mean that for millions of Americans the party symbol and label, and thus the party loyalties they arouse, dominate this set of choices in the American political system. In terms of the parties themselves, it is less than clear what it means to be an electoral party.

For one thing, the conventional references ought not to imply that the parties carry out their electoral activities with ease. The party organizations, at least, find it difficult to control the selecting of candidates, the taking of stands on issues, the fixing of campaign strategies, even the raising of money. Those aspects of the contesting of elections are controlled, in the name of the whole party, by its candidates — its party in government and the candidates hoping to join it. In many parts of the country the party candidates have, in fact, organized their own campaigns, recruited their own workers, hired their own campaign advice, and raised their own campaign funds. If it is true that the party in government controls the central and most visible activities of the party (at the expense of a frustrated party organization), can the party organizations reasonably achieve the goals their activists set for them?

At the same time that it stages an internal competition over the control of its electoral strategies, the party also faces the competitions of the other political organizations which also seek their political goals increasingly by interventions into the electoral processes. Over the past twenty years the non-party political organizations — the interest groups, party factions, personal followings, voluntary campaign committees, ideological organizations — have taken aggressive, overt roles in the nominating and electing of candidates. It is not uncommon now to read newspaper accounts of the electoral activities of trade unions, of the American Conservative Union, of *ad hoc* campaign organizations such as Citizens for Eisenhower, of public relations firms, and even of a nebulously defined "Kennedy organization." As they grow in electoral influence, the very pattern of party activities is threatened.

Such fundamental issues of control and competition in elections, both within the party and within the broader company of all the political organizations, raise the kind of questions to which generalizations and theories about the parties must ultimately be addressed. For these kinds of competitions go a long way in determining what the parties are and what they do in the political system. Throughout these coming chapters runs another theme close to those same basic questions: the impact of political instituticns on the forms and activities of the parties. For nowhere are the confining limits of political institutions on the parties clearer than in the electoral processes. The direct primary, for example, touches every attempt they make to control the nomination of candidates; it is, in fact, the primary that so often turns the control of nominations from the party organization to the candidates themselves or to other political organizations. Furthermore, the entire strategy of the quest for the Presidency is colored by the unique structural presence of the Electoral College.

In the chapters of this section we will, for the sake of orderly exposition, observe two sets of distinctions. The first is the common one between the nominating of the parties' candidates and the contesting of the general election. Even though the distinction between the two parts of the electing business may be analytically useful, it can be arbitrary and misleading if pressed too far. The interaction of one on the other makes them a single, indivisible process. What a party or a candidate does in one will affect, compel, or limit what it does in the other. Elections may be lost or won in the earliest informal steps to encourage candidates, and those steps may have taken place months or years before.

The special chapters set aside for the nomination and election of the American President reflect the second distinction. The contest for the Presidency is a special case in American nominations and elections and must be so treated. Although the direct primary dominates the formal nominating machinery for almost all American public offices, the convention system it replaced still functions in the nomination of presidential candidates. And the special election machinery of the Electoral College sets the presidential election apart from the simpler plurality elections that prevail elsewhere in American politics (Figure 1). Chapters Nine and

Figure 1
COMPARISON OF STEPS IN THE NOMINATION-ELECTION PROCESSES IN THE UNITED STATES

	Prenomination	Nomination	Election
Presidential Elections	Selection of delegates to national convention by state party action or presidential primary	By national party convention	By plurality vote within the states, and majority of votes in Electoral College
Other American Elections	Access to primary ballot by petition, request, or party action	By direct primary or (in few cases) by convention	By plurality vote at the general election

Ten describe the modal patterns of American electoral machinery and politics. Chapters Eleven and Twelve deal with the fascinating peculiarities of the processes by which Presidents are chosen. The final chapter of this group concerns the recruitment of the most important resource for the contesting of elections: money.

Chapter Nine

THE NAMING OF
THE PARTY CANDIDATES

Few Americans realize how indigenously American the direct primary is. Having devised it and adopted it almost universally for the nomination of candidates for public office, they seem unaware that the rest of the world has not followed their lead. The point is important, not because American political naiveté is unusually great, as a clue to the peculiar and even unique aspects of American politics and political parties. For no single fact goes so far to explain the differences between the American parties and those of the other Western nations than the direct primary. It has forced on them a new set of strategies in making nominations, in contesting elections, and in attempting eventually to maintain responsibility over what their successful candidates do in office.

In the virtually irresistible advance of the direct primary in the 20th century no state has been untouched. With the capitulation of Connecticut in 1955, the primary is now used or can be used to nominate at least some public officials in every state. The majority of states employ it in all nominations. For the present it should suffice to say that by the direct primary (or more simply "the primary") we mean a special election in which the party electorates choose candidates to run for public office under the party labels. At a later, conclusive "general election," of course, the total electorate makes the final choice from the nominees of the parties. That pattern of a direct primary for making nominations followed by plurality election at the general election is broken only by one great exception in American politics: the procedures for awarding the greatest electoral prize of them all, the American Presidency.

Even though the nomination step does not settle the electoral outcome, its importance is great. At the nomination the major screening of candidates takes place; here the choice is reduced to two in most constituencies. At this point a voter's preferred candidate may be rejected, or there may be formulated a "Hobson's choice" for the election. Especially in areas of one-party domination the real and effective choice will be made at the primary.

For the parties themselves the consequences of the nomination processes bulk very large. The images of its candidates are to some extent its images; their reputations and their stands on public issues may be identified as those of the party. Furthermore, the candidate with which it goes into the election campaign determines to a great extent its ultimate chances for victory. And if the party wants to assure the loyalty of its elected office-holders to the party program or if it seeks to reward faithful party workers with election to office, it must also control the key nomination process. The nomination of candidates, moreover, offers the party a major opportunity for uniting its wings and factions behind acceptable candidates. In short, it is obviously important to a political party who its candidates are, both for the success of its electoral competitions and for the building of internal unity and cohesion.

THE ADVENT OF THE DIRECT PRIMARY

As recently as the beginning of the 20th century the direct primary had come into use only in scattered communities in scattered states. For the first 110 years of the Republic the party caucus and then the party convention dominated the nominating of candidates for public office. Each gave way successively under the weight of criticism that they permitted, if not encouraged, the making of nominations by self-picked and irresponsible party elites. The history of the evolution of nominating methods in the United States above all is a story of the progressive triumph of the ethic and symbols of democracy. They have been shaped by the belief that in a democracy the greatest possible number of "party members" ought to take part in the nomination of the party's candidates.

Formal systems of nomination developed in the United States along with and as a part of the development of the party system. In fact, parties *qua* parties (rather than legislative associations) developed and evolved largely as nominators of candidates for public office. Local caucuses often met by the end of the 18th century to select candidates, and frequently caucuses of like-minded partisans in legislatures met to nominate candidates for governorships and other statewide offices. Similar congressional caucuses were meeting to nominate presidential and vice-presidential candidates. Ultimately the parties developed integrated caucuses which drew both on local activists and on legislators. But in whatever form, the caucus was chosen by co-optation — there was no machinery, no procedures, for ensuring even the participation of all of the powerful in the party. The Jacksonians attacked it relentlessly as an aristocratic device that thwarted popular wishes, and "King Caucus" was indeed an ample target.

In 1832 the Democrats met in a national convention for the first time and nominated, appropriately enough, Andrew Jackson for the Presidency. From then on the convention system quickly triumphed along with Jacksonian popular democracy, whose values it shared. It dominated the making of nominations for the rest of the 19th century. Broadly representative, the nominating convention was composed of delegates chosen by the local party organizations. But even though formally representative, the large and chaotic conventions were scarcely that in reality. Both in the picking of delegates and in the management of the conventions, the fine, guiding hands of party leaders were too obvious and too oppressive. Party insurgents, unhappy with the "bossism" of the conventions and with the alliance of the bosses and "the interests" — and unhappy with their own failures — belabored the convention system with moral fervor and political cunning. The Progressives led the movement and their journalistic handmaidens, the muckrakers, furnished the often shocking, often piquant, corroborative details.[1]

The cure of the Progressives, the direct primary, comported easily with their democratic norms. For it was an article of faith among them that for the ills of democracy one needed only to prescribe larger doses of democracy. It was appropriately one of Progressivism's high priests, Robert M. LaFollette, who ushered in the first statewide primary in the United States, that which Wisconsin passed in 1902. In the next fifteen years all but four states had adopted it, at least in part. By 1967 the record of progress was this: all states have adopted the direct primary for at least some offices, and forty of the states are committed to its use for all statewide offices.[2]

While it is true that the primary movement was intended to reform the nominating processes by "democratization," many of its supporters saw in it an instrument for crippling the political party itself. For them the primary was an attempt to cut back the power of the parties by striking at their chief activity as a party organization — that of nominating the party's candidates. While it is the "party as an electorate" which elects, the party organization had nominated under the caucus and convention systems. Primaries took from it the stipulation of who would participate in this nominating process, and in so doing they deprived the organization of the control of who would run under the party name and symbols. Regard-

[1] For the story of the convention system and the onset of the direct primary, see Charles E. Merriam and Louise Overacker, *Primary Elections* (Chicago: Univ. of Chicago Press, 1928). The writings and speeches of Robert M. LaFollette, Sr., also convey a great deal of the Progressive fervor for the primary and against the old-line political organizations.

[2] Two states, Indiana and Delaware, do not use the primary in statewide elections; eight others mix the primary and conventions.

less of the intentions and motives of the enactors of the primary laws, however, there is little doubt that they struck at the power of party organizations.

The quick success of the direct primary movement happened during the years of the greatest one-partyism in American history. Sectionalism was rampant, and one party or the other dominated the politics of many states. One-partyism meant that the nomination of the major party became crucial. Although the failings of the conventions might be tolerated when a real choice remained in the general election, they could not be borne when the nomination of the dominant party was in fact election. It could choose the weariest party hack without fear of challenge from the other party. And so the Progressives who fought economic monopoly with anti-trust legislation fought political monopoly with the direct primary.

VARIETIES OF THE DIRECT PRIMARY

The primaries of the fifty states are most frequently divided into a three-fold set of categories. The three varieties each demand a different degree of party attachment on the part of the voter.

THE CLOSED PRIMARY

Found in 43 states, the closed primary requires that the voter declare his party affiliation so that his participation may be limited to the primary of his own party. In most of these states when the voter registers to vote he specifies his party affiliation. Then at the primary election he is simply given the primary ballot of his party so that he may choose among his fellow partisans who seek the nomination for the same office. He may always change his party affiliation on the registration rolls, but the states require that this be done sometime ahead of the date of the primary.[3]

In the remaining closed primary states, the voter simply declares his party "membership" — or more accurately, his party attachments or preference — when he goes to the primary polling place. He is then given the primary ballot of his party. Should his declarations be challenged by one of the party observers at the polls, he may be required to take an oath of party loyalty. These oaths or tests differ (as does virtually all else!) from state to state. Some require him to affirm that he has voted for the candidates of the party in the past; some demand that he declare himself sympathetic to the candidates and principles of the party at the moment; and

[3] The reader should be aware that political idiom in some states uses the terms "open" and "closed" to describe primaries in an entirely different manner. The "open" primary in these cases refers to one in which the political party organization makes no endorsement and gives no support to any contestant for the nomination; it is a primary in which the party organization has left "hands off." The "closed" primary, in this usage, refers to one in which the party organization has intervened in some way to support a candidate or a slate of candidates.

others ask that he state his intention to vote for the candidates of the party at the general election. Needless to say, the secrecy of the ballot makes it impossible to challenge the veracity of such pledges. They depend entirely on the probity of the individual.

THE OPEN PRIMARY

In the six states of the open primary — Alaska, Michigan, Minnesota, Montana, Utah, and Wisconsin — the voter votes in the primary without at any time disclosing his party affiliation or preference. As he enters the polling place booth he is either given ballots for every party, one of which he selects in the privacy of the booth, or else he is given a single, consolidated ballot on which he chooses the section of the party he prefers. It is an "open" primary in the sense that any party's primary is open to any voter, regardless of his past, present, or future party loyalties. He may not, however, participate in the primary of more than one party.

The distinctions between open and closed primaries are easy to exaggerate. Such a simple dichotomy ignores the vast range of differences and nuances within the closed primary states, which do account after all for 86 per cent of the states. There is not such a great or critical distinction between an open primary and a closed primary which permits a voter to change his party affiliation on the date of the primary by taking a vague and unenforceable pledge that he plans to support its candidates at the approaching election.

THE BLANKET PRIMARY

The blanket primary, unique to the state of Washington, goes one step in freedom beyond the open primary. Not only does the voter need to disclose no party affiliation, he is free to vote in the primary of more than one party. In fact, the ballot form creates one aggregate primary by grouping all of every party's contestants under the office which they seek. The voter then votes for one of them, perhaps choosing among Democrats for one office and between Republicans in another. In less formal circles the primary has been called the "free love" primary for reasons which should be obvious.[4]

Among these forms of primary the parties clearly prefer the closed primary with party registration prior to the primary. It pays a greater respect to the right of the party itself to make nominations by limiting its primary electorate to its own party electorate. In addition, where there is the prior registration of party affiliation, the parties get an added bonus: complete lists of their partisans. And yet it is not quite that simple. Party registration tends to be at best an approximation of party loyalties at the moment. Especially since people are slow to change their party affiliations,

[4] See Daniel M. Ogden, Jr., "The Blanket Primary and Party Regularity in Washington," *Pacific Northwest Quarterly*, XXXIX (1948), pp. 33–38.

the party totals tend to lag behind the pattern of voting at the moment. Furthermore, the registration figures of the major or leading party tend also to be swollen by conformists and by a few "political rationalists" who want to vote in its crucial primary.

But the parties would gladly accept these uncertainties over what they regard as the more serious perils of the open primary. (The blanket primary enjoys even less favor.) Party leaders levy two charges against the open primary: "crossing-over" and "raiding." The terms are not always used differently, but a distinction will be made here. "Crossing-over" refers to the practice of voters choosing to participate in the primary of the party they probably do not generally support or feel any loyalty to. It is a drifting across party lines in search of the excitement of a pitched primary battle. "Raiding" refers to an organized attempt on the part of one party to send its partisans into the primary of the other in order to foist the least attractive candidates on it.

That "crossing over" happens in open primary states is beyond doubt. Take the case of primary contests in Wisconsin, cradle of the open primary and home of an especially rambunctious political tradition. In the 1952 senatorial primary Senator Joseph R. McCarthy, a highly controversial Republican engaged in a search for domestic Communism within the ranks of government, had scattered and well-publicized Republican primary opposition. So, while the Republicans later attracted only 54.3 per cent of the two-party vote at the general election, they had 79.2 per cent of the two-party vote at the primary — and this despite the fact that the Democrats had a close fight for the senatorial nomination in their own ranks! McCarthy was, of course, renominated with 68 per cent of the votes cast in the Republican primary. In general the exciting primary contests take place in the primary of the stronger party, and the drifting is to it; close two-party competitiveness tends to diminish drifting. But little evidence exists that the voters crossing party lines consciously try to saddle the party with a weak candidate; they largely vote for the candidate they would support if it were a general election. As for organized "raiding," there is precious little evidence to suggest it is more than a worrisome myth. Every party fears that voters drifting to the other party's primary will develop a habit of voting that will carry over to the general election. Furthermore, it must also be on guard lest the migration from its own primary permit its own primary contests to be settled by unrepresentative or irresponsible minorities. It has every reason, in other words, to encourage its loyalists to vote in their own primary.

THE PRIMARIES: RULES OF THE GAME

The distinctions of the last few pages concern the basic form of the primary election. But the states have found it necessary to surround the primary with additional clarifying legislation.

ACCESS TO THE PRIMARY BALLOT

The states must, first of all, deal with the problem of how a candidate gets on the primary ballot. Most of the states permit access to the ballot by petition (also called "nomination papers" in some areas). State statutes fix the number of required signatures, generally either a fixed number or a percentage of the vote for the office in the last election. In some cases it is sufficient for the would-be candidate to become a primary candidate by presenting himself to the clerk of elections and paying a modest fee. Finally, a few states put candidates on the ballot if they have formal party support. In Colorado and New Mexico, for example, any seekers after nomination who poll 20 per cent or more of the endorsement vote at party conventions are automatically placed on the primary ballot. These matters also have consequences for the parties. The easier access to the primary ballot, the easier it is for crank or dissident candidates to engage the party-supported candidate in a costly primary battle. Such arcane matters as the number of signatures a petition must have may materially affect the number of primary contests in the state.

CROSS-FILING — *entering both major party primaries*

Occasionally the states have confronted the question of whether to limit a candidate to seeking the nomination of a single party. Until 1959 California, alone among the states, permitted candidates to enter both major party primaries, a practice called "cross-filing." While it was in full flower, Earl Warren in 1946 won both party nominations for governor; in the general election Earl Warren, Republican, ran without Democratic opposition. Bowing to criticism that cross-filing destroyed a party's responsibility for its candidates and, in fact, destroyed the basic assumption of nominations by a political party, the state legislature abolished it. In California cross-filing worked to the advantage of the stronger party (the Republicans at that time), for that party's candidates tended to be better known.[5] Now the closest remaining practice is New York's willingness to permit cross-filing if — and the "if" is the crucial difference — the second party's organization for the constituency approves. The law thus permits electoral coalitions of the Liberal party and one of the major parties (usually the Democratic party) behind a single candidate or slate of candidates.

RUN-OFF PRIMARIES — *in only ten states, all Southern*

Finally, some states have tried to cope with the issue of primaries settled by less than a majority of the voters. In those cases in which candidates are nominated by only 35, 40, or 45 per cent, most states simply hope that the general election will produce a majority winner. But ten states, all

---

[5] R. J. Pitchell, "The Electoral System and Voting Behavior: The Case of California's Cross-Filing," *Western Political Quarterly*, XII (1959), pp. 459–484.

from the South and its borders, have run-off primaries, second primaries in which the two candidates with the highest vote totals face each other if the winner won less than 50 per cent in the regular primary. This Southern institution reflects the period of Republican impotence in which the Democratic nomination *was* in effect election and in which intense Democratic factionalism often produced three, four, or five serious candidates for a single office. Iowa has approached the same basic problem with a fresh solution. If no primary candidate gets 35 per cent of the votes cast, a party convention meets and selects the party's candidate.

THE NON-PARTISAN PRIMARY ~ *Minnesota & Nebraska*

Although of lesser importance in a study of the American political parties, the non-partisan primary is the occasion for nominating thousands of local officials, most judges, and even the legislatures of Minnesota and Nebraska. As the system of nominating that must (by definition) accompany the non-partisan election, the non-partisan primary groups all candidates for the office on one ballot on which no party designations appear. The two candidates receiving the highest number of votes at the primary become the candidates for the non-partisan general election. Although there are no party labels on the ballot, the party affiliations of various candidates may in fact be well-known. Party organizations may openly endorse and support candidates, especially in non-partisan mayoralty and city council elections. In those cases the distinction between a partisan and non-partisan primary may remain only for the voters who have little political information.

THE LINGERING CONVENTIONS

The convention as a device for nominating candidates faded quickly under early inroads by the direct primary. But decline has not meant death, and as of now the convention as a nominating device retains firm control over a significant number of public offices. The two parties, of course, nominate their national candidates in the best-known ceremonials of American politics, the quadrennial nominating conventions held in midsummer before presidential elections. As the major exception to the rule of the primary, they will be considered separately in Chapter Twelve.

Many states exempt the minor parties from the direct primary. The states are not anxious to carry the financial expense, and realism also suggests that minor party nominations are not especially important anyway. And the parties such as the Prohibition and Socialist Labor parties have difficulty enough finding even one candidate to run the futile race. Their candidates may, depending on state law, be chosen by party convention or simply by petition. In the one-party days of the South it was also common to exempt the Republicans from the primary for virtually the same reasons. Even with such freedom to select their own candidates,

Republicans frequently did not contest the general elections; even as late as 1964, twenty-eight Democrats won election to the House of Representatives from the Southern states without Republican opposition. Generally, the Republicans have not been exempted by name from the primary, but rather the state election code excuses those parties polling less than a fixed percentage of the vote for the office at the last general election.

Furthermore, a minority of states still keeps some offices, usually statewide offices, out of the coverage of the direct primary. In both Indiana and Delaware nominations for all statewide offices are still made in state party conventions. In others, such as Michigan, candidates for specific offices (e.g., the governorship) are so chosen. Until very recently, New York parties chose their statewide candidates in state conventions in which the ideological and geographic factions of the parties were propitiated and possibly even unified. In 1967, however, the state replaced convention nominations with a system which permits the state committees of the parties to designate their candidates; other would-be candidates may then challenge the committees' choices in a statewide primary.

Connecticut, the last state to embrace the primary, embraced it without a conspicuous show of affection. The Connecticut primary is like New York's, a "challenge primary," and it combines convention with primary. Each party holds conventions to nominate candidates, and if no other candidate "challenges" the party nominee, he goes directly on the ballot of the general election without an intervening primary. In the event of a challenge a primary is held — but the challenger must have sought nomination in the convention, must have amassed at least 20 per cent of the convention votes and must later have filed nomination petitions. Understandably, challengers have not been plentiful.[6]

Why has the convention survived in some of the states? It remains in a few states of strong, centralized party organization and of a political culture more accepting of the role of parties as robust, self-contained political organizations. As Lockard has written of Connecticut:

Why such protracted and successful resistance? Connecticut is not immune to political innovation. Although it may be known as "The Land of Steady Habits," it has nonetheless adopted an imposing array of progressive legislation, particularly in matters of labor law and social welfare. Still, matters of party concern are different — at least in Connecticut. For Connecticut parties are different from those of most other states; they are strong, centralized, and highly competitive with each other. The character of Connecticut party leadership — the power it has and the generally responsible manner in which it uses its power — constitutes the main reason why advocates of the primary made so little progress in Connecticut.[7]

[6] See Duane Lockard, *Connecticut's Challenge Primary: A Study in Legislative Politics* (New York: McGraw-Hill, 1960).
[7] *Ibid.*, p. 1.

Strong, centralized parties can, in other words, protect the sources of their strength, for in politics, too, "them that has, gets." Convention nomination enables them to maintain a control over candidates and office-holders, and it permits them to bargain within the party and to recognize the differences within it without airing them in public combat. And it is certainly no coincidence that in a state such as Connecticut in which parties as parties still control nominations, party cohesion in the state legislature is just about the strongest in the United States.[8]

THE THREAT OF THE DIRECT PRIMARY

The direct primary does not often realize the parties' worst fears about it, but occasionally it does. In 1962 a political novice from Cleveland with the promising name of Richard D. Kennedy managed to win the Democratic nomination for congressman-at-large in the state of Ohio in an eleven-cornered primary contest. Not only was he a novice with no support in the Democratic party, but he had run in the primary on a frankly segregationist program. A shocked Democratic party announced that it would not support him in the general election, and Democratic Governor DiSalle said he could not vote for him. And so, only nominally a Democratic candidate, Mr. Kennedy lost badly in the general election to Robert A. Taft, Jr., the Republican nominee.

Even though such total disaster befalls a party only rarely, the primary often causes it any number of lesser inconveniences, disruptions, and problems. Consider the threats it makes to the well-being of a political party:

> For the party which wants to influence nominations the primary greatly escalates the costs of politics. Contesting a primary, or supporting candidates in one, is considerably more expensive than holding a convention.

> The primary diminishes the power of the party organization to reward its faithful with nomination for public office. It thus makes less certain one of the rewards by which the party can induce service in its ranks.

> By curbing party control over nominations the primary denies the party a powerful lever for assuring the loyalty of its office-holders to the party platform or program. For if the party cannot control or prevent the reelection of the maverick office-holder, it really has no effective sanction for enforcing loyalty to its programs. The power of European parties to deny renomination to their recalcitrant parliamentarians contributes substantially to their maintenance of party discipline in Parliament.

[8] See Malcolm E. Jewell, *The State Legislature* (New York: Random House, 1962).

The primary permits the nomination of a man hostile to the party organization and leadership, opposed to their platforms or programs, or out of key with the public image the party wants to project — or all three! At the worst it may permit the nomination of a man under the party label who will be, intentionally or not, a severe embarrassment to it.

The nature of the primary creates the distinct possibility that the party will find itself saddled with an "unbalanced" ticket for the general election. In the hypothetical case of an electorate divided into X (50%), Y (30%), and Z (20%) — and let X, Y, and Z represent regions, races, religions, ethnic or national groups — the voters at the primary may select all or most of the candidates from X. (We are assuming considerable bloc voting, but that assumption, after all, lies at the base of party attempts to balance tickets.) Party leaders unquestionably would feel that a stronger ticket for the general election campaign would include a sprinkling of Y's and Z's.

Related is the fact that the primary may produce a "loser" for the party. The nominee may be a man who appeals to only a shade more than half of the dedicated 20 or 30 per cent of the electorate who votes in the party's primary. He may be a man of too limited an appeal — limited to an issue, a group, or an immoderate ideology — to win the support of the broader electorate of the general election.

Beyond all of these specific threats is the more general fear that the primary exacerbates party rifts, splits, factions, feuds, or whatever the headline writers choose to call them. It pits party man against party man, party group against party group.

A genuine primary is a fight within the family of the party — and, like any family fight, is apt to be more bitter and leave more enduring wounds than battle with the November enemy. In primaries, ambitions spurt from nowhere; unknown men carve their mark; old men are sent relentlessly to their political graves; bosses and leaders may be humiliated or unseated. At ward, county or state level, all primaries are fought with spurious family folksiness — and sharp knives.[9]

The resulting wounds are often deep and slow to heal. The cost to the health and strength of the party is considerable.[10]

Not even the gloomiest Cassandra expects all of these misfortunes to

[9] Theodore H. White, *The Making of the President 1960* (New York: Atheneum, 1961), p. 78.

[10] Andrew Hacker adduces evidence to show that a divisive primary battle does not appear to affect seriously the winner's chances in the general election. "Does a 'Divisive' Primary Harm a Candidate's Election Chances?" *American Political Science Review*, LIX (1965), pp. 105–110. His conclusions, however, do not rule out the possibility of a more general harm to and weakening of the party organization.

result from any given primary or even a series of them. But they are distinct possibilities for any party, especially the relatively weak and passive one. The parties recognize the danger, but they recognize, too, the futility of a direct assault on the primary. So, in the best American tradition of joining 'em if you can't beat 'em, some parties have in their various styles and capacities set out to control the primary and make it an instrument of party nominating. Others have lacked the will or the strength to do so; still others have lost ground to local political cultures which disapprove of a party role in the primary. The result is a range of party responses to the primary that extends from no response at all to complete party domination.

THE PARTY FIGHTS BACK

One axiom and a corollary deriving from it govern party strategy in the primary. The axiom is simple to the point of truism: the surest way to control the primary is to prevent competition in it with the party's choice. And the corollary is equally clear: the party must act as early as possible in the pre-primary jockeying of would-be candidates if it is to choke off unwanted competition in the primary.

In an informal sense the party interventions in a primary may have begun years before. Some party leaders may have begun to "groom" a candidate for an office. Or they may have earlier promised an ambitious partisan that if he would step aside to prevent a primary fight he would "get *his* chance" in the near future. And prospective candidates may have begun to build support and followings within a party two, three, even four years ahead of a primary election. As the primary draws near, specific decisions must be made within the party unless it is to remain neutral in the primary. It must decide on the candidates it will support, and the date of decision ought optimally to come before the period for filing for a place on the primary ballot. Otherwise, those not supported by the party will have already committed themselves to candidacy. Within the chronic minority party, "decision" or choice at this stage often means pleading with party workers to offer themselves as sacrificial candidates so that the party can go into the election with a full ticket of candidates; often the party officers themselves, failing to persuade others, must run.

Within some party organizations a powerful party leader or a few party oligarchs make the pre-primary decisions for the party organization. Or it may be a party executive committee or a candidate selection committee. If their sources of information are good, they will know who intends to run and who is merely considering the race. They may arbitrate among them, or they may favor and coax an unwilling man into the primary. If they command a strong and winning organization, their inducements to the non-favored to withdraw may be considerable. They may be able to offer him a patronage position or a chance to run in the future. Any would-be candidate understands the risks in running against a party choice. It is true that some men have begun and made political careers by "bucking" a party choice in a primary, but they are not legion.

This informal and often covert selection of candidate — communicated to the party faithful in the "word" (which is always "passed") or the "nod" — has been replaced within some parties by open, representative, publicized party conventions. A few states have formalized them, but in most cases they have prevented an unqualified endorsement. New Mexico and Colorado laws provide that all candidates who polled more than 20 per cent of a convention endorsement vote shall go on the primary ballot in the order of their vote percentage. Utah and Idaho direct the parties to nominate two candidates for each office. Conversely, a few states attempt by law to minimize the possibility or the power of endorsing conventions. California in 1963 prohibited party organizations from "officially" endorsing candidates for office. And other states, such as Wisconsin, have achieved substantially the same result — albeit with greater subtlety — by requiring party conventions to meet after the primary is safely past.

In most states, however, party endorsing bodies act informally and extra-legally — that is, without election law or party law taking notice of them. In Minnesota, for example, both the Republican party and the Democratic-Farmer-Labor party (the state's version of the Democratic party) hold a series of conventions to endorse candidates for statewide office and Congress. In some parts of the state, chiefly the urban areas, they also endorse local candidates and candidates for the state's formally non-partisan legislature. The instruments of endorsement, the conventions, grow out of the local ward and precinct caucuses mandated by state law. The required vote for endorsement, set by party rule, is 60 per cent within the GOP and two-thirds within the DFL. The party endorsement is, however, strictly unofficial. The endorsee must still go through regular procedures to get on the primary ballot, and the ballot nowhere gives him any preference or his endorsement any mention.[11]

If a primary contest does develop despite all plans and strategies, the party then falls back on its resources in conventional ways. It may urge party committeemen to help the anointed candidates circulate nominating petitions for the necessary signatures and leave the other candidates to their own devices. It may make money, know-how, party workers, and the party bureaucracy available to the chosen ticket. It may print advertisements announcing the party endorsees or issue handy little reference cards which the forgetful voter can take right with him into the polling booth. On the day of the primary the party organization may help to get

[11] On Minnesota see G. Theodore Mitau, *Politics in Minnesota* (Minneapolis: Univ. of Minnesota Press, 1960).

the party's voters to the polls. Whether the party organization acts overtly or covertly in the primary campaign depends both on the local political culture and the candidates' own appraisal of it. The party and/or the candidates may feel that voter sensitivity to party intervention ("boss-ism") may dictate that the candidates appear untouched by party hands.[12]

Of the frequency of party attempts to manage or influence American primaries, it is impossible to write authoritatively. Practices vary not only from state to state, but within states, and descriptions of local party practice are very hard to come by. One is probably safe in generalizing that the most common nominating activity is the recruiting of candidates to seek the nomination. County party leaders in Wisconsin and Oklahoma freely concede that they encourage qualified candidates to seek office. Yet they do not widely attempt the more demanding recruitment activities; only 10 per cent of the Wisconsin chairmen, and less than that in Oklahoma, tried to dissuade some would-be nominees.[13] The result is that in most parts of the country the political party is only one of a number of agencies seeking out and supporting men and women to run for office. It shares the recruitment with local business, professional, farm, and labor groups, with civic and community associations, with ethnic, racial, and religious organizations, and with politically oriented individuals and office-holders.[14]

There are, however, those party organizations which *do* control the recruitment of candidates and the other pre-primary processes. Generally they are the parties which intervene also in the primary itself. A recent study of legislative elections in 78 Pennsylvania constituencies found that party organizations regularly attempted to influence the primary in 116 (74 per cent) of the 156 primaries (one of each party in each of the 78 districts). In 88 (56 per cent) of them the interventions into the primary

---

[12] There have always been dark intimations of another party tactic in the primary: the instigation of "dummy candidates." They are candidates induced by the party to enter an already contested primary; their purpose is to divert and divide the support of the unendorsed candidates. Probably the tactic has been employed in American politics, but just as probably with an incidence far below some suspicions. The American parties generally are not sufficiently organized and/or sufficiently Machiavellian. Perhaps suspicions about "dummy" candidacies arise when rational men cannot otherwise "explain" a particularly hapless or inept candidate in the primary.

[13] Leon D. Epstein, *Politics in Wisconsin* (Madison: Univ. of Wisconsin Press, 1958), p. 93; Samuel C. Patterson, "Characteristics of Party Leaders," *Western Political Quarterly*, XVI (1963), p. 348.

[14] Lester G. Seligman, "Party Recruitment and Party Structure: A Case History," *American Political Science Review*, LV (1961), pp. 77–86. The interaction of party and non-party organizations may be complex. J. David Greenstone has illustrated Democratic party influence on COPE (AFL-CIO) endorsements for congressional seats in his "Party Pressure on Organized Labor in Three Cities," in M. Kent Jennings and L. Harmon Zeigler (eds.), *The Electoral Process* (Englewood Cliffs: Prentice-Hall, 1966), pp. 55–80.

were public and explicit.[15] Such determined attempts to control the primary are not the norm in other parts of the country, however. County chairmen in Kansas, Nebraska, North Dakota, South Dakota, and Iowa recently disclosed that they are not a part of Pennsylvania-style activities in the primaries. Some 40 per cent of them say they never openly support a candidate in a primary contest, and about two-thirds of them declare that their party organizations never endorse candidates before a primary.[16] Just what kind of party relationship to the primary is typical or modal across the United States at this time is virtually anyone's guess.

The role the party organization takes before and during the primary election appears to be a function of a number of factors. All data, first of all, point to a greater party role in urban and metropolitan areas. The political ethos of the cities seems to be more tolerant of party action in the primary; furthermore, the cities are also the sites of the strong and virile party organizations.[17] Secondly, in at least one study party intervention into the primary seems to be most probable in areas of two-party competitiveness. In one-party areas the majority party may tend to be smugly confident or it may be dominated by incumbent office-holders. The minority party tends to be helpless, and primary contests within its ranks are rare.[18] Finally, in the states of the Great Plains, at least, it appears that party control of the primary is more common within the Democratic party, even when one controls for urban-rural differences.[19] That would suggest differences between the two parties in intra-party expectations and ethos. Commentators on the styles and images of the two parties have often noted the more aggressively partisan style of the Democrats and, conversely, the "non-partisan," middle-class style of the Republicans. Very possibly these differences affect their approaches to the direct primary.

CANDIDATES AND VOTERS IN THE PRIMARIES

Candidates and voters inhabit the direct primaries along with the parties. And two facts about them are very much in favor of those party organizations and leaders who want to control the primary. First, the amount of competition — the sheer number of candidates — in the primary is rarely great. Secondly, the voter turnout at primary elections stays generally

---

[15] Frank J. Sorauf, *Party and Representation* (New York: Atherton, 1963), Chapter 5.

[16] Marvin Harder and Thomas Ungs, *Notes Toward a Functional Analysis of Local Party Organizations* (paper delivered at 1964 meetings of Midwest Conference of Political Scientists).

[17] Sorauf, *Party and Representation,* Chapter 5; Harder and Ungs, *op. cit.*

[18] Patterson, *op. cit.,* p. 349.

[19] Harder and Ungs, *op. cit.*

small also, and it is generally heavily populated by the party loyalists and activists most sensitive to the lead of the party.[20] Very possibly one or both of these conditions is of the party's making; the absence of primary candidates, for example, may reflect the skill and firmness of the party's pre-primary persuading and dissuading. Regardless of cause, however, the result tends to be limited primary competition for a limited electorate — and a nomination politics of limited scope. The result is also a nomination politics of greater manageability for the aggressive party organization.

Simple countings will confirm that in every part of the United States large numbers of primary candidates win nomination without contest and that the voter consequently, has no choice at all in the primary. Kirk H. Porter referred to it as the "deserted primary" after finding that there was no contest in either primary for any county office in 1944 in well over half of Iowa's counties.[21] A number of recent studies of primary contests in state legislative races suggest that matters have changed little since then. For example: [22]

> in the 1958 primaries for Pennsylvania legislative elections, 66.2 per cent were without contest.
>
> in Wisconsin from 1946 to 1956, 53.5 per cent of the state legislative primaries were not contested.
>
> 45 per cent of the legislative primaries in Ohio in 1948 were not contested.

And these data reflect a purely quantitative definition of competition (i.e., the number of candidates). If one adopts a qualitative standard of the closeness of the competition — to discount hopeless and frivolous candidates — the amount of genuine or "competitive" competition declines even further. In both the Wisconsin and the Pennsylvania data recounted above, only about three-fourths of the contests were decided by a margin of less than 30 per cent of the vote in the primary.

In the aggregate, competition in American primaries (measured by the number of contestants) is greater under certain rather predictable circumstances. Competition tends to flourish in primaries:

> of the dominant party; competition, in other words, tends to increase as the party's electoral prospects do, and aggregately it is greatest among the two parties of a district if they are closely matched.

---

[20] A recent study in Wisconsin finds the primary voters of that state are more interested, involved, and active in politics than the entire electorate, but that they do not (contrary to general assumption) assume more extreme ideological positions; Austin Ranney and Leon D. Epstein, "The Two Electorates: Voters and Non-Voters in a Wisconsin Primary," *Journal of Politics,* XXVIII (1966), pp. 598–616.

[21] Kirk H. Porter, "The Deserted Primary in Iowa," *American Political Science Review,* XXXIX (1945), pp. 732–740.

[22] Sorauf, *Party and Representation,* p. 111; Epstein, *Politics in Wisconsin,* p. 199; Key, *American State Politics* (New York: Knopf, 1956), p. 178.

in urban areas; competition tends to increase with increases in the percentages of voters living in urban or metropolitan places.

in which there is no incumbent office-holder seeking renomination and eventual reelection.

There are as well other factors influencing competition; the attractiveness of the office and the ease of getting on the ballot, for example. But the chief factor influencing it probably is the party's prospects for victory in the general election; large numbers of Americans do not fight for the right to go down to almost certain defeat. As for the power of the incumbent to discourage competition, it is one of the ironies of the primary. The primary really demands the kind of popular appeal and exposure which only the well-known incumbent often can muster. As a result, it creates the conditions that diminish its own effectiveness.[23]

The possibility remains that party organization activity — success in controlling access to the primary, that is — is responsible for the "deserted primary." But it is a striking fact that primary competition is greater in the very urban areas in which the parties are better organized and more apt to engage in nomination endorsements and recruitment. It is, of course, possible and even probable that the number of contestants would be even greater without party activities. Party interventions, however, clearly do not explain the lack of competition in the rural areas. It may be that the tradition of the office seeking the man is more powerful in rural areas or that the influence of informal community elites chokes off independent, self-serving candidacies. The greater competition of the urban centers may also reflect a greater value of public office, a greater desire to seek its social and economic rewards. Or it may reflect a more divided, heterogeneous, diverse society in which major groups tend to spawn their own special candidates.

If candidates are scarce at the primaries, so are voters. All evidence points overwhelmingly to one cardinal fact about the voting behavior of the American electorate at primaries: it does not vote. Take for instance Key's finding about voter participation in the gubernatorial primaries of fifteen non-southern states from 1926 to 1952: [24]

. . . in three out of four primaries not more than 35 per cent of the potential electorate voted in the primaries of one or the other of the major parties. That is, the total Democratic primary vote plus the total Republican primary vote did not exceed 35 per cent of the number of citizens 21 and over.

Or to use another base of measurement, primary turnouts frequently are less than half that at the following general election. For obscure local

---

[23] On the general causes of primary competition, see the references in the preceding footnote and also William H. Standing and James A. Robinson, "Inter-Party Competition and Primary Contesting: The Case of Indiana," *American Political Science Review*, LII (1958), pp. 1066–1077.

[24] Key, *American State Politics*, p. 134 and all of Chapter 5.

offices and reasonably non-controversial judicial races, the turnout may fall a great deal further.

Furthermore, the primary electorate has special characteristics of its own. A substantial sector of it generally comes from the party loyalists and activists. They are tuned to the cues of the party, but additionally they create problems for the party. They are often thought as a group to overrepresent issue and ideological concerns, and in statewide races especially they overrepresent the areas of the party's greatest concentrations. Even this generally interested electorate often, in the absence of reliable cues and information, lapses into erratic voting behavior. An inordinately large number of primary voters vote for the first name on the ballot, and political unknowns with magic names often do unexpectedly well in primaries. In the 1950's and 1960's a number of primary candidates with the surname of Kennedy — in addition to the sons of Joseph Kennedy — scored heavily. To these points one may add the clear instances of preference for ethnic names and local sons.[25]

For large numbers of voters in the primary the choice is more difficult than that at the general election. Since all of the candidates come from the same party, the voter's party loyalties cannot guide his decision. Nor can any reaction to "ins" and "outs." The primary campaign is brief, the candidates are not well-known, and the issues, if any, are often unclear. The voter's choice is, therefore, less well-structured and less predictable; the presence of an incumbent in the race may be the only continuing, stabilizing element. Consequently, many voter decisions are made right in the polling booth; the effect of the ballot position and the success of the famous "names" indicate that. Small wonder, then, that parties are never confident in primaries and that public opinion pollers prefer not to predict primary outcomes.

THE DIRECT PRIMARY AFTER SIXTY YEARS

More than sixty years have now passed since the introduction of the direct primary into American politics. Thousands of candidates have waged the necessary primary campaigns, and millions of weary voters have puzzled over obscure choices and no choices whatsoever. What difference has it all made? Has the primary "democratized" the nomination process by taking it out of the hands of party oligarchs? And has it materially increased popular participation and initiative in the selection of candidates for public office?

Basically the democratic hopes behind the direct primary ultimately

[25] A student once told me of a local party leader in Massachusetts who counseled his Italo-American voters always to select the candidate in a primary whose name ended in a vowel; his simple rule of thumb, however, contributed to the successful political career of a man named Shapiro.

falter on lack of competition and low voter turnout. The key to the primary is participation — both by candidates and by voters — if there are to be meaningful choices on meaningful alternatives. But the primary by its nature tends to diminish both. The need for broad public appeal, the cost of a contest, and the sheer difficulty of getting on the primary ballot — among other factors — discourage candidacies. And the sheer multiplicity of primaries with their unstructured, often confusing and unclear choices probably does its share to reduce both the quantity and the quality of voter participation. Clearly if mass participation in the nominating processes was a goal of the primary reformers, their hopes have not been realized.

The primary has, however, limited control of nominations by the party organizations, even though the realities of the primary favor the parties in their attempts to come to terms with it. When candidacies are expensive or difficult and where some measure of public support is necessary for nomination, the party gains an advantage. The candidate often needs the party organization, and an enormous advantage accrues to the party-supported candidate. And parties profit, too, from the traditionally small and selective voter turnouts at the primary and from the fact that a significant proportion of the primary voters are informed and motivated partisans. Let us, for example, assume a congressional district of 200,000 registered voters, 100,000 of whom are registered to vote in the primary of each party. In a 40 per cent vote turnout at the primary, 40,000 will vote in one party's primary, with 20,000 votes sufficient to nominate. The party then has a self-selected and restricted electorate at which to direct a campaign.

With these advantages at the disposal of the parties and with the threats of the primary to them so very clear, one may fairly wonder why so many default in initiative and control over the primary. The very size of the job deters many party organizations. The Jacksonian tradition of electing every public official even down to the local surveyor or coroner has produced an awesome proliferation of elective public officials. Understandably the organizations concentrate on a few of the most important legislative and executive offices, neglecting especially many local offices. The expense of supporting so many candidates — not to mention the expenditure of organizational energy and concentration — forces many parties to be selective in their primary interventions. The sheer size of the task also produces a scarcity of candidates and a "wearing thin" of voter attention. The primary when combined with a nomination task of such proportions merely disperses and exhausts the energies, attention, and resources of office-seekers, voters, and political parties alike.

Other factors also keep the party organizations aloof from the primary. Weakness or laziness may do this, although it is true, ironically, that the most futile parties are often forced into activity just to fill the party's ticket. But some with tired political blood lack the vitality to do even that. Others stand aside because a role in the primary threatens their internal harmony and cohesion. They may be paralyzed by the fear that their activity in the primary will open wounds or heat up old resentments. Still others are balked by local political cultures that resist overt party activity as an improper incursion on the spirit of the primary; indeed, party leaders themselves may reflect those norms.

The impact of the primary on the nomination process has, therefore, been an uneven one. In some instances it has effectively neutralized the political party as a nominator; in others it clearly has made little difference to the parties. Strong party organizations able to mobilize voters, money, and manpower are still the most effective determiners of primary outcomes.[26] But even for these parties the limits of the primary are tangible; the very presence of the primary electorate sets limits to what the parties can do. Many no longer find it possible to whisk any "warm body" through the nomination processes. For these parties the direct primary limits the parties by creating a veto body which must pass judgment on the work of the party nominators and by institutionalizing an opportunity for intra-party minorities (or even majorities) to take their case to the party electorate. The direct primary, therefore, has neither destroyed party control over the primary nor democratized the making of nominations. But it has forced the parties to operate semi-publicly and to reckon with the party electorate. Neither the parties nor American politics have ever been the same since its inauguration.

Finally, it remains to consider the more general impact of the primary on the political parties beyond the impact on the making of nominations. V. O. Key has argued that the primary leads to one-partyism by drawing both the voters and the attractive, prestigeful candidates increasingly to the primary of the dominant party. Little by little the majority party becomes the only viable instrument of political influence and the minor party atrophies, a victim of "the more general proposition that institutional decay follows deprivation of function."[27] The function of opposition then is shifted to contests within the primary of the majority party. However persuasive the argument, it is as yet unproved. One-partyism has receded in recent years, and much of it can further be explained in terms of changes in the characteristics of the American electorate. It probably is more likely that the direct primary has caused a more general atrophy or alteration in party organization, both in dominant and minority parties. Strong, centralized party organization continues noticeably

---

[26] For example, Phillips Cutright and Peter H. Rossi, "Party Organization in Primary Elections," *American Journal of Sociology,* LXIV (1958), pp. 262–269.

[27] V. O. Key, "The Direct Primary and Party Structure," *American Political Science Review,* XLVIII (1954), p. 24; the same argument reappears in Key, *American State Politics,* Chapter 6.

in states in which conventions either nominate or in which they make systematic, crucial pre-primary endorsements. Party organization will undoubtedly weaken and contract in those cases in which it loses vital functions and in which party officials and activists lose their reason for existing.

Furthermore, the direct primary has unquestionably altered the distribution of power within the party. When one speaks of "party" control of nominations he speaks of control by the party organization, and any weakening of that control obviously weakens the organization and enhances the power of the party candidates and the party in government. Their ability, especially as incumbents, to defy the organization's wrath and to win primary battles frees them from its discipline and, indeed, often calls them to positions of party leadership. In fact, the inability of party organization in the United States to control the party in government (as it does in so many other democracies) begins with the failure to control the nominations and to assure thereby that the party in government is recruited from the organization's ranks and thus from the ranks of partisans who share the goals of the organization and accept its discipline.[28] Failure to control nominations, therefore, weakens the party organization vis-à-vis the party in government, and at the same time it deprives the party of a meaningful activity on which the energies and aspirations of its activists might focus.

The concern of the Progressives and the other proponents of the primary was with extra-organizational controls over party nominations and with controlling the elites of the party organization. With the primary they created divisive forces within the party and thwarted the organization's quest for its own goals. Rather than achieve any real mass control of party nominations, they largely moved control from the elites of the organization to the elites of the party in government. They succeeded in multiplying the party oligarchies rather than democratizing them.

Finally, the direct primary has buttressed the prevailing decentralization of power in the American parties. So long as the candidates or incumbents can appeal to a majority of local primary voters, they are free from the control and discipline of a state or national party. Even so powerful a President as Franklin Roosevelt in 1938 met his greatest political defeat in trying to purge a number of Democratic senators and representatives in their local Democratic primaries; only one of his conservative targets was defeated. The primary plays on local loyalties and appeals to the local electorate, and the vast number of them are more than difficult for a centralized party organization to control.

If the advocates of the direct primary did indeed want to strike beyond

[28] Leo Snowiss notes differences in the ideologies, the voting records, the political ethos, and the party loyalty of congressmen nominated under various degrees of party organization control; "Congressional Recruitment and Representation," *American Political Science Review*, LX (1966), pp. 627–639.

the nomination process and hit the parties themselves, they found their target. The direct primary has in many instances weakened the parties' control of nominations, robbed their organizations of an important *raison d'etre*, and liberated their office-holders. It has in many important ways made the American political parties what they are today.

Chapter Ten

THE CAMPAIGN
FOR ELECTION

It used to be, in the old days when I went around the state with my grand-father, that what you needed to get elected to office was a big cigar, a shadbelly vest, and a constitution that permitted you to stand out in the hot July sun and talk for two and a half or three hours. Well, that day is gone. There is a new way of communicating with people and that is television.[1]

So observes Senator Thruston B. Morton, a Republican of Kentucky and former chairman of the Republican National Committee.

One observation neither makes nor documents a trend, but one could assemble many others to testify to the advent in American electoral politics of the mass communications media and their specialists in polling, advertising, and public relations. Not so long ago, for instance, a headline for an ad in the Los Angeles *Daily Journal*, a legal newspaper widely read by lawyers of the area, promised "You Can Be Elected State Senator." There then followed the announcement that a "Leading public relations firm with top-flight experience in state-wide campaigns wants state senator candidate." The advertising firm in question, Public Relations Center, and its affiliate, the Western Opinion Research Center, specialize in managing state and local campaigns in the volatile politics of Southern California. Its campaign strategy is generally simple: keep the candidate out of the public eye as much as possible and publicize his name with a "catchy" slogan or phrase.[2]

At the same time that the importance of the new communications media and their associated specialists is on the rise, a number of observ-

[1] *The New York Times*, July 16, 1967.
[2] *Ibid.*, January 6, 1966.

ers have noted the related decline of the party organization as the major planner and executor of campaigns. As one very urbane former candidate has put it: [3]

> With mass media which use a common language that everyone can read, people no longer need party workers to advise them how to vote. When a citizen can see and hear the candidate on a screen at home, and read news, written by the best journalists from a variety of points of view, about the candidate's public and private life, he does not heed what is told him by the precinct captain on his block. The media have done to the campaign system what the invention of accurate artillery did to the feudal kingdom — destroyed the barons and shifted their power to the masses and the prince. A candidate now pays less attention to district leaders than to opinion polls.

The argument, briefly, is that the party organization has become technologically obsolete — that it has been superseded by newer, more efficient, and more timely avenues and techniques of campaigning. Thus, the argument goes, the party organization has lost an important measure of control over the contesting of American elections and, ultimately, over its candidates elected to public office.

It is easy to exaggerate and even romanticize the days of machine-controlled campaigns. It is just as easy to overgeneralize about new trends in American campaigning even on the basis of a large number of reports, for it is the spectacular and the innovative which wins reports in newspapers and journals. And even if one concedes some degree of change, it is not necessarily true that the new men of the media have become masters rather than servants of the new campaigning. All of these reservations aside, however, some important innovations are clearly under way, and they threaten to affect the American parties profoundly. The new campaign skills are freely available to whoever can afford them, and they can easily, therefore, serve individuals and organizations who would like to diminish the control of the party organizations over the contesting of American elections.

The politics of the campaign for public office, however, takes place within a limiting context of legal regulation and definition. Prior to a discussion of the politics of campaigning and changes in it, therefore, it is necessary to discuss the shape of the electoral process itself. The strategies of the electoral game make sense only if one first understands the game itself.

THE ELECTORAL INSTITUTIONS

The legal framework which defines American elections also defines the "rules of the game" within which the parties and other political organiza-

---

[3] Stimson Bullitt, *To Be a Politician* (New York: Anchor, 1961), p. 65.

tions contest for public office. Each aspect of that framework, each rule of the game, places a strategic limitation on the campaign. The framework is not, therefore, a neutral or objective influence in the campaign and election, and each adjustment in any one of the "rules" may affect one party or candidate more than another.

Political parties around the world have not been slow or reticent in realizing the possible advantages to be gained by a careful, selective tinkering with election law, and the major American parties have been no exception. Yet, the American tinkerings have more generally been with the size and shape of the electoral districts; "gerrymandering" is a peculiarly American art form. The rest of the American electoral rules have remained surprisingly stable, even though they have been complicated by the usual state-to-state variations. The kind of repeated electoral tinkerings common in Europe in this century — the shiftings to systems of proportional representation and back again, and the experiments with second, run-off elections, for instance — have not been common here. The American parties have generally been content to make only changes which would make political life difficult for the third parties.

THE SECRET BALLOT

The American ballot is now uniformly secret, but it was not always so. Until the late 19th century the oral vote was common in many states and jurisdictions; the voter simply stated to electoral officials which of the candidates he preferred. During the 19th century it was gradually replaced by ballots printed by the parties or candidates. The voter brought the ballot of his candidate or party to the polling place and deposited it in the box. Since the ballots were by no means identical, his vote was often apparent to observers. Ballot reformers argued for the secret ballot as a way of curbing election corruption, especially vote buying; with the secret ballot, at least, the corrupter could never be sure the vote would be delivered. The secret ballot, named the Australian ballot after the country of its origin, quickly swept the day. By the beginning of the 20th century its success was complete, and it remains the status quo today. It is a ballot printed at public expense by public authorities, and it lists all candidates for office on its single, consolidated form. It is distributed only at the polling places and only to bona fide voters who then mark it in the seclusion of a voting booth.

Increasingly, especially in larger American cities, the voting machine is replacing the paper ballot. It does not, however, alter the basic form and premises of the Australian ballot. Only the mechanics of voting are different. The voter faces the machine within a small, draped enclosure and votes by moving levers next to the names of candidates or parties he chooses. These voters are formally recorded by the pull of a master lever which at the same time moves the levers back to neutral positions and opens the drapery for him to leave. Its advantages, so its makers assert, are its long-run economies in reducing election costs and its speed and accuracy in counting votes. It also thwarts certain forms of ballot box stuffing and dishonest counts. But technology never builds the perfect mouse-trap or voting machine, and innovation continues. When the computerized telephone capable of sending messages is perfected, voters may very well cast their votes by dialing a polling place and casting their votes by means of sensitized registration cards.

FORMS OF BALLOTS

The ballots in use in the United States fall into two main types. In about twenty states one finds the *office block* ballot on which the names of the candidates are grouped by the offices they seek (Figure 1). In the majority of states the *party column* ballot prevails; it is so named because the candidates of each party are grouped in vertical columns and by office only in horizontal rows (Figure 1). In other words, only in the party column ballot are the candidates of each party grouped so that the voter can visualize and perceive them as a "party ticket." By their very nature, of course, non-partisan elections employ the office block ballot.

All evidence indicates that the parties are correct in their belief that the party column ballot encourages and facilitates straight-ticket voting (i.e., voting for all of a party's candidates for all the offices being filled at the election). But the matter of straight-ticket voting also hinges on the presence or absence on the ballot of a single square or circle (or a single lever on machines) by which the voter can, in one fell swoop, cast his vote for the entire ticket. They are more commonly employed on party column ballots, but some states such as Pennsylvania combine them with the office block ballot (Figure 1). Then, it would seem, the ballot forms could be put into a diminishing scale of assistance to straight-ticket voting:

1. party column ballot with party circle or square
2. office block ballot with party circle or square
3. party column ballot without party circle or square
4. office block ballot without party circle or square.

The format of the ballot can in this and in other ways affect the way the voter sees the electoral contest and the nature of his own choices in it.

Two other aspects of ballot form deserve mention. Almost every ballot provides in some way for the insertion of "write-in" candidates, names not on the ballot. But the success of write-in candidates is so rare and unlikely that it is hardly a real question in American politics. Senator J. Strom Thurmond of South Carolina was, to be sure, elected initially in 1954 as a write-in candidate, but one political scientist has referred to that election as "one of the seven wonders of American politics," noting that "nothing of the sort had ever happened before in the history of the country." [4] Secondly, the order in which names of candidates appear in the office groupings on office block ballots may affect the outcome of the election. American voters have shown a notorious disposition to vote for the first name on a list of candidates.[5] The states differ in their responses to the issue of "who's on first"; some ask the candidates to draw lots for ballot position, others give the incumbent and the other majority party candidate the first and second places, and still others list names alphabetically. Perhaps the most equitable solution is the policy of rotating the names; if there are two candidates, for example, each will occupy the first position on 50 per cent of the ballots.

Finally, the American ballot is and has always been a "long ballot." Its length, to be sure, cannot be controlled by electoral or ballot law. It reflects the American tradition of electing (rather than appointing) a great number of state and local officials — judges, coroners, surveyors, sheriffs, jury commissioners, superintendents of public instruction, assessors, public utilities commissioners, clerks of the courts, party committeemen, and auditors and comptrollers. The one observable effect of the long ballot, especially in the office block form, has been a noticeable voter fatigue.[6] Many voters, either tiring or despairing, do not vote in contests at the bottom of the ballot. Partial voting (drop-off) of this sort can be high as 20 or 30 per cent of the voters at a given election.

STRUCTURE AND RULES OF THE CHOICE

Overwhelmingly, American elections are governed by the twin principles of single-member constituencies and plurality election. In other words, we elect only one man per constituency to a city council, to the House or Senate, to the local mayoralty. And the man who gets the most votes, even if it is not the majority of 50 per cent plus one, is elected. Even in those cases of multi-member districts — two-, three-, or four-man state legislative districts or at-large elections of local councils or commissions [7] — the principle is not altered. One casts the same number of votes as there are men to be elected from the district, and the plurality principle still governs. In a two-man state legislative district, for example, each

---

[4] William Goodman, *The Two-Party System in the United States*, 3rd ed. (Princeton: Van Nostrand, 1964), p. 440.

[5] Donald S. Hecock and Henry M. Bain, *The Arrangement of Names on the Ballot and Its Effect on the Voter's Choice* (Detroit: Wayne State Univ. Press, 1956).

[6] Jack L. Walker, "Ballot Forms and Voter Fatigue: An Analysis of the Office Block and Party Column Ballots," *Midwest Journal of Political Science*, X (1966), pp. 448–463.

[7] Maurice Klain has indicated that American state legislatures have far more multi-member constituencies than most of us would suspect; see his "A New Look at the Constituencies: The Need for a Recount and a Reappraisal," *American Political Science Review*, XLIX (1955), pp. 1105–1119.

Figure 1

EXAMPLES OF PARTY COLUMN AND OFFICE BLOCK BALLOTS:
WASHINGTON AND PENNSYLVANIA

A — PARTY COLUMN BALLOT: WASHINGTON

REPUBLICAN PARTY	DEMOCRATIC PARTY	OTHER PARTY
PRESIDENT AND VICE PRESIDENT (Name of candidate) } (Name of candidate) } ☐	PRESIDENT AND VICE PRESIDENT (Name of candidate) } (Name of candidate) } ☐	
UNITED STATES SENATOR (Name of candidate) ☐	UNITED STATES SENATOR (Name of candidate) ☐	
REPRESENTATIVE IN CONGRESS 3rd Congressional District (Name of candidate) ☐	REPRESENTATIVE IN CONGRESS 3rd Congressional District (Name of candidate) ☐	
GOVERNOR (Name of candidate) ☐	GOVERNOR (Name of candidate) ☐	
LIEUTENANT GOVERNOR (Name of candidate) ☐	LIEUTENANT GOVERNOR (Name of candidate) ☐	

REPUBLICAN PARTY	DEMOCRATIC PARTY	OTHER PARTY
SECRETARY OF STATE (Name of candidate) ☐	SECRETARY OF STATE (Name of candidate) ☐	
STATE TREASURER (Name of candidate) ☐	STATE TREASURER (Name of candidate) ☐	
STATE AUDITOR (Name of candidate) ☐	STATE AUDITOR (Name of candidate) ☐	
ATTORNEY GENERAL (Name of candidate) ☐	ATTORNEY GENERAL (Name of candidate) ☐	
COMMISSIONER OF PUBLIC LANDS (Name of candidate) ☐	COMMISSIONER OF PUBLIC LANDS (Name of candidate) ☐	
INSURANCE COMMISSIONER (Name of candidate) ☐	INSURANCE COMMISSIONER (Name of candidate) ☐	
STATE SENATOR (1st District) (Name of candidate) ☐	STATE SENATOR (1st District) (Name of candidate) ☐	
STATE REPRESENTATIVE (31st District) Position No. 1 (Name of candidate) ☐	STATE REPRESENTATIVE (31st District) Position No. 1 (Name of candidate) ☐	
STATE REPRESENTATIVE (31st District) Position No. 2 (Name of candidate) ☐	STATE REPRESENTATIVE (31st District) Position No. 2 (Name of candidate) ☐	
STATE REPRESENTATIVE (31st District) Position No. 3 (Name of candidate) ☐	STATE REPRESENTATIVE (31st District) Position No. 3 (Name of candidate) ☐	

(Names of other candidates should follow on the ballot in same form.)

B — OFFICE BLOCK BALLOT: PENNSYLVANIA

General Election Held on the 8th Day of November, 1955

To vote a straight party ticket mark a cross (X) in the square, in the Party Column opposite the name of the party of your choice.

A cross mark in the square opposite the name of any candidate indicates a vote for that candidate.

To vote for person whose name is not on the ballot, write or paste his or her name in the blank space provided for that purpose. This shall count as a vote without the cross mark.

To vote for an individual candidate of another party after making a mark in the party square, mark a cross (X) opposite his or her name.

For an office where more than one candidate is to be elected, the voter, after marking in the party square, may divide his or her vote by making a cross (X) to the right of each candidate for whom he or she desires to vote. For such office votes shall not be counted for candidates not individually marked.

If you make a mistake, do not erase. Ask for a new ballot. Use only pencil or indelible pencil.

Party Column

To Vote a Straight Party Ticket,
Mark a Cross (x) in this Column

DEMOCRATIC	
REPUBLICAN	X

Sheriff
(Vote for One)

Robert C. Hartley	Democratic	
Martin L. Kauffmann	Republican	

Prothonotary
(Vote for One)

Maurice F. Kelly	Democratic	
Arthur C. Barraclough	Republican	

Treasurer
(Vote for One)

William J. Moerschbacher	Democratic	
Edward R. Miller	Republican	

Register of Wills & Clerk of The Orphans Court
(Vote for One)

Charles F. Hipple	Democratic	
Harry R. Burd	Republican	

Recorder of Deeds
(Vote for One)

John W. Mills	Democratic	
E. K. Hibshman	Republican	

County Commissioners
(Vote for Two)

George H. McCormick	Democratic	
Jay Robinson	Democratic	
Harry V. Keeler	Republican	
O. P. McCord	Republican	

Coroner
(Vote for One)

Dr. Charles J. Cullen	Democratic	
Dr. Charles J. Cullen	Republican	

County Auditor
(Vote for Two)

Boyd E. Hazel	Democratic	
Harry C. Meyer	Democratic	
Howard M. Miles	Republican	
J. Thomas Mitchell	Republican	

County Surveyor
(Vote for One)

J. Thompson Henry	Democratic	
J. Thompson Henry	Republican	

voter casts two votes; the two candidates with the greatest number of votes (i.e., the plurality) are the winners. The effect is little different from a single-member district.

The American states have, therefore, experimented scarcely at all with the systems of proportional representation that so often enchant the other democracies of the world. In proportional representation systems — which are of necessity based on multi-member constituencies — the voter casts his vote for a party slate of candidates. The parties then share the seats according to the percentage of the votes they polled. In a five-man legislative district, for example:

Party A — 60% of vote — 3 seats
Party B — 23% of vote — 1 seat
Party C — 17% of vote — 1 seat
100%   5 seats

The possible combinations and modifications are virtually limitless in p.r. systems, but those endless complexities need not concern us here.[8] What is important is the political result of proportional representation schemes of any form. They encourage smaller, minor political parties by giving them a share of the elective offices. Ten or 20 per cent of the vote will rarely win any public offices in the plurality elections of American politics, but in the Fourth Republic of post-war France (1946–1958) it won parliamentary seats and cabinet positions for a number of parties. Secondly, proportional representation strengthens the hand of the party vis-à-vis its candidates. In strict party list systems, especially, the party fixes the order of the party list. To return to the above illustration of the five-man district under simple p.r., the leadership of Parties A, B, and C draw up the party list of five candidates. By placing a man first on the party list the leaders of a party virtually place him in public office; by placing him fifth on the party list they consign him to defeat. The prevailing single-member, plurality structure of American elections, on the contrary, reinforces both the two-party system and the independence of candidates and office-holders.

In a few instances, however, American states and localities have experimented with more-or-less exotic electoral systems. New York City adopted a system of proportional representation from 1938 to 1947, with a resulting growth and representation of minor political parties (Table 1). It was abandoned in 1947 after tension with the Soviet Union made the representation of the local Communist party increasingly intolerable for many New Yorkers.[9] Perhaps the classic case of statewide electoral exoticism

---

[8] For an excursion into some of the complexities, see Wolfgang Birke, *European Elections by Direct Suffrage* (Leyden, Netherlands: Sythoff, 1961).

[9] Belle Zeller and Hugh A. Bone, "The Repeal of Proportional Representation in New York City — Ten Years in Retrospect," *American Political Science Review*, XLII (1948), pp. 1127–1148. The data of Table 1 come from this article, too.

Table 1

THE EFFECTS OF PROPORTIONAL REPRESENTATION IN THE
NEW YORK CITY COUNCIL ELECTIONS: 1945 *

Party	Percentage of Vote	Council Seats
Democratic	59%	14 (61%)
Republican	15	3 (13%)
American Labor	10	2 (9%)
Communist	9	2 (9%)
Liberal	7	2 (9%)
	100%	23

* Source: see footnote 9.

has been Illinois' cumulative voting system. Since 1870 the lower house
of the Illinois legislature has been elected from three-man constituencies.
In order to facilitate representation of the minority party (of the two
major parties), the voter is permitted to cast his three votes in any one of
four different ways: all three for one candidate, one and a half for each of
two, one for each of three, and two for one and one for another. Party
committees in each of the constituencies determine before the election
(and the primary) whether the party in the district will offer one, two, or
three candidates for the three seats. They often·decide to contest only a
total of three seats (one party offers two candidates and the other party
only one), leaving the voters of the district no choice in the general election. The nature of the choices in the system, in other words, has encouraged the parties to adopt cautious, minimizing strategies that, in effect,
reduce competition between the two parties in the name of securing
representation for both of them.[10]

THE DATE OF THE ELECTION

Congress chose in 1845 to use its constitutional power to determine the
dates of presidential and congressional elections (Art. I, sec. 4; Art. II,
sec. 1). It provided that all states would select their presidential electors
on the first Tuesday after the first Monday of November; at the same
time it also provided that the same date be used for electing members of
Congress unless the state constitution provided otherwise. For many years
Maine chose to hold congressional elections in September, but all fifty
states now use the November date. Since considerations of economy dictate that the states hold state and local elections at the same time, they

[10] George S. Blair, *Cumulative Voting* (Urbana: Univ. of Illinois Press, 1960). On the
strategic possibilities, see Jack Sawyer and Duncan MacRae, Jr., "Game Theory and
Cumulative Voting in Illinois: 1902–1954," *American Political Science Review*, LVI
(1962), pp. 936–946.

have widely accepted the same date. So, uniformity in election date prevails, even though that date in this increasingly urban and industrial country is the one chosen originally to follow the fall harvests. No such uniformity on primary dates exists, however. Some come in April and May, some not until September. Consequently, the total campaign for public office may be six months or more in some states but only two or less in others.

ELECTION DAY

The states and localities set the hours and places of elections. In most communities the polls remain open for about twelve or thirteen hours; they open usually between six and eight o'clock in the morning and close at seven, eight, or nine o'clock in the evening. The polls usually are located in some public building — a school, a firehouse, a city hall — although they may be found in barbershops, auto showrooms, and private homes in some communities.

In each voting district, usually called the precinct, the administration of the polling place is in the hands of a group of publicly appointed judges, inspectors, or commissioners, as they are variously called. They check the voter's registration, give him ballots or see him into the voting machine, and make sure his vote is cast. Often they remain after the polls have closed to count the ballots, although centralized counting exists in some jurisdictions. The parties or candidates usually have the right to appoint poll watchers to oversee the administration of the balloting and the counting of the ballots.

Voting machines, of course, greatly facilitate the counting of ballots. Final totals are simply read off of a set of dials in the back. But in many precincts the job is still a laborious one often extending into the small hours of the morning. Weary polling officials must (often after twelve hours of work at the polls) decipher unclear marks and apply the often-complicated state law on what constitutes an invalid ballot. Does, for example, a check mark suffice as a substitute for an "X"?; in some states it does, and in some it does not. In a few close cases the count may be challenged, and a partial or total recounting of the ballots may result. The 1962 Minnesota gubernatorial election was in doubt for four months while a special three-man court supervised bi-partisan counting officials in a recount of every paper ballot cast in the state. The Democratic candidate, Karl Rolvaag, finally emerged a 91-vote winner. That and other recounts have testified to three conclusions about the marking and counting of ballots. There has been little or no dishonesty documented, first of all. Secondly, honest errors in counting and recording do occur; 10's become 100's, digits are inverted, the two parties' totals are reversed, for example. Thirdly, a significant number of voters do not correctly mark a ballot. In the 1962 election in Minnesota, for example, 389 voters voted invalidly for two candidates for governor, more than enough to decide the outcome that hinged on 91 votes.[11]

ABSENTEE VOTING

All states except New Mexico and South Carolina have some provision for voting by people unable to come to the polls because of illness, travel, service in the armed forces, studies or an occupation that take them away from home. There is, however, little uniformity in the details of the provisions for absentee voting. Some states permit it only for specific reasons, some permit it only for certain elections, and some permit it only if the person has left the boundaries of the state. The major controversial issue in the vote for absentees has concerned pressures on Congress to insure the serviceman's right to an absentee ballot in the face of the reluctance of some states to provide one. After a more forceful stand during World War II, in which it ordered the states to provide servicemen with absentee ballots for presidential and congressional elections, Congress now merely requests the states to permit servicemen to vote.

THE POLITICAL CONSEQUENCES OF ELECTORAL LAW

Perhaps the broadest impact of American political institutions on the politics of campaigning has been a focusing of attention on the candidates rather than the parties. The American electoral process is relatively free from institutions such as parliamentary-cabinet government or proportional representation that encourage the voter to see the contest between candidates in terms of the greater fortunes and future of their political parties. Non-partisan elections have in the United States even further reduced the visibility of the party in elections. Even such details of electoral law as the designating of incumbents on the ballot and the office block ballot itself tend to structure the electoral choice as a series of contests between individual candidates and not as a single, multi-faceted campaign between two great parties.

More specifically, the individual aspects of the electoral system are, therefore, only in part matters of efficiency or "good government," of carrying out democratic norms or of protecting against vote frauds. They carry grave and important consequences for the parties and for campaign politics in general. They may, in the first place, affect the voting behavior of the electorate:

All evidence suggests that the office block ballot does discourage *straight-ticket voting* and that the party column ballot does encourage

11 On recounts, see Ronald F. Stinnett and Charles H. Backstrom, *Recount* (Washington: National Document Publishers, 1964); Samuel J. Eldersveld and A. A. Applegate, *Michigan's Recounts for Governor, 1950 and 1952: A Systematic Analysis of Election Error* (Ann Arbor: Univ. of Michigan Press, 1954).

it.[12] So, too, will other electoral details, such as the presence of a party circle or square on the ballot.

Voter fatigue (or "roll-off"), the tendency to vote in only some of the contests on the ballot, appears to be in large part a result of the ballot itself; it is greater in areas using the office block ballot, and it tends to be greater the longer the ballot. The arrangement of the face of the voting machine will also affect it. Recent studies in the Minneapolis area show, for example, that in those eighteen communities with voting machines in the election of November, 1966, only between 33.9 and 78.3 per cent of the voters voted on a constitutional amendment up for ratification; but in seventeen communities with paper ballots the percentages varied between 92.2 and 100. (Since under the Minnesota constitution, the amendment had to be ratified by a majority of all people voting at the election, the effect of the "roll-off" vote was the same as a "no" vote.) [13]

To a great extent every ballot form discourages *write-in voting,* but some discourage it more than others. Generally it is especially difficult on voting machines, but even so small a detail as whether or not the state permits the attaching of stickers as a way of writing-in a candidate's name may be significant.

That such impacts on voting behavior clearly affect the parties and campaign strategies should require no more than to say that they alter and shape the voting responses of the electorates to which the parties and their candidates must appeal.

The impact of the electoral system, however, may fall more directly on the parties and campaign strategy. The states may limit the access of minor parties and their candidates to the ballot by requiring them to file petitions with large numbers of signatures. Electoral systems such as Illinois' cumulative voting, rare though they may be in the United States, drastically alter the nature of the campaign and choices in it; that particular system has, paradoxically, increased the party role in the election by forcing it to decide what number of the three seats in the constituency to contest while at the same time effectively reducing the amount of two-party competition. Even ordinary multi-member constituencies invite a party of limited strength to concentrate its voting strength on a single candidate by voting for him and no other candidate (a practice widely referred to as "bullet voting").

Furthermore, the facts and changes in American electoral law often do not touch the parties or candidates equally. If voting machines do confuse less well-educated, lower SES voters, and if office block ballots encourage greater voter fatigue ("roll-off") among less well-educated voters,[14] then

---

[12] Campbell, *et al., The American Voter* (New York: Wiley, 1960), p. 276.

[13] *The Minneapolis Star,* April 11, 1967; the story reports research findings by the Citizens' League of Hennepin and Ramsey Counties.

[14] Jack L. Walker, *op. cit.,* makes the latter point.

the disadvantages may accrue unevenly to the Democratic party which draws a larger share of its loyal electorate from those groups. And if the state refuses absentee ballots to students away at college or businessmen away on business, the disadvantages may well strike mainly the Republicans. Any ballot form which facilitates party ticket voting works to the advantage of the majority party in the constituency. And prime ballot position will help the incumbent and the majority party; so will designations of incumbency printed on the ballot. Even the hours and places for polling may have some marginal benefits for one party or the other.

Just how aware the parties and state legislators are of such possible advantages in refining electoral law is not easy to say. It is always difficult to establish the motives of legislators, especially when those motives might not be of the highest. But occasionally an attempt is just too persistent, too transparent, not to suggest the motives of party or political advantage. Jack L. Walker, for example, comments on Ohio's continuing development of the ballot form: [15]

In the state of Ohio the ballot has been changed six times during the twentieth century, and in each case the Republican majority tried to gain an advantage for itself by tampering with the election machinery. In 1940 Governor Bricker tried to avoid the influence of F.D.R.'s "coattails" by calling a special session of the legislature which approved a separation of the ballot carrying national races from the one on which state and local races appeared. Bricker reasoned that if a normally Republican voter who was determined to vote for Roosevelt had to use a second ballot in state races he would be less likely to vote a straight Democratic ticket (the ballots were later consolidated once again to capitalize on Eisenhower's coattails). In 1949 over $85,000 was spent in a campaign to substitute the Office Block ballot for the Party Column ballot in an effort to save Senator Robert Taft from defeat in the bitter 1950 election. . . . The Taft forces thought that by eliminating the party lever they would substantially reduce the number of straight Democratic votes and thus increase the Senator's chances among normally Democratic, working class voters. Key quotes Taft as claiming that the change "was responsible 'for something between 100,000 and 200,000' of his total majority of 430,000."

Doubtless, Democrats have acted similarly when and where the opportunity presented itself elsewhere.

Finally, in one way above all — the drawing of constituency lines — the American parties have tried repeatedly to steal an advantage in electoral politics. The general tactics have traditionally been two: constituencies of unequal populations and "gerrymandered" districts. The first and more obvious of the two, the districts of unequal populations, simply involves "stretching" the popular vote of the majority party by putting fewer people in districts in its strongholds than in the districts located in the other party's areas of strength. In the past the heavily populated districts were usually in urban areas, working to the disadvantage of Republicans in

[15] *Ibid.*, pp. 448–449.

the South and Democrats elsewhere. More recently, however, the new suburban and urban fringe areas, areas generally of Republican strength, have become the major underrepresented areas. The Supreme Court has, however, since 1962 cast an increasingly suspicious eye on unequal districts, and as it applies its "one man, one vote" rule to constituencies of all varieties, it closes off an indigenously American way of exploiting the rules of the electoral game.[16]

More subtle and less easy to detect, the gerrymander survives unimpaired. It consists of one party's drawing district lines in such a way as to use its own popular vote most efficiently while forcing the other party to use its vote inefficiently. That goal can be achieved in one of two ways: either by dividing and diluting pockets of the other party's strength to prevent it from winning offices, or (if its vote strength is too great for dilution) by bunching its strength into a few districts and forcing it to win elections by large and wasteful majorities. Frequently, but not always, the resulting constituencies, rather than being compact and contiguous, have been tortured into erratic, literally fantastic shapes. (The very term "gerrymander" was coined in the early years of the republic to describe a salamander-shaped congressional district drawn in Massachusetts when Elbridge Gerry was governor.) The gerrymander, of course, works to the advantage of the legislating party; it is that purpose which defines it. Which party reaps the advantage depends entirely on which party controls the legislature drawing the district lines.[17]

CAMPAIGN STRATEGY AND TACTICS

The folk wisdom about all aspects of American politics is more than ample, but in the one area of campaign tactics it is overwhelming. Much of it has been brought together into little books on campaigning which read like modern "how-to-do-it" manuals.[18] Since many of the recent books have been written by advertising and public relations specialists, much of their wisdom has a modern tone. The candidate is beseeched to powder his beard before a TV performance and to dwell on short and catchy phrases. He is warned not to seem academic or professorial; his handshake should be firm but not pulverizing.

There is much of value in the assorted, received wisdom about Ameri-

[16] See, especially on the political ramifications of apportionment, Malcolm E. Jewell (ed.), *The Politics of Reapportionment* (New York: Atherton, 1962).

[17] For an objective measurement of these characteristics of gerrymandered districts, see Ernest C. Reock, Jr., "Measuring Compactness as a Requirement of Legislative Apportionment," *Midwest Journal of Political Science*, V (1961), pp. 70–74.

[18] For examples of books on how to win office, see Frank R. Kent, *Political Behavior* (New York: Morrow, 1928); Maurice McCaffrey, *Advertising Wins Elections* (Minneapolis: Gilbert, 1962); and Paul Allyn and Joseph Greene, *See How They Run* (Philadelphia: Chilton, 1964).

can campaigning. Generally it represents the distillation of concrete experience. And yet it suffers from two deficiencies which are themselves
general warnings on the subject of the arts and crafts of political campaigning. The conventional wisdom seems to suggest, first of all, that most
political campaigns are run on a master battle plan adhered to with
almost military discipline and precision. In reality most American political
campaigns lurch along from one improvisation to another, from one immediate crisis to another. They are frequently underorganized, under-
planned, and undermanned — and consequently, often "played by ear" on
a surprising lack of information.

The folk wisdom would also suggest that there are principles of good
campaigning that have an almost universal applicability. In truth, however, optimum campaign strategy depends on a great number of variables,
and the only general rule is that there is no general rule. Strategy will
vary with:

the skills of the candidate: does he project on television, how does he
handle a press conference or an informal coffee hour?

the nature of the constituency: campaigning will differ if it is several
square miles of urban slum rather than 30,000 square miles of prairie.

the office being sought: a candidate for a judgeship must conduct a far
more restrained campaign than one seeking election to a city council.

the nature of the electoral system: is the ballot partisan or non-partisan,
the general election two or six months after the primary?

the party organizations in the constituency; to what extent can their
organized resources be counted on and what can they do?

the availability of political resources: how much manpower, skills, and
money will be available and when?

the nature of the electorate: what are their political norms, their party
loyalties, their perception of issues and candidates?

There are, of course, others. But the chief early task of campaign strategists remains the sober evaluation of these variables and the consequent
demands and limits they place on the nature of the campaign.

The two crucial steps in campaign strategy involve the gathering of information about the setting of the campaign (i.e., the variables above) and
the adapting of campaign techniques and tactics to the electoral setting.
Within the past generation great changes amounting to a revolution in
American political campaigning have reoriented each step. New sources
and methods for gathering political information and new techniques of
campaigning have, indeed, modified and streamlined much of the old wisdom of American politics and modified as well the role of the parties in
the campaigning. At the base of these changes lie modern communica-

tions skills and the related arts of public relations, advertising, and opinion research.

NEW KNOWLEDGE

The development of modern social science has opened up new sources of information and knowledge to the candidate. Data processing systems permit a party to keep records about constituencies or to process that information rapidly — although very few avail themselves of the opportunities. Carefully kept records will usually yield a faster and more accurate answer to "how the 21st ward went four years ago" than will even the most conscientious party committeeman. Then, too, scholars are building a body of systematic knowledge about the voting behavior of the American electorate — wily parties and candidates have, for instance, found especially valuable the data on the demographic bases of Republican and Democratic strength. The campaign managers of John F. Kennedy's presidential campaign, for example, commissioned a simulation of the 1960 electorate as an aid to campaign planning. The simulation attempted, with the aid of computers, to coordinate and correlate knowledge about the American electorate and to project the effects which various events of the campaign might have on it.[19]

No new avenue to political knowledge has, however, been more fully exploited than the public opinion poll. It may be employed at the beginning of a campaign to assess the political issues uppermost in the minds of voters. Questions about leading public issues, about awareness of current problems, or just about what issues the voter thinks or worries about will yield information about which themes the candidates should develop for greatest effectiveness. Early polls can also develop "candidate profiles," information about the way the voting public views the two opponents. If it develops that many voters think a candidate too bookish or intellectual, he may be sent to plowing contests, athletic events, or a weekend fishing trip. Polls can also indicate whether the campaign ought to capitalize on party loyalties or whether the candidate would be better advised to divorce himself from an unpopular party or a President or gubernatorial candidate at the top of the ticket. During the campaign a poll or two can chart its progress and impact; it may also indicate where time and resources ought to be concentrated in the waning days of the campaign.

Parties and candidates have not been uniformly willing to avail themselves of such new techniques. For one thing, much of the knowledge, especially of voting behavior, thus far accumulated derives chiefly from presidential campaigns and elections and has only limited applicability

[19] Described in Ithiel de Sola Pool, Robert P. Abelson, and Samuel Popkin, *Candidate, Issues, and Strategies* (Cambridge: MIT Press, 1964). A fictionalized version can be found in Eugene Burdick, *The 480* (New York: McGraw Hill, 1964).

to local elections. Much of it, too, would be beyond the resources of many local campaigns. But the difficulty runs deeper. American political campaigns, despite popular impressions to the contrary, have rarely been run on a solid base of information. Thousands of party organizations around the country do not and never have kept even their basic voting data by precincts, wards, townships, cities, and counties. Frequently, what passed and what passes for such information are the hazy impressions of a few party officials. So, such a shift to the "new knowledge" would involve a basic commitment to knowledge itself, as well as to diverting the resources which knowledge costs in money and manpower. But statewide campaigns — and even some local ones — have increasingly moved toward a more systematic gathering of information about the campaign task and situation. In at least one recent set of congressional campaigns, for example, the AFL-CIO's Committee on Political Education put the polling services of Louis Harris at the disposal of selected congressional candidates for pre-campaign polling on issues and candidates.

THE NEW TECHNIQUES

Campaigns are basically exercises in mass persuasion, and increasingly the commercial arts of persuasion have been applied to them. There was a time when strong party organizations were available as the great persuaders in American campaigns, but changes in them and in American politics have diminished that role. Party organizations, even where they continue in something like the form of earlier days, do not "control" votes and turn them out as they once did. Nor have they been quick to pick up new campaign and communication skills. Into the vacuum have come skilled candidates, their advisors and personal staffs, and even public relations firms specializing in the management of political campaigns in the "new style." [20]

Predominant among the new techniques has been the increasing role of the mass communications media. Frequently now a candidate takes the time and effort to address a rally or meeting largely in the hope that it will produce a news report or a brief film clip on the local TV news. (Of course, the question of whether it produces a news report is not left to chance; the staff prepares news releases and copies of the speech for the local papers and other news media.) But often candidates have to buy their time and space in the media. Early in the campaign candidates may vie to commit choice TV time and billboard space for the concluding weeks of the campaign. And as the campaign progresses the candidates' faces, names and slogans blossom on billboards, newspaper ads, radio and TV spot announcements — even on lawn signs, the bumpers of automo-

[20] The early success of one of them, California's Whittaker and Baxter, is told in Stanley Kelley, *Professional Public Relations and Political Power* (Baltimore: Johns Hopkins Press, 1956).

biles, and construction fences. Full TV or radio coverage of a speech is in
most instances an extravagant waste of money, but candidates may take
longer media time for talkathons or "open mike" shows in which they
answer the questions and challenges of all comers.

The new campaign techniques also involve the new arts of communication. Their impact may be no more revolutionary than a new haircut and
suit of clothes for the candidate, or a Dale Carnegie course for the cam-
paigner. But it may also involve a new awareness of audience limits and
propensities, a new sensitivity to "communicating" with the semi-political
men and women in the electorate. The search for an appropriate theme,
slogan, or issue goes on more systematically than before; in this regard,
the problem is not greatly different from that of launching an advertising
campaign for a commercial product. The emphasis is on simplicity in the
campaign: a few themes, brief speeches, uncluttered (and often uncom-
municative) ads, quick and punchy spot commercials.

Nelson Rockefeller's race for reelection as governor of New York in
1966 may well have been the archetype of the "new" campaign. Aided by
jets and helicopters, the candidate visited all 62 counties of the state. He
retained a New York advertising agency which has built its reputation on
an ability to "restore" or "rehabilitate" products and clients (it had re-
furbished Braniff Airlines by putting an end to the "plain plane.") The
Rockefeller campaign, furthermore, was variously described as having
put between 3,000 and 4,000 TV commercials on the stations of the state.
In all of these plans and logistics the Governor was aided by a staff of
some 300. To be sure, there were the traditional bouts of handshaking and
the traditional pictures of the candidate eating blintzes on New York
City's Lower East Side, but something relatively new had clearly been
added to the old.

All of this is not to argue that the traditional campaign techniques are
obsolete. Handshaking on the streets and in the stores, speeches before
anyone who will listen, endorsements by local groups and party organizations — these are still much employed campaign techniques. Nor is it to
argue that the media-centered campaign has swept the boards. Certainly
it is too expensive for many candidates; a minute of prime TV time for a
political spot announcement can easily cost $500, and a large billboard in
a good city location may well cost the same figure per month. It is also
inefficient for many local candidates; the radio, television, billboard, and
newspaper space they purchase is wasted in great part on readers and
viewers and listeners who cannot vote for them.

Consequently, the impact of the new style in American political campaigning has been uneven. It is more likely greater among the better
financed candidates for state and national office and less common for local
offices, especially in the less concentrated electorates of the rural areas.
An absence of data on campaign practices makes it difficult to map the
exact extent of its incursions. Probably the best documentation we have of

its impact is the data on campaign finance, for observers and data agree that the rising costs of campaigning in the United States are a result primarily of media-centered campaigning.[21]

THE PROBLEMS OF THE CAMPAIGN

While the resources and tactics of candidates differ widely, the well-run campaign is, according to the lights of many practitioners, characterized by the successful solution of certain standard strategic problems.

TIMING

Campaigns have no real beginning in time. For the office-holder, such as a congressman, the campaign may begin with the first political speech after the last election; for the challenger it may have begun with earlier preparatory (if losing) candidacies. The great danger in the long campaign, however, is that the campaign will lose momentum after "peaking" too early. The candidate tries to build the campaign in a gentle crescendo, pacing the campaign, not hurrying it, not overexposing himself or his message, not tiring himself, and not using up his resources too early.

STYLE

An extravagant oratorical style mixed with a rural folksiness has long prevailed as the dominant political style in many parts of the American South. In much of the urban North it would strike voters as foreign and a bit "cornball." Similarly, the rough-and-ready, old-style city politics has given way in the suburbs to the middle-class gentility of coffee hours in private homes and good-natured handshaking in supermarkets. But whatever tone or style of campaigning the political traditions and culture of the constituency demand, the campaign must meet it. Striking the right style in a mixed constituency may mean altering the style from one part of the district to another; it may also mean striking one political tone for the general electorate and quite another for the party activists and loyalists.

MORALE

Morale can, perhaps, be thought of as the belief that victory is at least possible. Nothing so quickly mires a campaign than the conviction of the workers or voters that the candidate cannot win; it is, of course, also the end of any successful fund-raising. The fight against the loss of morale has always been a campaign problem, but since the development of public opinion polling it is far more severe. The newspaper poll, whether authoritative or not, now carries an aura of certitude about it, and it can seriously hurt the morale of any campaign by announcing a few weeks before the election that the "other" candidate leads by seven or ten per-

---

[21] See Chapter 13 for the full details on trends in campaign finance.

centage points. It is to counteract this deadly effect that so many candidates cite contrary results of "private polls." It has, in fact, been cynically noted that there are not pollsters enough to execute all of the "private polls" taken during political campaigns.

SELECTIVITY

The campaign strategy must define the audience, and that is the problem in selectivity. For the candidate to spread his scarce time and resources evenly over a constituency is in effect no campaign strategy at all. He and his managers essentially face a problem in the maximization of scarce resources — decisions where the return in votes will be the greatest for each unit of campaign resources expended. Will he work on areas normally loyal to the other party in hopes of cutting his losses there, or will he hammer at the party strongholds? He must also tailor his appeals and campaigning for different parts of the electorate; for the party loyalists there must be appeals to party identification, but for other segments of the electorate there must be non-party appeals of personality and issue. He will also have to apportion his resources between the demands of his party activists and the voters in general. Many candidates find that they must spend time during the campaign to restimulate the loyalty and will-to-work of the people in the party or campaign organization; they may even give speeches on the ideological issues important to the activists. For the more general electorate the "gut" issues, the issues of immediate personal (especially economic) interest, are more in order.[22]

There are also other recurring problems in virtually all campaigns. An increasingly major one, money, receives a chapter of its own later, and the problem of organization will be taken up in the next section. Behind all of the universal problems and conventional wisdom about campaigns in American politics, however, there remain two cardinal, overriding rules. The first is as obvious as it is ignored: it is better to have a campaign plan built on a knowledge of the electorate and political realities and on an efficient budgeting of available political resources than to yield to day-to-day improvisation and its uncertainties, hunches, and inefficiencies. The second rule follows logically: the candidate is better advised to follow his own campaign plan than to react to the strategy of his opponent. The campaign that merely reacts to the opposing campaign loses force, timing, and morale; it is constantly on the defensive, and it runs the danger of helping the opponent call attention to the candidate's weaknesses.[23]

[22] A number of writers have suggested that the problem of campaign strategy is one which can be approached through existing "maximization" models, such as that of game theory; see John H. Kessel, "A Game Theory Analysis of Campaign Strategy," in M. Kent Jennings and L. Harmon Zeigler (eds.) *The Electoral Process* (Englewood Cliffs: Prentice-Hall, 1966), pp. 290–304.

[23] For a general approach to campaign strategy, see Lewis A. Froman's essay, "A Realistic Approach to Campaign Strategies and Tactics," in Jennings and Zeigler, *The Electoral Process,* pp. 1–20.

A final and persistent problem in American campaigning is the one of ethical standards. It is a problem which, perhaps, concerns the American electorate as much as the candidates, for the opinion is common that American politics are "dirty" and that the candidates and parties do a major share of their "dirty work" in campaigns for public office. In an area of considerable difference of opinion, there appears to be a consensus of disapproval on two kinds of practices:

electoral fraud. Whether it takes the form of buying votes or stuffing ballot boxes (or other election-day frauds such as "long counts" or voting the graveyards), these practices fall well outside of the common bounds of political morality.

misstatements or misrepresentations of fact. In recent years the most celebrated case of these practices was the "composite" photograph used in the campaign to defeat Senator Millard Tydings of Maryland in 1954. During a campaign which charged Senator Tydings of complacency about the internal Communist conspiracy there appeared a photo which purported to show the senator in earnest and friendly conversation with Earl Browder, formerly the national chairman of the American Communist party. The photo was later identified as a fake, and a public relations expert in the employ of Tydings' opponent owned up to the work.[24]

But beyond cases such as these there is only ethical chaos, for one man's "dirt" is often another man's debating point. What, indeed, constitutes a "smear" in a campaign? The very imprecision of the term suggests the ethical uncertainty behind it. By far the most troublesome ethical questions involve the campaign charges or assertions that wound by suggestion, by innuendo, or by implication. They may suggest that another candidate is a member of the Ku Klux Klan or the Communist party, or even more hazily, that he is "sympathetic" — consciously or unconsciously — with their aims, or that he is unwittingly serving their purposes. These are usually attempts to associate candidates with unpopular causes or people without directly charging — and certainly without establishing — a real association with or loyalty to them. It is this kind of hinting or implying a condition or fact without assuming the responsibility of alleging it clearly that in many ways raises the most troubling ethical problems.[25]

It would be comforting to conclude that such campaign practices are always rebuffed by a stern and judicious electorate. Often they are, for most American voters have a fine sense of fair play, but often the facts or the reaction come too late to hurt the perpetrator at the polls. Perhaps it

[24] This milestone in political public relations is recounted at greater length in Kelley, *Professional Public Relations and Political Power.*
[25] On the subject in general, see Bruce Felknor, *Dirty Politics* (New York: Norton, 1966).

is somewhat reassuring to conclude that such practices are probably no more common today than they were in earlier periods of American history. After all, the annals of presidential campaigns have long been marked with breathless tales of mistresses and illegitimate offspring. And the vocabulary of today's campaigning seems almost effete compared with the terms in which the Federalists and the Jeffersonians berated each other. Most of the most questionable campaign practices have always involved more-or-less unscrupulous attempts to play on the fears and insecurities of American voters — regardless of whether they were fears of Oriental hordes, the Pope in Rome, or an international Communist conspiracy — and so long as the fears remain, so, too, the temptation to exploit them.

CAMPAIGN ORGANIZATION

The political campaign for the House of Commons in Great Britain is in the hands of 630 Labour party and 630 Conservative party election "agents." The parties employ the agents, train them in the direction of campaigns, and place them in the individual constituencies as managers of the local campaign for Parliament. English law buttresses their authority by making them legally responsible for the observance of all election laws and the management of the moneys spent in the campaign. The parties are, therefore, guaranteed a guiding role in the parliamentary campaigns. Not so the American parties. Nothing, either of law or tradition, assures them even a prominent place in the campaign. They must compete constantly for a role in the campaign, just as they fought to control the politics of the nominations. Their adversaries in this struggle are would-be-independent candidates, the *ad hoc*, personal campaign organizations they are wont to create, and the new professional (and commercial) managers of campaigns.

Some American political campaigns are run literally from under the hat of the candidate. He may raise his own funds (often on his own local credit rating), write his own speeches and press releases (which his wife may type), drive his own car from speech to speech. These one-man campaigns are found chiefly in campaigns in small constituencies, in rural areas, and for less noted offices — the campaign of a rural candidate for state legislator or less important county office, for example. More common and perhaps the modal campaign organization in American politics is one including the candidate, his campaign manager, perhaps an office manager, and a small number of faithful political friends who devote part-time or leisure time to major campaign tasks. Together they constitute something of a general council for the campaign. Basically candidates adopt these modest campaign organizations for one or both of two reasons. Organization costs dearly, and many candidates cannot afford it.

Secondly, the style of campaigning which many offices and many political cultures demand does not require a large organization; minimal campaigning demands only minimal organization.

The other extreme in campaign organization is the complex organization with full bureaucratic panoply. In its "ideal," textbook form it is headed by a full-time campaign manager, a man of political experience and preeminent organizational skills. The rest of the campaign organization is then broken into functional units. A research staff examines the political characteristics of the constituency, researches the stands and speeches of the opponent, prepares material for the candidate's speeches, and oversees the gathering of information during the campaign. Canvassers, often a veritable army of them recruited by the party organization, contact voters in person or by phone; they must be coordinated by some individual or a small staff. A speakers' bureau may be necessary to provide speakers in addition to the candidate. A small group of public relations and mass media specialists will prepare press releases, ads for the media, printed literature, and in general handle the relationships with representatives of the media. A finance committee, possibly supplemented by a treasurer, centralizes the raising of funds, the budgeting of expenditures, the paying of bills, and the keeping of records (especially where state law requires reporting). Finally, a bureaucracy of a few secretaries and staff people maintain the candidate's headquarters, answer the phone and mail, and organize the sending of large mailings.

If he can afford it, the candidate can in many states now "rent" a full-scale campaign organization. The archetype of this variety of professional campaign organization in recent years has been Spencer-Roberts, Inc., of Los Angeles, prominent in a number of recent California contests, especially Ronald Reagan's primary and general election campaigns for the governorship of the state in 1966. The assets of an organization like Spencer-Roberts are many and impressive; they have a detached professionalism and experience, they are familiar with all the arts and crafts of advertising, public relations, and the mass media, they have expensive mailing lists of Republican activists and loyalists in California, and they have good ties to local Republican workers and luminaries. The scope of the operations of the firm can best be seen by sketching their exertions on behalf of Nelson Rockefeller in the 1964 presidential primary in California. In that election the Goldwater forces had almost completely tied up the regular Republican organization; the Rockefeller forces were forced to begin virtually from scratch.

With absolutely zero troops of their own to start with, Spencer-Roberts had to use money to recruit troops; by opening 40 to 50 Rockefeller headquarters across the state (6 in Los Angeles alone) to show the flag and banner where moderate volunteers might rally; by publishing a newsletter whose circulation rose from 4,500 to 25,000 in a few months; by direct mail techniques; by billboards, advertisements, television and the drenching of radio, which in auto-mobile-happy California has a dimension of its own.[26]

In addition, S-R organized local committees for Rockefeller, made all of the arrangements for local rallies and handshaking receptions, and set up phone campaigns to reach registered Republicans shortly before the primary date. On major matters of strategy it apparently dealt directly with Rockefeller's New York advisors.

These campaigns run by "maximum" organizations — whether professional or not — still are not the norm in American politics. For some campaigns they may be desirable; for others they would be a form of organizational "overkill." But regardless of the size and complexity of the campaign organization the key man unquestionably remains the campaign manager. Most candidates find it necessary to shift the burdens of directing the campaign so that their time, physical energy, and concentration can all be expended on the campaigning itself. But the relationship between the candidate and his manager is frequently a difficult one. Few candidates care to abandon control of their campaigns, even to a talented veteran of campaigning. But the candidate must clearly delegate at least administrative authority to the manager, or else there is no advantage in having a campaign manager. The major point of tension arises over whether the candidate can and should surrender any control over major strategic decisions to his manager. In reality few candidates do, and on these questions the campaign manager assumes the role of the candidate's closest advisor.

To What Effect the Campaign?

More than one candidate, surely, has wondered what the impact and the effect of the campaign's sound and fury was. The barrage of words and pictures is staggering, but is anyone listening or watching? Do the handshakes, the literature, even the canvassing make any difference in the ultimate voting decision? No one really knows for sure.

Logical deduction leads one to some plausible and probably reliable answers. We know that the American voter exposes himself to the campaign with great selectivity. He tends, first of all, to surround himself with friends, literature, mass media reports, and even personal experience (such as rallies and meetings) that support his perceptions and loyalties. He tends, furthermore, to perceive what he is exposed to in terms of stable, long-term values, the most stable of which appears to be his loyalty to a political party. Therefore, what we think of as "a campaign" may to some extent be two campaigns — one party and its candidates shouting

[26] Theodore White, *The Making of the President 1964* (New York: Atheneum, 1965), p. 127.

at their supporters and the other doing the same. Logically, therefore, a good deal of American campaigning has the effect of stimulating, activating, and reinforcing "given" political predispositions. Far less of it actually achieves any changes that might be called "political conversions." And much of it, too, is directed more to getting people out to vote than to altering or affecting the nature of the voting decision itself.[27]

We can also make some deductions about the effectiveness and impact of campaigns just from the data we have about the exposure of the voter to them. Only a minority of the American adult public report being contacted by a party worker in presidential election campaigns; for example only 8 per cent had been contacted in the 1948 study in Elmira and only 26 per cent report being approached in person or by phone by a campaign worker in the 1964 campaign.[28] Media exposure similarly reaches only a minority of the electorate. Asked after the 1964 campaign whether they had heard, seen, or read about the campaign on radio, television, and magazines, only 12.4 per cent reported they had "a good many" exposures to the campaign via radio, 9.8 per cent through magazines, and 41.3 per cent through television. Significantly, 56.5 per cent of the respondents thought they got most of their political exposure via the TV set.[29]

Therefore, we do know that most American electoral campaigns are carried on by limited means within limited ranges of attention and perception. And even if it does "reach" a voter, the campaign may not dent his fixed and stable loyalties to a candidate, to a party, or to an attitude position. Moreover, events outside of the campaign — wars, depressions, inflation — may have a far greater impact than the campaign on voting decisions. One cannot, therefore, expect even the most dazzling campaign to achieve a full measure of persuasiveness, for it is a political universe and not a college debating society to which it is directed.

Beyond these generalizations it is extremely difficult to document the impact of a campaign. For one thing, there are all manner of methodological difficulties. The "campaign" is a whole congeries of events and activities — some of them are the activities of the parties and candidates, and some are not. Consequently, it is difficult to say just what part of the total impact can be attributed to any part of the total. It is also difficult to determine what part of it the individual voter has been aware of and how he has perceived it.

---

[27] On the campaign effects of reinforcement, activation, and conversion, see Paul F. Lazarsfeld, Bernard R. Berelson, and Hazel Gaudet, *The People's Choice* (New York: Duell, Sloan, and Pearce, 1944).

[28] The Elmira study is reported in Bernard R. Berelson, Paul F. Lazarsfeld, and William N. McPhee, *Voting* (Chicago: Univ. of Chicago Press, 1954); the 1964 data are from the Survey Research Center of the University of Michigan.

[29] These data also come from the Survey Research Center; like all of the SRC for 1964 they were available through the services of the Inter-University Consortium for Political Research.

One study has indicated that personal contacts are a more effective activator of political apathetics than mailed propaganda. The setting of the study was a local referendum, however, in which there was a low level of information and no activation by party loyalties.[30] Other research has shown in varying degrees that traditional precinct work by party committeemen does have an impact on voting behavior (an impact that seems to be in the magnitude of about a 5 per cent change in the vote). They suggest furthermore that the effect of the precinct work may be greater in local elections than in the media-centered presidential ones; in local elections there may be fewer alternative cues and sources of information.[31] But beyond these scholarly fragments one cannot go very far. The entire question of what kinds of campaign strategy and campaign technique are most effective and their variations in effectiveness as the nature of the election and the political environment change remains largely a matter of conjecture and the abundant popular wisdom of American politics.

THE PARTY'S ROLE IN THE CAMPAIGN

The realities of American politics force the candidate to run under party symbols that will help him attract the votes of a party electorate. Nothing forces him, however, to let the party organization control or even participate in the campaign. The candidates (and, thus, the party in government) have long waged a tense competition in the American parties with the party organizations over control of the campaigning. It would probably be no exaggeration to say that this competition is, along with their competition for control of nominations, a contest over which sector will dominate the party and its decisions.

That competition frequently begins in the primary election, and if the candidate without the support of the party organization wins there, he often carries his independence of the organization into the general election. Such a case was that of Milton Shapp, a Philadelphia industrialist, who sought the Democratic nomination for the governorship of Pennsylvania in 1966. The state's formidable Democratic party organization was supporting a 34-year-old lawyer, Robert P. Casey. In what was billed as a battle of "exposure versus organization," the Shapp campaign (on the side of "exposure") employed some 7,000 spot radio commercials, 34 half-hour

---

[30] Samuel J. Eldersveld, "Experimental Propaganda Techniques and Voting Behavior," *American Political Science Review*, L (1956), pp. 154–165.

[31] Phillips Cutright and Peter H. Rossi, "Grass Roots Politicians and the Vote," *American Sociological Review*, XXIII (1958), pp. 171–179; Daniel Katz and Samuel J. Eldersveld, "The Impact of Local Party Activity Upon the Electorate," *Public Opinion Quarterly*, XXV (1961), pp. 1–24; Raymond E. Wolfinger, "The Influence of Precinct Work on Voting Behavior," *Public Opinion Quarterly*, XXVII (1963), pp. 387–398.

television shows on prime time, an assortment of more than 30 pamphlets and leaflets, more than 60 campaign headquarters across the state, and a single mailing of one large brochure to a million and a half voters (estimated cost: $75,000). The total cost of the primary campaign, financed in large part from Shapp's personal fortune, ran over a million dollars. But in the end, exposure did beat organization, and Shapp won the Democratic nomination. A similar reliance on polls, direct mailings, and television — even on campaign pictures with well-known athletes (who were paid up to $500 for permitting their pictures to be taken with Shapp) — continued into the general election. This second expensive, media-centered campaign was to no avail, for Shapp lost the governorship to Raymond Schaefer.

Shapp's victim in the primary, Robert Casey, declaring that he was wiser than he had been a year earlier, observed about the Shapp primary campaign: [32]

Politics is changing tremendously. The old ways no longer work. From that election, I learned that these days you need a combination of two things. First, the traditional grass-roots effort, the telephoning and the door-knocking. But more than that, you have to do what he did. You have to use the new sophisticated techniques, the polling, the television, the heavy staffing, and the direct mail. You can't rely any more on political organizations. They don't work any more. These days, who wants a job in the courthouse or with the highway department? Why, the sons of the courthouse janitors are probably doctors or professional men. You can't give those jobs away any more. We're at the tag end of an era in Pennsylvania.

Party organization, however, still retains assets in some parts of the country which make it indispensable for the campaign. If it can command the armies of local workers, it can provide the candidate with a campaign vehicle (or "medium") that costs him little while assuring success. These organizational campaigns occur chiefly in one-party urban areas in which parties control primaries and in which voters have been habituated to accept the party ticket in the general election; canvassing and "turning out" the vote are still relevant there. Furthermore, the candidate himself is much more apt to be a creature of the party organization, nominated by the organization through its control of the primary and thus its creature in the general election campaign.

Yet, where they can, the candidates find it strategically useful to rely on a separate campaign organization composed of friends, followers, and non-party groups. A personal organization may exploit the willingness to work and to contribute of people who may be chary of party ties or who may consider themselves of the "other" party. It enables the candidate to widen his appeal beyond the party, and to draw support on his own personality and charisma. It permits him more easily to develop a campaign

[32] *National Observer,* September 26, 1966.

that surmounts party lines both in its organization and in its impact. And in some states a reliance on his own non-party groups may help him avoid the restrictions the state places on expenditures by party organizations during a campaign. Finally, by running his own campaign (and paying for it) the candidate frees himself of gratitude and dependence on the party organization. Should he be elected, he will be more his own man and less the organization's.

The candidate has always had certain "liberating" advantages on his side in the competition for control of campaigns. The sheer number of campaigns, coupled with the feebleness of many party organizations, forced those organizations to surrender control of the campaigns by default. Electoral institutions, from the direct primary to the office block ballot, have been on the side of the candidates, and so have the political norms of many sections of the American electorate. Now, additionally, the candidate has in his favor a whole new set of campaigning skills for which he does not have to depend on the party organization. If he can afford them — an important *caveat* which gives political advantage to men of wealth — he can employ strategists, a campaign organization, and ways of communicating with voters. In other words, the party organizations some fifty or sixty years ago came close to monopolizing the knowledge, skills, and manpower necessary for a successful campaign. They do so no longer; new sources of knowledge, skills, and manpower are available "for hire."

It is probably a mistake to conclude, as have some of its victims, that a new style campaign is indispensable. Campaigns in the Shapp and Rockefeller manner are still very much the exceptions — at least in the magnitude of their reliance on the new knowledge and techniques. It is still possible for the careful candidate to win elections without important help from either the party organization or the media men. Many candidates, indeed, are as suspicious of the new practitioners as they are of the organization. Listen to the campaign manager of a successful congressional candidate: [33]

During our first campaign, some fellows from big P.R. outfits who live out here came around and volunteered their time and their talents. We talked with them and looked at the campaign material they'd put together, and we were scared witless. As far as they were concerned, facts and statistics were simply things to be changed. . . . Basically, the P.R. approach is different. Politics has a deeply negative quality. We're convinced that most people vote against somebody. . . . And that's what we concentrate on — making them vote against our opponent. The P.R. crowd feel they have to sell something positively. . . . We believe in being amateurish. Our brochures look as if they were got up in our

[33] Richard Harris, "How's It Look?" *The New Yorker* (April 8, 1967), p. 63; the entire article is an excellent case study of a congressional campaign which relies neither on party organization nor on the new techniques and specialists.

basement. But the P.R. men want to put out four-color brochures with dazzling artwork and their idea of how the Gettysburg Address should have read.

All one can say at the present is that the new skills are far more often thrown on the side of the candidate than the party organization. (The reluctance of party organizations to master the new techniques is in itself a startling instance of political conservatism.) That tends to be true whether they modestly supplement a conventional campaign or whether they shape one largely in their image.

The interests of candidate and of the party organization in the campaign do not ever completely converge. That is the basic truth behind their struggle for its control. The candidate, unless he has been dragooned to fill a ticket in a lost cause, takes himself and his candidacy seriously. Even the longest shot among candidates tends to think he will win; the degree of his ego-involvement in the campaign almost demands it. The party, on the other hand, wants to be selective in its use of campaign resources. It may see some races as "lost"; these candidates, indeed, it may be glad to turn loose for their own independent campaigns. (On "lost" races: more than 40 per cent of the seats in the House of Representatives in 1964 were won with percentages of the popular vote greater than 65 per cent.) Party organizations want to set over-all priorities and allocations of scarce resources; they want to eliminate the inefficient and uneconomical (and wastefully overlapping) use of all the resources of the campaign. Furthermore, the party organization by its nature campaigns on the activation of party loyalty, and candidates may not care to. It may also want to protect a platform and a program, help a presidential or gubernatorial candidate, or win control of a legislature. But these need not be the goals and interests of individual candidates.

To be sure, there are potent advantages to a party-led series of campaigns on behalf of an entire ticket. Such planning can eliminate the embarrassment and futility of two candidates' competing for audiences in the same small town. It can arrange the distribution of campaign literature for a number of candidates at the same time. And it alone can mount the major election-day activities: setting up operation headquarters, providing cars and baby sitters, checking voter lists and alerting the non-voters late in the day, and providing poll watchers to oversee the balloting and the counting. "Efficiency" and "integration" of the campaign does, however, often threaten the interests of specific candidates. While the party organization may prefer to raise money and prevent unseemly competition for the political "buck," an individual candidate may well believe he can raise more on his own. And although the party may prefer billboard posters which celebrate the full party ticket of candidates, some among them may prefer to go it alone.

Out of this pulling and tugging for control of the campaigns emerges a considerable overlapping of campaign organization. Of course, there are those campaigns in which the party dominates and those in which the local party is too weak even to want to exert any control. In many campaigns, however, both party and candidate organizations run parallel campaigns, each supplementing and often duplicating the other. Non-party groups — interest groups and ideological associations, for example — may aid either one or both; it is not uncommon for them to contribute to specific campaigns and to the party, too. And candidates spawn a series of voluntary and *ad hoc* committees: Democrats for Jones, Republicans for Smith, Educators for Miller, Italo-Americans for Burns, and so on. So, the struggle and tension for control of the campaign is really a four-cornered one involving the candidate, non-party groups and specialists, the local party organization and the state-national party organs. Which one dominates depends largely on which one controls the resources — the money, the men, and the skills — the campaign requires.

· · ·

Thus, in the two American major parties, dominated though they are by a concern for contesting elections, the party organizations have had the greatest difficulty in controlling those electoral activities. The ability of the candidates and the party in government to control these processes has in many parts of the country permitted them to dominate the party organization itself. If these are electoral parties and the groups other than the party organizations control the electoral processes — the picking of candidates and the staging of campaigns — then those groups control the parties.

Their failures inevitably frustrate the party organizations. Domination by candidates and incumbent office-holders mattered little when the partisans of the organization wanted only patronage and preference. They and the candidates could agree that electoral victory was their common goal on whatever terms were necessary to win it. The victory itself, and its later fruits, were all that mattered. The tension between these two sectors of the party becomes far greater as the organization recruits ideological and issue-oriented activists. The electoral goals of the new activists include more than mere electoral victory; they would like to control electoral choices so that they might expound issues and select candidates loyal to them. The inability of the organization to control nominations and election campaigns means simply that it, of all the sectors of the party, has the greatest difficulty in achieving its goals and rewards at the election.

Through their ability to control nominations and election campaigns, the candidates are freed of organizational domination, both in the affairs of the party and in the decisions of public office. But the failures of the party organizations also enhance the competitive position of the non-party political organizations which want to play electoral politics. And it is easier than ever before for them to influence nominations and elections, for they now can acquire the new techniques and skills to compete with the parties. Success in the competition goes to him who can mobilize the necessary resources, and now (with enough money) non-party groups can get the knowledge, skills, and manpower with which to compete on even terms with the political parties.

Chapter Eleven

PRESIDENTIAL POLITICS:
THE PRELIMINARIES

It has often been said that the American Presidency is the "biggest," most demanding job in the world. Its size and responsibilities are in part a reflection of the power and concerns — the global involvements and the domestic tasks — of the government of the United States in the 1960's. In part also they reflect the unique institution of the Presidency itself, for the United States is virtually alone among the major powers of the world in choosing a national executive from a national constituency in free and competitive elections. And as if to match the prodigious demands and responsibilities of the Presidency, the American people have evolved a process of nomination and election to that office that for sheer length, expense, attention, and gaudy extravaganza is certainly without peer in the world. It commands front-page coverage in most of the world's newspapers, and media coverage in the United States alone reaches enormous proportions. One need note only that in 1964 the three major television networks lavished about $15,000,000 of television coverage on the two nominating conventions alone.

Furthermore, the quadrennial American presidential campaign and election have become the focal points of all of American politics. It is an election whose results radiate out to affect others — strong presidential winners carry other candidates into office on their "coattails." Its candidates and rhetoric tend to shape party loyalties and identifications, and its regular four-year cadence marks the basic pulse of American politics. The presidential election is also the great centralizing moment in American politics, the centripetal force against the decentralizing, centrifugal tendencies of American politics. It is the brief but influential hour of the parties as national parties. And, finally, for many American citizens, often apathetic to local politics, its salience and prominence make it virtually the whole of American politics.

Appropriately, such a singular campaign and election process pivots around two very singular American political institutions: the nominating conventions of the summer before the presidential election and that constitutional anachronism, the Electoral College. Those two institutions combine to create a presidential politics of baroque complexity and an electoral process which remains an insoluble puzzle to many of the world's observers. It is a politics that is, to say the least, peculiarly American.

The Rules of the Presidential Game

If the American President and Vice-President were elected directly by a simple plurality of the American electorate, presidential politics would be vastly different — and undoubtedly easier to understand. But the presidential constituency, the one national constituency in American politics, is not composed simply of all American adults. It is a complicated constituency from which is chosen an 18th century deliberative body which no longer deliberates. And just as any formal electoral system does, this one gives a special form and cast to the political competition that goes on within it. Electoral institutions, as we have noted before, are the rules of political competition, and they determine the skills and the strategies of the players.

The Electoral College as it is set down in the Constitution rests heavily on the structure of American federalism.[1] Each state receives in it a number of electors equal to its total representation in the two houses of Congress; that is, to the fixed quota of two senators one adds the number of the state's representatives in the House. The votes of the states in the Electoral College, therefore, extend from a fixed minimum of three (two senators and one representative) to an open-ended maximum, currently the 43 of New York. In addition, since the ratification of the 24th Amendment, the District of Columbia has had three electoral votes. The total membership of the College thus presently is 538, the sum of the membership of the Senate (100), the House (435), and the three votes of the District of Columbia.

The Constitution further provides that the President and the Vice-President must be elected by an absolute majority of the votes of the College; at present that requirement means 270 votes. Should the Electoral College not be able to elect a man by this absolute majority, the Constitution proceeds to set up what is in effect a "super-electoral college." The election of the President would be settled by the House of Representatives choosing among the three candidates with the greatest number of votes in the Electoral College. However, while state delegations in the

[1] Article 2, section 1, as amended by the 12th Amendment.

House would decide whom the state would support (and would not be bound by the popular vote of the state), each state would have only a single vote in the balloting. The emergency procedure was twice employed in the early 1800's but not since then. In view of its uncertainty and its drastic redistribution of political power, it is an eventuality that the major parties would prefer to continue avoiding.

Originally the framers of the Constitution intended the Electoral College as a genuinely deliberative body. The choice of a President, argued Alexander Hamilton

. . . should be made by men most capable of analyzing the qualities adapted to the station, and acting under circumstances favorable to deliberation, and to a judicious combination of all the reasons and inducements which were proper to govern their choice. A small number of persons, selected by their fellow-citizens from the general mass, will be most likely to possess the information and discernment requisite to such complicated investigations.[2]

Not all of the Founding Fathers were as fearful of direct popular election as was Hamilton, but the majority seems to have accepted the wisdom of selection by a body of respected notables who were in turn to be chosen by the state legislatures. The transformation of the Electoral College began in the early years of the republic with the shift to a popular election of the electors; then the rise of political parties completed the transformation. Slates of electors began to run in the states pledged to support a party's set of presidential and vice-presidential candidates. Voters, in other words, began to know that the ties of party loyalty assured them that a vote for a specific set of electors was in effect a vote for a pair of candidates. As soon as that practice of pledged slates became widespread, the Electoral College ceased to function as an independent and deliberative body. Rather it became a filter through which the popular vote for presidential candidates was translated into the more complicated electoral vote for the same candidate. And so the Electoral College today is perhaps the world's most important non-meeting governmental body. In most states the electors meet briefly over lunch or dinner in the state capitol to register their vote formally. Some official of the state then transmits it to the President of the Senate in Washington, and the collective preferences of the Electoral College are recorded without the inconvenience of a single meeting of the College as a whole.

The workings of party slates and loyalties on the Electoral College have had another transforming effect. The fact that parties offer full slates of electors has undoubtedly influenced the states to make (by law) the choice of the electors an "all or nothing" race. A plurality edge of just a few votes or a few thousand votes carries all of a state's electoral votes. In no

2 Number 68 of *The Federalist* (New York: Modern Library Ed., 1937), pp. 441–442.

state are the electoral votes shared according to the percentages of the vote won by the slates of the various candidates. This "winner take all" effect has in turn had two consequences. First of all, it has forced the parties and the candidates to appeal to the voters of the large and competitive states with the big, indivisible blocs of electoral votes. To fail to carry Nevada or Delaware, with their three electoral votes, is not a major loss; to fail by a few thousand in New York (43 electoral votes) or in California (40) is distinctly a major setback. Secondly, it has greatly magnified the possibilities of the loser in the national popular vote being, nonetheless, the winner and new President by reason of the distortion of the popular vote that takes place in the Electoral College. That possibility can come about if a candidate wins state blocs of votes by narrow margins and loses others by landslides.[3] Indeed, since the Civil War two men have been presidential losers even though winners in the popular vote — Samuel J. Tilden in 1876 and Grover Cleveland in 1888.[4]

Although party ties have robbed the Electoral College of its deliberative quality, they have not made it completely automatic and predictable. Electors in most states are not legally or constitutionally bound to vote for the presidential candidate under whose name they have run. In 1956 an Alabama elector pledged to Adlai E. Stevenson shocked a good many Democrats by abandoning his candidate at the "moment of truth" to vote for an unknown local judge, Walter B. Jones; in 1960 an Oklahoma Republican deserted Richard M. Nixon and voted for Senator Harry F. Byrd of Virginia, not even a member of his party. Furthermore, rebellious state parties may exploit this lack of binding tie for their own purposes. One of them may deny the voters of its state a chance to vote for the national candidates of the party by running either a different slate of candidates or an unpledged slate under the state party label. In 1948, for example, J. Strom Thurmond, the Dixiecrat candidate for the President,

---

[3] For example, to reduce the problem to three states of equal voting population and electoral vote:

    State A — population of 2,000,000 and 10 electoral votes:
        Democratic vote: 900,000
        Republican vote: 1,100,000
    State B — same population and electoral vote
        Democratic vote: 950,000
        Republican vote: 1,050,000
    State C — same population and electoral vote
        Democratic vote: 1,300,000
        Republican vote: 700,000

So here the Republican candidate leads in the electoral vote, 20 to 10; the Democratic candidate, however, leads the popular vote by 300,000.

[4] On the Electoral College generally, see Lucius Wilmerding, *The Electoral College* (New Brunswick: Rutgers Univ. Press, 1958). Also: Ruth C. Silva, "State Law on the Nomination, Election, and Instruction of Presidential Electors," *American Political Science Review*, XLII (1948), pp. 523–529; Robert G. Dixon, "Electoral College Procedure," *Western Political Quarterly*, III (1950), pp. 214–224.

rather than Harry S. Truman, appeared as the Democratic candidate for
the Presidency in a number of Southern states; Mississippi Democrats in
1960 and those of Alabama in 1964 ran unpledged slates of electors under
the Democratic party label. A combination of party decentralization and
state control over the presidential ballot and election, therefore, stands as
a limit to the development of a national, popular election of the American
President.

Each of these characteristics and consequences of the Electoral College
has produced a body of criticism and reform proposals. One school of
thought, concerned about its artificiality and the possibility of a "minority"
President, would abolish it in favor of a direct, popular election of the
President. Others, alarmed by its emphasis on the indivisible "big state"
votes, have proposed various systems of dividing the electoral votes of
the state; most of them involve either dividing the electoral vote propor-
tionally according to the candidate's percentage of the popular vote, or
electing some or most of the electors in the congressional districts of the
state. Still others have sought to check the uncertainty of its operation —
the possibility of unpledged slates, of state ballots without a national
candidate, or of local slates intended solely to deadlock the Electoral
College. Yet, despite a torrent of polemics and tomes of argumentation,
operation of the College remains untouched.[5] It changes today as it has in
the past — by custom, tradition, and state law.

Behind all of the attempts to reform or abolish the Electoral College lie
broader questions of political power and ideology. Electoral systems, like
other political institutions, are allocators of political power in that they
create political advantages for some which they deny to others. In defining the national constituency of the President and the Vice-President, the
Electoral College enhances, in the over-all, the political power of the
large, pivotal, urban, industrial states.[6] To put the matter another way, it
creates a presidential constituency that is markedly different from the
sum of all the congressional constituencies. Because of the equal state
representation in the Senate, regardless of population, and the remaining
overrepresentation of rural areas in the House of Representatives, the political power of the rural and small city electorates is magnified in the
Congress. Presidents have, as a result of their different national constituency, more often in the last generation espoused the "liberal" social and
economic programs favored by the people of the urban areas. Not surprisingly, the desire of political conservatives to reduce the power of the
large urban, industrial states lies behind some of the attempts to alter

---

[5] Except of course for the obvious changes of the 12th and 23rd Amendments.

[6] There is a paradox here. In formal terms the Electoral College would appear to
have done the opposite: given the rural states greater power by overrepresenting them
(through the inclusion of Senate representation in the formula). However, the "winner
take all" tradition, and its consequent big-state bias, overcomes this formal bias in
practice.

the College, especially those concerned with dividing the electoral votes of the individual states.[7] And the desire to preserve that power lies behind a great deal of the opposition to change.

The other chief issue behind reform of the Electoral College is no less than the issue of direct, popular democracy itself. Unquestionably the Electoral College has in the last 130 or 140 years evolved into something very close to a *de facto* popular election of the Presidency. In every presidential election since 1888, it has secured the Presidency for the candidate with the greatest number of popular votes in the country; and that, too, has been the period of the spread of democratic norms and the constant broadening of the suffrage. Some of the reform attempts try to protect and further that evolution, either by institutionalizing the popular election of the President and Vice-President, or by preventing individual states or state parties from thwarting popular choice and popular will. Into this category fall both the attempts to abolish the College and those less drastic proposals to limit state party control over the ballot choices and to force electors to vote for the candidates they ran pledged to support.

Despite all the talk of change and reform, the Electoral College remains much as it has always been — an archaic bit of political Americana reformed only by custom and the rise of the two-party system. Therefore, its form continues to set the major rules of the game of presidential politics, and its influence marks all steps in the quadrennial pursuit of the Presidency. Its composition is reflected in the composition of the great nominating conventions themselves. It underlies their propensity to pick presidential candidates from the large, pivotal states with the big electoral votes. The "big state" arithmetic it fosters influences much of the strategy of the subsequent campaign. Its nature offers opportunities for minor parties such as the 1948 Dixiecrats (who hoped to deadlock the Electoral College) or Southern slates of uncommitted electors, and it is the reason for talk of a Wallace candidacy in 1968 which would duplicate the Southern strategy of twenty years before. So important is the Electoral College as an influence that the entire range of presidential politics makes little sense to those who fail to understand it.

FIRST STEPS TOWARD THE NOMINATION

The national conventions of the two major parties resolve and conclude the complicated process of nomination. It is, however, far more difficult to say just when that nominating process begins. For some especially am-

[7] For an analysis of the possible impact of one of these plans, see Ruth C. Silva, "The Lodge-Gossett Resolution: A Critical Analysis," *American Political Science Review*, XLIV (1950), pp. 86–99. On this point and also for a general review of the impact of the Electoral College, see Allan Sindler, "Presidential Election Methods and Urban-Ethnic Interests," *Law and Contemporary Problems*, XXVII (1962), pp. 213–233.

bitious and far-sighted men it may have begun in their own political career planning some six or eight years before. Already in the late 1960's there is talk of the 1972 Democratic nomination and the interest of Robert Kennedy and Hubert H. Humphrey in it. Within the party defeated at the last presidential election, jockeying for the next nomination begins the morning after defeat. In a more formal and easily identifiable sense, the nomination process may well begin as the first "advance men" for would-be candidates straggle into New Hampshire to enter their candidates and delegates in that earliest of the presidential primaries.

Basically the business of the pre-convention part of the nomination process is that of the selection of delegates to the conventions. The major would-be candidates within each party seek the selection of delegates bound to them — or at least committed or inclined to them. Conversely, delegates or heads of state delegations want to remain unbound and uncommitted so that their bargaining power will remain unexpended until the convention meets. Typically in this country, the party organizations control only part of the picking of delegates to their own conventions. They fix the number of voters in the convention and apportion them out to the state organizations. That is to say, the national committee of each party decides what percentage of the total votes in the convention each of the fifty state delegations will have. State legislatures, however, decide the equally crucial matter of how those delegates will be chosen. They decide whether they will be chosen in a presidential primary or by a convention or committee of the party.

THE APPORTIONMENT OF VOTES AND DELEGATES

In apportioning the voice in their conventions to the state party organizations, the Democratic and Republican national committees deal in "votes" rather than "delegates." The Democrats in particular have had a long tradition of permitting the state party to send more delegates to the convention than the number of its assigned votes — with the understandable result that some delegates have cast bizarre fractions of a single vote at the convention. To assign the number of votes to the state organizations each national committee employs a formula that is almost unconscionably complex. Fundamentally, each formula is based on the state's electoral college vote augmented by extra votes for the states in which the party has shown strength in recent elections.

In late 1966, for example, the Republican National Committee announced that the apportionment of delegates (and thus of votes) to the party's 1968 national convention would observe the following formula:

Each state receives a base grant of four delegates.

An additional six delegates go to states which the GOP ticket carried in 1964 or which have a Republican governor or senator.

An additional delegate is awarded for each congressional district in which the presidential nominee or congressional candidate received at least 2,000 votes in the last election; a second extra delegate is added if the vote was over 10,000 in the district.

Under the plan every state was given at least eight delegates, and New York has the greatest number, 92. Basically, the formula (and similar ones within the Democratic party) creates a distribution of power similar to that on the party's national committee. It tends in general to overrepresent the smaller states and the areas of party strength, which in the case of the Republicans tend to be the same states. Recent party victories in the South mean that delegates from the eleven states of the Confederacy, plus Kentucky and Oklahoma, account for 27 per cent of the 1968 GOP convention votes, the highest percentage of all time. The effect, thus, is to create for the Republicans a convention structure which underrepresents the party goals and organizations of the large, pivotal states.

THE PRESIDENTIAL PRIMARIES

Even though only a minority of the states choose their convention delegates in presidential primaries, it is by far the better known of the selection methods. In 1964, in fact, only fifteen states and the District of Columbia elected some or all of their convention delegates in ways that also offered voters of the state some opportunity to express a preference for the presidential nominee of the party.[8] Together the delegates from these states cast 41.4 per cent of the votes at both the Democratic and Republican conventions. Additionally, New York elected at primaries unpledged delegates to the two conventions; there is, however, no way in New York's election that the voter can indicate his preference among the contenders for his party's presidential nomination. Alabama permits the parties to elect delegates at primaries if they so choose.[9]

To speak blithely of "presidential primaries" is, however, something of an oversimplification. No two of them are alike. The major source of their variety lies in their two-part character: they can be (but need not be) devices for selecting delegates to the national conventions and/or for showing a preference among contestants for the party's nomination. In the way they combine or divide these two separate functions — the selection of delegates and the designation of a presidential preference — the

[8] The 15 states are: California, Florida, Illinois, Indiana, Maryland, Massachusetts, Nebraska, New Hampshire, New Jersey, Ohio, Oregon, Pennsylvania, South Dakota, West Virginia, and Wisconsin. For a general study of the primaries, see James W. Davis, *Presidential Primaries: Road to the White House* (New York: Crowell, 1967).

[9] If one includes New York, the 16 states and D.C. primaries are located in states accounting for 49 per cent of the votes of the Democratic convention of 1964 and 48.4 per cent of the Republican. The percentages of this paragraph, however, overestimate the percentage of delegates actually elected, because small numbers of delegates in some of the states are appointed by party organs.

assorted presidential primaries fall into four logical categories: those in which only delegates are chosen, those in which the voters may only show a presidential preference, those with the two features integrally combined, and those with separate delegate selection and presidential preference polls.

1. *Delegate selection only.* In Alabama and New York the primary is solely a vehicle for the election of delegates to the national conventions. There is no place on the ballot for the names of the contenders for the party nomination, and the delegates do not run pledged to any contender. The ballot is, therefore, innocent of any names except those men and women who seek election as delegates.

2. *Presidential preference only.* In two states — Maryland and Indiana — the presidential primary is nothing more than a presidential preference poll. The voter confronts the names of his party's worthies who have entered the primary and merely indicates which he would prefer to represent his party in the November presidential contest. The state committees of the parties then pick the delegates to the respective conventions. Those delegates are, however, required to support the candidacy of the winner of the state's presidential poll.

3. *The two elements combined.* Five states — California, Florida, Ohio, South Dakota, and Wisconsin — combine the presidential poll and the election of delegates by a simple device: the delegates may pledge themselves to support specific candidates for the party's nomination. That pledge and the name of the national candidate is, of course, linked with the delegate's name on the ballot. In some of the states the association with a candidate appears with each delegate's name — for example, the statement under his name "pledged to support John Smith for President." Other states, such as Wisconsin, provide that full slates of delegate-candidates be entered under the name of a seeker after the presidential nomination. Of these states, however, some do permit delegates to run unpledged and uncommitted if they prefer.

4. *The two elements separated.* Illinois, Massachusetts, Nebraska, New Hampshire, New Jersey, Oregon, Pennsylvania, and West Virginia — eight states in all — and the District of Columbia include the two features of the primary but separate them. The ballot in these states has a separate presidential preference poll in which the party's hopefuls may compete for the favor of partisans within the state. It is also an occasion for picking delegates to the conventions in a distinct and separate section of the ballot. Confusion and diversity of practice, however, surround the relationship between the two parts. In only Oregon do the results of the preferential polls bind the delegates selected; in the other states they are only "advisory." But in Oregon and some of the other states the would-be delegates may also choose as individuals to run pledged to a presidential candidate. The result, of course, may be conflicting advice from the

voters, and in the case of Oregon the delegate could be bound to a man other than the one he pledged himself to.

In outline these are the presidential primaries. There are, though, still other dimensions to the differences among them. First, the convention delegates in some are elected from the state at large, in others from the individual congressional districts, and in still others from both. Such a seemingly minor variation, however, can have major political conse- quences. For example, the chances of a divided state delegation (and its attendant intra-party squabbles) are much greater when delegates are chosen by congressional district. The district system also puts much greater campaigning strains on the candidates for the presidential nomi- nation, for in effect they must contest little elections in every congres- sional district of the state.

Secondly, some states in their primaries elect all of the delegates the parties will send to the conventions. Some, however, elect only part of them. In Pennsylvania, for example, about a quarter of the delegates to national conventions are chosen by the parties' state central committees. Such a provision helps meet one of the parties' major objections to the presidential primary by permitting them to make sure (through their own state committees) that the important leaders of the party organizations will go as delegates to the national conventions of their parties.

Thirdly, the states vary, too, on the issue of whether a presidential hopeful must give his consent before he is involved in the state's primary. Most, but not all, require his approval (or permit his disapproval) before his name is entered in a presidential preference poll or before delegates run pledged to him. In Oregon the primary law entrusts to the Oregon secretary of state the delicate decision of putting on the preference poll the names of all candidates "generally recognized in the national news media" to be candidates for the presidential nomination. Increasingly the states are forcing contenders for nomination into difficult choices. Ne- braska voted in 1965 to gives its secretary of state the same authority that his counterpart has in Oregon; the only way a candidate can keep his name off the Nebraska ballot is to file an affidavit stating that he is not and does not intend to become a candidate for the Presidency. In 1967 the Wisconsin legislature amended its primary law to create an eleven- member committee to decide the names of the active candidates and order them placed on the ballot. The total effect is clearly to make it less possible for potential candidates to avoid some of the primaries and also to "heat up" the politics of the presidential primaries.

Fourthly, the presidential primaries differ in the nature of the commit- ment of the pledged or "bound" delegates. In some cases the pledge of a delegate to support a certain candidate for the nomination is buttressed only by his enthusiasm for his candidate or his own code of honor — or his sense of the political value of integrity. In other states the delegates are required by law to take a pledge of loyalty to the candidate. Wisconsin, for instance, specifies by law the content of the pledge:

I will, until released by said candidate, vote for his candidacy on the first ballot of the said party convention and vote for his candidacy on all ensuing ballots, provided, however, that if on any ballot said candidate shall receive less than ten per cent of the total vote cast on such ballot, I am released from this pledge and shall thereafter have the right to cast my ballot according to my own judgment.[10]

Finally, while all of the other states and the District of Columbia hold their presidential primaries under the conditions of the closed primary, Wisconsin holds it in an open primary. The possibility that voters who would normally support Democratic candidates at the general election might drift into the Republican presidential primary — and vice versa — creates an additional uncertainty and unpredictability for the candidates who might want to enter the primary in Wisconsin.

DELEGATES CHOSEN BY THE PARTY ORGANIZATIONS

The presidential primaries are dramatic, and they are reported in the most intricate detail. Nonetheless the great majority of the states — as well as the Democratic parties in the Canal Zone and Guam, and both parties in Puerto Rico and the Virgin Islands — permit the parties to choose delegates by assorted internal party processes. Those processes are most frequently combinations of state and congressional party district conventions; the Democratic parties often simply hold district caucuses during the state convention, but Republican national party rules require the holding of separate district conventions. Generally, the district conventions choose a fixed and equal number from each district, and the state convention selects the remainder from the state at large. In a few states some or all of the delegates are chosen by the state central committee of the party.

Delegates so chosen by party processes may also be instructed by the state party. The mechanics of instruction vary. Some conventions pass resolutions instructing the delegates to support one specific contender for the party nomination. Some, indeed, mandate their chosen delegates to work actively for his nomination in addition to voting for him on the convention roll calls. In other cases the resolution of the convention may state nothing more obligating than a preference or recommendation. Often the process of instruction is less formal. The personal loyalties and preferences of the would-be delegates may be very well known; they may campaign for selection on the basis of their support for a particular presidential nominee. Those personal loyalties bind more securely than a dozen party resolutions. Often, too, the delegates themselves lead in writing the resolutions which instruct themselves, thus giving party sanction to their own preferences.[11]

[10] *Wisconsin Statutes,* Chapter 5.38.
[11] The mechanics and politics of choosing convention delegates are discussed more

The Politics of Selecting Delegates

It is only a truism to say that the politics of winning a presidential nomination depends ultimately on enlisting the support of a majority of the delegates at the national convention. No aspiring presidential nominee can escape that logic. The strategies of the aspirants will, however, differ in the way and the time in which they make their move for delegate backing. But as front-running candidates increasingly attempt to influence the selection and instruction of delegates — attempt, in other words, to wrap up the nomination before the convention convenes — the meaningful and significant part of the politics of nomination shifts to the pre-convention phase. The intensive pre-convention campaigns for delegates by John F. Kennedy in 1960 and Barry Goldwater in 1964 successfully beat off their challengers and assured them their parties' nominations on the first ballot of the convention.

Even though the intensive pre-convention campaign becomes more common, it is a strategy which makes sense only for some contenders for the presidential nomination. Front-runners well-known to the political public — and who can muster the resources — may feel they have no alternative but to make a show of strength and come to the convention with a majority of delegates firmly in grasp or at least in sight. Other candidates, partially in response to the front-runner's activity, may feel they have to contest the selection of some delegates if only to block him short of a majority of the delegates. The moral of the dithering inactivity of moderate Republicans in 1964 while Barry Goldwater went on accumulating delegate support is not apt to be forgotten in the near future. Still other candidates may contest the delegate selection in a few states for assorted reasons — to garner enough convention votes to have a substantial voice in its deliberations, or to extract a political *quid pro quo* (the vice-presidential nomination or a cabinet seat, perhaps). And other candidates, the true "dark horses" who lack a publicized name and a political following, may avoid contests in the states in order to remain acceptable to all wings of the party should a deadlocked convention think of turning to them.

The pattern of contesting before the convention may be determined within a party by a number of factors; among them:

the presence of a President. When Presidents are eligible for another term, they are in a commanding position to dictate their own renomina-

---

fully by Gerald Pomper, *Nominating the President: The Politics of Convention Choice* (Evanston: Northwestern Univ. Press, 1963), Chapter 3. Also on the pre-convention strategies, see Nelson W. Polsby and Aaron B. Wildavsky, *Presidential Elections* (New York: Scribner, 1964), pp. 59–77.

tion and to eliminate competition. Even Presidents who are not candidates for renomination (such as Truman in 1952 and Eisenhower in 1960) may be their late decisions or solid support for a successor influence the politics of nomination.

the number of candidates and their strength. Two leading candidates (such as Rockefeller and Goldwater in 1964) force a different form of strategy and counter-strategy than will four or five evenly matched candidates.

the resources of the candidates. Candidates such as Hubert H. Humphrey in 1960 can be sorely pressed by lack of time and money; Humphrey was tied down in Washington by his Senate leadership responsibilities and limited in his campaigning by a shortage of money.

the degree and nature of commitment of state leaders and parties. In some years large numbers of state parties and their leaders may be committed to a candidate even before the selection of delegates, as were many Democratic organizations committed to Adlai Stevenson in 1956; but in other years the levels of commitment may be lower and the pre-convention politics can then go on in a freer, more open political environment.

Within these general political configurations, the candidates must also make personal strategic assessments. They face a common problem: the allocation of scarce time and resources to those places where it will do the most good. A candidate may be forced to greater pre-convention activity to counter a popular impression that he cannot win or that he does not enjoy party support. Or he may feel compelled to prove to the skeptical that his campaigning skills, his handshake, and his smile (and perhaps those of his wife) are durable enough for the presidential race. He may want to counter the feeling that his popularity is regional. John F. Kennedy in 1960 entered the presidential primary in Protestant West Virginia to prove that his Catholicism would not hamper him in a presidential campaign. Above all, the candidate's decisions may be governed by his estimates of probable success. No law or political tradition forces a candidate to contest every presidential primary or state convention, and only a foolhardy one would try.

The candidates are not alone in having interests at stake in the selection of delegates to the conventions. So also do the party organizations and leaders in the states, and their interests often run counter to those of the aspiring presidential nominees. For the local and state parties, a hotly contested selection of delegates is often an occasion of intra-party conflict. Battles between Rockefeller and Goldwater for the Republican delegates in 1964 — both in primaries and in state conventions — created rifts in the party which have been slow to heal. Twelve years before, many of the same state organizations were torn by Eisenhower-Taft competition for their delegates. That convention of 1952, indeed, was forced to decide between slates of delegates pledged to Taft and slates loyal to Eisenhower in three separate states. A slightly different peril befell some Democratic organizations in 1956. Estes Kefauver, a Tennessee senator who became a national figure because of his chairmanship of well-televised investigations into organized crime, entered a number of presidential primaries against the wishes and opposition of state Democratic leaders. The delegates he selected to run pledged to him were, therefore, often unknowns or members of dissident party factions. When his delegate slates won, the state party leaders were often denied positions as delegates to the national conventions.

The interests and goals of the parties in selecting delegates to the national conventions go further than the avoidance of conflict, however. The state party organization (or one of its leaders) may want to pursue its own goals at the convention. It may want to preserve its bargaining power to affect the platform, to win a cabinet seat for a notable of the state party, to affect the vice-presidential choice, or just to enhance its value in the presidential nomination. Its interests may also be the parochial ones of a state party; a number of state Democratic parties were cool to Kennedy in 1960 for fear of losing the votes of Protestants in the state and thus hurting the state ticket.

For these reasons, the leadership and organization of state parties would generally prefer to "de-politicize" the process of selecting delegates. If conflict looms, the party chieftains may agree on an uncommitted slate of delegates or one loyal to a "favorite son" candidate rather than chance deep and lasting divisions. Or if there is a presidential primary in the state, they may do as Wisconsin Republicans did in 1964. Faced with intra-party conflict between Goldwater and Rockefeller forces, they negotiated a settlement by which all the major contenders for the GOP nomination agreed to stay out of the Wisconsin presidential primary. Wisconsin Republicans then elected the only slate on the ballot, one carefully composed of Republicans of various loyalties and ideologies and pledged to a "favorite son" non-candidate, Congressman John Byrnes. Frequently, therefore, the pressure within the state party for commitment comes from volunteer groups loyal to one national contender or another, from ideologues in the party, and from the contacts and advance men of the contenders. The pragmatic organization men, the "pros," tend often to oppose it.[12]

Apart from the interests of parties and candidates, however, has it really made any difference whether delegates to the national conventions

[12] Theodore H. White's two volumes on the 1960 and 1964 elections contain excellent journalistic accounts of the pre-convention politics of those two years; *The Making of the President 1960* (New York: Atheneum, 1961) and *The Making of the President 1964* (New York: Atheneum, 1965).

have been chosen by primary or party processes? Do the 40 to 50 per cent of the delegates chosen by primary behave any differently than those chosen through party bodies? Do the presidential primaries have an impact on the nominations commensurate with the time and money spent in them?

By their very nature the presidential primaries involve large numbers of party voters (as distinguished from party activists) in the selection of delegates to the national convention. They will tend to be more attuned to the personality, the fame, the "public image" of the candidate than his party "regularity" or his acceptability to party organizations. The primaries offer roads to the nomination to men such as Estes Kefauver whose strength in the 1952 and 1956 Democratic conventions was built largely on primary victories. And yet perhaps the most important fact of the Kefauver bids is that he did not, despite his demonstrated primary popularity, win his party's nomination.[13] The presidential primary has rarely by itself offered access to the nomination. And yet victories in them may be more important than the number of delegates acquired would indicate. Victories may prove to pragmatic state politicians that the would-be candidate can win; success in them may, therefore, stimulate support in the non-primary states. So, the impact of the primaries may be both more and less than meets the eye. They have been enormous opportunities for candidates to display their popular political assets and build blocks of influence, but they have had their greatest importance in the context of and related to a total strategy that cultivates other sources of influence over the nomination as well.

Perhaps the most important difference between the two methods of selecting delegates, suggest the authors of the major study of presidential nominating politics, is in their timing.

In the party process systems the selection and mandating of delegates remain largely open until near the final moment of choice in the responsible party body. Voter opinion may then be assessed in terms of its current manifestations, as well as of manifestations that may have occurred in earlier stages of the process. It can be flexibly taken into account both in the choice of delegates and in the related decisions on whether to instruct formally and to what extent.

In the presidential primaries, by contrast, there is a tendency to cut arbitrarily into early phases of the campaign and often to compel premature decisions as to who shall go on the ballot. This is conspicuously so when presidential candidates must be named on the ballot with their own formal consent. On a lesser scale, the same problems are involved when would-be delegates with known preferences must decide long in advance whether or not to file.[14]

Beyond that strategic consideration, the differences are not as sharp as one might imagine. Data from the most thorough study of any set of

---

[13] He did win the vice-presidential nomination in 1956.

[14] Paul T. David, Ralph M. Goldman, and Richard C. Bain, *The Politics of National Party Conventions* (Washington: Brookings, 1960), p. 268.

national nominating conventions (1952) reveal that differences between delegates chosen by primary and those chosen by party processes were not great. Primary-chosen delegates in each party seemed to be committed and uncommitted in the same percentages as the other delegates — and committed in the same ratio to leading and non-leading candidates, too. Furthermore, Senator Taft in 1952 actually cornered a larger percentage of his committed delegates in the primary states (40.3 per cent) than did the popular hero, General Eisenhower (37.5 per cent). In the 1952 Democratic convention Senator Kefauver, preeminently the child of the primaries, did get 156 of his 202 committed delegates in the primary states; indeed, he got others only in Maryland and his home state of Tennessee. But state organizations managed to stop the Senator even in the primary states; a gigantic 322 delegates picked in primary states went to the convention uncommitted. With all of his effort the Senator won less than 30 per cent of the delegates chosen in the primary states.[15]

The sanest judgment on the impact of the primaries is probably the well-hedged one. Only some of them, such as Oregon's, favor the popular candidate without party ties and party approval. That is to say, party electorates, rather than party activists, play an important role in only some of them. Small presidential primary turnouts, especially were there is no lively contest, leave the activists in control. Furthermore, the "tribune of the people" is blocked in some states by the nature of the primary. There simply is not, for all practical purposes, a great deal of difference between electing delegates at a state convention and putting the unpledged names of party leaders (as does New York) on a primary ballot. Nor indeed may there be much difference if the separate presidential preference poll is merely "advisory." Illinois in 1952, for instance, was the scene of a Kefauver triumph in the Democratic advisory poll, but the delegates to the national conventions supported Stevenson.

A SYSTEM IN NEED OF REFORM?

The briefs against both the presidential primaries and the party selection of delegates are long and weighty. In fact, they seem to so outweigh the briefs in favor that the observer might easily conclude that once again in American politics he is choosing between the lesser of two evils. However, the debate has broadened recently to include a third option: a national presidential primary. Its specific form varies with specific proponents, but all proposals outline a single primary election to be held in all states and in which each party would choose, not its delegates, but the presidential nominee himself. Since it would replace the nominating convention, its consideration can await the discussion of the convention in the following chapter.

[15] *Ibid.*, p. 253 and pp. 518–521. The 1952 study is reported at greater length in five volumes: Paul T. David, Malcolm Moos, and Ralph M. Goldman, *Presidential Nominating Politics in 1952* (Baltimore: Johns Hopkins Press, 1954).

Because the nominating conventions appear likely to remain on the American political scene, the more pertinent question at this point concerns the selection and mandating of delegates. Or to put the issue more pointedly — ought the presidential primaries as we know them be expanded or abolished? The case against them is impressive:

> They consume an enormous amount of time, energy, and money before the presidential campaign has ever begun. Leading contenders for the nomination often run through a series of primary campaigns from February through June, arriving at the party convention personally and financially exhausted.

> They put a tremendous premium on the well-known, familiar name and face — which is to say, often, on the financial and other resources necessary to build that political familiarity. Consequently, their existence makes it difficult for the party to consider less well-known or reluctant candidates. (They have not, however, made it impossible; Adlai Stevenson entered nary a primary in 1952.)

> Their importance may easily be distorted or puffed out of all perspective. In the mass of publicity surrounding them, candidates and voters alike fail often to assess them soberly. Wendell Willkie, for example, bowed out of 1944 Republican contention after a loss to the Dewey slate in Wisconsin; Dewey, however, polled only 33 per cent of the Wisconsin Republican vote (conducted in an open primary at that). While primaries may be deemed measures of a candidate's popularity, in reality they may be measures of popularity among the voters of the party. They are simply primaries and not general elections.

> Their results are too often colored by the particular quirks that mark some or all of them. In some, for example, the candidate may be involved even against his wishes. In Wisconsin the state's open primary adds another capricious element. And in all of them a winner may be determined by plurality; Henry Cabot Lodge carried the New Hampshire Republican primary in 1964 with about 36 per cent of the votes.

> The presidential primaries frequently provide the occasion for the internal division of state party organizations, for divided and warring delegations to the national conventions, and for delegates not representative of the party organization and leadership in the state. Like any other primary which takes important party processes out of the control of the organizations, it weakens them.

The list of arguments against the presidential primary could be extended, but these are its chief ingredients.

The charges against the party convention or party committee selection of a state's delegates to the national convention come almost entirely from outside of the party. The burden of the argument is the old and traditional one against party processes — that they are too easily controlled and manipulated by a handful of party oligarchs. Furthermore, in these states it is said that the party electorates are excluded from an important and often crucial step in the picking of a president. And it is undoubtedly true that in these states the political ambitions of national figures get less attention, and the interests of the state parties *qua* parties get more attention, than they do in the presidential primaries.

Debating points aside, however, no great changes seem likely in the selection of delegates. What was a generation or two ago an impetus toward the presidential primary has slackened off. By 1916 at least twenty-three states were holding presidential primaries at least periodically, but by 1965 the number had dropped well below twenty even though the total number of states had increased by two.[16] Yet it seems unlikely that the presidential primary will completely fade away. Increasing media coverage has spotlighted its role in the nomination process. And its basic rationale — the twin democratic norms of mass popular participation and fear of party oligarchies — seems still powerful in many states. Some state parties may attempt to clarify and strengthen the process of instructing convention-chosen delegates; others may alter the state convention procedures. But for the moment few drastic changes seem likely at any point.

The presidential primaries have come to serve a popularizing and informing — even a legitimizing and democratizing — function in American presidential politics. They are a testing of major presidential aspirants — physically, intellectually, and politically. And at the same time, the party-controlled selection of delegates in other states creates another kind of testing — one more dependent on party organizational skills and contacts, on the pragmatic trading and compromising of American politics. The peculiar mix of the two tests adds something unusual, and probably something important, to the politics of the presidential nomination. If the mix does not score high in logic and consistency, one can only say that a good deal of the rest of American political processes does not either.

· · ·

The fifty state organizations of the major American parties have only the one opportunity every four years to act as a national party. The quest for the Presidency is their single national task, and the archaic boundaries set by the Electoral College form their single national constituency. Their attempts to act as a single, unified, national party are, ironically, disturbed and complicated by a pre-nomination politics which in length and in method divides individual state organizations and sets state party against state party. In part that friction develops from institutions such as the presidential primary. It derives in greatest part, however, from the fact that the American parties are disunited, heterogeneous conglomera-

---

[16] For the early development of the presidential primaries, see Louise Overacker, *The Presidential Primary* (New York: Macmillan, 1926). For example, Montana and Minnesota discontinued their presidential primaries by state legislative action in 1959.

tions of state parties and that they are welded into national parties, even for a brief task, only with the greatest difficulty.

Even at these early stages of presidential politics one also sees the beginning of the repetition of an old theme in American politics. It is difficult for the party organizations to control the presidential nomination, just as it is difficult for them to control other party nominations. In part, again, the presidential primary weakens organizational control and shifts it to the would-be candidates. In part, too, the organizations are weak because they have no means of uniting or coordinating their own preferences prior to the nominating conventions. So, candidates with rational and unified national strategies find it easy to take the initiative from individual state party organizations in this phase of presidential politics. And to the extent that they are able to win the commitments of enough delegates to capture the nominations — as the candidates did in 1960 and 1964 — then the nomination is captured by the candidates and the party in government before the party organizations ever gather themselves together to act as a "national party" at the convention.

Chapter Twelve

PRESIDENTIAL POLITICS:
THE CRUCIAL DECISIONS

That cynical observer of recent American politics, H. L. Mencken, especially loved the challenge of reporting a national nominating convention. Wrote the Sage of Baltimore, ruminating on the Democratic convention of 1924 and the 103 ballots it took to nominate John W. Davis: [1]

. . . there is something about a national convention that makes it as fascinating as a revival or a hanging. It is vulgar, it is ugly, it is stupid, it is tedious, it is hard upon both the higher cerebral centers and the *gluteus maximus,* and yet it is somehow charming. One sits through long sessions wishing heartily that all the delegates and alternates were dead and in hell — and then suddenly there comes a show so gaudy and hilarious, so melodramatic and obscene, so unimaginably exhilarating and preposterous that one lives a gorgeous year in an hour.

Such judgments, however amusing and diverting, are not unexpected from Mencken. More surprising are the equally severe judgments of less cynical observers. Former President Dwight D. Eisenhower in mid-1965 called the conventions "a picture of confusion, noise, impossible deportment, and indifference to what is being discussed on the platform." The banner-waving demonstrations that so typify the carnival gaiety of the conventions he dismissed as "spurious demonstration[s] of unwarranted enthusiasm." [2]

Scarcely a convention goes by, indeed, without evoking a series of tongue-clucking appraisals in the serious journals, and calls for convention reform come as regularly as the conventions themselves. And yet the national conventions persist, the chief hold-out against the domination of

---

[1] Malcolm Moos (ed.), *H. L. Mencken on Politics* (New York: Vintage, 1960), p. 83.
[2] *New York Times,* June 29, 1965.

American nominations by the direct primary. How is it that so maligned an institution has so successfully resisted the impetus of change? Has it, indeed, become an indispensable political institution? And perhaps more relevantly, has it, while possibly offending the canons of taste and decorum, really managed to function effectively as a recruiter of Presidents?

THE STRUCTURE OF THE CONVENTION

Although the states control the selection of delegates to them, the two conventions per se are completely the creatures of the parties' national committees. They are subject to no congressional or state regulation, and the total range of planning for a convention is a major responsibility of the party's national committee and its staff.

Planning for the quadrennial conventions begins at least a year before the event with the selection of a host city and the related matter of arrangements for TV coverage. The choice of the site reflects a wide spectrum of considerations, from the size of the "financial package" of the bidding cities (Atlantic City and other New Jersey groups gave $625,000 to the Democratic national committee to bring the 1964 deliberations to the Boardwalk) to the matter of time zone changes for evening television coverage.

After the national committee maps out the number of votes and delegates the convention will have, it apportions the votes and delegates to the states. In 1960 the Democrats authorized the casting of 1,521 votes and the Republicans 1,331. Four years later the Democrats permitted the convention votes to soar to 2,319, while the Republicans held the line at 1,308. Within the Republican party the rules of 1960 and 1964 authorized the state parties to send one delegate and one alternate delegate for each allotted vote, producing a maximum of more than 2,500 delegates in each year. The Democrats, however, have in recent years authorized the state parties to send close to twice as many delegates as they had votes in the convention. In 1964 they authorized the sending of:

> 2,944 delegates from the states (representing 2,319 "votes")
> 108 national committee delegates
> 2,211 alternates (one alternate for each of the 2,319 "votes"
>   minus the 108 of the national committee members)
> _____
> 5,263 total delegates and alternates.

The total authorized number of delegates and alternates clearly set a record for American national conventions.

Why such gargantuan conventions? Largely because the national committees are under tremendous pressure from the state party organizations to increase the number of delegates. Party workers in the state cherish the prestige and experience of attending a convention; many of them happily give up summer vacation time and pay hundreds of dollars of their own to do so. The state parties, therefore, find the positions of delegates and alternates excellent rewards for party service. The experience of being a delegate will also likely stimulate the activist to work and contribute in the campaign which follows. State organizations have found that the larger the number of delegates, the fewer difficult choices they will have to make and the fewer the number of people they will have to disappoint. Finally, the national committee itself may well want a large number of delegates and alternates to create a mass rally atmosphere for television coverage. Especially when the convention will certainly renominate an incumbent President — as the Democratic convention of 1964 did — the "rally" aspects of the convention replace its deliberative duties.

Like all other major American institutions — both political and non-political — the conventions function in part through committees. Generally the chief ones are four:

1. *Credentials.* This committee accepts the credentials of delegates and alternates and makes up the official delegate list of the convention. Its prickliest duty is that of deciding contests (two delegates or slates vying for the same seats) and challenges (of the qualifications of any delegate or alternate).
2. *Permanent organization.* It selects the permanent officials of the convention: the permanent chairman, the secretary, the sergeant at arms. Generally its work provokes little controversy.
3. *Rules committee.* It sets the rules of the convention, most particularly the specific procedures for the selection of the presidential nominee. Ever since the Democrats abandoned their two-thirds rule in 1936 and joined the Republican practice of nominating a candidate by an absolute majority of votes, the main procedures have been fixed and customary. Yet the rules committee struggles at every convention with rules such as those concerning the length and number of speeches of nomination, the number of non-delegate demonstrators that will be permitted on the convention floor, and the method of polling delegations should controversy arise within them.
4. *Resolutions.* The resolutions committee presents a series of resolutions to the convention — thanks to the host city, salutes to fallen party leaders, etc. — and, more importantly, drafts the party platform.

The personnel and chairmen of these committees, too, are selected by the national committee. Early appointment is necessary if only because they begin to function before the convention convenes. The platform committees, indeed, have recently begun to scour the party and the nation for ideas several months before the convention opens.

The first three of these committees — credentials, permanent organization, and rules — make decisions which define the structure and procedures of the convention. These decisions are no less important for being procedural, however. Often they have enormous impact on the substantive decisions the convention will make on the nominees or the platform. Like all other procedural rules or institutions within the parties they affect the distribution of power within it. The abandonment of the two-thirds rule by the Democratic convention in 1936 — to take a prime example — drastically diminished the power of the party's Southern wing. Under the rule, two-thirds of the votes of a convention were necessary to nominate, and the "one-third plus" strength of the South in the convention gave it a virtual veto over the presidential nomination. For these reasons the national committee picks the members of these committees with an adept sensitivity, usually making sure that major sections, candidate followings, and ideological currents are represented.

In recent years it has been the credentials committees of both parties whose decisions have had the gravest repercussions. Senator Robert A. Taft and General Eisenhower's contest for the 1952 Republican nomination embroiled the credentials committee in deep controversy. Pro-Eisenhower forces (many of them Democrats until shortly before) from Louisiana, Georgia, and Texas challenged the pro-Taft delegates from these states on the general grounds that they were excluded from the conventions and party meetings that chose the delegates. They had then held conventions of their own to select Eisenhower slates. Initially the national committee voted to seat temporarily the Taft delegates from Georgia and most of them from Louisiana and Texas. After the convention voted to exclude them from even temporary seating, the credentials committee countered by supporting the national committee's decision. Ultimately, however, in scenes of bitter recrimination the convention as a whole seated the pro-Eisenhower claimants from the three states. Had Senator Taft had the votes of the delegations from those states he would have led Eisenhower on the first ballot of the convention. Similar kinds of credentials problems, growing largely out of ideological and factional splits in state parties, have afflicted conventions of both parties periodically.

A somewhat different problem in credentials has plagued the Democratic conventions since World War II: Southern state delegations unwilling to take the *pro forma* pledge of delegates to support the candidates and platform of the convention they are about to attend. In popular parlance it is the issue of the delegate "loyalty oath." In 1948 all of the delegates from Mississippi and half of the Alabama delegation marched out of an evening session of the convention after Northern liberals "nailed" a strong civil rights plank onto the platform. Many of those delegates and their state parties later supported the Dixiecrat party ticket; more heretical than that, four state parties put the Dixiecrat slate on their state presidential ballot as the ticket of the Democratic party. Following the rebellion of 1948, delegates from a few Southern states appeared at the 1952 and 1956 conventions with instructions from their state parties that qualified their pledge of loyalty. In 1952 the Democratic convention temporized and seated three delegates who refused to sign its loyalty oath after receiving some verbal assurances of loyalty from most. The conventions of 1956 and 1960 made no attempt to impose an oath.

The loyalty issue erupted again at the 1964 convention when the largely Negro Freedom Democratic Party of Mississippi challenged the seating of the Mississippi delegation on the grounds that Negroes had been prevented from participating in the selection of national convention delegates. After demonstrations, hassles, intervention from the White House, and ultimately the withdrawal of the Mississippi and Alabama delegations, the credentials committee and the convention accepted a compromise. The Mississippi delegates were forced to pledge loyalty to the party ticket and two at-large delegates of the Freedom Democratic party were seated as regular Mississippi delegates. Most significantly for the long run, the convention announced that beginning in 1968 no delegations would be accredited if in their states, any person was excluded because of race or color from the party processes which chose them.[3]

Finally, to complete the organization of the convention the national committee selects the temporary chairman, who usually also delivers the extravagantly partisan "keynote" address. His qualifications are only two — an aloofness from the major contestants for the nomination and a telegenic oratorical style — but the candidates are many. They remember that Alben Barkley's oratorical flights in praise of the Democratic party literally won him the vice-presidential nomination in 1948.[4] But even at lower levels of ambition the assignment is an ideal publicity showcase which does no man's political future any harm.

Such is the formal structure or organization of the convention. Its description, of course, fails to convey anything of the ambience or the atmosphere of the convention. Born of a rough-and-tumble political tradition and related to the institution of the boisterous convention in other areas of American life, the national party conventions are part carnival, part "fling at the big city," and part (a large part, actually) serious party conclave. At one and the same time they mix phony, well-rehearsed "spontaneous" demonstrations with serious thought about "presidential stature," the conferences of the powerful king-makers with the aimless amblings of ordinary delegates, the perfunctory afternoon oratorical "fillers" with the often eloquent messages of the party worthies. The convention is in many ways two conventions — one of them the surface patina of

[3] On the issue of the loyalty oath see Allan P. Sindler, "The Unsolid South: A Challenge to the Democratic Party" in Alan Westin (ed.), *The Uses of Power* (New York: Harcourt, Brace, 1962); Abraham Holtzman, "Party Responsibility and Loyalty: New Rules in the Democratic Party," *Journal of Politics*, XXII (1960), pp. 485–501.

[4] On the contrary case they may remember that General of the Army Douglas MacArthur disappointed his supporters by failing to light any fires with his keynote speech before the Republicans in 1952.

bogus fun, hoopla, earnest platitudes, and devotion to party symbols, the other the less public world of bargaining, influence, and negotiation through which agreement is achieved and choices made.

THE DELEGATES

The delegates to the Democratic and Republican conventions are in no sense a cross-section of American citizenry. They are as a group over-whelmingly white and male — about 90 per cent male and 98 per cent white in the 1952 conventions.[5] They are Protestant, although less dom-inantly so within the Democratic party. They are, furthermore, well-educated and well-off; 1948 data indicate that the median income for both parties' delegates was between $10,000 and $11,000. A large per-centage are lawyers (over 35 per cent in 1948) and either public officials or high-ranking party officials. As a group they appear to be representa-tive of activists in the two parties. All data we have about them paint a composite picture quite similar to a composite portrait of county and state committee members across the country. These are, in other words, the men and women with the time, the money, the knowledge, and the incentives to be politically active.

Ideologically, the delegates are very probably more committed, more aware of issues and issue-positions than the ordinary voters of their party. They also tend more to the ideological poles than do the electorates of their parties; they are more apt to be identifiably "liberal" or "conserva-tive" than even the identifiers of the parties.[6] Furthermore, the ideological commitment of the delegates may well be increasing. The 1964 Republi-can convention clearly broke with the rule of pragmatic compromise and opted for an explicitly ideological candidate and program. The ideological gap between convention delegates and the party's rank-and-file voters results both from the differences between activist and non-activist and from the way in which the apportionment of delegates at the conventions overrepresents the areas of the party's weakness across the country and thus overrepresents some of the party's electors. That gulf has raised especially acute problems for the Republicans. Ever since 1936 their con-vention delegates have clearly had their hearts to the right of their candi-dates; if it had been purely personal choice they would have probably preferred Senator Taft in the 1940's and 1952 and large numbers were

[5] Paul T. David, Ralph M. Goldman, and Richard C. Bain, *The Politics of National Party Conventions* (Washington: Brookings, 1960), pp. 327ff for these and the follow-ing data. See also Dwaine Marvick and Samuel J. Eldersveld, "National Convention Leadership: 1952 and 1956," *Western Political Quarterly*, XIV (1961), pp. 176–194.

[6] Herbert McClosky, Paul J. Hoffmann, and Rosemary O'Hara, "Issue Conflict and Consensus among Party Leaders and Followers," *American Political Science Review*, LIV (1960), pp. 406–427.

favorably disposed to Senator Goldwater in 1960. In 1964 the heart won out.

What leads these men and women to give up the time and money to trek off for a week of convention-going?[7] On one level it is the excitement and novelty of the political experience, the prestige of being a delegate, the age-old fascination with politics. The lure may also be the publicity and contacts with which to promote a political career. And more than one delegate has parlayed a convention trip into a brief moment of glory (and high Nielsen rating exposure) on national television. These we may call the personal goals. On another level there may be the support for a candidate — indeed the delegate may be legally bound to one — and/or an ideological position. They may also come to reach local goals — to promote local candidates, to boost a local leader for national office, to improve their access (and possibly patronage) by backing a "winner," even to fight out local factional disputes. And as participants in the national party they come to pick a President, to measure the would-be candidates against their understanding of the demands of the office. They also come to pick a winner — to pick the men and means for victory.

As tangible and important as the individual delegates are, the real unit of the conventions is the "delegation." Delegates live and communicate at the convention as a delegation; and their goals, commitments, and outlooks are often the same. They caucus periodically, and they react together to leadership within the delegation and to pressures outside of it. They are often bound together by loyalty and political indebtedness to the same governor, senator, or state party chairman.[8] The cohesiveness of state delegations is especially great in the Democratic convention, for the rules of the Democrats have historically permitted the invocation of the "unit rule." State delegations operating under it — under specific instructions of the state party — cast all of the state's votes for the candidate or option favored by a majority of the delegates. Republican conventions do not permit the use of the unit rule.

THE BUSINESS OF THE CONVENTION

The convention begins in low key with stiff formalities and the business of organization, warms up with the keynote address, tries to maintain momentum and expectation through the platform consideration, and reaches a dramatic peak in the nomination of the presidential and vice-presidential candidates. This general format remains basically the same

[7] David et al. discuss the problem of convention costs and support for delegates on pp. 334–337.

[8] For perceptive studies of the state delegations to the 1960 conventions, see Paul Tillett (ed.), Inside Politics: The National Conventions, 1960 (Dobbs Ferry, N.Y.: Oceana, 1962), pp. 112–251.

convention after convention. TV coverage has necessitated some rear-
rangement into a more compact convention and one with the events of
major interest reserved for prime evening transmission time. The traditional building up to the nomination creates something of a dramatic
problem for the party of the President eligible to succeed himself — the
likelihood of his renomination is so great that the spectators know "how
the play is going to end." President Lyndon B. Johnson himself solved a
good share of the problem in the 1964 Democratic convention by creating
suspense and uncertainty over his vice-presidential choice. The Republicans never really solved the problem in 1956, although bursts of opposition to Vice-president Nixon's renomination created some suspense.

Aside from the rites of nomination the drafting and approval of the
platform is the convention's chief business. The platform committees begin hearings long before the convention opens so that the platform will
be in draft form for convention hearings. Those hearings before and during the early phases of the convention are often spiced by the appearance
of leading contenders for the nomination. Governors Rockefeller and
Scranton and Senator Goldwater all appeared before the Republican
platform committee in the days before the opening of the 1964 convention. The finished document then is presented to the convention for its
approval. That approval is not always *pro forma*, for some of the most
spirited recent convention battles have come over it. The Dixie withdrawal from the 1948 Democratic convention came after the platform
plank on civil rights legislation was toughened on the floor of the convention in a revolt of the party liberals led by Hubert H. Humphrey, then the
mayor of Minneapolis. In 1964 the Republican conservatives beat off last-
ditch attempts by the party's moderates to soften the platform's conservatism.

Few aspects of American politics so openly invite skepticism and cynicism as do the party platforms. They are long and prolix; the Democratic
platform of 1964 ran to about 20,000 words (or about a 75-page, double-
spaced typewritten manuscript). They are not often read; the congressional party generally ignores them, and even presidential standard-bearers
usually reserve the right to disagree with them (some of Adlai Stevenson's
pronouncements on the Taft-Hartley Act seemed to fall short of his party's
demand for total repeal in 1952). Basically the problem is that platforms
are the instruments of ideology, and the two major American parties have
not been explicitly ideological. They really have no persistent sets of political principles, no total political philosophies which unite their followers. The American party platform, rather than being a statement of the
party, is much more apt to be a statement of the presidential candidate
and/or the wing of the party in control of the convention. An incumbent
President seeking renomination virtually writes the platform himself, and
strong contenders for the nomination (such as Barry Goldwater in 1964)
can often make sure that their forces are in firm control of the resolution

committee. And if it happens that the man likely to be nominated disapproves of the platform, he may insist on its modification. Vice-President Nixon in 1960, clearly about to receive his party's nomination, bowed to the criticisms of the draft platform by Governor Nelson Rockefeller of New York, rushed to New York to confer with him, and then hurried back to Chicago to press revisions on a very unhappy committee.[9]

Part of the cynicism about the platforms grows from the impression that they are often less than forthright — that they are exercises in semantic virtuosity. Words and phrases often are intended to obfuscate rather than clarify; compromise may indeed be achieved by phrases that can mean all things to all people. But overlooked generally is the possibility that the platforms of splintered and heterogeneous parties may be *too* specific in their attempt to offer something for everyone. In 1964, for example, the Republican platform addressed itself to "the handling of oil shale patent applications," and the Democrats felt compelled to discuss the kilowatts of non-Federal hydro-electric generating capacity licensed recently by the Federal Power Commission.[10] Probably the one frequent charge the platforms are not guilty of is the charge of identity. They have in recent years differed over social security, labor-management relations, farm price support programs, the conduct of the Korean war, defense policy in general, and medicare programs. Certainly no one reading the Democratic and Republican platforms of 1964 could have the impression that one was merely reiterating the other.[11]

Finally the conventions confront a third major task: the governance of the party. They select the members of the national committees, although in reality they merely ratify the choices of the state parties. As the highest authority in the party, the convention may also alter the structure and procedures of the national committee and supervise its work. However, the conventions hold a very loose rein over the activities of the national committee, chairman, and offices. And in the matter of picking a new national party chairman it defers to the personal choice of its presidential nominee.

FINDING A PRESIDENTIAL CANDIDATE

The main attraction, the political *pièce de résistance*, of the convention — the picking of a presidential candidate — begins as the secretary intones

[9] The story of the drafting of party platforms in one year is told by Edward F. Cooke, "Drafting the 1952 Platforms," *Western Political Quarterly*, IX (1956), pp. 699–712. See also Tillett, *Inside Politics*, pp. 55–111.

[10] All of the party platforms are available in one volume: Kirk H. Porter and Donald B. Johnson, *National Party Platforms, 1840–1964*, 3rd ed. (Urbana: Univ. of Illinois Press, 1966).

[11] See Gerald Pomper, *Nominating the President: The Politics of Convention Choice* (Evanston: Northwestern Univ. Press, 1963), pp. 71–75 for a discussion of differences in the party platforms.

the litany of the states: Alabama, Alaska, Arkansas. . . . Thus begins the process of placing before the convention the names of candidates for the presidential nomination. As each state is called, the head of the state's delegation responds in one of three ways — he may yield his position in the roll call to another state for the purpose of placing a name in nomination, he or some other delegate from his delegation may come forward to offer a candidate, or he may pass. So, as the secretary works his way through the states, the contenders for the nomination are entered, each one by a formal speech of nomination and shorter seconding speeches.

It is at this point that the convention reaches back by tradition to a 19th century political style. The speeches of nomination roll out in great Victorian periods, often seeming to be parodies of nominating speeches and usually ending (after many references to "the man who") with a dramatic "revelation" of the name of the nominee. The seconding speeches, carefully chosen usually to provide a cross-section of the party — are, in style, often vest-pocket versions of the main speech. After each set of nomination speeches the supporters of the nominee burst out in well-planned demonstrations, usually augmented by young and tireless non-delegates. The demonstrators snake their way, often for close to an hour, through the crowded aisles of the hall, singing and chanting, waving banners and signs, and generally disporting themselves in the carnival spirit. As a result the process of getting the names of all the candidates before the convention often took a day in former years. Recently, however, the party managers have tried to reform and shorten the hi-jinks, for what seemed colorfully traditional in the hall itself looks mildly grotesque on the TV screen.

Once all of the names have been presented to the convention, the task of settling on a single presidential nominee begins in earnest. The secretary of the convention starts again through the states (and the District of Columbia, the territories, and the dependencies), asking each delegation to report how it votes. If no candidate wins the necessary absolute majority of votes, the convention presses on to another ballot. A number of nominations have been settled on the first ballot, but in 1924 the Democrats plodded through 103 ballots in sultry New York's Madison Square Garden before nominating John W. Davis. Since 1948 no nomination contest in either party has consumed more than three ballots (Table 1); and in 80 per cent of both parties' conventions, nomination has been on the first ballot. Furthermore, the conventions in the same period have averaged only two candidates who polled more than 10 per cent of the convention votes on any ballot (Table 1). That trend may be attributable to a number of factors — the Democratic party's abandonment of the two-thirds rule, more intensive pre-convention campaigning, and the pressures on delegates that follow the increased publicizing of the events of the convention.

Table 1

NUMBER OF BALLOTS TO NOMINATE AND NUMBER OF CANDIDATES
POLLING TEN PER CENT OF VOTES IN
DEMOCRATIC AND REPUBLICAN CONVENTIONS: 1948–1964 *

	Democratic Conventions		Republican Conventions	
Year	Candidates over 10%	Number of ballots	Candidates over 10%	Number of ballots
1948	2	1	3	3
1952	4	3	2	1
1956	2	1	1	1
1960	2	1	1	1
1964	1	1	2	1

* Source: Congress and the Nation (Washington: Congressional Quarterly, 1965).

The casting of the votes takes place in a context of some of the most intense political activity in all of American politics. Even before the opening of the convention, representatives of the various contenders have been stalking uncommitted or wavering delegates across the country by mail, by phone, and by personal visit. Once the convention opens, the process is stepped up. Of the 1960 Kennedy organization, Theodore H. White has written: [12]

In all, some forty delegate-shepherds were assigned each to a particular state delegation that was theirs to cultivate; each was given packets of name cards listing the assigned state delegates by name, profession, hobby, children, wife, peculiarity, religion, and sent out to operate. They were instructed, as they found shifts in any delegation, to report such changes to a private tabulating headquarters in Room 3308 at the Biltmore; and there, every hour on the hour from Friday through balloting day, a new fresh total, accurate to the hour, was to be prepared. For five days, the shepherds were told, they were not to sleep, see their wives, relax, frolic or be out of touch with 8315. Each morning, for the five Convention days from Saturday to the Wednesday balloting, they were to gather in Room 8315 for a staff survey at nine A.M., then disperse to their tasks.

Such organizational thoroughness probably has never been seen at conventions before or since, but front-runners generally know they must win quickly. To do so means convincing the uncommitted delegates and those committed to minor candidates that the time has come to climb on the bandwagon or forever endure the consequences. The pressure on the delegates thus increases as the front-runner inches closer and closer to the majority total.

Once the convention has passed through an unsuccessful ballot, nego-

[12] White, The Making of the President 1960 (New York: Atheneum, 1961), p. 157. See also Tillett, Inside Politics, pp. 25–54.

tiations renew with even greater intensity. The leading candidates must take care to prevent a chipping away of their supporters — a genuine danger if they fail to increase their votes on a second or third ballot. New support comes more easily from minor candidates or uncommited delegates, since data suggest that delegates bound to candidates are too loyal to those commitments to be lured away.[13] The favorite son candidate, for his part, faces the delicate decision whether to cast his lot with a front-runner, or hold tightly and maintain (either alone or in concert) a defensive action. The danger of the latter option is the danger of holding the line too long and seeing one's political bargaining power suddenly become worthless. It is in these negotiations that the minor and unsuccessful candidates seek their *quid pro quo* and that the leader in the balloting makes his commitments or promises. It is, in fact, at this point that the formation of Cabinets is widely thought to begin.[14]

Following the naming of the presidential nominee, the party begins the roll call ritual once again for the selection of the vice-presidential nominee. In most conventions that has merely meant the ratification of the choice of the presidential nominee. In a few instances conventions have rebelled briefly against the judgment of their presidential candidates; for instance, in the Democratic meetings of 1944 the supporters of Vice-President Henry Wallace briefly, but futilely, resisted the decision of President Roosevelt to replace him with Harry S. Truman. Moreover, in 1956 Adlai Stevenson convulsed the Democratic convention by refusing to name a vice-presidential candidate. Senator Estes Kefauver was chosen on the second ballot in the "hands off" free-for-all. More typically, however, presidential candidates make the choice, often to balance and strengthen the ticket by representing other centers of party power than their own.

THE "AVAILABILITY" OF PRESIDENTIAL NOMINEES

There is a bland and misleading term in American politics used to describe the personal, social, and political characteristics the parties seek in their presidential nominees. If a man possesses them, he is said to be "available." Contrary to popular use, the word in this idiomatic sense has nothing to do with the candidate's willingness to be a candidate; the assumption seems to be that in that sense every native-born American adult is "available" for the Presidency.

The concept of "availability" sums up the qualities the parties believe make a politically appealing and acceptable — and thus a "winning" — candidate. (Such a concept, of course, does not preclude the possibility

[13] David *et al.*, *The Politics of National Party Conventions*, p. 379.
[14] On the strategies of presidential politics generally, see Nelson W. Polsby and Aaron B. Wildavsky, *Presidential Elections* (New York: Scribner, 1964).

that he will have the abilities and personal qualities necessary to fill the presidential office successfully, but it does not guarantee it. The qualities necessary for electoral success may not be identical with those which assure effective in-office performance.) In part the canons of "availability" reflect the distribution of political power in presidential politics. It is said, for instance, that the presidential candidate must come from a large state — that is, from a state with a large electoral vote which he can be presumed, by reason of local loyalties, to command (and as they have in more than 70 per cent of the cases from 1896 through 1964). From 1896 to the present only four of the twenty-one men who were originally nominated for the Presidency by a convention have come from the smaller states. The other seventeen have come from seven large states: seven from New York, four from Ohio, two from California, and one each from Illinois, Texas, Massachusetts, and New Jersey. None of the four from the smaller states — Landon of Kansas, Davis of West Virginia, Bryan of Nebraska, and Goldwater of Arizona — won the Presidency.[15]

In part, too, the concept of "availability" is a codification of widely held expectations in the American electorate of what a President should be. It is an aggregate of the characteristics the parties think the American electorate would prefer a President to have — and would, therefore, vote for in a presidential candidate. Some years ago it was commonly said that for a man to be considered seriously for the office he had to be:

a personal success in business or public life;

happily married and blessed with an attractive family;

a reasonably observant Protestant;

a white male in his late 40's or 50's;

of Anglo-Saxon or north-northwestern European ethnic background;

the product of small city or rural life.

Although there is considerable validity to such a list as a description of past presidential nominees, it is dangerous to project it into the future. The lore of acceptability shifts with changes in social attitudes and what is socially acceptable. Adlai Stevenson, a divorced man, was nominated in 1952 and 1956; and the second urban, Catholic candidate, John F. Kennedy, was nominated in 1960. Those nominations probably indicate, at least in part, the declining social stigma attached to divorce, the life of the "big city," and Catholicism in contemporary America.

Finally, related to the issue of availability, but somewhat different, is the question of career pattern. Although not all presidential candidates have had prior governmental or office-holding experience, most have. The

---

[15] If one uses the 1964 electoral vote as a measure, none of the seven "large states" referred to here had an electoral vote smaller than fourteen; none of the "small" states had one greater than seven. In the same year only seventeen of the fifty states had electoral votes greater than ten.

question, then, is frequently raised about what positions provide the best access, the best "jumping off" point, for the Presidency. What public positions grace a man with an aura of governmental success and competence and yet give him a fruitful base for building party and public support? From 1900 through 1956, nineteen different men ran for the Presidency on the Democratic and Republican tickets; eleven of them had been governors (McKinley, Theodore Roosevelt, Wilson, Hughes, Cox, Coolidge, Smith, Franklin Roosevelt, Landon, Dewey, and Stevenson). Only two, the luckless Harding and Harry Truman, had been senators. It had come to be a commonplace in American politics that the Senate was the graveyard of presidential ambitions. Senators, it was said, were forced to cast too many politically sensitive votes and create too many political enemies; they also were thought to lack the opportunities for national popularity and image.

In 1960 and 1964, however, all four nominees had been senators. In fact, the 1960 Democratic convention featured a battle among five senatorial contestants: Kennedy, Johnson, Symington, Humphrey, and Russell. The shift in recruiting to the Senate (assuming it continues) may well reflect changes in the offices of governor and senator and in the public perception of them. Undoubtedly senators find it easier now to keep themselves in the public view, especially with the easy access to the media they enjoy; and a senator determined to build a national following finds jet air travel a boon to making speeches and contacts in all parts of the country. The very nationalization of American politics may also have convinced large numbers of Americans that a senator's coping with issues of national importance is a good apprenticeship for the Presidency. The governors, on the other hand, have found themselves in political difficulties in their states in recent years. Problems of taxation and budgeting, racial tension and rioting, and legislative reapportionment — as well as the more conventional political conflict resulting from the spread of two-party competitiveness — have caught many of them in a damaging political cross fire.

Let it be added, finally, that conventions collectively and delegates individually do consider the general abilities of the contenders to fit the demands of the Presidency. One can roam convention hallways and hear it said repeatedly that this man or that man does or does not "measure up." These considerations increasingly apply to vice-presidential candidates as well. The illnesses of President Eisenhower and the assassination of President Kennedy have reminded the parties and the American electorate that Presidents are mortal. The matter became, in fact, a minor campaign issue in 1964. President Johnson repeatedly emphasized that he thought his vice-presidential choice was of presidential caliber, and many Democrats and newspaper editorials argued that the Republican vice-presidential choice was not.

Conventions: Yesterday and Today

It is unlikely that small bands of national "kingmakers" huddling in "smoke-filled rooms" ever did control the national conventions to the extent that popular myth would have it. Even the celebrated negotiations at the Republican convention of 1920 — in the course of which Warren G. Harding "emerged" — took place in a convention deadlocked by other candidates with large popular and delegate followings. But whatever power the kingmakers may have had in the past, it appears increasingly that it is declining. They and the convention delegates find that the pre-convention campaign has dictated their choice or drastically narrowed their options. More nominations are decided in the first ballot these days, and the chances of a party's picking an "unknown" candidate diminish.

But if they have lost some of their freedom and deliberative character, it is too soon to say that they have lost it all. The unlikelihood of lightning striking the unknown statesman does not signal the complete decline of the convention. As one observer has expressed it: [16]

Conventions will reach their decisions quickly, avoiding prolonged contests and exhausted nominations of unknown but inoffensive compromise choices. The party's designation will go to an aspirant who has already established himself as a major possibility among the electorate and the party leaders. The convention's decision will be largely one of choosing from a number of major hopefuls — but, in many years, this will still be a decision for the convention to make.

The choice, that is, may still remain in the convention, even though it is somewhat restricted. And if the choice must be made among the well-known "major hopefuls," it may more likely be made by the majority of delegates at the convention rather than a small number of "kingmakers." But regardless of where the locus of power in the conventions rests, the convention as a nominating institution has suffered some decline in recent years.

At the same time, the conventions have been converted increasingly into massive party rallies and pageants; they have become "spectaculars," intended as much for the national radio and TV audience as for the delegates in attendance. Sensitive to the new audience, convention officials have rescheduled the major events for prime viewing time and preached good convention deportment; they have given key convention roles increasingly to telegenic partisans, speeded up roll calls and polls of delegations, and virtually eliminated the conduct of serious business in the daytime hours.[17] The television coverage offers each party a priceless op-

[16] Pomper, op. cit., p. 197.

[17] For a fuller study of the impact of television on the conventions, see Herbert Waltzer, "In the Magic Lantern: Television Coverage of the 1964 National Conventions." Public Opinion Quarterly, XXX (1966), pp. 33–53.

portunity to reach voters and party workers and to launch its campaign with maximum impact. So, not completely but perceptibly, the function of the convention shifts from the conduct of party business to the stimulation of wider political audiences.

REASONS FOR THE CHANGES

These changes in the nature of the presidential nominating conventions derive from more basic changes in American politics and especially in presidential politics. Among them one can cite the following:

1. Seekers for the party nominations have stepped up their pre-convention activity, attempting both to tie up delegates and to enlist popular support for their aspirations. Greater organization, resources, jet transportation, polling, and media exposure all permit it; John F. Kennedy's pre-convention campaign of 1960 may very well have ushered in the new era in campaigns for the presidential nomination. As a result, the pre-convention period may reveal a popular favorite, or it may discourage other candidates. Accompanying the candidate activity is more intensive reporting; press services keep count of the number of delegates committed to various candidates, and the Gallup poll and its competitors report the state of public enthusiasm for them. Both candidates and delegates have today far fuller information about the entire nomination process before they get to the convention than they ever did before. Consequently, the crucial bargaining and trading of support, the committing of some and the weeding out of the others, take place increasingly at the pre-convention stages. The political metabolism of the nomination process has, in other words, been greatly accelerated with the result that the crucial point of decision may come before the convention.

2. Political power in the party has shifted away from the state and local party leaders who at one time came as ambassadors to the convention for the purpose of negotiating within a fragmented, decentralized system. Power in the parties in mid-20th century is less decentralized as national leadership, national candidates, Presidents, and Congresses dominate the political loyalties and perceptions of voters. National party figures and national concerns — and party identifications shaped by national politics — have cut into the complete independence of the state leaders.

3. The enormous escalation of media coverage during the conventions has transformed them. Major candidates become national figures, and information on the slightest defection of support is daily news. The convention itself is no longer a private meeting; its diplomacy must be conducted in public. Even the formerly sacrosanct hagglings of resolutions and credentials committees are done in the public eye. Over 5,000 media credentials were issued at each of the 1964 conventions; in that same year CBS alone had a total staff of over 600 at the Republican convention in San Francisco.[18] Broadly based wishes and expectations — especially pop-

[18] *Ibid.*

ular choices in the pre-convention politics — now must be weighed more heavily in the deliberations of the conventions.

Taking a broader overview one may put the matter of change another way. Aided by mass media-based and reported campaigning and by the results of periodic polling, the process of nominating a President has fallen under the spell and evolving influences of a national, popular democracy. More and more people are aware of the candidates and the choices before the party, and more and more of them have views about those choices. To nominate an unknown candidate today is, therefore, doubly dangerous — dangerous first for the seeming affront to the popularly supported contestants, and dangerous if only for the handicap of running an unknown candidate against the very well-known candidate of the other party. (That kind of "publicity gap" was one of Adlai Stevenson's main problems in 1952.) To the extent that closed, secretive party conventions were incompatible with the "democratization" of the presidential nominating process, they had to change.[19]

Change and declining power may beset the conventions, but the parties are not about to abandon them. They will gladly make those compromises and trimmings necessary to use radio, press, and television coverage more effectively. But even in its altered condition the national convention of the 60's and 70's is too precious an institution to surrender. It is the only real, palpable existence — the only "symptom," indeed — of a national political party. It is the only occasion for rediscovery of common traditions and common interests, the only time for common decision-making and a coming together to celebrate old glories and achievements. The convention also stimulates the workers and contributors to party labors, and it encourages party candidates in the states and localities. Its rites may not mean a great deal to the majority of Americans passively peering at the TV screen (and a bit sullen over missing the summer re-runs), but they do mean something to the men and women of the party organization. They are, in short, a vital, integrative force in the life of the American national parties.

Not surprisingly, the parties have resisted the varying proposals for a national presidential primary advanced over the last several generations. The proposals fall into two categories: those which would replace the nominating conventions with a national primary for nominating presidential candidates, and those which would retain the convention but extend the elections of pledged delegates to all of the states. They are aimed in major part at the manipulation of national conventions by small groups of supposedly irresponsible men. Their rationale is the general rationale of the direct primary as a system of nominations. Ironically, it is in this case

[19] William G. Carleton offers another reinterpretation of the national conventions in "The Revolution in the Presidential Nominating Convention," *Political Science Quarterly*, LXXII (1957), pp. 224–240.

directed at convention conditions that were far more prevalent fifty or eighty years ago than they are today.

The problems involved in instituting a national presidential primary — the problem of a uniform date, for example — are as great as the objections, and the proposals have come to naught. There is, first of all, the objection that the national presidential primary would deprive the parties of the organizational benefits of the convention. There is, too, the staggering burden in time and resources that a nomination campaign in fifty states would place on the parties and candidates. (And very possibly it would encourage the growth of a pre-primary endorsement politics in which the leading contenders would seek the endorsement of the various state organizations.) But above all, most scholars and political leaders are unconvinced that a national presidential primary would result in the selection of more able candidates for the Presidency. There seems little reason to think it could elevate — as did the conventions — less known but able men such as Wendell Willkie and Adlai Stevenson. And there is reason to suspect that it might not pick the strongest candidates from the party's point of view. It might very well select men like Estes Kefauver, who enjoyed little support within the party and among its activists. Like any primary, it might also result in the nomination of a presidential candidate whose appeal was limited to the hard-core party voters. In a pragmatic political system one of the greatest advantages of the convention is its ability to pick candidates who unite rather than divide the party and who make the broadest possible appeals to the American electorate.[20]

The Presidential Campaign

Tradition has long dictated that the presidential campaign open in early September. After the July or August conventions the presidential and vice-presidential candidates rest and map strategy for the approaching campaign. Then, it all begins with the Democratic candidate's traditional opening speech in Detroit on Labor Day.

The campaigning for the Presidency is in many ways the generic American political campaign "writ large." Its main problems and tasks are different in degree but similar in kind. The candidate and his campaign managers must still raise money, print literature and flyers, contract for ads and media time, schedule travel and speeches, put together an integrated campaign organization, and amass the necessary research. The candidate also faces similar strategic choices. Is he to rely on personal appearances or radio-television speeches, or, more likely, on what mixture of the two? What timing will he adopt — the "full speed from the beginning" strategy of Kennedy in 1960, or the pointed, paced build-up favored

[20] For a defense of the convention, Aaron Wildavsky, "On the Superiority of National Conventions," *Review of Politics,* XXIV (1962), pp. 307–319.

by Nixon in the same year? Will he play primarily on the appeals of the party, the candidate ("I like Ike," "All the way with LBJ"), or issues and ideology (of Barry Goldwater: "In your heart you know he's right," or Kennedy's promise to "get the country moving again")? And like candidates all over the country he faces problems in presenting himself to voters — Nixon's problem in overcoming a reputation for deviousness; Kennedy's problems of youthfulness, Catholicism, wealth, and family; Goldwater's reputation for impetuous "shooting from the hip"; and Johnson's for the ruthless exercise of political power ("arm-twisting").

Yet, many of the usual campaign problems are heightened by the nature of the presidential office and constituency. The candidate's problem in keeping posted on how the campaign is going, on his progress with the electorate, is tremendous. The expanse of the country, the variety of local conditions, and his isolation from the "grass roots" make any kind of assessment difficult. In this dilemma the presidential candidates have recently relied on professional pollers to supplement the reports of the local politicians. That same expanse of continent when joined to the length and pace of the campaign puts exceptional physical strains on the candidate. During the 1960 campaign the Republican candidate lost valuable time because of a knee injury, and the Democrat was plagued with hoarseness in the early phases of the campaign. Virtually every presidential candidate comes to election day on the fine edge of exhaustion. Finally, there are the special problems of the candidate who must run against an incumbent President and thus run against all of the publicity, public exposure, and media attention a President has commanded and continues to command. Perhaps these developments in the presidential campaign can best be illustrated by the changes of a century. In 1860 Abraham Lincoln never left Springfield, Illinois, during the campaign; in 1960 the two candidates together travelled more than 100,000 miles and gave almost 600 speeches during the campaign.

The Electoral College and the American parties shape the presidential campaign — and the candidates' problems in organizing it — in at least two additional ways. Because of the Electoral College, presidential candidates allocate their time and resources in a special way. In all other American constituencies a candidate can pick up useful votes even in his areas of weakness, even in those areas he will lose. Not so in the Electoral College, where the candidate gains only if he can win at least a plurality of the vote in a state. The strategy of a presidential campaign is, therefore, drastically altered, and presidential candidates generally pick a group of states which they feel they can carry and then devote their time to them. Presidential campaigns have tended to be concentrated as a result in the close, two-party states, with the candidates largely avoiding each other's areas of strength. Increasingly, however, as virtually all of the states are becoming competitive, two-party states, fewer and fewer states can be avoided. The sheer physical burden of the campaign may thus increase within the next decades. Richard Nixon in 1960, in fact, fulfilled his pledge to campaign in all fifty states — an awesome precedent for future candidates.

The rambling, decentralized character of the American parties places special problems of its own on the campaign, chiefly on its organizational aspects. Here one finds the same issues of professional versus amateur, of party committee versus voluntary personal organizations, that one finds in the organization of any campaign. But in the case of the presidential campaign there is the extra complication of the decentralized American party system. The national committee can do little to control the whims and activities of state parties. The party's ticket may find state organizations opposed to it — Harry F. Byrd, autocrat of the Virginia Democrats, rebuffed Adlai Stevenson in both 1952 and 1956. The problem, then, is one of deciding whether to rely on a weak national committee to unify the various state and local parties, or whether to build a largely voluntary, *ad hoc* organization. A candidate such as Lyndon Johnson successfully transferred the power of the Presidency to the national committee and made it an effective part of his campaign organization. His opponent, Barry Goldwater, simply merged his personal organization with the Republican national committee by placing his men in positions of formal party power. Adlai Stevenson, at the other extreme, set up his own campaign organization in 1952 with its headquarters in Springfield, Illinois.[21]

RADIO, TELEVISION, AND THE THIRD ESTATE

For a series of special reasons presidential campaigns depend more heavily than most others on campaigning through the mass media — radio, newspaper, and television ads and appearances. The "special reasons" are, among others, these:

> Even though media exposure costs dearly (example: the two presidential candidates in 1964 spent over $11,000,000 on radio and television alone), presidential candidates find it easier to raise the "big money" than other candidates.

> Media exposure is more "efficient" for presidential candidates. They have none of the usual problems of paying for an audience that lies partly outside of the candidate's constituency.

> The presidential candidates have a more receptive audience for a media-centered campaign. The voter who wouldn't by-pass the TV wrestling show for a congressional candidate may do so for a presidential aspirant.

[21] Theodore H. White, *The Making of the President 1964* (New York: Atheneum, 1965) gives a full description of the Johnson campaign organizations in 1964 from pages 366 to 371.

The size of the presidential constituency dictates that this is the only practical way for the candidate to reach large numbers of voters.

So the dependence of presidential campaigners on the media grows, and there is no end in sight. To a greater extent than in most other campaigns the masters of the media — public relations men, pollsters, ad agencies, TV production experts — form a new political elite in the presidential races.

No candidate can escape the opportunities the media offer him. A good deal of his media exposure will come without cost or effort; every speech or foray, no matter how trivial, will be reported. Even some of this kind of exposure can be controlled, however. Barry Goldwater's campaign managers persuaded him to forego press conferences during the 1964 campaign in order not to be goaded into rash and ill-considered retorts. In their commercial uses of the media, however, the candidates have full control of its uses. They can control its major and minor impacts — right down to the cases of a specially coiffed Kennedy (to alter the boyish mop of hair) and the specially made-up Nixon (to conceal a heavy beard). Candidates may choose their form of exposure — will it be full speeches or spot announcements (the former runs the danger of boring voters, the latter have been criticized for merchandising Presidents)? Then, too, the candidate must find a congenial personal style for the media, and he must master its little arts — the reading of the teleprompter (a repeated pitfall for Eisenhower in 1952), or the timing of the speech (a skill Adlai Stevenson never mastered). For the candidate who has had little experience with it, the problems of coping with television add one more very wearing pressure to the strains of the campaign.

Something of an apogee in the trend toward the media-centered presidential campaign was reached in the Great Debates of 1960. The networks had laid the way early in 1960 by offering to give free TV time during the campaign to the Democratic and Republican candidates if Congress would free them from the legal necessity of granting "equal time" to the other, minor party presidential candidates. Congress obliged them for the 1960 campaign and that one only. Senator Kennedy proposed the debate format, and Vice-President Nixon agreed; together with network representatives they worked out the protocols. The format was this: four debates, spaced from late September to late October; opening statements from each candidate in the first and last debate; the remainder of these two and all of the other two debates given over to two-and-a-half-minute responses to the questions of reporters. Some 85,000,000 Americans saw at least one of the debates, and the audiences averaged about 70,000,000 per debate. The composition of the audience was as remarkable as the size; candidates perpetually face the problem of speaking largely to their committed supporters, but a debate such as this brought each candidate before partisans of the other party and before the self-defined independent and undecided voters.

Most observers seem agreed that the Debates of 1960 did more for Kennedy than Nixon. They offered Kennedy the opportunity to close the "publicity gap" between himself and the better known Vice-President, and they also afforded him the opportunity of showing his intellectual maturity and his grasp of public issues. The debates certainly set no new records for elevated, rational debate of public issues, but they did give the voters a chance to watch the candidates face, under conditions of stress, a series of intellectual demands. A CBS poll conducted by Elmo Roper suggested that a margin of Americans perhaps as large as two million chose Kennedy over Nixon largely on the basis of the debates alone.[22] President Johnson showed no enthusiasm for the debate format in 1964, and it seems unlikely that incumbent Presidents will often be lured into it. In fact, there may not be many presidential elections in which both candidates will think it to their advantage to debate. And public pressure does not seem great enough at the moment to force them.

The media-centered campaign raises new issues and creates new dimensions for the entire range of presidential politics. It forces the parties to consider the voice and appearance of the presidential candidate; it will always be held against Richard Nixon, unhappily, that his profile, beard, and dark eyebrows do not look well on television. It has certainly multiplied the costs of a presidential campaign and created new problems in money-raising. It has also raised repeatedly the question of the political biases of the media. In 1952 and 1956 the Democratic party had well-publicized difficulties in hiring an advertising agency to handle its presidential campaigns, and in the same years there were charges that the "one-party press" gave far more coverage and far more favorable coverage in its news columns to the Republican candidate.[23] In 1960 and 1964 the Democrats seemed to have no problems on either score. By 1964, in fact, the party had retained the prominent Madison Avenue agency of Doyle Dane Bernbach, creator of the much-admired Volkswagen ads, and won the support of a good majority of daily newspapers in the poll of *Editor and Publisher*.[24] The Democrats' experience seems to have proved

---

[22] White, *The Making of the President 1960*, p. 294. On the Great Debates of 1960, see Sidney Kraus (ed.), *The Great Debates* (Bloomington: Indiana Univ. Press, 1962) and Stanley Kelley, "Campaign Debates: Some Facts and Issues," *Public Opinion Quarterly*, XXVI (1962), pp. 351–366.

[23] Nathan B. Blumberg, *One-Party Press?* (Lincoln: Univ. of Nebraska Press, 1954) reports a survey of the 1952 coverage in 35 large dailies; he finds only mild bias toward the Republican party and candidate. The study, however, includes most of the country's most respected and responsible newspapers. Very probably bias was greater among the smaller city dailies.

[24] *Editor and Publisher*, October 31, 1964; some 60 per cent of American daily newspapers responded to the poll with these results: 440 for Johnson, 359 for Goldwater, and 237 independents.

once again that in politics, as in the rest of life, nothing succeeds like success.

· · ·

These are, as we have reiterated, not esoteric campaign problems. Many candidates face them. They are more differences of degree than of kind — of quantity rather than quality. For, despite the exalted magnitude of the office, presidential politics grow out of American political norms, styles, and traditions. And of the entire process of presidential politics, the campaign phase is probably the most typical, the least unusual, phase of all. Certainly it is not marked by the special procedures and institutions that the earlier phases are. The art of presidential campaigning is the basic art of American political campaigning — the art of defining and specifying the various audiences of the campaign and then reaching them most efficiently and most effectively.

The National Party

If there is a "national" party in the United States — despite all of the influences which fragment the parties into fifty state parties and innumerable local autonomies — it must materialize, if only in passing, as the parties contest the one national election in American politics. And if there is a national party, it must be able to function as one and to identify some goals and interests beyond those of the state and local parties. Does, then, the quadrennial race for the Presidency serve as the stimulus or the occasion for the emergence of a national party?

If by a "national" party one means a national party organization, then clearly there is no national party. The national committees, even during the presidential campaigns, are usually weak, often unused, auxiliaries of the campaign organizations of the parties' presidential candidates. The candidates have the right to appoint the chairmen of the national committees, and that traditional right in many ways symbolizes both the deference paid to the wishes of the candidate and the subordination of the national committee to him. In fact, the entire business of nominating and electing a President is dominated by the candidates to a degree greater even than the usual domination of the candidates in the rest of American politics. If there is, therefore, a national party, it is almost exclusively the party of office-seekers and office-holders (i.e., the party in government), and we have every right and reason to call it the "presidential" party.

The best indication that the state parties cannot build national organizations or find a national voice comes in the politics before and during the nominating conventions. Even though they are nominally preparing for a national election, the state parties and their activists continue to weigh heavily the interests of state and local parties. In the honest words of a New York delegate to the 1960 Democratic convention: [25]

Politics is business. We figure Senator Kennedy for a winner who will help the local ticket. My first preference is Lyndon Johnson but party considerations come first. DeSapio, who is in trouble back home, and Michael Pendergast are the real leaders. Sure, we have Governor Harriman as the Honorary Chairman and Mayor Wagner as the chairman of the delegation — we had to give Harriman a place of distinction and the mayor just wants publicity and is only protecting his own political future in New York City.

That theme of the dominance of state and local organizational interests could be repeated over and over with the lore of the conventions. While nominating national candidates and writing national platforms, the delegates pursue the organizational interests and goals of their state parties and the state party leadership. They want to make sure that the process of choice (both before and during the convention) will not create factions in the organization or in any other way threaten its organizational well-being. They want to protect their bargaining power so that they can maximize the achievement of their particular goals (e.g., the promotion of the aspirations of a state leader). And they want to make sure that the presidential candidate and platform of the party will assist the party in winning state and local office.

Much of this localism, even during the period of Presidential politics, results from the localism of political incentives. The incentives of patronage and preferment, of political career and social advantage, depend on the winning of state and local elections and the maintenance of an effective state party organization. The goals and incentive of party activists, however, appear to be shifting from these locally-rooted incentives to those of issue, interest, and ideology. And these tend by nature to be national, since the great issues of public policy with which they are involved tend to be national issues which will be resolved by national political institutions. The party worker must, therefore, look to national politics — to the election of a President and a Congress — for the achievement of these goals. That trend is probably also matched by an increasingly national focus within the loyal party electorate; the political information and goals of the American voter, as well as his party identification, are increasingly dominated by the competitions, personalities, and issues of national politics.

There are, therefore, forces making for a national party and those resisting it. The conventions themselves illustrate that ambivalence. In some

---

[25] Quoted by Bert E. Swanson in Tillett (ed.), *Inside Politics*, p. 193. The case studies of the behavior of state delegations to the 1960 conventions reported in this collection are full of similar instances of the strength of the state party interests in the process of choosing a presidential nominee. It is, in many ways, the theme which unifies the case studies.

states the state organizations may be strong enough to send delegates to the convention who will protect the interests of the state party. In other cases the delegates may be loyal primarily to a would-be candidate and committed to support him, regardless of the competing interests of the state party. They may even be people of little experience in the party; the Goldwater delegates in the Republican convention of 1964 generally had less party experience than delegates usually have. The result is an unstable amalgam of state-oriented and national-oriented presidential politics in the conventions.

With the state party organizations and delegates so divided between local and national outlook, and with the national committees unable to function effectively, the national party, such as it is, is easily dominated by the presidential candidate and his followers. The only viable national organization is his — either his pre-convention organization or, should he win the nomination, his campaign organization. It is the only organization with purely national goals and incentives. And frequently the activists in the states whose incentive to action is a national personality or a national ideology find their best avenue to national political involvement in the voluntary organizations (e.g., Citizens for Eisenhower), the campaign organizations, or the personal followings (e.g., the Robert Kennedy personal organization) of the present or potential presidential candidates. The would-be candidates collectively dominate an ever-growing portion of the pre-convention politics; they have thus destroyed the control the state party organizations and their leaders (the fabled "kingmakers") once held over the nominations in the conventions. Presidential candidates no longer emerge as the result of bargainings among representatives of state party organizations. And the candidates more and more raise the enormous sums of money needed for the campaign itself; the setting of campaign strategy and tactics is also entirely in their hands.

What is, therefore, loosely called the national party is really a party of the presidential candidate. His main political problem in presidential politics, in fact, is to override and unite all of the local, separatist interests and loyalties within the party. He must nationalize the attention of voters and the activities of party activists for at least the brief time of the presidential campaign. And he must do so in a constituency (as defined by the Electoral College) which is in itself not quite national, for it is more exactly a constituency which is, like the parties themselves, an aggregate of state units. In solving these problems of "nationalization" the candidates have in their favor the absence of a competing national organization; they reign supreme in the national party. They also have on their side their own increasing visibility as political personalities, the increasingly national focus which the party loyalties of large numbers of voters have taken, and a concern for national issues and ideologies among increasing numbers of political activists.

The American party is, therefore, something of a hierarchical hybrid. It combines a party organizational structure that remains steadfastly decentralized with a politics in which the focuses — in party identifications, personalities, and issues — are increasingly national and centralized. These centralizing influences are represented by the candidates, the officeholders, and the issues and conflicts they decide. The party in government thus becomes the focus of these nationalizing tendencies, just as it furnishes (at another level) a centralizing impetus in states where local city and county organizations have undercut centralized organizational power within the state. The American party, taken as a national entity, is an illogical, even contradictory, mixture of a decentralized party organization and an increasingly centralized party in government. Such an unlikely combination raises, finally, the question of how long the party organizations will be able to remain so determinedly decentralized at a time when all other influences in American government and politics are thrown on the side of nationalization and centralization.

Chapter Thirteen

FINANCING THE CAMPAIGNS

At some time in the future it may ultimately be possible to draw up a great balance sheet for the parties in which all of the inputs of manpower, skills, and money — all of the resources they recruit — are balanced against the resources and assets they expend and the purposes for which they are spent. This kind of resource accounting, when and if we ever achieve it, will suggest different patterns from state to state and locality to locality in the total value of the resources, in the kinds of resources employed, in the nature and motives of the contributors, and in the uses and "expenditures" to which the resources have been put. That kind of input-ouput accounting is, however, beyond us at the moment; and so, therefore, are the kinds of analysis of the parties it would sustain.

The discussion earlier (in Chapter Four, especially) of the recruitment of manpower and skills into the party organizations approached the question of such an account, however fragmentarily, for the party organizations. It suggested at least the rewards and incentives the organizations had at their command and the manpower resources they recruited with them. But the party organization is only one sector of the complex American major party, and it does not account for all the resources the party gets and spends. The party candidates and public officials — the party in government, in other words — recruit and spend another substantial sum of political resources. And since it is the contesting of elections that most concerns the party in government, and since it dominates the party's role in those activities in most parts of the country, the collective campaign for public office affords the most logical occasion for assessing its resources.

Again, in the best possible of all scholarly worlds, we might some day be able to account for all of the contributions to the campaigns for nominations and elections — to account, that is, for all of the man hours of work, all of the goods, all the skills and expertise, and all of the cash contributed. But difficult as they may be to identify, the cash contributions are easier to outline than the others, and this chapter will be largely limited to them. That limitation is one forced largely by sheer lack of information, but one can build a substantive rationale for it, too, even at the risk of seeming to make a virtue of necessity. While the assets of the party organizations have been largely in valuables (goods and services) other than cash, those of the party in government have to a much greater extent been based on cash contributions.

The shift from organization control of electoral contests to control by the party in government has, therefore, meant a shift to a reliance on political assets the candidate must purchase or rent with cash. As candidates progressively free themselves from the organizations, they find they must solicit cash contributions for the political information, skills, manpower, and organization which the party organization once furnished them for no charge other than some mortgage on their political loyalties. Some of those assets the party organization may have purchased and may still purchase with cash contributed to it; the party organization, too, may commission public opinion polls or rent billboards. But much of the organization's campaign assistance — the door-to-door canvassing, the phone calls, the taking of voters to the polls — came without cash expenditure.

Finally, the increasing importance of money as a political resource can easily be documented — and thus its special consideration justified. There is abundant evidence scattered through this chapter that the cash inputs into American political campaigning are rising steeply. There is no comparable evidence that the value of non-cash inputs is increasing or, at least, increasing at such a pace. One can only conclude, consequently, that cash inputs, especially in the campaign activities dominated by the party in government, are increasing in relative importance.

How Big Is the Big Money?

A forbidding secrecy veils the budgets of parties and candidates. The secrecy results from a number of considerations: the hesitance of contributors to be publicly identified, the fear of candidates that they might (knowingly or unknowingly) be violating some law regulating political finance, and a general fear by all concerned that even the most modest political contributions and expenditures will seem to be profligacy to a suspicious public.

Even if one pushes past the barrier of secrecy, the problems in identifying sums of money in politics do not disappear. American parties and politics are decentralized and fragmented, and so are their finances. The welter of overlapping, semi-autonomous party and candidate organizations all have budgets, and they often transfer sums among each other — occasionally, one suspects, to obscure purposely the total picture of political finance. Furthermore, it is often difficult to allocate expenses to a specific candidate or campaign; how, for example, does one apportion the costs and value of a billboard supporting a number of candidates? It is also difficult to distinguish between campaign and non-campaign expense; is the salary of a secretary in a congressman's office to be charged as a non-campaign expense, even during the last few weeks of the campaign?

Despite all of these and other difficulties, Alexander Heard and Herbert Alexander, the two most authoritative experts on the question of money in American politics, have made estimates of the total campaign expenditures — for all offices, at all electoral levels, and at both primaries and general elections — for the presidential years: [1]

> 1952 — $140,000,000
> 1956 — $155,000,000
> 1960 — $175,000,000
> 1964 — $200,000,000

In just twelve years, therefore, total expenses in presidential years increased by more than 40 per cent. The total campaign bill for the years in between would, of course, be smaller.

Not surprisingly, the single most expensive campaign for public office in the United States is that for the Presidency. Just to win the party nomination — that is, the right to run — may cost several million dollars. Governor Nelson Rockefeller of New York, a man of very considerable resources, is said to have spent almost five million dollars in his ill-starred pursuit of the 1964 Republican nomination. The victor in that contest, Barry Goldwater, spent even more. Even a semi-serious favorite son candidate may spend $50,000 in the nomination campaign. And an indecisive or unaggressive candidate, such as Adlai Stevenson, can mount a costly campaign; just two national committees working for his renomination in 1956 spent almost $800,000.

The presidential campaign itself raises the ante conspicuously. In 1960 the total spent at the national level was just about $25,000,000; by 1964 the tab had increased to $34,800,000 (Table 1). That figure for 1964 represents a more than doubling of the 1956 total of $17,200,000. The two parties taken together spent about $29,000,000 nationally, or about 41 cents per vote for their November aggregate. Those figures include, it should be clear, both direct expenditures and transfers to state and local committees.[2]

[1] The data from 1952 and 1956 come from Alexander Heard, *The Costs of Democracy* (Chapel Hill: Univ. of North Carolina Press, 1960); those for 1960 and 1964 are from Herbert E. Alexander's two studies, *Financing the 1960 Election* and *Financing the 1964 Election*, both published in Princeton, New Jersey, by the Citizens' Research Foundation, a non-partisan organization devoted to studies of money in politics.

[2] The data from this paragraph and Table 1 come from Alexander's two studies, *Financing the 1960 Election* and *Financing the 1964 Election*.

Table 1

NATIONAL SPENDING IN PRESIDENTIAL ELECTIONS
OF 1960 AND 1964

	1960	*1964*
Democratic Party	$10,587,000	$11,973,000
Republican Party	11,300,000	17,187,000
Labor and Misc.	3,127,000	5,628,000
Total	$25,014,000	$34,788,000

It is difficult to generalize about the cost of a race for the Senate, but it is not unheard-of to spend several million dollars in one. In their 1964 contest in New York, Robert Kennedy and the incumbent, Kenneth Keating, were estimated by the *New York Times* each to have spent close to two million dollars. But more typically, Senate races in fairly competitive areas may cost between $200,000 and $500,000; it is, of course, possible for a firmly entrenched senator from a small state to spend considerably less. It is no easier to generalize about the cost of House campaigns. The campaigns of many candidates in competitive urban districts run up costs exceeding $100,000. Other more fortunate candidates may manage for 10, 20, or $30,000 — or for some figure between $10,000 and $100,000. Costs also fluctuate erratically in successive congressional campaigns. It is not unusual for a successful candidate for the House to spend twice as much beating the incumbent than he will in his first defense of the office two years later.

Beyond these quests for national office, there are the thousands of campaigns for state and local office. Hard information is rare, the generalizations questionable. Many of them involve almost unbelievably small sums; each year hundreds of candidates win office in the United States in campaigns that involve cash outlays of a few hundred dollars. On the other hand the mayoralty campaign in a large American city may cost a candidate and his supporters several hundred thousand dollars. Campaigns for governor of the larger states often exceed $500,000. And Nelson Rockefeller spent more than $5,000,000 winning reelection in 1966; it was very likely the most expensive non-presidential campaign in the history of American politics. Campaigns for referenda in California, the home of the most elaborate non-candidate campaigns, have been known to reach a million dollars; the various groups on both sides of the 1964 pay-TV referendum are estimated to have spent over $2,000,000.

To repeat, all of these figures reflect only cash outlay. Therefore, they do not reflect the true economic costs of the campaign. They do not include the gift or loan of goods or services. Volunteer workers contribute time for canvassing, typing envelopes, plotting campaign strategy, writing press releases, and dozens of other campaign jobs. Business or trade unions may, in fact, donate the services of specialists to a party or candidate for the length of the campaign. Partisans may also donate goods: free paper for literature, the use of a plane or auto, or their home and their refreshments for fund-raising parties. Nor do these totals include the costs of campaigning borne by the public treasuries. In cities and states with old-style patronage systems, the city hall and county court houses and all of their employees may be a vortex of campaign activity for the weeks before elections. Senators and congressmen customarily use their offices, their staffs, and often their franking privileges for campaign help. Heard suggests that these additional contributions (exclusive of part-time volunteer labor) would add another 5 per cent to the bill; the value of contributed labor seems greater but it is virtually impossible to estimate.[3] One might venture the opinion, however, that these non-cash expenditures form a larger chunk of local campaign costs and that with a shift from party organization campaigning (non-cash) to media campaigning (cash), the percentage of non-cash costs is, on the aggregate, declining.

The costs of campaigning are on the rise. Heard, writing in 1959, plotted the rises in costs from 1940 through 1956 and concluded that the increases of 54 per cent in that period were no greater than increases in the price level — that is, no greater than increases in the general cost of living.[4] Since then, however, the increases have far exceeded the rise in the price level; between 1956 and 1964 the aggregate sums increased by 29 per cent, while the price level rose only 4.5 per cent. So, while the myth of rising campaign costs is an old one, the phenomenon is actually fairly new. Most observers would attribute the rise to greater dependence on the mass media, especially television. It can also be put more broadly in the terms suggested in the last paragraph. Campaigning in the United States has increasingly depended on avenues and mechanisms requiring cash rather than donated labor and goods.

These then are preliminary answers to the question of how big the political money is. Unanswered is the more difficult question of how big it *really* is — how big it is when measured by relative values and utilities rather than the fixed measure of the dollar sign. In the affluent American economy the $200,000,000 figure represented about .03 of 1 per cent of the gross national product in 1964. If one is looking for comparative benchmarks, it becomes clear that many smaller countries spend far more on political campaigns (measured by money per voter) than does the United States. A country such as Italy may spend four times what American parties and candidates do per voter,[5] and the two candidates in the Philippine presidential elections of 1965 spent just a bit more than the

[3] Heard, *The Costs of Democracy*, p. 372.

[4] *Ibid.*, p. 376.

[5] The entire edition of the *Journal of Politics*, XXV, No. 4 (November, 1963), was devoted to studies in comparative political finance; see especially the article by Arnold Heidenheimer, "Comparative Party Finance: Notes on Practices and Toward a Theory," pp. 790–811.

two American contestants of 1964. And that $200,000,000 total for 1964 is just about what Procter and Gamble spends per year on an advertising budget for some 42 different products. The top ten advertisers in the United States alone spent more than a billion dollars in 1965.

PATTERNS OF EXPENDITURES

The modern arts of mass communication — and especially the television tube — have revolutionized American political campaigning. In so doing they have, of course, upset and restructured the patterns of expenditures in campaigns. In 1948's presidential election there were no expenditures for television, but sixteen years later in 1964 the campaigns of Barry Goldwater and Lyndon B. Johnson together spent, by conservative estimates, $9,000,000 for television time. Additions of those magnitudes not only go to explain the absolute rise in campaign costs in recent years; they also reflect shifts and dislocations in the percentage portions of campaign budgets going for various purposes.

Table 2
TOTAL RADIO AND TELEVISION EXPENDITURES
IN ALL GENERAL ELECTIONS [a]

Dollars (in millions)

Year	Democrats	Republicans	Total [b]
1956	$ 4.1	$ 5.4	$ 9.8
1960	6.2	7.5	14.1
1964	11.0	13.0	24.6

[a] Source: Alexander, Financing the 1964 Election, p. 52.
[b] The total includes small sums spent by other parties and groups.

The reports of the Federal Communications Commission to Congress permit a more-than-usually precise definition of radio and television campaign costs. As Table 2 suggests, the total Democratic and Republican election costs have increased more than two and a half times between 1956 and 1964. (And the figure of $24,600,000 for 1964 could also be swelled by the additional $10,000,000 spent on TV and radio in the 1964 primaries.) Part of the increase reflects the spread of television sets and stations; part, however, reflects a growing reliance on TV. As for the jump between 1960 and 1964, it should be remembered that the presidential candidates in 1964 had to pay for their TV time. In 1960 they received between $4,000,000 and $5,000,000 in free coverage; the four Great Debates alone amounted to a two-million-dollar largesse. Congress did not waive the "equal time" rule in 1964, and the parties paid.

The radio and TV costs have, furthermore, continued to increase enormously ever since 1964. In 1962 the parties and the candidates spent $21.8 million on all radio and TV campaigning in both the primary and general election campaigns. The comparable comprehensive total for 1964 (for all candidates, in both the primaries and the general election) was $34.6 million. But by 1966, the year of another "off-year" election, total radio and TV costs were at $32 million, an increase of 60 per cent over 1962's totals and a figure very close to that of the 1964 presidential year.

Television expenditures, however, do not fall evenly on all candidates and party levels. Presidential campaigns rely far more heavily on them than do the others. While the 1964 presidential campaign accounted for only 17.5 per cent of total campaign costs in that year ($34.8 of $200 million), the bills of the presidential campaign ($11 million) explain 32.1 per cent of the total radio and TV bill for all of 1964's politicking ($34.6 million). Some other campaigns do match this concentration of funds on radio and TV; Senator Robert Kennedy allocated over half of his 1964 expenditures for radio spots and television presentations, some $900,000 on TV alone. But campaigns for the Senate and House — not to mention state and local office — rarely rely to such an extent on radio and TV. For many — such as the congressional candidate whose district is a small patch of a great urban center — TV time is a costly, inefficient, buckshot method, striking only perhaps one in eight or ten listeners who can vote for him.

Other costs related to the shift to media campaigning are also greater in the presidential campaigns. The arts of opinion polling do not come cheaply — private polls at all campaign levels in 1960 were estimated by Elmo Roper to have cost $1,500,000 — and a proportionately greater cost is probably borne in the presidential races. Advertisements on the printed page can also cost thousands of dollars; an eight-page insert in the *Reader's Digest* cost the Goldwater forces about $300,000 in 1964. Given the nature of the presidential office, the campaign for it involves far greater costs for travel and communication; jet fares, postage, long-distance phone bills, postage, and telegrams are major items. The costs of moving presidential entourages — advance men, press contacts, speech writers, diction coaches, friends, advisors, and family — increase not only because of the greater traveling but because of the greater costs of jet travel itself.

On the other hand, state and local campaigns rely more on newspaper advertisements and campaign literature. Other sources of communication — the lapel button, the bumper sticker, the signs on the lawn or in the window, for example — can also account for a sizeable part of the candidate's expenditures. The state and local campaigns also bear heavy costs in salary and expenses of staffs and in maintaining headquarters or offices. In almost every campaign, in fact, the major categories of expenses are two: communication costs and overhead and staff costs.

Finally, what if any differences are there in party expenditure patterns? The evidence of recent presidential years is that the pattern of the distribution of expenditures does not differ between the parties; they both, for example, spend approximately the same percentage of their expenditures for radio and television. But while general patterns are the same, the level of Republican expenditures has stayed above that of the Democrats. Even if one includes the transfers that Democratic national committees make to state and local committees and the labor spending on behalf of Democratic candidates, it appears that the Republicans at the national level have been spending between 10 and 20 per cent more than the Democrats. What is more, the level of Republican spending held up even in the 1964 campaign, despite the discouraging poll results, the obvious division within the party, and the difficulties of running against an incumbent President. It may well be, however, that greater non-cash expenditures by the Democrats — volunteer labor and work by party activists and patronage-holders — would narrow the margin if they could be calculated.

SOURCES AND WELL-SPRINGS

Political expenditures are comparatively obvious; the voter sees them in the very nature of the campaign directed at him. Not so with the political "input"; its sources are not apparent even to the fairly sophisticated citizen. The mechanics of fund-raising, the ways in which the parties and candidates get their money, may be no great secret, at least in part. But the nature of the contributors who avail themselves of those avenues and the nature of their motivation are. To most American political-watchers they are shadowy subjects for speculation, and their motives are the objects of the greatest suspicion.

The techniques or means by which the parties and candidates raise their funds are limited only by their ingenuity and by the prevailing political norms. The chief methods would include these:

Personal solicitation. Personal visits, phone calls, personal letters, door-to-door solicitation, or any other personal approach by the candidate himself or his solicitors raise substantial sums for the party. This is the method most generally used to reach the big contributors, the so-called "fat cats" of American politics. The success of these solicitations depends, of course, on the skill of the solicitor and on his access to men who contribute. The problem of access may be easily solved by the solicitor's range of acquaintances; given the well-known propensity of many "fat cats" to give and give again, it may only be a matter of getting the "right list."

Access arrangements. Increasingly the parties are dressing up the old-fashioned solicitations by adding the extra inducement of access to and association with men of power. Both President Kennedy and Johnson had a similar President's Club, in which a $1,000-a-year political membership fee entitled the members to periodic dinners with the President and briefings by high-level governmental officials on policy issues of the day. One of these closed dinners in 1964 attracted 1,000 guests (representing a million dollars in revenue) to break bread with President Johnson. Governor Rockefeller of New York calls his version the Governor's Club; entrance to it costs only $500. Not to be outdone, the House Republican Campaign Committee set up the Boosters Club; $3,000 acquires a founding membership in it, and a sustaining membership costs a thousand dollars.

Mail and newspaper-periodical solicitation. Candidates and parties seem constantly hopeful that the supporter sitting in the privacy of his home will be touched to the depths of his checkbook by a letter or advertisement of solicitation. It rarely seems to happen this way, however, and the results of these solicitations have been disappointing. However, the Republicans in 1964 had great success with direct mail appeals; almost a third of their revenue came in this way, and another 14 per cent came in response to TV appeals by Republicans such as John Wayne and Ronald Reagan. Republicans purchased or borrowed various mailing lists (including those of veterans groups, credit card holders, members of the American Medical Association, and stock market analysts), and then using market research techniques, planned the specific and tailored appeals for funds. In all, 15 million mailed appeals were sent out, and with them the Republicans demolished the traditional wisdom that no substantial political money could be raised with mail solicitations.

Dinners. As unlikely as it may seem, a considerable amount of the fiscal stability of American politics has been built on a foundation of banquet chicken, mashed potatoes, and half-warm peas. For a "ticket" price, usually between $10 and $100, one has dinner in a large banquet room and listens to endless political exhortations, rubs elbows with the other party faithfuls, and perhaps observes a senator, a Cabinet member, or a President. It is an "occasion"; it offers something in return for the contribution, and it may also permit some expense account sleight-of-hand. The sums raised are significant; senators or a state party may net between $50,000 and $250,000 with the right "name" guest as a drawing card. Party committees also traditionally use the dinner for fund-raising; the Lincoln Day dinners of the Republicans and the Jefferson-Jackson dinners of the Democrats are traditional annual events all around the country. Recently a variant of the political dinner — a dinner for people less interested in pure politics — has begun; called the "gala," it substitutes assorted entertainments for the usual fusillade of political oratory.

Other diversions. Taking their cue from the success of the political dinner, money-raisers have begun to rely on related occasions — the cocktail party, the theater party, the reception, the wine-tasting party, the beach party, and the trip-to-the-races. They are adaptable to all levels of giving, and they are especially apt for local candidates who cannot risk the pretentiousness of a "dinner."

Patronage. Although patronage has virtually passed from national politics, there continue to be charges that civil servants are subjected to various indirect forms of pressure to contribute, especially by purchasing tickets to political dinners. There has been little or no evidence of anything more than an occasional over-zealous salesman, however. Patronage does yield contributions in many states and localities in which the holder of a public job may be expected to contribute a fixed percentage of his salary at campaign time. In Indiana, the state patronage holders are referred to as the "two per cent club." [6] Heard reports that in some states close to two-thirds of state-level campaign funds came from state employees. Crude as it may seem, the patronage system comes close to governmentally-financed campaigns in a few American states. In addition, of course, the patronage workers make an even more substantial non-cash contribution in their labors for the party, some of which may occur during the hours of their patronage employment.

Miscellaneous. One can only suggest the richness of the ingenuity with which other sums are raised. Syracuse Democrats in 1960 offered trading stamps (at a rate higher than that of the supermarkets) for contributions. Rummage sales and raffles have been used many times. In 1964 the Goldwater enthusiasts opened retail shops in some cities to sell the usual campaign buttons and stickers, Goldwater sweatshirts, tumblers, and pens. The Democrats in 1964 sold a souvenir booklet, dedicated to John F. Kennedy, at their national convention for $10; the major revenue of the project, however, came from the advertising which cost up to $15,000 for a full-color page. Flushed with the success of that project, they put out a salute to the Congress in 1965 ("Toward an Age of Greatness") at the same advertising rates. The project raised some $600,000, but criticisms of the solicitations of the advertisers (e.g., some of them were large government contractors) were so great that the Democratic national committee turned over proceeds to the American Heritage Foundation for a nonpartisan voter education project.

Finally, the budget of any single candidate or party committee may as well show two other sources of campaign funds. One is a transfer from another political committee; large numbers of candidates for the Senate and House, for example, receive sums from their party's campaign committees in the Congress. Some, too, may rely in the short run on debt. But both of these sums must ultimately be raised in the ways suggested above.

Whatever may be the form, the occasion, or the spur for the contribution, some individual or a group of individuals has for some political goal or reason added to the political assets of a candidate or party. But who are these individuals and how many of them are there? The 1960 and 1964 studies of the American electorate by the Survey Research Center

[6] On Indiana party finance, see Robert J. McNeill, *Democratic Campaign Financing in Indiana, 1964* (published jointly by the Institute of Public Administration, Indiana University, and Citizens' Research Foundation, 1966).

found about 11 per cent of American adults claiming they had made a political contribution in that year's campaign; in the aggregate, that would
be about 10 and 12 million political contributors in the two years. They
are not, however, evenly divided between the two parties. Even though
there were far fewer Republican identifiers and voters in the 1964 national sample, about 60 per cent of the contributors were Republicans.
Or, to put it another way, 19 per cent of the Republican identifiers and
only 7 per cent of the Democratic identifiers said they made contributions in the election.[7]

Table 3
PERCENTAGES OF NATIONAL LEVEL CONTRIBUTIONS IN
AMOUNTS OF $500 OR MORE: 1960 AND 1964

	1960	1964
Democrats	59%	69%
Republicans	58%	28%

Notwithstanding that seemingly broad base of political giving — one so
broad, in fact, as to make one wonder if the SRC's respondents did not
inflate their political generosity — candidates and parties have always relied heavily on the big contributor (Table 3). In 1964 about $2,200,000
was raised by the two parties in gifts from individuals contributing more
than $10,000 apiece; both in 1960 and 1964 about 100 Americans con-
tributed at least $10,000 to one or both parties. In 1964, the national
Republicans raised more than two million dollars from the Republican Associates; an "Associate" is defined by a contribution of at least $1,000. The
President's Club of the Democratic party required the same membership
fee, and it was even more successful; the Club probably had at least some
3,500 members. Even at the lower political levels (where a large contribution often is defined as a minimum of $100 rather than $500), many state
and congressional candidates rely on large contributors for more than 50
per cent of their political campaign funds.[8]

Large contributions also come from organizations. The Committee on
Political Education (COPE) of the AFL-CIO spent more than a million
dollars in 1964 on preelection voter registration drives which were, of
course, based on the assumption that most of the new registrants would
be Democrats. COPE also spent close to another million dollars in the
election, largely in congressional races. Individual international unions
have political education committees which spend money supporting indi-

---

[7] Alexander, *Financing the 1964 Election*, pp. 68–69.

[8] Data of this paragraph and Table 3 are from the Alexander studies of 1960 and
1964.

vidual campaigns. Other business and professional groups contribute — to mention only a few examples of the 1960's, the American Medical Political Action Committee, the Council for Abolishing War, the Committee on American Leadership (the lumber industry). Their support varies; some give to candidates, some to party committees, some to Democrats, some to Republicans, and many to both.[9]

Sporadic efforts to broaden the base of party finance had not had a notable success before 1964. Sometimes the effort was less than enthusiastic, but on occasion, with strong local leadership, it succeeded. The Democratic national committee during the 1950's and 1960's tried to mount "Dollars for Democrats" drives, door-to-door solicitations for party funds. Exact figures on the returns were never published, but no one seems to have considered them a success.[10] In 1958 a well-advertised campaign for the two parties sponsored by the American Heritage Foundation and heralded by the Advertising Council yielded a grand total of less than $500,000 — roughly what three or four moderately successful dinners might have netted. In 1964, however, the Republicans staged the only really successful solicitation of small amounts in all of national politics, receiving approximately 650,000 contributions of less than $100 in response to a bevy of appeals. The response to mail solicitations continued successfully into 1965 and 1966.

Yet, the parties and candidates have never ignored the small contributor. His contribution, even if a minor one, is often crucial; moreover, one of the surest ways to recruit a worker is to induce a voter to make a contribution first. But the "big money" has rarely been raised in small amounts. Many Americans will not contribute to their party even if asked. Nor have the parties learned how to solicit and collect small contributions. If the parties have trouble finding volunteers for door-to-door voter canvassing, they will surely have trouble finding workers for door-to-door financial solicitations. To be sure, there have been sporadic successes. Minnesota Republicans in their Neighbor-to-Neighbor Drive of 1960 brought in more than $200,000 from the whole state, $94,000 of it from Hennepin county (Minneapolis and suburbs). But successes have not been common, and despite the success of the Republican national campaign with mail solicitation in 1964, local candidates still find that many of their solicitations do little more than cover the costs of printing and postage.

The elections of 1964 marked a sharp turn in the parties' patterns of contribution. The Democrats, who had long accused the Republicans of being the party of big money and big business wealth, turned to curry

[9] See especially the Congressional Quarterly Special Report, *1961–1962 Political Campaign Contributions and Expenditures* (Washington: Congressional Quarterly, 1963).

[10] On attempts to tap the small contribution, see Richard F. Schier, "Political Fund Raising and the Small Contributor: A Case Study," *Western Political Quarterly*, XI (1958), pp. 104–112, and Bernard C. Hennessy, *Dollars for Democrats, 1959* (New York: McGraw-Hill, 1960).

those very contributions — and successfully, too. The Republicans, for their part, not only raised the great bulk of their money in small contributions, but despite the disadvantages of being the "opposition" party and a "long-shot" chance at that, they raised more money than the Democrats. The change in the pattern reflects a number of factors: the political style and campaign of President Johnson, the fact that "big" money tends to be pragmatic ("smart") money, and the disaffection of many businessmen and big contributors with the Goldwater conservatism (especially the Eastern Republican money). The ideological nature of the Goldwater appeal perhaps attracted more middle-class and upper middle-class contributors; giving was for many of them an act of ideological faith rather than an investment in victory and power.

COMPETING FOR THE DOLLAR

The solicitation of political money is as decentralized and dispersed as the American parties and campaigning are. Chaotic organization, inefficient overlap and multiple solicitations, and even an unseemly scramble for cash ensue. In this competition the parties find themselves hard-pressed to raise money as parties; the individual and personal appeal of a candidate or office-holder is far more effective. In part the party organizations' problems are merely a reflection (and a cause) of the basic difficulty that the parties have in controlling and coordinating campaigns for office. But the problems also spring from the fact that it is much easier to raise political money for campaigns (the power and goal-oriented activity of the parties) than it is to raise it for the continuing, monthly costs of party organization. Most American party organizations consequently limp along on small budgets; it is not uncommon, for example, for a state party's organizational costs for a year to be just about the cost of a single senatorial campaign (i.e., between $100,000 and $500,000). Periodically parties try to establish a list of regular monthly contributors to a sustaining fund or to make levies on candidates, but in the long run they often fall back on the funds from a few dinners and a hand-to-mouth existence.

The competition for the political dollar has another dimension: the uneasy fiscal relationships among the national, state, and local levels of the party. The national party committees have periodically tried to assess quotas on the state parties; the Democratic national committee, however, has a typical history of inability to collect the funds from the state parties or to do anything about it. In one way or another, therefore, the movement of money in American politics has been from the bottom and middle levels to the top — exactly as one would expect in a decentralized party. The implications, then, are tremendous when an incumbent President such as Lyndon Johnson succeeds, through the President's Club, in reversing the direction of flow by collecting funds that otherwise might have gone to local fund-raising and then dispersing it back to state and

local party campaigns. Any device or practice which manages to centralize permanently the financing of American politics will shake the parties
to their foundations.

Historically the Republicans have coped more effectively than the
Democrats with this competitive chaos. Since the middle 1930's the Republicans have attempted to centralize fund-raising in a National Republican Finance Committee, with parallel finance committees at the state
and county levels. The national committee, composed in part of the state
chairmen, negotiates a budget for the national organs (the national committee, the two congressional committees, and the independent television
committee), and their negotiations also set the sums it will seek to raise.
The national finance committee in turn assigns to each state committee a
quota for it to raise in its behalf. Ideally the state Republican parties are
encouraged to organize their committees' activities and candidate needs —
and they in turn levy quotas on the county finance committees which,
having no remaining committees to squeeze, raise it themselves. It is
ideally a system which has two great advantages: it will budget for competing candidates and committees at the same party levels, and it will
eliminate a great deal of overlapping solicitation. The "price" — so great
that many state and local party leaders hesitate to pay it — is one of a
considerable centralization of recruitment (and thus of control) of one
important party resource.

For many years the Republican financial organization apparently
"worked" or worked in substantial part. Republican finances were put on
a regular, year-around basis, and the party established an image of sound,
business-like political finance. Especially because the party chose men of
business and financial substance for its finance committees, it appeared to
take party finances out of the hands of working party leaders and put
them into the hands of men with status in the non-political world. However, the ideal remained only that in many states; in the late 1950's perhaps only two-thirds of the states and territories had a financial system
compatible with the model.[11] By the 1960's, however, the system had
deteriorated badly, even at the national level. The congressional parties
increasingly went their own way; the organization of the Congressional
Boosters Club (at $1,000 a Booster) was symptomatic. Then, too, the fac-
tional division within the party in 1964 undermined centralized finance;
moderate Republicans preferred not to contribute to the Goldwater-
controlled national committee, and moderate and conservative Republicans competed with each other in a number of states. The ideological
satellites of the party — such as Republicans for Progress and the Free
Society Association — augmented the competition for Republican money.[12]

[11] Heard, *The Costs of Democracy*, p. 218.
[12] Walter Pincus, "The Fight over Money," *The Atlantic Monthly* (April, 1966),
pp. 71–75.

No such degree of coordination ever marked Democratic money-raising efforts. With the exception of voluntary cooperation — the agreement of two candidates to share receipts from a fund-raising dinner or reception — it is virtually every man or committee for himself. What little coordination there is nationally has come through the personal force and influence of the treasurer of the Democratic national committee, the man most concerned with finance at the national level. Men of the party prestige and fund-raising acumen of Edwin Pauley, the California oilman, and Matthew McCloskey, the Philadelphia contractor, have brought some order and centralization. In 1960 the Democratic national committee created a national finance committee patterned somewhat on the Republican experience; it was also, like its Republican counterpart, to organize state finance and help collect the state quotas for national committee support (an especially pressing problem at the time for the Democrats). But these attempts at centralized finance came to naught. And within most state Democratic parties the traditions of financial decentralization remain similarly unbroken. The nationalizing impact of the President's Club in 1964 stands dramatically against this Democratic party history, and it represents control by the presidential party rather than by the national party organization.

The differences in organizational pattern between the two parties are clear. The explanation is not. Perhaps to some extent they reflect a difference in party "styles." The Democrats, in their general organization and in their conventions, have never put the premium on order, neatness of authority lines, and managerial competence that the Republicans have. They have always been the scramblers and scratchers of American politics. But very likely more important is the reason Heard suggests: [13]

The Republican system functions most successfully in a sympathetic business community. In presidential elections generally, and in states of vigorous party competition especially, businessmen offer infinitely better hunting for Republican than Democratic solicitors. This is so much the case in many places that it has seemed pointless, or impossible, for Democrats to organize a systematic canvass of business and financial enterprises. They have fallen back instead on individuals who know the politically unorthodox businessmen and the companies and industries where Democratic sympathizers may be found.

That explanation, too, would suggest that the Republican financial apparatus fell apart in 1964 at least in part because the party could not rely any longer on the solid sympathies of the business community.

The main obstacle to centralized party finance, however, remains the voluntary campaign committees. Party organizations may rationalize their solicitation of funds, but they cannot control the solicitations of candidates and their committees. The failures of the party organizations in

[13] Heard, *The Costs of Democracy,* p. 230.

finance merely reflect their loss of control of electoral politics to the parties in government. The problems of the Republicans in 1960 are typical of those which both parties face at all levels: [14]

The relationship between the Republican Party and the volunteer organizations was typified by the independent fund-raising effort of the latter. Walter N. Thayer, finance chairman of the Volunteers (for Nixon–Lodge), accepted the position on condition that the Volunteers would not be asked to clear potential contributor lists with the regular party finance committees; he indicated the impossibility of adequately financing the Volunteers' effort if the party wanted such clearance. Citizens for Eisenhower lists of contributors from earlier years were used. Over 23,000 persons contributed, and the Volunteers raised $2.3 million, more than $400,000 over their goal.

Similarly, Republicans found in 1964 that the ideological split within the party further increased the number of contributions going directly to the Goldwater campaign instead of to the Republican Finance Committees (whose budgets support Republicans of all stripes and varieties).

THE CONTROL OF CAMPAIGN FINANCE

No one is pleased with the present system of financing campaigns for public office. No aspect of American politics excites the moral sensibilities of the American public as quickly as its financing. The feeling gnaws, and not completely without foundation, that money is influence, and that its givers exercise an unhealthily large influence in the election of candidates and over their decisions in office should they be elected. Nor does the system endear itself to the candidates. They care neither for the importunities of contributors nor for the popular suspicion that they may have compromised their integrity. Apart from these problems, the candidate often finds himself either badly underfinanced during a campaign or deeply in debt after it.

If the feelings and doubts have been strong, so have the legal reactions. Few governments, if any, have taken the steps toward legal control of campaign finance that the government of the United States has. A brief checklist indicates the following chief restrictions:

1. *Restrictions on sources of money*

> no contributions from corporations and labor unions.

> no contributions by an individual having a contractual relationship with the United States government.

> no sale of goods, commodities, advertisements, or articles of any kind for the benefit of candidates for federal office.

[14] Alexander, *Financing the 1960 Election*, p. 51. Former President Dwight D. Eisenhower made a contribution of $500 to the Volunteers.

no solicitation of federal employees on the job or by another federal employee (nor such solicitation of state or local employees whose activities are in whole or part financed by loans or grants from the federal government).

Of these restrictions only the ones controlling the solicitation of federal employees can be said to have had appreciable success. Even its attempted protections of state and local employees working with federal funds has had only partial success. The restrictions on corporation giving are by-passed by widespread giving by their officials as individuals, and that on labor by the creation of semi-autonomous "political action committees" thoroughly controlled by them. Everyday observance documents the sale of buttons, gadgets, and other articles for candidates, although the fiction may be maintained that proceeds go to voluntary committees rather than the candidate.

2. *Restrictions on size of the contribution*

no contribution of more than $5,000 to or on behalf of any candidate or his organization (with the provision that contributions to state and local committees are exempt).

This restriction has been universally interpreted to mean that no contribution of more than $5,000 may be given to the candidate himself or to any one committee. It is easily avoided, therefore, by giving to a number of committees, or by contributing (in the case of presidential elections) to state committees, such as, for example, the New York Volunteers for Nixon-Lodge.

3. *Restrictions on expenditures*

no interstate (i.e., national) political committee may spend more than $3,000,000 in any year.

no candidate for the Senate may spend more than $10,000, and

no candidate for the House of Representatives more than $2,500. (However, if the state places a lower limit, that limit applies; the maximum sums may be raised to $25,000 and $5,000 depending on a formula computed in terms of votes cast in the election; and, finally, the figures are to be computed without considering expenses for a vast number of items, among them travel expenses, stationery, postage, and printing.)

The first of these restrictions is met simply by proliferating the national committees so that each can stay below the magic maximum. The second is interpreted in American political folklore to apply only to the candidate himself, and not to committees and groups working in his behalf. He is presumed to be innocent of their activities. Finally, the exemptions are so substantial that they can account for a goodly portion of a campaign's expenditures; they are pre-radio and television, however, and do not exempt those expenditures.

4. *Control by publicity*

national political committees attempting to influence any national election must list contributors of more than $100, expenditures of more than $10, and all receipt and expenditure totals in a report to the Clerk of the House of Representatives.

any individual who spends more than $50 a year in two or more states to influence any senatorial or congressional election must also file a report with the Clerk of the House.

candidates for either house of Congress must file reports with that house in which they list contributions and expenses that they personally handled or which were handled by their agents.

Since these publicity provisions do not involve questions of legal behavior, their impact and effectiveness is far more difficult to judge. But only the rankest political Pollyanna could argue that they have met the goals of their authors. They are founded on the hope that public knowledge of financial excesses will produce a chastening defeat. But the reports are sketchy, some candidates do not file them, and they are often long, confusing, or inconsistent. Worse than that, they may reflect little and big dishonesties, the most common of which is the listing of "dummy" contributors, willing partisans who publicly "contribute" the sums that more reticent contributors furnish. Furthermore, they are misleading in their incompleteness. Candidates file reports, but their committees do not, and state and local committees — which often contribute thousands of dollars to national elections — do not file either. But perhaps most basic among the problems, they are not filed until *after* the election. Retribution then depends on the voters' long memories — six years long in the case of senatorial candidates.[15]

To that arcane maze of federal legislation must be added the assorted state attempts to regulate money in politics. The majority of them limit or prohibit political expenditures by corporations and labor unions; these laws are as easily evaded as the federal law. And most have some sort of laws prohibiting certain kinds of election-day expenditures; all prohibit bribery and vote-buying, and others prohibit such practices as paying for a voter's poll tax, his transportation to the polls, or a drink on election day. Over forty states also have some sort of publicity requirements; they are generally even less well-observed and less effective than federal reporting laws. And while only a handful limit the contributions of individuals, about two-thirds have some ceiling on expenditures by candidates. In

[15] This summary of federal legislation relies heavily on Heard, *The Costs of Democracy*, Chapter 13.

most states they apply, as does the federal law, only to the candidate himself. In the aggregate they do not succeed in doing what the federal law
fails to do.

The record, then, is not one of success. And most observers would argue that in addition to its failures, the mass of regulatory legislation
has had unfortunate additional effects. It has stimulated the proliferation
of party committees and the decentralization of party finance. A multiplicity of committees has become necessary to avoid three limitations: the
limit of $5,000 per contribution and the expenditure limits on national
committees and congressional candidates. Furthermore, it encourages —
as does any failure in legal regulation — a cynicism about the motives of
the regulators and the regulated and a feeling that hypocrisies are involved and laws evaded. Perhaps more serious are the two lacunae in the
legislation. All the legal limits scarcely reach the process of nomination —
and this despite the fact that most experts judge the power and impact of
political money to be greater in securing nominations than in winning
elections. Secondly, they generally reach only the question of money in
campaigns, leaving untouched the area of contributions and expenditures
between election campaigns.

Despite the failures, the search for an effective and yet realistic approach to campaign finance goes on. President John F. Kennedy appointed
a Presidential Commission on Campaign Costs which reported in mid-
1962 with a bevy of recommendations which included, among many, proposals for: [16]

the encouragement of bi-partisan fund-raising.

the provision of income tax incentives (either a deduction from taxable
income or a credit against tax owed).

the repeal of the present futile limits on expenditures.

the extension of reporting requirements to all committees (as well as
candidates).

the requirement that reports of expenditures be made *before* elections.

The recommendations of President Kennedy's Commission illustrate both
the informed thinking of critics of the status quo in political finance and
the fate their proposals have generally met. The Commission's proposals
were hardly novel or extreme (even though it did explore the possibility
of soliciting for political contributions in the supermarkets of America),
but they nonetheless received no serious congressional attention.[17]

Similar results have marked the persistent talk of reform during the
Johnson administration. President Johnson in 1966 revived a great many

[16] Report of the President's Commission on Campaign Costs (Washington: Government Printing Office, 1962).

[17] For the less orthodox approaches, see Herbert E. Alexander, *Money for Politics:
A Miscellany of Ideas,* also published by the Citizens' Research Foundation.

of the proposals of four years earlier: abolition of the ceilings on expenditures, a $5,000 limit on individual contributions to a single campaign for federal office (regardless of the number of committees the contribution was divided among), full disclosure of the sources of all funds, and a deduction for political contributions of up to $100 from an individual's taxable income (rather than gross income). A year later the President urged a bolder step: a direct federal subsidy by congressional appropriation to the campaigns for the Presidency. These proposals, too, came to naught.

One other proposal did, however, briefly catch the congressional fancy. In 1966 the Congress authorized individuals filing federal income tax returns to put one dollar of their tax (by checking a box on the return) into a presidential campaign fund to be divided equally by the two parties. (Minor parties were not to share in the fund unless they had polled 5,000,000 votes at the previous presidential election.) The contribution would thus come from the taxpayer's tax liability and in that sense "cost" him nothing; he could not, however, earmark it for one or the other party. It was expected that the fund would yield up to about $30 million each for the Democratic and Republican tickets in 1968. Before the plan could go into operation, however, it was repealed in 1967. Congressional motives were unclear, but apparently the Congress had reservations and second thoughts about the strengthening of the national committee under the control of the presidential candidates, about the omission of the minor parties, and about the absence of controls or limitations on the funds. Perhaps, too, they feared the unknown consequences of a venture into publicly supported campaigning — its effects on two-party competition, for example, or on the relationships between the national party and state and local parties.[18]

RESOURCES AND THE FUTURE OF THE PARTIES

The uncommon combination of dissatisfaction and inaction on the present state of political finance in the United States can be viewed on a number of different levels. Most immediately it reflects a conflict between the norms of the parties (and their candidates) and those of the broader American public. Large numbers of Americans tend to view the question of political money with a mixture of unrealism and self-righteousness. If a candidate (or his family) finances his own campaign, he is accused of "buying" office; the Kennedy campaign for the Presidency, for example, was dogged by references to "Jack's jack." If the candidate relies on large contributions from labor, business, or professional groups, he may be accused of "selling out" to special interests. As for the "little man," he is

[18] Jasper B. Shannon considers the entire issue of reform in campaign finance and the Norwegian experience with political finance in *Money and Politics* (New York: Random House, 1959).

generally unwilling to make political contributions himself, and he appears to be overwhelmingly opposed to direct government support for political campaigning. One can only suppose, therefore, that large numbers of Americans think that a political stork brings campaign funds. And their attitudes, furthermore, forestall realistic and dispassionate thinking — not to mention remedies — about the problem. They foster within the parties and campaigns exactly the secrecy and hypocrisy which reinforce the original suspicions about political finance.

To put the matter more broadly, this is another skirmish in the long-run conflict between the goals of the parties and a general American political culture which remains unfriendly to those goals and the activities the parties employ to pursue them. It is, furthermore, a conflict which divides the activists of the parties — both in the organization and the party in government — from substantial parts of the loyal party electorates. On issues such as these the support of the party electorates is at best uncertain, for they do not identify fully with the values, interests, or even the goals of the party activists.

Beyond these considerations of political ethics and norms, the question of financial contributions concerns the very basic issue of influence in the parties and the electoral processes. Political contributors have political goals and incentives, just as do activists who contribute their skills and labor to the party organization or to a candidate's campaign. Large numbers of Americans wonder what kind of demands or expectations accompany their financial contributions, what kinds of rewards they seek. Money is obviously a major resource of American politics, and its contributors clearly acquire some form of political influence. What we have not been able to decide is the nature of the influence and the differences, both quantitative and qualitative, between it and the influence which results from non-money contributions to the parties and politics.

It is not easy to specify with certainty the goals or incentives that motivate the financial contributor. Very likely they come from the same range of incentives that bestir the activist to contribute his time to the party organization: patronage, preferment, a political career, personal social or psychological satisfactions, and interest, issue, and ideology. Unquestionably the chief one is the combination of interest, issue, and ideology — the desire, that is, to influence the making or administration of some kind of public policy. The desire may be for direct access, for the ear of the powerful. More commonly, it is for no more than a desire to elect public officials with values and preferences which promise a sympathy for the goals of the contributor. The demands of the contributor are, therefore, largely indirect; certainly very few contributors seek a direct *quid pro quo.* But it is unlikely that they will continue to support the political career of a man who has indicated that his preferences are out of harmony with theirs.

Looking at the question broadly again, the goals of Americans making "inputs" into American party politics appear to be increasingly policy-oriented. The shift of incentive patterns in this direction among the activists of the party organizations has already been commented on; those of financial contributors have probably been shifting similarly for the same reasons (e.g., the decline of patronage and preference). And the consequences of that shift appear all the greater in view of the sharply rising amounts of money being recruited now into political campaigns.

Two brief footnotes to the subject of financial contributors and their goals ought to be added. These contributors are not a group completely separate from non-money contributors; many of the smaller contributors, especially, are also activists who give time, skills, and labor to the party. It appears likely, however, that a smaller percentage of the large contributors make similar non-cash contributions. Secondly, the general concern for the goals of contributors is accentuated in American politics because of the failure of the American parties to develop either non-political or widely distributed sources of money. The British Labour party, for example, distributes the burden of finance more widely through individual and group payment of membership dues. Some local Labour parties also raise substantial sums by running soccer pools; contributors to the parties through such devices have the special advantage of not making any political demands on them.

Thirdly — to shift the level of analysis once again — the status quo in American political finance clearly supports the parties in government and helps them, thereby, to maintain their independence of the party organizations. As long as they continue to finance their own primary and general election campaigns, they block the organizations' control of access to public office. Unquestionably the reluctance of Congress and state legislatures to disturb the present patterns of political finance with meaningful legal reform grows in large part from their satisfaction with it and with the political independence it assures them.

Even more controversial recently have been the successes of officeholders in raising funds for political expenses between elections. A considerable number of senators and congressmen raise money from their supporters for continuing political expenses such as trips home for weekends, entertaining constituents in Washington, and political bulletins and newsletters. In 1952, disclosure of the $18,000 per year fund of Senator Richard M. Nixon, the Republican vice-presidential candidate, forced Nixon to take to radio and television with an explanation. In 1967 the Senate censured one of its members, Senator Thomas Dodd of Connecticut, for using funds received at political dinners and during the 1964 campaign for his own personal expenses (e.g., travel, membership dues in clubs, restaurant bills).

Leaving aside the difficult question of whether senators such as Dodd use political funds for purposes other than those for which they were given, there still remains the increasing tendency and ability of some members of the party in government to finance not only their own campaigns, but other political and personal expenses as well. To the extent that an office-holder does so, he further releases himself from ties to the party organization. At the same time he assumes the necessity of satisfying, however indirectly, the political goals of his financial supporters.

Finally, the status quo in American political finance raises issues of competition among the political organizations. Within the party system and its competitions, the Republican party has generally found it easier to tap the sources of political money, largely because its issue positions and leadership entitle it to the confidence of people of financial substance. That Republican facility was for a long time roughly counter-balanced by the greater Democratic success in recruiting resources into both the party organizations. But with shifts in incentives and the skills needed in party organization, the Republicans may find it easier than the Democrats to recruit resources into both the party organizations and campaign efforts. (More than one observer has suggested this as an explanation for Republican eagerness to repeal the income tax check-off plan in 1967.) In any event, should the Republicans establish an overall superiority in the recruitment of all political resources, that advantage would to a considerable extent offset the advantage in party loyalties in the electorate which the Democrats presently enjoy.

Competition for political resources comes also from outside the party system, and money is the one political resource that most non-party political organizations have at their command. Furthermore, purely political organizations of an ideological bent — the American Conservative Union, the Free Society Association, and to some extent the John Birch Society, for example — have unquestionably become competitors with the parties, especially the Republican party in this instance, for financial resources. If it is true that cash is accounting for an increasing percentage of the total American political resources recruited, and if it is also true that political skills and organization are increasingly available for rent or purchase, then new political opportunities are available to the non-party organizations for influencing the electoral processes and the decisions of public office-holders.

· · ·

Aided by political institutions such as the direct primary and the office block ballot, and supported by their own ability to recruit the political resources they need, the parties in government (including the candidates for office) have often been able to escape the control of party organizations. They have even, in many state and local parties, been able to dominate the party organization. But at what price? Certainly at the price of a loss of cohesion as a party in government — for example, in the loss of a unified presence as party representatives in American legislatures. Certainly, too, at the price of a weakening of party organization, not only vis-à-vis the party in government, but internally in terms of its ability to achieve the goals (and thereby provide the incentives) of its activists. For increasingly the activists of the organization seek goals of ideology and interest that can be achieved only by public policy and thus by the co-operation with the party in government. If the party organization per se cannot achieve that rapport, its activists will surely be tempted to leave the organization and associate themselves with the followings of individual candidates and office-holders.

At stake in the competition between the party organization and its candidates and office-holders also is the very nature of the political party. Its broad base — in the number of contributors of resources to it as well as in the number of its loyalists — made the political party the archetypical political organization of the democratic era. It organized the large numbers of newly enfranchised citizens, and it drew them as well into the mechanism of the party itself. It capitalized on the sheer weight of numbers to offset the organized political power of limited oligarchies and aristocracies with vast resources. If, however, the American party must shift increasingly to a "cash economy," it is threatened with a new elitism unless it can broaden the base of its financial contributions. So far, at least, the American parties have had no success in cultivating public subsidy, small-sum contributors, dues-paying members, or any of the other means by which it might escape the dilemmas it faces as it increasingly relies on a relatively small number of men and women for an increasing percentage of its total resources.

PART FIVE

Party in the Government

No observer of the American political parties has described more pungently their inability to govern than E. E. Schattschneider:

> . . . when all is said, it remains true that the roll calls demonstrate that the parties are unable to hold their lines on a controversial public issue when the pressure is on.
>
> The condition . . . constitutes the most important single fact concerning the American parties. He who knows this fact, and knows nothing else, knows more about American parties than he who knows everything except this fact. What kind of party is it that, having won control of the government, is unable to govern? [1]

The parties put their resources and energies into a concerted bid for office, and they try to convince the American electorate that it does matter that they, rather than the opposition party, win office. But can it really matter if, when a party wins office, it cannot guarantee that its officeholders will carry out the dictates of a party program? Above all, the inability of the American parties to govern once they win office raises the question of the purpose or goal they have in their strivings for office. Is electoral victory and the capture of office an end in itself? Is the political party indifferent to the uses to which its representatives put the powers of government? Or is it simply powerless to enforce its wishes?

It is not at all easy to say why the two major American parties want to

[1] E. E. Schattschneider, *Party Government* (New York: Rinehart, 1942), pp. 131–132. Italics in the original have been eliminated.

325

capture and control governmental offices. In searching for the answer one must again distinguish among the three sectors of the party which are brought together in the search for power at election time: the party organization, the party in the electorate, and the party in government and its candidates. Each has its separate set of goals or purposes in the quest for public office. The candidates and office-holders seek the office, its tangible rewards, its intangible satisfactions, its opportunities to make public decisions. The party activists of the organization may seek to translate an ideology or program into policy, but they may also seek patronage jobs, other forms of reward or preference, the sensations of victory for themselves or the party, the defeat of incumbents or a hated opposition. The party's voters may be stimulated by an issue, a program, or an ideology (no matter how vaguely conceived), but they may also be responding to personalities, to the incumbents ("time for a change"), to abstract and traditional candidate or party loyalties, or to the urging of friends, family, and associates. But in any event none of these three components of the party is committed wholly — or possibly even predominantly — to the capture of public office for the working out or enacting of public policies. None of the three is, in other words, wholly or largely committed to governing.

The endemic difficulty the American parties have in governing has stimulated a school of thought in American political science committed to building for them a more positive role in policy formation. Its advocates have called the role either "party government" or "party responsibility." In the late 1940's an *ad hoc* committee of the American Political Science Association, echoing their views, called the profession to arms in a report entitled *Toward a More Responsible Two-Party System*. The committee's position, however, has found more than the usual sprinkling of academic criticism, and the dialogue over the possibility and/or desirability of "party responsibility" has been especially spirited over the past generation.[2] The central debate has been over the prospect of the American parties' taking more forthright stands on public issues and holding their elected candidates responsible for carrying those stands into public policy. That issue involves, in turn, a series of related questions about the composition of the American parties, the goals and incentives of political activists and organizations, the political behavior (and especially the voting behavior) of the American electorate, and the operation of American executives and legislatures.

Ultimately the question of "party government" or "party responsibility"

[2] The report of the Committee on Political Parties of the American Political Science Association was published by Rinehart in 1950. The literature "pro" and "con" the demand for party government (or party responsibility, or whatever term one prefers) is too lengthy to cite here in its entirety; it will be discussed at some length in Chapter Sixteen.

becomes one of the American democracy itself. If the parties were to become policy initiators, then they would assume a central representative role in the American democracy. They would join great, amorphous majorities in the American electorate to groups of office-holders by means of some kind of party program or platform. They would forge a new representative link between the mass democratic electorate and the few men of power in government. Or to put the issue another way, responsible parties would bring electorates closer to the choices of government by giving them a way, a mechanism, for registering approval on policy alternatives. In part those choices might be "before the fact" (and thereby represent the mobilization of grass roots support behind proposed programs), and in part they might be *post facto* judgments on the stewardship of two different and distinguishable parties in government. Ultimately at stake in the proposals is the question of restoring initiative and significant choice to the great number of voters and, for that purpose, the creation of two great parties responsible to them for the exercise of government power. Implicit, too, would be the decline of the power of "non-responsible" political organizations (such as interest groups) to affect the exercise of governmental power.

The critics of proposals for party government have concentrated on one insistent theme: the non-ideological, heterogeneous, and pragmatic nature of the American parties makes agreement on, and enforcement of, a coherent policy program very difficult, if not impossible. Yet the party organizations are becoming increasingly oriented toward programs and ideology — and thus toward the uses of governmental authority for specific policy goals. There was a time when the activists of the party organization contested elections for the "spoils" at stake — jobs, contracts, honors, access, and other forms of special consideration. It made little difference to them what uses public office-holders made of the governmental power in their hands. That time is, however, passing. As more and more citizens are attracted into the party organizations (and also into the party electorates) for policy reasons, an important intra-party pressure builds up for some measure or variety of party responsibility.

In fact, the build-up of issue commitments among party activists, party contributors, and some members of the loyal electorates raises the question of the consequences — in disenchantment alone — if the institutions of American government and the dispositions of the American electorate cannot accommodate the policy-oriented goals and motives within the party. The question of the "desirability" of greater party responsibility, therefore, becomes two questions: desirability for government and desirability for the parties. And the issue of possibility broadens to include the issue of inevitability.

The general question of the role of parties within the institutions of government is really two questions. It is, as the debates over party responsibility suggest, a debate about the contribution of the party to the decision-making of public officials and ultimately about the role of the party in a democratic political system. These concerns one may call the issue of the party's impact on the broader political system. But the relationship of party to government is also a question of the impact on the party itself. Political parties are, as we have reiterated, purposive, goal-oriented organizations. The achievement of those goals (both of the party organization and the party's loyal electorate) we have always supposed to be largely related to the holding of governmental power. But in what way? What, to put it bluntly, does governmental power do for the parties? What kind of rewards does it generate for the men and women who have invested so much in politics and the party, and how does it contribute to the health and vitality of the party and its various sectors?

Concern over the party role in government is in many ways only an extension of the conflict between the party organization and the party in government that began earlier in the nomination and election processes. The very idea of party government presumes that the decisions of the party in government will be congruent with (or subordinate to) the wishes of an entire party which agrees on ideological or programmatic essentials, and yet the organizations find it difficult to foster or force that congruence. Tension between the party in government and the party organization, however, is not uniquely American. Throughout the history of the Western parties one finds a recurrent conflict between the party in office (especially the party in the legislature) and the desire of the personnel of the regular party organization to provide policy leadership. In view of this separateness of the party in office from the party organization, therefore, do the rewards of electoral victory and governmental office flow to the activists of the party organization? Or do the party men in office use their party organization or role exclusively for themselves, their followers, and the electorates of their individual constituencies? How indeed is the party organization to exert any control, any discipline, over the uses of the governmental power it fought to win? Is there any hope of merging the interests of the party organization, the party electorate, and the party's office-holders in the use of the policy-making machinery of government?

Much of the talk about more centralized, more ideological, more disciplined political parties — for that is certainly the implication of any shift to policy- or issue-oriented political parties — has raised the specter of the dogmatic European parties. For it has been the European parties that have achieved the strength of central organization and the commitment to ideology which in turn insure a high order of party discipline in the parliaments. So strong is party control over their legislative representatives — and over the entire policy-making process — that European scholars complain of the decline of parliaments and journalists write darkly of "partyocracy." Ironically, it is not uncommon to hear in these circles envious talk of the flexible, non-dogmatic American parties.

Reform of the American parties, or their own self-propelled development, to achieve greater "responsibility" or issue-orientation, however, will probably follow no conventional route, European or otherwise. The peculiar institutions of American government, if nothing else, insure that. The role the parties have now in American politics and the new roles to which they are moving will be as uniquely American as the institutional complex of American federalism, the separation of powers, electoral processes, and the parties themselves are.

The first two chapters of this part examine the present role of the political party in the organization and operation of the three branches of government. They are basically concerned with the degrees of party direction or party cohesion in legislative and executive policy decisions. (Needless to say, most Americans would consider party direction in judicial decision-making grossly improper.) They deal also with the relationship between party organization and the party in government, especially with the ability of the latter to achieve the goals of the former. They deal, in short, with the impact of internalized party loyalties and external party influences on the public official. The last of the three chapters of this part confronts the general question of party government, its desirability and its possibility. It will be especially concerned with the question of whether increasingly ideological orientations within the party sectors are creating the conditions necessary for and hospitable to the development of party government.

Chapter Fourteen

PARTY AND PARTISANS
IN THE LEGISLATURE

The political party assumes an obvious and very public form — and yet a very shadowy role — in the American legislatures. In the legislatures of forty-eight states and in the United States Congress, the political parties organize majority and minority power, and legislative leaders and committee chairmen are party oligarchs.[1] And yet despite the appearance and panoply of party power, voting on crucial issues often crosses party lines, not to mention party pledges and party platforms. The party in many forms stalks the American legislatures, and yet the effect and the consequences of party effort is often less than obvious. On this paradox turns much of the scholarly effort and the reformist zeal expended on the American legislature.

The character of the American legislative party has been deeply affected by the American separation of powers. In the parliamentary regimes, such as that of Great Britain, the necessity of party majorities or coalitions in the parliament to unite and cohere in support of the cabinet (and its government) creates a constitutional presumption and pressure on behalf of unity within the legislative party. When legislative majorities crumble in their support of the cabinet, the cabinet falls. A reorganization of the cabinet or a reshuffling of the legislative coalition supporting it may ensue, or the parliament may be sent home to face a new election. No such basic institutional and constitutional pressures weigh on American legislators. They may divide on, dispute with, or reject executive programs — even if that executive be of their own party — without similar

---

[1] The legislatures of Minnesota and Nebraska are elected in non-partisan elections. On the considerations of most of this chapter, see the bibliography of Charles O. Jones and Randall B. Ripley, *The Role of Political Parties in Congress* (Tucson: Univ. of Arizona Press, 1966).

consequences. In these American legislatures, unlike those of the parliamentary systems, party role in the legislature has not been institutionalized. The legislature may not run as smoothly without party cohesion and discipline — or without party leadership — but it can nonetheless proceed without it.

PARTY ORGANIZATIONS IN AMERICAN LEGISLATURES

In all but two of the fifty-one American legislatures the members come to their legislative tasks after having been elected as a candidate of a political party. The ways in which they form and behave as a legislative party, however, differ enormously. In some American states the legislative party scarcely can be said to exist; in others it dominates the legislative process through an almost daily regimen of party caucuses. And anomalies abound. Party organization is at its weakest in the overwhelmingly dominant party of the one-party states, and yet in officially non-partisan Minnesota the legislators align themselves into Liberal and Conservative caucuses which look more like Democratic and Republican caucuses with each passing year.

Party organization in the United States Congress stands as something of a benchmark for our observations of the American legislatures because it is the best known of them. Both parties in both houses of Congress meet as the party caucus at the beginning of each congressional session to select the party leadership: a party leader, an assistant leader, a whip and assistant whips, and a party policy (or steering) committee. In addition, the party caucus presents its candidates for the position of Speaker of the House and President Pro Tempore of the Senate, and it sets up procedures for the appointment of party members to the regular committees of the chamber. In effect, then, the basic unit of party organization, the caucus, begins the business of organizing the chamber; from its decisions there rises the machinery of the party as a party (the leaders, whips, policy committees) and the organization of the chamber itself (the presiding officer and the committees).

Once the session of Congress opens, however, the party caucuses fade into relative inactivity and disuse. They meet very rarely during the session. When the party caucuses or conferences (the Republicans prefer the latter term) do meet on important issues during the session, they no longer undertake to bind the individual members. And the parties have not devised any substitute representative body for setting policy and determining the party legislative strategy. The policy committees set up in the Reorganization Act of 1946 have not by general consensus succeeded as broadly based instruments of party policy-making or strategy-setting, even though they were created for the "formulation of overall legislative policy of the respective parties," as the act puts it. One study of them found that they lacked any internal agreement on party policy and that, instead of becoming a collective party leadership, they had lapsed into representing the assorted blocs and wings of the party.[2] Furthermore, they have become organizational and communication instruments of the party leadership. Despite any original hopes, the policy committees have operated primarily as advisory boards and channels of communication between the party leaders and influentials and the full party membership.[3]

Dissatisfaction with leadership control of the policy committees breaks out periodically, especially within the liberal wing of the Senate Democrats. Senators William Proxmire (Wisconsin) and Albert Gore (Tennessee) tried in 1959 and 1960 to enlarge the Democratic policy committee, make it more representative of the party in the Senate, and convert it into a formulator of party policy. In 1963 Senator Joseph Clark (Pennsylvania) included strictures about conservative and leadership domination of the same policy committee in his attack on the "Senate Establishment."[4] In the same year the overthrow of Representative Charles Halleck, the Republican leader, by Rep. Gerald Ford was accompanied by an increase in the number of younger Republicans on that party's policy committee in the House. But despite the agitation, the policy committees remain at best a means for increasing consultation and communication within the legislative party; they are a very long way from becoming the authors of party policy in the legislature. The Democratic liberals of the House — in the absence of a House Democratic policy committee (Speaker Sam Rayburn successfully thwarted it) — have formed something of their own caucus or policy committee: the Democratic Study Group. The DSG does some staff research, takes policy stands, and represents the liberal views of its members; it has even developed its own whip system.

The initiation and formation of party policy in both houses of Congress, therefore, remains largely the function of the party leadership. The floor leaders, and the powerful men of the party consult widely throughout the sectors and centers of power within the party, but the final codification of party policy, the sensing of a will or consensus, rests primarily on their judgment. If they are of the President's party, their actions and decisions are limited by his legislative program and his influence within the Congress. Within the non-presidential party the leadership in the House and Senate not only acts without continuing check by the legislative party, but it also acts without the continuing check of any party organ or spokes-

[2] David B. Truman, *The Congressional Party* (New York: Wiley, 1959), pp. 126–130.

[3] For the leading study of one of the policy committees, see Charles O. Jones, *Party and Policy-Making: The House Republican Policy Committee* (New Brunswick, Rutgers Univ. Press, 1964).

[4] Joseph S. Clark, *The Senate Establishment* (New York: Hill and Wang, 1963).

man. Senate party leaders such as Lyndon Johnson in the 1950's and Everett Dirksen in the 1960's, in fact, established themselves as spokesmen for both the legislative and the national party.

The power of the party leaders is chiefly a personal power, the product of their knowledge, their organizational skill, their persuasiveness, their sense of the wishes and temper of their fellows, and their use of the vast legislative powers at their command. They may speak for the norms of the legislature, for the group values and social group of the chamber, for personal friendships and obligations, for a vague party loyalty, for a presidential program, for a clique or faction within the party, or for a personal vision of the national well-being. They and their whips organize majorities behind legislative proposals that reflect these and other goals and values; only in part at best are their decisions guided by the programs and interests of their political party. And furthermore, they tend to be brokers of majorities and agents of compromise rather than creators or enforcers of an *a priori* party policy. Not surprisingly, therefore, studies of their votes on congressional roll calls have placed the party leaders in the fluid middle or moderate point of a party's bloc voting structure.[5]

Among the state legislatures there are those in which daily caucuses, binding party discipline, and autocratic party leadership make for a party far more potent than exists in the two houses of Congress. But there are as well those legislatures — especially those of the traditional one-party states — in which party organization is perceptibly weaker than that in the Congress. Even in states with the complete apparatus of party organization the parties fail more frequently than the congressional parties to make it operate effectively. The party caucuses in Congress at least maintain cohesion in their initial organizational tasks; they always agree on candidates for the presiding officers. But in January of 1965, the Democrats of the New York legislature, the majority party in both houses, split so badly that they could not agree on a single set of leadership candidates. After a hiatus of a month — during which the unorganized legislature could conduct no business — the Republicans threw their votes to one of the Democratic factions and thus elected leaders for both chambers. State legislative parties have, in other words, on occasion found themselves too riven by factional differences to organize for action.

The party caucus has little excuse for being in a one-party state. Disagreement over organization, leadership positions, and policy issues in these states often falls along factional lines within the party or along the lines of the personal followings of powerful personages. In the heyday of

[5] Truman, *The Congressional Party*. More generally on party leadership in the Congress, see Ralph K. Huitt, "Democratic Party Leadership in the Senate," *American Political Science Review*, LV (1961), pp. 333–344; Randall B. Ripley, "The Party Whip Organizations in the United States House of Representatives," *American Political Science Review*, LVIII (1964), pp. 561–576.

the Long Dynasty in Louisiana, one Democratic faction adhered to the Longs, and others followed the competing political king-pins. In this particular case, and in others as well, factional lines built on personal and family followings coincide with differing regional loyalties. Alternatively the legislative caucuses in one-party states may reflect ideological lines; from 1910 to the 1930's in Wisconsin the LaFollette Progressive Republicans organized one legislative caucus, the conservative Republicans another, and the very feeble Democrats a third. Of course, the party caucus as the basic party unit in the legislature prevails in a majority of the states, generally in those states of two-party competition. In some they meet no more frequently than the congressional caucuses; in others they meet almost every day during the legislative session, often binding their members by majority vote. A state of active party caucuses, such as Pennsylvania, may even spawn caucuses within the party caucuses; both the Pittsburgh and Philadelphia Democrats occasionally caucus separately in addition to attending the Democratic caucus.[6]

Party leadership — in those state legislatures which the parties organize — assumes a number of forms. The traditional floor leaders and whips exist in most. In others the Speaker of the House or a spokesman for the Governor may mobilize the party's legislators. State party officials, unlike the relatively powerless national party officials vis-à-vis Congress, may have a powerful voice in the legislative party. In the Connecticut lower house

. . . the "outside" party leaders are in daily attendance at the capitol and can be seen in corridor conferences with the great and small alike. Each party chairman sits in on his respective party policy conferences and not infrequently he is the real leader of the conference. With few exceptions the men who reach the party pinnacle of the state chairmanship can expect (and they certainly receive) proper deference from their fellows in the legislature. . . .[7]

And the legislative party leaders in the states are no more bound or checked by the rank and file of the legislative party than their counterparts in Congress. They generally control the caucus in those states in which it meets frequently, and smaller, representative party steering or policy committees are rare in the states.[8]

PARTY ORGANIZATION: EFFECTS AND INFLUENCE

In the United States Congress and many state legislatures, then, the parties have erected imposing organizations. But for what? For organizing

[6] On caucuses in state legislatures, Malcolm E. Jewell, *The State Legislature* (New York: Random House, 1962), pp. 89–92.

[7] W. Duane Lockard, "Legislative Politics in Connecticut," *American Political Science Review*, XLVIII (1954), p. 167.

[8] See Belle Zeller (ed.), *American State Legislatures* (New York: Crowell, 1954), pp. 194–195.

party support for a set of party programs or merely for parceling out the perquisites of legislative office? Or does the legislative party seek both policy and perquisites?

The party organizations in the United States Congress have amply illustrated over the last century that they can muster explicit party discipline on only one issue: the failure of a member of the legislative party to support its presidential candidate. A congressman or senator can freely vote against the party's platform, majority, or leadership — or against the program of his party's President. Party leadership will freely concede that a member of the legislative party may, if faced with the choice, please constituents rather than please party or President. But he risks punishment if he undercuts his party's presidential candidate. The Republican caucus in the Senate in 1925 expelled Senators LaFollette, Ladd, Frazier, and Brookhart after they had supported LaFollette and the Progressive ticket in the 1924 elections; that decision also robbed them of their Republican committee assignments and seniority. In 1965 the Democratic caucus in the House invoked a lesser measure of sanction on two Democrats from the South who supported the Republican presidential candidate, Barry Goldwater, in the 1964 elections. While they were not expelled from the party, they were stripped of their legislative seniority and placed even below the new congressmen of the '64 class in committee seniority. Some liberal Democrats favored stiffer sanctions, but the majority chose the lesser punishment, at least in part in hope of not making martyrs of them. Disloyalty in presidential elections is not always punished, however. Senator Harry F. Byrd of Virginia openly supported General Eisenhower in 1952 and maintained his "golden silence" about the Democratic party candidates in 1956 and 1960 without suffering any consequence.

Even though the party organizations in Congress seem to be limited to these sporadic formal disciplinary actions, they do also offer a vehicle for informal pressures. The President's wishes and influence are often funnelled through his party's leaders; they confer with him and carry his proposals and battle plan to the Congress, and they accept his initiative — they are often called "his" leaders in the Congress. They may even occasionally report and transmit the feelings of national party leaders outside of the Congress; rarely, however, do they directly represent the views of the national chairman and committee. What appeals the congressional leadership makes to party loyalty is to the party of the legislature and to the symbols of party unity and to the necessity of preserving a responsible and constructive "image" of the party. Their success is usually limited and personal, for behind the spurs to party loyalty there are very few sanctions. So long as local voters control primaries and general elections and the seniority system controls entree to the major positions of congressional influence, the party apparatus in the two houses of Congress will be without control over the uses of legislative power.

In many state legislatures party leadership and organization operate far more effectively than they do in the Congress. Positions of party leadership and committee power much more frequently go to legislators loyal to the party and to its program. Furthermore, either party leaders, the party speaking through a periodic caucus decision, or the party's governor or state committee may expect the legislator to support the party program or the party "stand" on a particular issue. Whether for an earlier programmatic commitment or for the issue of the moment, they stand ready to enforce party discipline. For example, a survey of the states in the 1950's revealed that in more than a quarter of them the majority caucus in the legislature met frequently and attempted to maintain discipline on behalf of a party program.[9] For excessive lapses of party loyalty the state legislator may suffer sanctions inconceivable in the United States Congress. His influence may wane in the legislature, and he might ultimately lose his positions of power. He might in a patronage state find that the applicants he sponsored fared less well than formerly. He might also find that in the next election campaign he no longer got campaign funds from the state or local party, or worse yet, that the party was supporting a competitor in the primary.[10]

Clearly the party organizations in those competitive, two-party state legislatures have advanced the art of party discipline in the legislative process far beyond its state in the Congress. In probing for the reasons for greater legislative party vigor in the states, we probe in reality for the conditions and determinants of organizational discipline itself. The reasons for the disciplinary superiority of the parties in state legislatures would have to include the following.

ABSENCE OF COMPETING CENTERS
OF LEGISLATIVE POWER

In the Congress the committees have traditionally been the centers of legislative power. A vast amount of the real business of the Congress goes on in them; they are in a genuine sense a set of screens which sift through the great mass of legislative proposals for those relatively few nuggets of legislative metal. And power and influence within the committee system come not from party decision but from the automatic workings of the principle of seniority. The result is the creation of important centers of power in the Congress that owe nothing to the parties and do not necessarily reflect the party organization or aims. (In fact, one can argue that since seniority and its power accrues to the congressmen from the one-party areas, they are definitely unrepresentative of the party in the country at large.) In the states on the other hand, legislators accumulate less

9 *Ibid.*, p. 194.
10 Duane Lockard in *New England State Politics* (Princeton: Princeton Univ. Press, 1959) details the discipline ("spanking") in Connecticut on pages 297 to 302.

seniority (turnover is greater), and the deference to seniority in allocating positions of power is far less common. In the 1950's, for example, a survey of the state legislatures concluded that seniority "figured prominently" in the selection of committee chairmen in only fourteen senates and twelve lower houses in the states.[11] The parties are freer to appoint their loyalists to positions of legislative power; the committees and other legislative agencies generally operate as instruments of party power in a way they cannot in Congress. Legislative oligarchs, such as Judge Howard Smith, long-time chairman of the House Rules Committee and staunch in his ability to bottle up the programs of his own Democratic leadership in the House, have no real counterparts in the states.

THE AVAILABILITY OF
PATRONAGE AND PREFERENCES

Patronage and other forms of governmental preference still exist in some states to a far greater extent than they do in the national government; more than one-third of Indiana's employees, for example, are patronage appointees. Especially in the hands of a vigorous and determined governor these rewards may be potent inducements to party discipline in state legislatures. The legislator who "bucks" his party, if it is the party of the governor, may not be able to secure the political appointments that his constituents and local party organization have been waiting for. In a party system and political culture keyed to the "pay off" of a political job, such failure may cost dearly. Conversely, the loyal and faithful party legislator can be amply rewarded. Little such patronage remains with which to induce party discipline in the Congress; it may well have died there in the early 1930's as Franklin Roosevelt mustered what remained of the federal patronage and told his patronage chief, Postmaster-General James A. Farley, not to dole out the jobs until the voting records were in from the first congressional session.

THE ALLIANCE OF THE STATE PARTY ORGANIZATION
AND THE LEGISLATIVE PARTY

The state legislator is subject to far more sanction and control from his state party organization than is the member of Congress from the feeble national committee of the party. In the states the party organization and the legislative party are far more apt to be allies. State party leadership may inhibit the political ambitions of party mavericks or deny them advancement within the party, especially where they control the nomination processes. They may even prevail on local parties to deny renomination to the disloyal. State party leaders may indeed sit in positions of legislative leadership; powerful party figures such as the Democratic Speaker of the California Assembly, Jesse ("Big Daddy") Unruh, combine state party

[11] Belle Zeller (ed.), *American State Legislatures*, p. 197.

influence with legislative leadership. And Lockard reports that the Republicans in Rhode Island "have a policy committee comprised of important senators, a few representatives, the state party chairman, and a few members of the state central committee." [12] By contrast the national political party is relatively powerless in dealing with its congressional parties. Even so powerful a party figure as Franklin Roosevelt failed in his 1938 attempt to purge a group of conservative Democrats for failure to support his program. To put it briefly, congressmen are protected by decentralized, federalized party power. State legislators are not.

THE ELECTORAL DEPENDENCE OF STATE LEGISLATORS

State legislators are far more dependent on the local and state party for nomination and election than are the members of Congress. And what the local party hath given, it may taketh away. Congressmen and senators may and do build up their own political organizations, their coterie of local supporters, and their own sources of campaign financing. But state legislators are politically unknown and therefore politically more dependent; in some states the parties so control the election of state legislators that these positions approach an "elective patronage" which the party awards to loyal toilers in its organizational ranks. (About 70 per cent of the candidates for the Pennsylvania House of Representatives in the election of 1958 had held some party office.) [13] Party irregularity may cost the legislator that crucial local support — either through the local party's unilateral action or at the behest of a powerful state party organization.

THE GREATER POLITICAL HOMOGENEITY

Greater party cohesion and discipline in some state legislatures reflect also the greater homogeneity of state than national parties. While a legislative party in Congress reflects a full range of views within the national boundaries, that party in a given state embraces a narrower spectrum of interests and ideologies. This greater political homogeneity of the states produces legislative parties in which the ranges of differences and disagreements are smaller and in which there are fewer sources of internal conflict. The political culture of the state also is more homogeneous, and in some cases more tolerant of party discipline over legislators than would the national constituency be. Legislative party strength has, for example, traditionally flourished in the northeastern part of the country (Rhode Island, Connecticut, Pennsylvania, New Jersey, for example), the very states of party strength, patronage, the weakness of the primary, and, one infers, a political culture tolerant of the exercise of political muscle or "clout."

In summary, therefore, the parties in some state legislatures exert far

12 Lockard, *New England State Politics*, p. 218.
13 Frank J. Sorauf, *Party and Representation* (New York: Atherton, 1963), p. 86.

more discipline than they do in other states or in the United States Congress, and the differences may be explained by a number of factors. State legislators may be subject to far more impressive party sanctions: the loss of legislative influence, committee positions, patronage, party influence, a political "future," and ultimately even the loss of the legislative seat. Secondly, the party in state legislatures generally faces no other institutionalized system of power within the legislature of the sort the seniority system represents in Congress. Finally, the general distribution of political interests and the political culture produces in some states homogeneous, relatively unified parties operating in a political culture which offers more latitude to their legislative discipline.

PARTY COHESION IN LEGISLATIVE VOTING

The operation of the party organization in the legislature — with its caucuses, leaders, whips, and policy committees — is only the most apparent, overt manifestation of the party in the legislature. It is immediate and palpable because it is the party organized for legislative action, and its efforts on behalf of party unity and discipline among its legislators are tangible, even if difficult to document. But the question of party influence in the legislature is broader, more pervasive, than the enforcing activities of the legislative party. Party pressures on legislators come from other sources: from state parties, from the executive branch, and from the party electorate of the constituency. "Party" also in a broader, more figurative sense may operate "within" the legislator as a series of internalized loyalties and frameworks for organizing his legislative decisions. To speak of party only in the organizational sense of leaders and caucuses, therefore, is to miss the richness and complexity of its influence in the legislative process.

The multiplicity of "party" pressures on the legislator may even afflict him with conflicting or confusing influences. The cues, even the articulated demands, he gets from the party electorate in his constituency may differ from the demands of the more ideological and more militant souls who make up the constituency party organization. And one or both may be at odds with the presidential or gubernatorial voice in the party. Then, too, party pressures often conflict with non-party pressures, including those of non-party organizations and the legislator's own belief system. The dilemmas arising from these conflicts are the staple of legislative conflict; they are typified by the problem facing many Democrats in 1965 as they considered their President's proposal to redeem the party's platform pledge of 1964 to repeal that section of the Taft-Hartley law permitting the states to forbid union shop contracts (the so-called state "right to work" laws). Constituency pressures and personal inclinations appeared to be strongly against repeal, and party loyalties and party commitments lost out. It is, of course, always possible that party pressures will be absent or relatively weak on a number of issues. Traditionally in the legislatures of Great Britain and the United States, for example, issues touching personal morality and religious conviction have remained outside of party discipline; nor do party pressures concern themselves either with legislation affecting only a person or a specific locality (e.g., legislative grants of citizenship).

Gauging or measuring the complexity of party influences on legislative behavior is no easy matter. But the collective consequences — the proof of the pudding, in the old cliché — of party influence ought logically to be apparent in the actions of the legislative parties. At issue in the arguments over party government and party responsibility are the results and consequences of party action — the ability of the legislative party to vote cohesively behind legislative proposals and in support of the programs, budgets, and appointments of its executive (whether President or governor).

THE INCIDENCE OF PARTY COHESION

Answers always depend on the terms of the question, and so it is with the question of just how much cohesion or discipline the American parties generate in legislatures. The answer depends entirely on the operational definition or index of "cohesion" or "discipline."

One more-or-less classic measure of party discipline in legislatures has been that of the arbitrary definition of a "party vote." It classifies as a cohesive "party vote" any legislative roll call in which 90 per cent or more of the members of one party vote "yes" against a 90 per cent or more of the other party voting "no." [14] By such a rigid test party discipline appears frequently in the British House of Commons, but far less so in the American legislatures. Julius Turner found that from 1921 through 1948 only about 17 per cent of the roll calls in the House of Representatives met such a criterion of party discipline. A comparable average for the British House of Commons from 1924 to 1928 was 95 per cent. [15]

Although the "90 per cent vs. 90 per cent" standard discriminates between British and American party cohesion, it is too stringent a standard for comparisons within the American experience. Scholars of the American legislatures have increasingly opted for less demanding criteria. Whatever the criterion one accepts, it may also be used to describe both the overall incidence of cohesion in the legislatures and the party loyalty of individual legislators. That is, one may make statements about the per-

[14] The origins of these measures and indices are admirably discussed in Malcom E. Jewell and Samuel C. Patterson, *The Legislative Process in the United States* (New York: Random House, 1966), Chapter 21.

[15] Julius Turner, *Party and Constituency: Pressures on Congress* (Baltimore: Johns Hopkins Press, 1951), p. 24.

centage of instances in which the majority (or 80 per cent) of one party opposed a majority (or 80 per cent) of the other; alternatively, one can count the percentage of the time that an individual legislator votes with his party in the total number of instances in which party opposes party. In their study of American legislatures, Jewell and Patterson have collected data from various studies and sources on party cohesion in state legislatures, drawing on a number of these measures of party cohesion (Table 1). The table indicates the enormous variation in party cohesion in the decisions of a number of state legislatures. It illustrates especially the high degree of cohesion in the urban, two-party states of the northeastern section of the country.[16]

Table 1

PARTY COHESION ON NON-UNANIMOUS ROLL CALLS IN SELECTED STATE LEGISLATURES (IN DIFFERENT YEARS)

State and Year	% Roll Calls with Majority vs. Majority		% Roll Calls with 80% versus 80%	
	Senate	House	Senate	House
Rhode Island (1931, 1937, 1951)	96%	96%	92%	88%
Connecticut (1931–1951)	90	83	71	77
Massachusetts (1931, 1937, 1951 *)	82	87	36	56
Pennsylvania (1951)	34	43	25	30
Michigan (1962 *)	56	61	24	43
Illinois (1949–1957)	. .	. .	32	26
Missouri (1945–1946 *)	23	36	. .	. .
California (1959 *)	31	49	. .	. .
Washington (1945 *)	71	51	. .	. .

* In states and years marked with the asterisk the percentages exclude not only the unanimous votes but also those in which 10 per cent or less of the legislators are in a minority (i.e., they are "virtually unanimous" votes). The effect, of course, is to raise the percentages by excluding an additional category of roll calls from the base figures.

By similar measures the degree of party cohesion in the United States Congress falls somewhere in between the extremes of party cohesion among the states. In recent years the two houses of Congress have been

[16] Table 1 is adapted from Table 17.1 of Jewell and Patterson, *The Legislative Process in the United States*, pp. 420–421.

pitting majorities of Democrats against majorities of Republicans in between 40 and 60 per cent of the roll calls (Table 2).[17] Or to express the
same question of party cohesion in terms of the individual member of
Congress, in 1965 the average Democrat in the Senate voted 63 per cent
of the time with his party in those roll calls in which party majority opposed party majority. For the average House Democrat the figure was 70
per cent, and it was 68 per cent for Senate Republicans and 71 per cent
for House Republicans.

Table 2

PARTY COHESION IN U.S. CONGRESS: 1960–1965
(PERCENTAGE ROLL CALLS WITH MAJORITY vs. MAJORITY)

Year	Both Houses	Senate	House
1960	42%	37%	53%
1961	58	62	50
1962	43	41	46
1963	48	47	49
1964	41	36	55
1965	46	42	52

THE OCCASIONS FOR COHESION

The incidence of cohesive voting among members of the same legislative
party varies significantly among the types of issues and questions the legislatures face. Studies in the Congress and the state legislatures find that
three kinds of legislative concerns are most likely to stimulate high levels
of party discipline: those touching the interests of the legislative party as
a group, those involving support of or opposition to an executive program, and those concerning the socio-economic issues and interests that
tend to divide the party electorates.

The interests of the legislative parties *qua* parties — of the parties as
interest groups, one might say — often spur the greatest party militancy in
legislatures. The range of this type of issue is broad. It includes, especially in two-party legislatures, the basic votes to organize the legislative
chamber. In the Congress, for example, one can safely predict 100 per
cent party cohesion on the early session votes to elect a Speaker of the
House and a President Pro Tem of the Senate. Discipline runs high in the
state legislatures over issues such as patronage (and merit system reform),
the laws regulating parties and campaigning, the seating of challenged
members of the legislative chamber, election and registration laws, or the
creation or alteration of legislative districts. But whatever form these issues take, they have in common the fact that they touch the basic inter-

[17] The data come from the *Congressional Quarterly Almanacs* for each year; the
reader should note that these data are for all roll call votes.

ests of the party as a political organization. They threaten some aspect of the party status quo — the party's activists, its internal organizational structure, its system of rewards, its electorate, its assorted activities.

Secondly, legislators of a party rally around the party's executive, or they unite against the executive of the other party. Perhaps the reaction to an executive program is not as predictable as it is in a parliamentary system — American Presidents freely court the support of the other party — but it is nonetheless a significantly partisan issue even in the American context. The *Congressional Quarterly* periodically devises a measure of the support the partisans of each legislative party give to the President on those issues which he has clearly designated as a part of his program (Table 3).[18] The fact that the years of 1958 through 1960 were the years of a Republican President is readily apparent. At least under a Democratic President it also appears, both from the data of this and Table 1, that the House recently has been a more partisan chamber than the Senate. This executive-oriented cohesion that one finds in the Congress and also in the state legislatures reflects a number of realities of American politics. It may result from the executive's control of political sanctions — patronage in some states, his personal support in fund-raising and campaigning, his support of programs for the legislator's constituency. It also results from the fact that the executive increasingly symbolizes the party and its performance. A legislator of the President's party or the governor's party knows that he hurts his party and his own political future should he help make the executive look "bad" or ineffective.

Table 3

PERCENTAGES OF TIMES THE MEMBERS OF CONGRESS SUPPORT
BILLS FROM PRESIDENT'S PROGRAM, 1958 THROUGH 1965

Year	Senate Dems.	Senate Repubs.	House Dems.	House Repubs.
1965	64%	48%	74%	41%
1964	61	45	74	38
1963	63	44	72	32
1962	63	39	72	42
1961	65	36	73	37
1960	43	66	44	59
1959	38	72	40	68
1958	44	67	55	58

Finally, legislative cohesion remains firm on some policy issues, especially those bearing directly on the socio-economic interests of the electorate. Especially in those states in which the SES foundations of party

[18] These data come from the *Congressional Quarterly Almanacs* of the respective years. Truman in *The Congressional Party,* p. 91, finds a similar unity in support of the administration.

loyalties produce an issue-oriented politics, that fact is not surprising. In more specific terms these issues include those of labor-management relations, aids to agriculture or other sectors of the economy, programs of social security and insurance, wages and hours legislation, unemployment compensation, and relief and welfare programs. These issues involve, in the oversimplifications of American politics, the "welfare state," or the whole complex debate over government responsibilities which we sum up in the liberalism-conservatism dualism. For example, on issues the AFL-CIO's Committee on Political Education (COPE) considered a test of labor-liberal positions between 1947 and 1960, the Senate Democrats supported the COPE position 70.9 per cent of the time, the Senate Republicans 27.5 per cent of the time. Something of the limits to party cohesion can, however, be gathered from the same indices; among the Senate Republicans, scores varied from the 82.1 per cent mark of Senator Jacob Javits of New York to the zero score of Senator Barry Goldwater of Arizona. A similar variation existed also between Northern and Southern Democrats.[19]

To single out these three groups of issues is not to suggest that they are the only occasions of party cohesion. The structure of the choice itself may also encourage or discourage cohesion. In the Congress (and probably in the states, too) party discipline seems to be easier to maintain on the complex, almost invisible procedural issues before the chamber. Apparently the simple, substantive questions attract publicity and thus attract the attentions and activities of non-party pressures. In the House of Representatives, at least, party leadership finds its task easier when it is working on an obscure issue.[20]

THE CONSTITUENCY BASIS OF COHESION

Party cohesion in legislative voting is greatest in those states of competitive, two-party politics. One-partyism in a state legislature invites the disintegrating squabbles of factions and regional or personal cliques within the dominant party. Traditionally, the South has in recent years been the area of the least cohesive legislative parties. But this is perhaps to labor the obvious; the very concept of cohesive parties and party government presumes two healthy, competitive parties locked in the competitive struggle to make public policy.

Party cohesion, furthermore, is at its maximum in the legislatures of ur-

[19] William J. Keefe and Morris S. Ogul, *The American Legislative Process: Congress and the States* (Englewood Cliffs: Prentice-Hall, 1964), p. 276. Unquestionably there is considerable overlap between this issue category and the previous one of support for or opposition to the executive; cohesion in reaction to the executive may very well be in part an artifact of issue consensus.

[20] See Lewis A. Froman and Randall B. Ripley, "Conditions for Party Leadership: The Case of the House Democrats," *American Political Science Review*, LIX (1965), pp. 52–63.

ban and industrialized states (Table 1). The key to explanation here — and perhaps the main key to the riddle of legislative party cohesion — is in the types of constituencies the parties represent. In these urban and industrial states the parties tend to divide the constituencies along urban-rural and SES lines, and they develop an issue-oriented politics which reflects those lines. Party cohesion in the legislature, therefore, reflects the relative homogeneity of the constituencies the party represents and the homogeneity of interests and demands of its loyal electorate. It reflects also the fact that the other party represents a different configuration of interests in different constituencies. The legislators of the two parties may themselves have different background characteristics and different life styles; that is to say, their own values and experience reinforce and strengthen the party differences in constituencies. On the other hand, in the two-party competitive states with fairly homogeneous SES populations, there is no reinforcing constituency basis for a persistent, issue-related disagreement between the two legislative parties.

There do exist urban, industrial states with relatively little legislative party cohesion. California has become the most famous example. California's two parties represent districts which are by the usual SES measures fairly mixed. The Democratic party, for instance, has an important rural wing, a possible result of the long-time overrepresentation of rural areas in the state legislature. Similarly in essentially rural and small city states, such as Iowa and Kansas, the party division of the state's constituencies, even though the division is close, does not reflect a rough dualism of interest differences.

Within the legislature of a particular state the degree of any individual legislator's party loyalty also appears to be related to constituency characteristics. Party cohesion is greater among those legislators of the party who represent the "typical" or "modal" constituency when typicality or modality is measured by some index of SES or urbanness. In the example of MacRae's study of the Massachusetts legislature, Republicans tended to represent districts with a high rate of owner-occupancy housing; Democrats tended to come from areas in which fewer people owned the homes they lived in. Republicans from low owner-occupancy areas and Democrats from high owner-occupancy districts — that is, legislators from the districts not typical of those their party generally represented — tended to be the party mavericks on roll calls.[21] In concluding this point it might be appropriate to point out that this kind of analysis pointing to the influence and limitations of constituency loyalties proceeds on the assumption that each party has differing "typical" or modal districts and that differences are chiefly in SES interests. In short, we appear to be

---

[21] Duncan MacRae, "The Relation Between Roll Call Votes and Constituencies in the Massachusetts House of Representatives," *American Political Science Review*, XLVI (1952), pp. 1046–1055.

examining here the same constituency effect on the individual legislator that we saw working on entire legislative parties in the paragraph before last.

Clear and unmistakable though the constituency bases of party regularity may be, they do not explain all party cohesion in the state legislatures. The parties as operating political organizations do account for some — daily caucuses, state party chairmen roaming the legislative corridors, and the party pressures of a vigorous governor do count for something, even though it is difficult to measure their influence. But measurement or none, few observers of the state legislatures deny their influences. What actual organizational pressure the legislator feels, however, probably comes from the state party, the party in the executive, or from within the legislative party itself. It rarely comes from the constituency party, which, if it makes any demands on him at all, generally makes them on purely local, service issues. Limited evidence from Pennsylvania even points out that legislators whose selection was most firmly controlled by the local party — and who, one might suppose, were most obligated and beholden to it — showed no greater party cohesion on legislative roll calls than legislators elected without the help of a party organization.[22]

Party regularity also appears to be related to the political competitiveness of the legislator's constituency. Those legislators from the unsafe, "marginal" seats — districts with finely balanced parties — are more apt to defect from the majority of their fellow partisans than are those from the safer districts.[23] It is, to be sure, both possible and likely that many of these marginal districts are also the districts of SES characteristics atypical of the parties' usual constituencies. But marginality may also be a product, even in a "typical" district, of the organizational strength or appealing candidates of the opposing party. Hence the legislator representing the district may be forced to be more sensitive to constituency pressures, to be more fearful of them, and thus to permit them to countermand his party loyalties more freely.

The northeastern states provide, in summary, the archetype of the state legislature of greatest party cohesion. They are largely competitive, two-party states. Drawing on urban-rural lines and the SES differences of a diverse population, their major parties represent fairly homogeneous and markedly differing clusters of constituencies. Their differences give rise to a politics of issue and even of ideology, and these are in turn reinforced

[22] Sorauf, *Party and Representation*, p. 144.

[23] The scholarly evidence on this point is not unanimous, but support for it can be found in the two sources of the two preceding footnotes and in Samuel C. Patterson, "The Role of the Deviant in the State Legislative System: The Wisconsin Assembly," *Western Political Quarterly*, XIV (1961), pp. 460–472; Pertti Pesonen, "Close and Safe State Elections in Massachusetts," *Midwest Journal of Political Science*, VII (1963), pp. 54–70; and Thomas R. Dye, "A Comparison of Constituency Influences in the Upper and Lower Chambers of a State Legislature," *Western Political Quarterly*, XIV (1961), pp. 473–480.

by the similar axes of national politics. These are also the states of old-line, vigorous party organizations and party control of nominations; here, too, one finds that the hardship politics of favors and patronage has armed the parties with impressive arsenals of sanctions and rewards. Organizational strength carries over, too, into the legislative chambers where regular caucuses and the apparatus of party discipline are often in evidence. Here, too, party differences and party conflict have a greater salience for the individual legislator. In a recent study of four state legislatures, the legislators were asked to indicate the kinds of conflict that were important in their legislature; 96 per cent of the members of the New Jersey lower house designated party conflict as "important"; comparable percentages for Ohio, California, and Tennessee were 49, 26, and 23, respectively.[24]

It is not easy to place the United States Congress into this discussion of the conditions leading to cohesion in legislative voting. Among the American legislatures it is *sui generis;* there is nothing with which to compare it. Perhaps because of the unique scope of its politics and its powers as a legislature, it does not lend itself to the relatively simple generalizations we have made about the state legislatures. The members of Congress come from fifty different political systems, not one, and the diversity of the constituencies and constituency politics they represent may be too great for a continuous, simple set of party battle lines to encompass. The parties in Congress suggest a more complex pattern of party cohesion than do the state legislative parties. Because of the southern regional special case the Democratic party achieves varying degrees of cohesion on various issues. The Republicans manage often a greater cohesion on foreign policy issues than on the conventional "welfare state" issues of domestic politics. And it is not until one narrows the Congress to deal only with northerners that the constituency bases of party cohesion appear.[25] So sticky does the issue of the bases of party cohesion in the Congress appear that David Truman has suggested that party voting may be better understood in terms of stable blocs *within* each of the parties. These blocs reflect regional differences in economy, in attitudes, and in political traditions, and they appear to reflect as well the cohesiveness and pressures of state party delegations.[26]

LEGISLATIVE PARTIES AND PARTY GOVERNMENT

Even though party cohesion in American legislatures falls far short of the standards of some parliamentary parties, it still remains the single most

[24] John C. Wahlke, Heinz Eulau, William Buchanan, and Leroy C. Ferguson, *The Legislative System* (New York: Wiley, 1962), p. 425.

[25] Lewis A. Froman, *Congressmen and Their Constituencies* (Chicago: Rand, McNally, 1963). See also David R. Mayhew, *Party Loyalty Among Congressmen* (Cambridge: Harvard Univ. Press, 1966).

[26] Truman, *The Congressional Party.*

powerful determinant of roll call voting in American legislatures. Party affiliation, in other words, goes further to explain the legislative behavior of the average American legislator than any other single factor we may adduce. His normal disposition seems to be to support the leadership of his party unless some particularly pressing commitment intervenes. All other things being equal (i.e., being quiescent and not demanding) party loyalty usually gets his vote.

That disposition toward party loyalty on the part of American legislators is, however, easier to identify than explain. While a good deal of the scholarship on it looks to constituency explanations, no one would want to restrict his explanation to that variable.[27] Obscure though its origins may be, this disposition to party cohesion appears to grow out of at least five forces:

1. The force of executive programmatic leadership tends to polarize a legislature "for" and "against" — not only in response to the nature of the policies proposed, but also out of an awareness that success or failure of an executive affects the political fortunes of both parties. And as Presidents and governors combine new political and governmental power with greater personal leadership, their influence on legislative parties grows.

2. The natural condition of two-party competition itself creates a loyalty to party, a tension between the two parties, and a rejection of the symbols and traditions of the other party.

3. Party discipline may as well be enforced or maintained by a series of systems of rewards and punishments. They may be in the hands of an executive (patronage), a party organization (defeat in renomination or a stunted political career), or the legislative leadership (denial of positions of influence or defeat of legislative projects).

4. Loyalty to the legislative party also springs naturally from the group life of the legislature and the legislative party (and in the Congress, of the state delegation within the party). The legislative party's leaders are men of influence and persuasiveness; the legislator values their esteem and support as well as the esteem and camaraderie of his fellows.

5. Finally, the cohesion of the legislative party stems from a homogeneity of interests, outlooks, experiences, and even ideologies within it. In a large number of states the districts one party represents differ from those of the other, with the result that the legislators of one party represent a set of political interests different from that of the other party. Those differences may also be reinforced by the differing political styles and cultures they represent — as, for example, in legislatures in which urban Democrats face rural and small town Republicans.

Yet, for all the talk of party cohesion, the fact remains that most Ameri-

[27] Thomas A. Flinn, "Party Responsibility in the States: Some Causal Factors," *American Political Science Review*, LVIII (1964), pp. 60–71, makes the point very well.

can legislative parties achieve only modest levels of cohesiveness — and then only fitfully. Party lines are often obliterated in the coalitions which enact important legislation. Interest groups, powerful governors, local political leaders, the mass media, influential legislative leaders all contend with the legislative party for the ability to organize legislative majorities. In this system of fragmented legislative power the legislative party may only occasionally govern. Indeed, it may find itself in conflict with other party voices in the struggle to mobilize majorities in the legislature. The governor or President as a party leader and expounder of the party platform may find himself repeatedly at odds with legislators of his party whose roots are deeply emplanted in local, semi-autonomous electorates and local party organizations.

Once again also the fragmenting institutions of American government have their impact. With the separation of powers there is no institutionalized need or pressure for party cohesion. Two recent studies of Canadian parties suggest, indeed, that it is primarily the presence of a parliamentary system which accounts for the greater cohesion of legislative parties in Canada.[28] It is possible for government in the United States to act — to govern — without disciplined lines of support in the legislature. In fact, at those times when the same party does not control both houses of Congress and the Presidency — or both houses of the state legislature and the governorship — it would be impossible to govern if high levels of party cohesion to an *a priori* program did prevail.

Even where one finds party cohesion or discipline in an American legislature, however, party government or party responsibility need not result. Cohesion is a necessary but not sufficient condition of responsibility, and that's the rub. The American legislative party tends to have only the most tenuous ties to the various units of the party organization. The legislative parties of Congress do not recognize the equality — much less the superiority — of the party's national committee; a number of state legislative parties similarly escape any effective control, or even any persistent influence, by their state party committees. Nor do the legislative parties have a great deal of contact with local party organizations. Many legislators depend on personal organizations for reelection help, and even those who rely on the party at election time receive no continuing advice from the party "back home." The local party organizations are usually preoccupied with local issues, local crises, and local services, and furthermore, they do not often sustain enough activity between elections to keep even the most fleeting supervisory watch over their legislators.

The American legislative party, therefore, has often found it easy to re-

[28] Leon D. Epstein, "A Comparative Study of Canadian Parties," *American Political Science Review*, LVIII (1964), pp. 46–59; Allan Kornberg, "Caucus and Cohesion in Canadian Parliamentary Parties," *American Political Science Review*, LX (1966), pp. 83–92.

main aloof and independent from the party organization and even from the organization's platforms and program commitments. It creates the major part of its own cohesion, employing its own persuasions, sanctions, and rewards. What discipline it commands generally serves a program or a set of proposals that originate in the executive or within the legislative party itself. More particularly, they may originate in the policy preferences within, or the constituency pressures on, the party leaders. Only rarely is the legislative party in any sense redeeming earlier programmatic commitments or accepting the overriding discipline of the party organization. As a legislative party it is politically self-sufficient; it controls its own future and rewards to a considerable extent. So long as its members can protect their own renomination and reelection, they may keep the party organizations at arm's length.

This freedom — or irresponsibility, if one prefers — of the legislative party grows in large part from the fact of its unity and homogeneity of interests in a total party structure where disorder and disunity prevail. The legislative party and executive party are wary and suspicious allies in the party in government, and the decentralized party organization (decentralized even within the states) can define no common goals or interests. Even if a group of local party organizations were to establish supervisory and instructory relationships with their legislators, no kind of party responsibility would result unless those relationships were unified and integrated within the state as a whole. There is, in other words, no unified political party which might establish some control over and responsibility for the actions of its legislative party. There is only a party divided geographically along the lines of American federalism, functionally along the dimensions of the separation of powers, and structurally by the differing goals and commitments its various participants bring to it.

If the legislative party is relatively free to go its own way and pursue its own interests in its legislative activities, what then of the goals of the activists of the party organization? Their incentives may not depend on legislative action; patronage and preferment are controlled by executives, and many of the other personal and political incentives are administered by the party organizations themselves. But if their incentives are those of issue and ideology, they depend at least in great part on legislative action, and the inability of the party to guarantee the commitment of its legislative party on some issues or a simple ideology can only mean frustration and disappointment for them. Their only response and defense is a selectivity of commitment within the party — a willingness to work only for those candidates or causes whose issue positions they are confident of. They may form ideological factions or groups within the party organizations, associate themselves with this candidate or that, and opt out of those activities and commitments of the party that give no promise of returning the rewards they seek. These are the activists who, as we earlier suggested, make the local party organization a "pool" of potential activists who can be activated only selectively and differentially. Since the party cannot vouch for an ideology or a set of issue positions, they attach their loyalty to those within the party who can.

At the most, therefore, the American legislative parties are tied to the rest of their parties by some agreement on an inarticulate ideology of common interests, attitudes, and loyalties. And in many state legislatures and in the United States Congress the mute "ideology" of one party and its majority districts differs enough (even though imprecisely and roughly) from that of the other party to promote the tensions of inter-party disagreement and intra-party cohesion. These modal sets of interests and attitudes may or may not find expression in platforms, and they may or may not be articulated or supported by the party organizations. Legislative parties may in the short run even ignore them. They are nonetheless there, and to some extent they unite the three sectors of the party; they are the chief centripetal force in a political party which has difficulty in articulating a central set of goals for all of its activists and adherents. Whether this inarticulate ideology can produce a measure of party responsibility is, however, another question, and it will wait until the considerations of Chapter Sixteen.

Chapter Fifteen

PARTY IN THE
EXECUTIVE AND JUDICIARY

The American involvement of the executive and the courts in the matters of party politics stems in considerable part from the traditions of 19th century popular democracy. The belief that democratic control and responsibility could best be guaranteed through the ballot box led to the "long ballot" on which judges and all manner of administrative officials (from local coroners to state auditors) were elected rather than appointed. Popular election led easily to party influences in those elections. At the same time the dicta of Jacksonian democracy supporting the spoils system and the values of turnover in office also justified the use of party influence in appointments to office. Thus in the name of popular democracy access to public authority was often opened to men who enjoyed the support of a powerful party. And that access was opened in the executive and judicial branches with a frequency quite unknown in the other Western democracies.

However, it is one thing for the political party to influence — or even control — the recruitment or selection of men to office, and it is quite another for it to be able to mobilize those office-holders in the exercise of their powers to office. The parties have had only very partial success in mobilizing that power in American legislatures. The pertinent question here is whether they have been equally successful with executive and judicial branches. To put the matter another way: In the decisions that affect us all, has it made any difference that the men have been party selected? Do they carry party programs or values into effect? Or are the rewards of office merely theirs for past service to the party? Does the pursuit of public office by the political parties serve only their internal organizational needs for rewards and incentives — or does it promote the

352

enactment of party programs and platforms? For what purpose the party pursuit of power in executives and judiciaries?

THE EXECUTIVE AS PARTY LEADER

The 20th century has often been proclaimed as the century of mass political leadership, both in the democracies and dictatorships of the world. In the democracies electorates have expanded to virtual universality among adults, and at the same time the revolutions in mass media and communications have brought political leaders closer than ever to them. In the United States these changes have culminated in the personal leadership of the American Presidency in the 20th century — a trend summed up merely in the listing of names such as Wilson, Roosevelt, Eisenhower, Kennedy, Johnson, names that signify both executive power and a personal tie to millions of American citizens. Even the parliamentary systems and their prime ministers have been energized by the growth of personal leadership; clearly it is no longer true in any realistic sense that the British prime minister is merely "first among equals" in the cabinet.

Unquestionably one important ingredient of executive leadership in the United States has been its dependence on concomitant leadership of a mass political party. When Andrew Jackson combined the search for executive office with leadership of a new popular political party he began a revolution in both the American Presidency — and governorship — and the American political party. The Presidency ceased to be the repository of elitist good sense and conservatism that Hamilton saw in it and became, slowly and fitfully, an agency of mass political leadership and representation. It was ultimately the President rather than the Congress who became the Tribune of the People in the American political system. Popular democracy found its two chief agents — a popularly elected leader and a mass political party — merged in the American chief executive, the power of the office reinforced by the power of the party.

It is easy to speak glibly of the American chief executive as the leader of his party. The chief executive — whether President or governor — wears many hats at once, and one of them surely is the hat of party leadership. Leadership of his party is, that is to say, both one of his major tasks and also one of his major sources of executive power and influence. His party is both his burden and his support; it demands his time and concern, and yet it supports his dealings with his administrative underlings and the legislative branch. But the specifics of executive leadership of a party are more elusive, for the President and governors are rarely formal party leaders. National and state party chairmen hold that responsibility. The role of "party leader" is for the chief executive really a subtle and complex combination of a number of overlapping roles.

PARTY LEADER AS REPRESENTATIVE
OF THE TOTAL CONSTITUENCY

James MacGregor Burns has written of an American four-party system
composed of the two "presidential parties" and the two "congressional
parties." [1] But even if one does not see the basic divisions of the American
party system in executive-legislative differences, it is evident that the
President alone represents the national constituency. Perhaps more importantly, the national constituency he represents differs from the sum
total of the congressional constituencies. While their constituencies are
local and particularistic ones which collectively overrepresent the rural
areas of the country, his overrepresents the urban, industrial states on
which the Electoral College places such a premium. His constituency is
more concerned with the problems of the big cities, their industrial workers, and the racial and ethnic minorities which live in them. It is a constituency so defined as to make its incumbent more "liberal," more committed to government social welfare programs than his congressional
party. He symbolizes both the recognition of national problems and the
national power to deal with them. Furthermore, since his is the only really
national constituency — especially in contrast to the localism of the congressional party — it is the presidential candidate who *is* the national
party. Apart from its national convention, he is its only manifestation.

Many of the same observations may be made of the American governors. They, too, represent the entire state in contrast to the local ties of the
state legislators. Other public officials may also have state-wide constituencies (the fathers of the states have seen fit to elect treasurers, attorneys
general, and state insurance commissioners), but unlike his less well-
known and less public fellow executives, the governor embodies the party
on the state-wide level. He is, to put it briefly, the "political executive"
and so recognized by the voters of the state. His constituency, too, weighs
the urban centers far more heavily — i.e., equally — than have the historically rural-dominated legislatures. Like the President, most governors
must make political and policy records more appealing to the voters of
the urban centers, and like him they symbolize concern for the problems
of the whole constituency.

PARTY LEADER AS ORGANIZATIONAL LEADER

At the same time the American executive may choose to be concerned
with the organizational, internal life and affairs of his political party. Or
he may, like President Eisenhower in the 1950's, choose not to be. But
even though he "preferred to leave the operation of the political machinery to the professionals," [2] not many other recent Presidents have.

[1] James M. Burns, *The Deadlock of Democracy* (Englewood Cliffs: Prentice-Hall,
1963).
[2] Sherman Adams, *First-Hand Report* (New York: Harper, 1961), p. 25.

The opportunities for organizational leadership are, however, generally greater for governors than for the President. Their constituency and political power coincide with a viable level of party organization. In the state party organization there is an organization worth leading and capable of being led. The President, confronted with an often-divided and usually futile national committee, is less fortunate. Not all governors assert themselves in positions of party leadership, of course; they may have no taste for party organizational leadership, or they may even represent a dissident faction within the party. But many governors do lead. Their control of the state patronage establishes them as party leaders, since they control a major element of the party's reward system. Powerful county chairmen must pay them periodic homage. And at the national conventions of their parties, the governors can often be seen leading their state's delegation.

The President unquestionably asserts his organizational control over his national committee; its chairman, if not his personal choice, must be acceptable to him. In his relationships with the state and local organizations of his party he may be less secure. Ought he to take sides, however covertly, in a deep-seated split within one of the party's state organizations? That unpleasant question confronted both Presidents Kennedy and Johnson in the 1960's as they trod lightly through the debris of battle between the New York Democratic organizations and the reformers. In general the President faces the question of how to allocate his political resources — the dwindling patronage, his own presence, the prestige of his Vice-President or Cabinet members — among the parties within his party. Traditionally in this century Presidents have relied on the Cabinet position of the Postmaster-General as the place for an advisor knowledgeable in the intricacies of the party's many organizations. Franklin Roosevelt relied on James Farley, and Dwight Eisenhower chose Arthur Summerfield — both had extensive party organizational experience and both served as the national party chairman. It was that tradition that Lyndon Johnson honored in 1965 by appointing Lawrence O'Brien, his predecessor's shrewdest political counselor, as his Postmaster-General. In addition to seeing that the mail was delivered, Mr. O'Brien was apparently expected to help the President feel his way through the treacherous labyrinths of local organizational politics.

PARTY LEADER AS ELECTORAL LEADER

The chief executive is often a party leader in the additional sense that his electoral successes or failures affect the electoral fortunes of other office-seekers within his party. In some cases the effect may be unintentional and unavoidable. Presidential "coattails" are widely thought to carry in a certain number of congressional and state candidates with them. Although specific candidates may be able to isolate themselves — by reason of special organizational support, the cultivation of non-party support, or special constituency care — from the effect of the presidential or gubernatorial success or failure, many do not.[3] The basic nature and mechanism of the effect are obscure — is there, for example, a "downward" coattail effect as well as an upward one? — but the relationship is often present. In the 1964 Democratic landslide, for example, North Dakota Democrats won a house of the state legislature and half of the state's congressional delegation for the first time in history. In Iowa the Johnson sweep turned the state's congressional delegation from six Republicans and one Democrat to six Democrats and one Republican; while the President garnered 62 per cent of the vote and the popular Democratic governor, Harold E. Hughes, won 68 per cent, none of the Democratic congressmen won even 54 per cent. Thus the evaluations of executives or candidates for executives — the evaluations of the men at the head of the tickets — tends to wear off on other party candidates. In other words, the short-term judgment on a party that grows out of executive performance or potential can to some extent overcome the patterns of voting that stem from long-term party identifications.[4]

More delicate and more uncertain is the ability of Presidents and governors to intervene consciously and overtly in specific elections. Certainly the experience of this century indicates that Presidents cannot successfully intervene in primaries; Franklin Roosevelt's rebuffs in his 1938 attempts to urge Democratic voters to defeat conservative Democratic incumbents such as Senators George and Tydings stand as a case in point. Governors may have some greater success, especially in those states of strong party caucus control of legislative roll call voting. In general elections, the executive's main options center on those elections in which he is not running — i.e., the "off-year elections." Again here, popular wisdom generally overestimates the executive's power. President Eisenhower's appeal in 1958 for a Republican Congress with which he could work more effectively met total defeat. While the Democrats had held 54 per cent of the seats in the House of Representatives before the 1958 elections, they raised the percentage to 65 in those elections.

The attempts of Presidents to intervene in specific local elections often end in embarrassing ineffectiveness. Lyndon Johnson at first stayed aloof from the 1965 New York Mayoral contest among Republican John Lindsay, Democrat Abraham Beame, and Conservative William Buckley, but after his silence had been interpreted as a lack of enthusiasm for the Democrat, the President, if a bit belatedly, threw his prestige and per-

[3] Malcolm Moos, *Politics, Presidents and Coattails* (Baltimore: Johns Hopkins Press, 1952).

[4] On the general subject of the "coattail effect," see the Moos book cited above; Warren E. Miller, "Presidential Coattails: A Study in Political Myth and Methodology," *Public Opinion Quarterly*, XIX (1955), pp. 353–368; and Charles Press, "Presidential Coattails and Party Cohesion," *Midwest Journal of Political Science*, VII (1963), pp. 320–335.

sonal support behind Beame. Lindsay nonetheless scored an amazing upset victory. Perhaps the safest conclusion to make is that apart from coattail effects, the impact of the executive on specific primaries and elections will be close to negligible unless it is exercised through a party organization. Executive appeals directly to the voters seem not to have a great deal of effect, no matter how great the popularity and personal strength of the executive. All the traditions and pulls of localism in American politics are against him.

PARTY LEADER AS SYMBOL OF THE PARTY

Closely related to his effect as electoral leader is the executive's role as the symbol of his party, for the President or the governor stands as its most trenchant and salient representative. His programs are in the public's mind the party's programs. His successes and failures are its successes or failures; his imaginativeness and vigor are the party's, too. He is, for a public which understands and grasps politics chiefly in personal terms, the personification of the party. And in parties that find it notoriously difficult to enunciate clear statements on public issues, his program is the party's. It is in this sense that the chief executive is a party leader by virtue of being a chief executive. He can choose not to lead his party organization, not to lead his party in the Congress, not to intervene in local or congressional elections, not to cater to the national constituency — but he cannot avoid his symbolic impact on his party. For that impact springs not from his intentions, but from the voters' perceptions of his success in the Presidency.

Again, however, it is easy to overestimate the impact of the executive on the party. During the Eisenhower years, for example, the President's personal popularity rode high, and yet the survey data on party identifications for that period indicate only a slight Republican increase — certainly in dimensions far below the President's personal popularity.[5] In the long run, popular chief executives such as President Eisenhower do not convert their personal popularity to their political party *unless* they succeed in altering either the ideological and voter coalition supporting the party or its organizational structure and leadership.

However, if one looks not for presidential impact on long-run party identifications, but on short-run voter choices, the effect is clearer. The material of Table 1 suggests graphically that a sag in a President's popularity may be almost directly reflected in his party's electoral fortunes.

To separate all of these closely-linked facets of the executive's role as a party leader is to do them violence. They buttress and reinforce each other, and the skillful party leader draws on one to be effective in another. They should more properly be thought of as intertwined and inter-

[5] The point is more fully discussed in the consideration of party identification in Chapter Six.

Table 1

RELATIONSHIP BETWEEN POPULARITY OF
PRESIDENT LYNDON JOHNSON AND THE
VOTE INTENTIONS OF AMERICAN VOTERS: 1965–1966 *

		Percentage Approving Johnson Conduct of Presidency	Percentage Intending to Vote for Democratic Congressional Candidates
August,	1965	. . %	58%
September,	1965	65	. .
January,	1966	. .	57
February,	1966	61	. .
April,	1966	55	. .
May,	1966	. .	55
June,	1966	46	. .
July,	1966	56	. .
August,	1966	. .	55
September,	1966	48	52

* Sources: The data on the President's popularity come from the Gallup Poll reported in the Minneapolis Tribune of September 17, 1966; the data on the vote intentions for 1966 Congressional elections come from Louis Harris and were reported in the Minneapolis Star of September 15, 1966.

dependent aspects of the single phenomenon of executive leadership in the party.

Imposing as these ties between the chief executive and the party may be, they are not, however, without their very real and tangible limits. The executive may be, first of all, limited by his own political experience and taste for political leadership. There are those Presidents and governors who do not want to lead a party, or whose view of the executive roles does not include great exertions as a partisan leader. And even those whose role perceptions do include them may find that the representational demands of the office — the pressures to be a President or governor of "all of the people" — limit their partisan work and identification.

The President or governor may find, too, that he leads only part of the party. He may, especially in the case of governors from one-party states, lead only a faction of the party. He may, too, share leadership of the party with other party notables. Presidents not especially secure in national party affairs may find that the more experienced leaders of the congressional party are asserting major leadership in the national party. Governors, too, may find senators and congressmen of their party pressing parallel leadership claims over the state party. They and state party leaders may fear that the governor — or any other single person — will use party control for his own political ambitions.

Both Presidents and governors may be limited in party leadership by a paucity of resources on which to base their leadership claims. Patronage is available only to some, and many of the others have precious few inducements or incentives with which to lead. The President may employ the almost endless prestige of his office and its almost limitless powers of communication with the electorate, but governors are less able to catch the public eye or ear. And both are limited by the general knowledge that their day on the stage of power is carefully marked out. And while eight years may give a President ample time to establish himself as a party leader, one-third of the governors are limited to four years in office.

For What Purpose Party Leadership?

Only in a somewhat special sense is a governor or a President a leader of his party. A good deal of the impact he has on his party is either unintentional or unavoidable; it is an inevitable by-product of his own personal successes and failures in and out of office. Only sporadically and tentatively do the American executives seize and exercise an actual organizational leadership over the parties as party organizations. And yet the fact remains that the executive does exert, in varying degrees, a powerful influence on his party, and from that influence he derives his very considerable power within it. Ironically, however, the power he acquires as a party leader is almost invariably expended on his goals and tasks as a chief executive. Only rarely does he use it for the purposes of the party *qua* party. The power of the executive in the party, in other words, will be converted into executive power or personal political power rather than the power of the party. The President and the governors use their leverage in the party to further their own political careers, to win success for their programs in the legislature, and to coordinate the work of the executive agencies and departments. More often than not, to take an example, patronage appointments will be used for these purposes rather than for the building of party organization. The "executive party" thus does not differ greatly from the legislative party; it is an instrument of the executive and his goals, just as the legislative party is an instrument of its goals. Like the legislative party it has only tenuous ties and commitments to the interests, needs, and programs of the broader party organization.

There is, of course, an old and honorable argument that the goals of the executive and those of the party coincide in partisan administrative appointments. It is an argument heard when the two parties exchange the American Presidency, and thus it was last heard nationally in 1952. After years in the wilderness of opposition the Republicans swept into national power led by a military hero turned presidential candidate. Republican party worthies eyed eagerly what remained of the federal patronage, while at the same time they argued that a new and fresh Republican policy approach would be thwarted by "hold-over" Democratic appointees (or public servants conditioned by long years of Democratic rule) if they were not replaced by Republicans loyal to the GOP platform and program and to its newly elected administration. And in the early years of the Eisenhower administration thousands of top-level (and some not so top-level) administrators were replaced or appointed in positions exempted from the operation of Civil Service.[6]

In fact, the partisan use of top administrative appointments proceeds on the tacit assumption that a patronage appointment at this level can at one and the same time serve the party purpose of rewarding a loyal worker and the executive's purpose of coordinating administrative policy-making and implementation. But it rarely works out that way. Often the political appointees are men loyal to the President and his own personal interests; one need only look at the appointments of Presidents such as Kennedy and Johnson to see that they have often been "President's men" — personal friends, confidants, state party leaders who supported him — rather than party men in the broader sense. Furthermore, the job demands for skills and experience in administrative appointments are often so great that Presidents, governors, and parties must be satisfied if the appointee's party credentials go no further than loyalty or identification.[7]

And so it is that the uses of the President's or governor's leadership position are complex and difficult to untwine. In part they are for the purposes of the party as a party, and in part they are for the personal political purposes of the chief executive. But in great part his party powers are the executive's ally in support of his own policy program. In the classic American separation of powers, decision-making power is fragmented and scattered among the three branches. And in his attempts to hold his own in this system of fragmented power the executive frequently suffers a genuine paucity of constitutional powers. Indeed, the proverbial Man from Mars, should he obtain a copy of the U.S. Constitution, could not imagine from its niggardly awards of constitutional powers to the President what the office has come to be. Inevitably, the President has come to depend on his extra-constitutional powers as head of a popular, mass political party. It is the party that is his major source of strength, his instrument of political leverage, as he attempts to shape the making of policy within the complex processes of government.

PARTY POWER AND EXECUTIVE-LEGISLATIVE RELATIONSHIPS

For that area of policy-making reserved to him, the executive is free to pursue his understanding of public wisdom. But for most executives the

---

[6] Schedule "C" of the Civil Service rules exempts positions which are policy-making or which involve close personal relationships with the chief policy-making officials of an agency. See Harvey C. Mansfield, "Political Parties, Patronage, and the Federal Government Service," in *The Federal Government Service* (New York: The American Assembly, 1954), pp. 81–111. Also see Cornelius Cotter and Bernard Hennessey, *Politics Without Power* (New York: Atherton, 1964), pp. 144–145.

[7] Dean E. Mann, *The Assistant Secretaries* (Washington: Brookings, 1965).

area of policy-making autonomy is not large. Aside from the President who enjoys such a primacy in the fields of defense and international relations, there is, in fact, little substantial policy reserved for making by the executive himself. What impact he is to have on the making of policy, on the choosing among alternative programs, or on the enacting of a party program or stand must in great part be felt through the formal actions of the legislature. And in this pursuit of policy by influencing a legislature the President and the governors turn repeatedly to their identification with, and their embodiment of, their political party.

By far the most important institutional barrier to the coordination of legislative and executive decision-making under the aegis of a unifying political party in the American system is the separation of powers. Very simply, the President or the governor may find that at least one house of the legislature is in the hands of the other party or of another faction of his own party. Between 1931 and 1952 more than two-thirds of the American states experienced some period of divided party control of the governorship and the state legislature; only the Democratic one-partyism of the Southern and border states (which accounted for twelve of the fifteen states not experiencing any divided control) saved the percentage from being much higher.[8] Those divided regimes reflect a number of causes — overlapping terms of office, differing constituencies, the impact of a politics of personality and localism, and legislative malapportionment. At such times the executive has no choice but to minimize or limit his partisan appeals, but the problems he faces in times of divided control do not differ fundamentally from those of other times. Given the closeness of the party split in many legislatures and the unreliability of some legislators of his own party, he must in most instances curry the favor of some legislators of the opposing party. Thus the President or the governor follows a mixed strategy: partisan appeals and sanctions for his own party, and non-partisan or bi-partisan politics for those of the opposition.

The role of the President vis-à-vis the Congress is too well known to bear a great deal of rehearsal here. His power in the party is not usually organizational in nature. He may use a little of the lingering federal patronage for legislative purposes, but he has little direct organizational power that can affect the political careers or responses of a senator or representative. Congress responds, however, to the power he has over the symbols, the public prestige, of the party. Members of his party know that if they make him "look bad," they to some extent also make themselves "look bad." They cannot, in other words, escape the fact that he will head the party's ticket and that in that position he may very well have some impact on their own fortunes and on the fortunes of the party. Presidential power derived from party leadership consists very largely in

[8] V. O. Key, *American State Politics* (New York: Knopf, 1956), p. 55.

a President's ability to represent the enterprise of the party in its broadest terms. The President rarely can threaten a recalcitrant congressman with defeat at the polls, nor does he control many of the other rewards and incentives for which the average congressman seeks public office. He may, of course, hurt a congressman simply by exposing him to his scorn or criticism, or by denying him various executive favors. But these are sources of presidential power that seem not to spring from the political party.

Governors, on the other hand, are frequently in a position to exercise far greater and more direct party organizational power over the legislators of their own parties. In many states their legislatures are unbound by the traditions of seniority, and governors may take an active part in the selecting of committee chairmen and influential party floor leaders at the beginning of the session. The party floor leaders of the governor's party may in a very real sense be "his men," chosen by him to steer his program through the legislative waters. Governors may as well attend party caucuses and even direct the strategy of the party's legislative leaders. The governor may also lead a powerful, on-going state party organization. To cross him may be to run the risk of falling from party favor; a legislator's career in the legislature, not to mention his future ambition, may be at the mercy of a determined, politically skillful governor. To put it another way, the average governor has a far greater control over party rewards and incentives than the President — he may control party patronage far beyond that in the hands of a President, he can exercise greater control over political careers, and he may even be able to control the rewards of the legislature itself. But on the other hand, in the symbolic aspects of party leadership the governor usually exerts far less influence than a President. His political sanctions and organizational power may be more impressive, but he suffers from under-sized political coattails.

PARTY POWER AND ADMINISTRATIVE POLICY

Increasingly legislatures have, under the weight of complex realities, delegated greater and greater discretion to administrative agencies. Such agencies now regulate vast areas of the economy — the railroads, atomic and nuclear energy, radio and TV, for example — under only the vaguest legislative mandates. Even the question of tariff barriers, long and traditionally the occasion for bitter and protracted congressional politicking, has largely been sloughed off to the President, the State Department, and the Tariff Commission. Obviously, then, any concept of "party responsibility" or party government cannot be restricted merely to legislatures. The administration clearly shapes policy in its application, and party programs require sympathetic administrative leadership to be effective.

There are, however, substantial limits on the chief executive's use of his position of party leadership to unify his administration and hold it responsible to him and to his party's program.

1. The legislature may place administrative positions outside of executive control by stipulating terms of appointment that last beyond a President's or governor's term, by limiting the executive's power of removal, by placing policy-makers under merit system and tenure. It may extend a special legislative protection to others; so potent are the legislative supporters of the Director of the Federal Bureau of Investigation, J. Edgar Hoover, that he must be reckoned as independent of presidential authority as a matter of fact.

2. Special precautions may also be taken to thwart partisan control of an administrative agency. Federal agencies such as the Securities and Exchange Commission, the Federal Trade Commission, and the Civil Aeronautics Board are headed by five-man commissions or boards, but not more than three of the members of each may be of the same political party. Republican Presidents often meet that formal bi-partisan requirement by appointing conservative Democrats, while Democrats often seek out liberal Republicans. In the name of bi-partisanship, therefore, the search often goes on for atypical and unrepresentative partisans.

3. In a number of states the top administrative positions are, like the gubernatorial office, filled by election. That may at worst mean members of both parties in an uneasy executive alliance. Even if the other positions are filled by men of the governor's party, they are often politically and constitutionally independent of him. They build personal followings, and often the nature of their office allows them to publicize their name or control a minor administrative patronage. They may and do clash with governors over policy matters, and they guard their administrative independence pugnaciously. They often outlast even the hardiest governor; in Minnesota in 1965, for example, the incumbent Democratic governor had first been elected in 1962, but the state treasurer (a Republican) had first won his office in 1950, the secretary of state in 1954, and the state auditor (a Republican) in 1930! Thus the governor may confront a number of entrenched "executive parties" as he enters office; they may even be there as he leaves.

4. American executives furthermore suffer some diminution of political power as their terms of office come to a pre-determined halt. The 22nd Amendment to the U.S. Constitution limits the presidential terms of office to between eight and ten years, and twenty-four of the states limit the gubernatorial time in office, either by providing that the governor cannot succeed himself (fourteen states) or by limiting him to two consecutive terms (ten states).

5. Finally political realities may force an executive to share the instruments of party leadership with others. His appointments may be subject to the close scrutiny of party or legislative leaders; in the case of the

President, he must temper his choices to satisfy the dictates of senatorial courtesy should the appointment lie within the boundaries of a state represented by a senator of his party. Other leaders or factions within his party may also press in on him. Senator Robert A. Taft, the leader of the conservative wing of the Republican party, extracted an early commitment from President Eisenhower that in making his appointments the President would not discriminate against the Taftites of the party and that he was "determined to maintain the unity of the entire party by taking counsel with all factions and points of view" [9] within it.

Establishing control of the executive branch is far more complex than simply putting fellow partisans into positions of power and influence. Control over their operations and decisions comes with the greatest difficulty. Legislatures may limit the chief executive's power to dismiss even his own appointees, or they may limit his budgetary control over the agency's operations. Moreover, the chief executive faces essentially the same problem in enforcing party discipline on his administrative underlings that a party leader in the legislature faces. The problem in both cases is prior constituency loyalties. Just as the legislator identifies with the problems and outlooks of the citizens he knows and represents, so, too, does the administrator often identify with the problems and outlooks of the groups and individuals with which his agency deals. And just as the legislator must depend on the "folks back home" to protect his political "neck," so, too, the top-level administrator knows that the support of his client groups are his best personal political protection and the only protection for his agency, its mission, and its budget. And the pressure of party loyalties and party sanctions overcomes these loyalties to administrative constituencies with only the greatest difficulty. For in the executive as well as the legislative branch, the party has less to give and less to take away than does the constituency.

In that small sector of the administrative establishment closest to the chief executive, then, the party may function as an agency of "party responsibility." It may, through the person of the governor or President, hold top administrative officials responsible to a party mandate. But that sector often extends not far beyond the personal staff and appointed cabinet of the executive. And here, too, personal responsibility may be more important to the chief executive than a vaguer party responsibility or loyalty. Yet, at these top administrative levels the appointee has often been politically active and associated actively with a political party; he has very likely come to recognize the validity of the claims of the party organization and developed a commitment to (and awareness of) party goals and programs. The Cabinet of a President such as John F. Kennedy illustrates the combination of party and governmental experience and

⁹ Robert J. Donovan, *Eisenhower: The Inside Story* (New York: Harper, 1956), p. 104.

loyalty to the President himself. Secretaries Freeman, Hodges, and Ribicoff had been governors; they and others had had vast governmental and political experience. Yet the personal and political ties to the President bound them together. Secretaries McNamara, Day, and the President's brother, Robert, were old associates, and Secretaries Udall, Freeman, Goldberg, Ribicoff, and Day, as well as the President's brother, had all been active on behalf of Kennedy in 1960 presidential politics.

But when one looks a step below that level in the administrative structure to the "assistant secretary" level, party and governmental experience dwindles. These are men most often chosen for their skills and experience in administration and only very secondarily for their political credentials; their recruitment process may have included the political party only incidentally. In fact, in the selection of many of them the role of the party organization may not have extended beyond determining whether they were politically acceptable (i.e., inoffensive) in their home states. Generally speaking, the partisans seeking these positions through the party organizations lack the basic job qualifications, and the party role in appointment suffers therefore because executive and managerial considerations weigh more heavily than the political with most Presidents. The hope and assumption that one can serve both the political party goals and the executive-administrative goals with a single man often turns out to be no more than a hope.[10]

In assessing the executive party as a part of the broader political party, two related facts stand out. First of all, there is a constant tension between the demands of the party organization for the patronage and preference the executive controls on the one hand and the desires of the executive to build a cohesive administrative organization which will support his goals and programs. While the President, for example, may heed the demands of the party to represent the various factions and wings of the party in his Cabinet, the result, while building party cohesion and unity, may be to thwart the administrative and executive goals of the President.[11] Secondly, however, the executives, and not the party organizations, tend generally to claim the prime loyalty of the executive party. The executive may, to be sure, share the rewards of office with the party organization, but he more typically builds an executive party with administrative skills necessary to the executive task and with political goals and loyalties compatible with the executive's political purposes. Furthermore, in some American jurisdictions the usefulness to the party organizations of his appointments may be further diminished by laws requiring the political neutrality of the appointees. Within the administrative establishment of the national government, the Hatch Acts effectively prevent some politi-

[10] Mann, *The Assistant Secretaries.*

[11] Richard F. Fenno, *The President's Cabinet* (New York: Vintage, 1959), pp. 180–187.

cal appointees from continuing their activities within the political party which secured the office for them.

Unquestionably the chief tie between the broader party and the executive party is the tie of recruitment. The party organization has attracted, brought to public attention, perhaps even "indoctrinated" the men of the executive party; it has served as an authenticator of partisan bona fides. As a result the men and women of the executive party may well share (as does the legislative party) some general and loose concern for the values, the programs, and the outlooks of the party. What responsibility or party government that is possible, grows in part from that homogeneity of purpose and value and in part from the effort of the chief executive. For even though the executive party resembles the legislative party in its dependence on constituency, in its concern for its own job and responsibilities, in its reliance on its own system of rewards and status, and in its independence of the party organization, it is different in one very crucial respect. Unlike the legislative party, it has a powerful — politically and governmentally powerful — head: the governor or the President. Since the party organization must therefore deal with the executive party almost solely through the chief executive, it is almost powerless in the face of an aloof or hostile governor or President.

THE MYSTERIOUS CASE OF THE JUDICIAL PARTY

Nothing illustrates the difficulties of evaluating the party in office quite so clearly as those examples of cohesive "party voting" in American appellate courts. Several recent studies point to the presence of party-rooted blocs in state appellate courts in cases such as those involving workmen's compensation. Another broader study cutting across a number of states finds that Democratic and Republican judges differ significantly in the ways they decide certain types of cases. The Democrats on the bench tend, for example, to decide more frequently for the defendant in criminal cases, for the government in taxation cases, for the regulatory agency in cases involving the regulation of business, and for the claimants in workmen's compensation, unemployment compensation, and auto accident cases.[12] Certainly no one suggests that the incidence of party cohesion in judicial decision-making approaches that in legislatures. The relationships

[12] On the general subject of party blocs or voting affinities within justices of the same party see Sidney Ulmer, "The Political Party Variable on the Michigan Supreme Court," *Journal of Public Law*, XI (1962), pp. 352–362; Stuart Nagel, "Political Party Affiliation and Judges' Decisions," *American Political Science Review*, LV (1961), pp. 843–850; and Glendon Schubert, *Quantitative Analysis of Judicial Behavior* (Glencoe; Free Press, 1959), pp. 129–142. Similar differences in decision-making in the federal judiciary are reported in Sheldon Goldman, "Voting Behavior on the United States Courts of Appeals, 1961–1964," *American Political Science Review*, LX (1966), pp. 374–383.

appear only in certain types of cases, and the sheer amount of disagreement within an appellate court that can be explained by party division falls far below the amount of legislative division that party can explain. But, in any event, there is an apparent party cohesion in the American judiciary.

It may infrequently happen that some American judge is swayed by some subtle persuasion of his political party, but if it does happen, it hardly happens frequently enough to explain the party cohesion of which we spoke above. Rather the explanation undoubtedly rests in the different and coherent sets of values, even the different ideological stances, which the major parties represent. Quite simply, judges of the same party vote together on cases for the same reasons of ideology and outlook for which they chose to become affiliated with the same political party, or because they have been socialized into the goals and values of the same party. Two judges, that is, vote together on an issue of the administrative regulation of utilities because of deep-seated values about the relationship of government and the economy which they share in common; those same values or perceptions led them some years earlier to join the same political party, or they developed out of experience in the same political party.

The impact of the party on the decision-making processes of the judiciary is largely, therefore, its impact as a representer of basic attitudes. That this should be so ought not to surprise anyone, for the appointment of judges in the United States has classically taken the values and attitudes of judges into account. While we have only recently accepted in any overt way the notions of limited judicial "law-making" — the notions that in some instances judges have options and that in these choices they may at least in part reflect their own prior experiences, perceptions, and values and attitudes — we have acknowledged it implicitly for some time. President Theodore Roosevelt, considering a replacement for Justice Horace Gray on the Supreme Court wrote Senator Henry Lodge inquiring about a certain Judge Oliver Wendell Holmes of the Massachusetts Supreme Court:

. . . In the ordinary and low sense which we attach to the words "partisan" and "politician," a judge of the Supreme Court should be neither. But in the higher sense, in the proper sense, he is not in my judgment fitted for the position unless he is a party man, a constructive statesman, constantly keeping in mind his adherence to the principles and policies under which this nation has been built up and in accordance with which it must go on. . . .

. . .

Now I should like to know that Judge Holmes was in entire sympathy with our views, that is with your views and mine and Judge Gray's, just as we know that ex-Attorney General Knowlton is, before I would feel justified in appointing him. Judge Gray has been one of the most valuable members of the Court.

I should hold myself as guilty of an irreparable wrong to the nation if I should put in his place any man who was not absolutely sane and sound on the great national policies for which we stand in public life.[13]

Congress, too, has often implicitly examined such issues in approving appointments to the federal judiciary. The Senate in 1930 rejected an appointee to the Supreme Court, John J. Parker, on the grounds that he was unsympathetic to the causes of Negro rights and organized labor.

If it is within the province of the President or a governor to consider such matters in proposing judicial appointments, the appointee's political party loyalties serve as some indication of his values and attitudes. It is, indeed, one of the reasons that American Presidents have in the last century appointed to the federal bench a preponderance of men from their own parties. They have, in fact, generally chosen more than 90 per cent of their appointments from the ranks of their own parties, and in every case since Cleveland the percentage has been above 80 (Table 2).[14]

Table 2

PERCENTAGES OF JUDICIAL APPOINTMENTS FROM THE PARTY
OF THE PRESIDENT: GROVER CLEVELAND THROUGH JOHN F. KENNEDY

Cleveland	97.3%	Coolidge	94.1%
Harrison	87.9	Hoover	85.7
McKinley	95.7	F. Roosevelt	96.4
T. Roosevelt	95.8	Truman	90.1
Taft	82.2	Eisenhower	94.1
Wilson	98.6	Kennedy	90.9
Harding	97.7		

That overwhelming percentage is, to be sure, the result of other pressures. For one, the President's information network and his own personal acquaintanceships — his whole mechanism for recruiting appointees — quite naturally flows through his party and his own acquaintances in the party. Furthermore, there is an old and honorable tradition in American politics that judicial appointment constitutes one of the most desirable, high-level rewards for good and faithful service to the party or to a candidate of the party. Executives are under strong pressures to find their qualified judicial appointments within the ranks of the attorneys who have labored for them or the party.

In the majority of the states, the judiciary is not appointive; it is filled

[13] The Roosevelt letter is quoted more fully in Walter F. Murphy and C. Herman Pritchett, *Courts, Judges, and Politics* (New York: Random House, 1961), pp. 82–83.

[14] The data of Table 2 were drawn from two sources: Evan A. Evans, "Political Influences in the Selection of Federal Judges," *Wisconsin Law Review* (May, 1948), pp. 330–351, and Hugh A. Bone, *American Politics and the Party System*, 3rd ed. (New York: McGraw-Hill, 1965), p. 266.

either at partisan or non-partisan elections. In the partisan elections of twenty states, of course, the man is elected as a member or candidate of a party, and one can reasonably suspect that his party tie may represent certain generalized value positions. But in these elections the state parties vary greatly in the active way they contest them; in a few states the party organizations make primary endorsements and actively support energetic partisans for the judgeships. They would, in other words, make the position a form of "elective patronage." Other state parties pay far less attention to judicial elections, so that in some cases the same man — often with the endorsement of the state bar association — will even run on both party tickets.

Party pressures and activities are far less obvious and important in the non-partisan elections. But regardless of the election process and politics, the judge still may come to the bench with the values that a party represents, and party lines may even be apparent in the divisions of a non-partisan judiciary, too.[15] Judicial terms tend to be so long and judges tend to stay in office so long that many elective judgeships in fact become appointive. Death often takes a man off the bench in mid-term, and the vacancy is filled before the next election by a gubernatorial appointment. The political considerations attending such appointments may then prevail, and with the advantage of even a brief period of incumbency the appointed man usually wins a full, regular term at the next election.

The point, then, is a simple one. There is no way to eliminate the values and preferences, the important frames of reference, that judges bring to their work. Judges have been men of the world; they know the issues of their times and the ways the parties relate to them. Furthermore, given the tradition of the political activity of the American lawyer, there is a good chance that the judge has had some active, political party experience. Beyond this, the political party has an opportunity for more active and overt influence in the selection process through the initiatives of governors or Presidents of the party or through the usual processes of a partisan election. In these latter selection processes the party has the opportunity, which it sometimes takes advantage of, to select men for the judiciary who are especially sensitive to the ideological issues for which the party stands and whose ideological positions have been reinforced through years of service to the party.

The use of the federal or state bench as a desirable bit of political patronage obviously opens the American courts to a degree of politicality

---

[15] Even in a state in which judges are chosen on a non-partisan ballot partisan blocs may be apparent in some kinds of issues. In Minnesota, for example, the state supreme court has in recent years shown a high degree of party cohesion in two celebrated, "political" issues: an important question of procedure in the early stages of the recount of the state's 1962 gubernatorial election, and the question of the authority of the governor to veto a legislative reapportionment.

unthinkable in many other political cultures. But the relationship between judge and party may even extend beyond the politics of appointment. In some parts of the country the local district or county judge still may retain some hidden ties to local politics; he is in some American counties the *eminence grise* of the party, slating candidates behind the scenes, directing party strategy, arbitrating among the conflicting ambitions of the party's candidates. Moreover, the local administration of justice occasionally opens new reservoirs of patronage for the party. The judge, loyal member of a political party, may parcel out guardianships, receiverships in bankruptcy, and clerkships to loyal lawyers of the party. In the 1966 battle between the party-designated candidate and the reform candidate (supported by Senator Robert Kennedy) for the Democratic nomination for a judgeship in Manhattan's Surrogate Court, it developed that the Surrogates had in the preceding year issued 428 guardianships, with lawyers' fees running into many millions, in that one borough of the city alone. Many commentators and journalists, and many party officials, believe that those and similar appointments go chiefly to attorneys active in the party ranks.[16]

How is it that the tie between the judiciary and the parties is so substantial in the United States? The factors are complex and mixed. The phenomenon of the elective judiciary, compounded by the political appointment process, is one. Then, too, we have no career vocation, no special training process or examination for the judiciary — any lawyer can be a judge; by contrast in many continental European countries the career of judging requires special preparation, study, and apprenticeship, and one enters it by special civil service examination. In this context, then, the additional factor of the dominance of American politics by the legal profession is free to operate. Lawyers are everywhere in American political and public life, and many of them hope for ultimate reward and retirement to the bench. And within the American tradition, access to the bench is a dream they can realistically entertain. The bench, then, is a perfectly understandable part of the universe of rewards and incentives on which the American parties depend.

SUMMARY

Surprisingly, the influence of the political party on the executives and judiciaries of the American political system, while they differ in degree, do not differ in kind. The main avenue of party influence is indirect and in both cases it stems from the kinds of commitments and values which membership in a party — or loyalty to one — represents. It depends, in

16 On judicial patronage see Charles E. Merriam and Harold F. Gosnell, *The American Party System*, 4th ed. (New York: Macmillan, 1949), and Herbert Jacob, *Justice in America* (Boston: Little, Brown, 1965), pp. 87–89.

other words, on the ideological impact or presence of the party *within* the men who hold administrative or judicial office. It is an influence that is difficult to supervise — and in the case of judges very, very difficult, because of both long terms and the dominant concepts of judicial ethics. If a party cares to activate it, it had better do so at the selection point.

Furthermore, in both the executive and the judiciary one observes the conflict between the policy purpose — even when pursued within the limits of judicial propriety — and the demands of the party. For every executive and legislature that would like to use party as an indication of future decision-making in office, there are countless pressures from the party to use the positions for party rewards. The administrative position or the judgeship remains one of the few available positions with which to reward a party leader, and the party is not anxious to have it pass to a party "nobody." When that happens the party suffers doubly; no one is rewarded, and even worse, the party's inability to control the positions for rewarding purposes is spread on the record for all to see. In the filling of positions in both branches one sees again the struggle between the party's own, important needs for organizational incentives and the desire, however guarded, to affect the making of public policy. For the American parties it is a dilemma without end or resolution.

Chapter Sixteen

THE QUEST FOR
PARTY GOVERNMENT

The political parties are everywhere in American legislatures and executives, and even in American judiciaries. All American executives, almost
all American legislatures, and about half of the American judiciaries are
selected in processes that weigh the party affiliation and loyalty of the
office-seeker heavily. Moreover, the appearances of party power are more
than plentiful in the party leaders and whips of the legislatures and the
clearly partisan cast of many executive appointments. Even the elemental
struggle between "government" and "opposition," "ins" and "outs," largely
follows political party lines in the American system, just as if the parties
controlled cohesive government and opposition parties in office. And yet,
despite the trappings and portents of power, the American major parties
do not govern in the sense of mobilizing cohesive groups of office-holders
behind programs and ideologies to which the parties, and their guiding
organizations and activists, have committed themselves.

The discontent with this inability of the American parties to "govern"
is an old one within academic political science.[1] But the dissatisfactions
are with more than the American parties; they extend to the entire American political system and its fragmented centers of authority, its tendency
to blur political alternatives and differences, and its built-in barriers to
strong and vigorous governmental initiatives. The critics, many of them
admirers of the cohesive parties and the ease of mobilizing party majorities in the British political parties, long hoped that by joining electoral
majorities and office-holders to party programs they could surmount the
diffusion of power in the American polity. They found an official profes-

[1] Austin Ranney, *The Doctrine of Responsible Party Government* (Urbana: Univ. of
Illinois Press, 1962).

sional and academic platform by the late 1940's in a committee of the American Political Science Association; and the 1950 report of the committee, *Toward a More Responsible Two-Party System*,[2] gave the controversy its major recent stimulus. While the ensuing academic controversy has slowly simmered down, it is by no means quiescent today.

While the controversy over "party responsibility" and "party government" has embroiled academic political science for the past twenty years, a similar and parallel concern has agitated much of the American political world. From the ideologically oriented activists in both parties have come wails of dissatisfaction with the issuelessness of American politics and the tendency of the major parties to take similar centrist positions in support of the status quo. They complain, much as did Lord Bryce some seventy years ago, that the American parties are as Tweedle-dee and Tweedle-dum. In recent years the greater concern has been within the Republican party's conservative wing; its leaders have inveighed against the "me-too-ism" of the party's liberals and moderates, and in working for the nomination of Barry Goldwater in 1964 they pleaded for "a choice, not an echo." Others have attempted to get at the fundamental inhibition to an ideological politics, the presence in each party of differing ideological positions, by advocating a gradual realignment of partisan loyalties to produce sharply differing, frankly "liberal" and "conservative" parties.

At first blush it may seem that the somewhat hermetic controversy over party "responsibility" has not a great deal to do with the development of a distinct and different ideological personality for the parties. One would not in any event ordinarily expect such a conjunction of academic debate and popular political controversy. But the two questions are to some extent the same one. The scholarly schools favoring party government and/ or responsibility have come to realize that the conditions necessary for the achievement of responsibility — party-led enactment of a party program by party office-holders — can be achieved only with the development (at least to a limited extent) of ideological political parties. And the political activists who seek ideological clarity and ideological alternatives in American parties want those ideological parties to govern, to carry their ideological imperatives into public policy. Ideological clarification is probably a necessary condition for party government, and conversely party government or responsibility is certainly the implicit role of the ideological party.

THE LOGIC OF THE RESPONSIBLE PARTY

Despite the nomenclature, the doctrines of party government and party responsibility are only secondarily concerned with political parties. They

[2] Committee on Political Parties of the American Political Science Association, *Toward a More Responsible Two-Party System* (New York: Rinehart, 1950).

are fundamentally doctrines of democratic government — or, more precisely, doctrines advocating one particular variety of American democracy. Much of the debate over them has in fact been a debate over the
kind of democracy we are to have. The whole movement for party government has sprung from a discontent over what some scholars and citizens have seen as the ills of American democracy. Part of the blame for
those ills they have laid at the feet of the major American parties, and a
good many of their hopes for remedying the ills rest on the possibility of
reconstituting and revitalizing the parties. The parties are to be the instruments or mechanisms — perhaps even the "panaceas" — for curing the
maladies of American democracy.

The proponents of party government [3] begin with a belief in strong,
positive government as a very necessary force for the solution of problems
in the American society and economy. And like so many of the advocates
of positive government in the contest of the American separation of powers, many of them see a need for strong presidential and executive leadership if the whole complex governmental apparatus is to move forward
with some vigor and semblance of unity. Yet, they know all too well that
the institutions and traditions of American government diffuse, disperse,
and divide governmental power in ways that prevent the generation of
aggressive and responsive governmental programs. Theirs is the old complaint that American political institutions, suited perhaps for the minimal,
gingerly governing of the 18th and 19th centuries, are far less adapted to
the present century's need for positive government action. And, clearly,
decentralized political parties, each of them divided by a vast diversity of
interests and points of view, only accentuate the problem of diffusion.

A second thread of argument also runs through the political diagnoses
of the proponents of party government. It is their concern for the miniscule political power of the individual in a mass, popular democracy. Contemporary government becomes large, complex, and remote, and the
individual, beset with his own personal concerns, finds it hard to have the
time, attention, and political knowledge for an active role in the political
system. He is often bewildered, alienated, and politically ineffective. He
finds it especially difficult even to know and judge what his elected
representatives have been doing in public office. And into the political
void resulting from his ineffectiveness and ignorance rush well-organized
and well-financed minorities — local elites, interest groups, party bosses,
or *ad hoc* alliances. Consequently, so the argument goes, important decisions are frequently made by public officials and organized minorities

[3] A word of semantic distinction may be helpful here. "Party government" refers
to leadership by a majority political party in the important decision-making processes
of government; the "responsible" party is one able to organize majorities and officials
behind party programs and thus be responsible to its voters for the conduct of office.
It is not, therefore, a gross oversimplification to say that the "responsible" party is one
capable of "party government."

without the participation or even the *post hoc* judgment of the great majority of individual citizens. The individual, for his part, drifts from one meaningless decision to another; he does not know for what the candidate stands when he first elects him, and he has no standards or information for judging his performance in office when he comes up for reelection.[4]

This sense of alarm about the American democracy, to be sure, is by no means limited to the proponents of party government. Theirs is an analysis which countless other scholars, journalists, and public figures would in varying ways subscribe to. It is a more-or-less "standard" critique from those quarters of American life committed to the "liberal" confidence in the usefulness of a broad governmental role and to the "liberal" belief in the rationality and desirability of citizen involvement in a popular democracy.[5] What sets the school of party government apart is its reliance on the organizing and consolidating powers of the competitive political party. A reconstituted (and "responsible") pair of political parties will, it is hoped, bring together masses of voters behind meaningful party programs and candidates loyal to them and then hold the elected candidates to the obligation of carrying those programs into public policy. The responsible political party thus bridges the gulf between the politically disoriented individual and the distant, complex institutions of government. At the same time it assists, through the force of loyalties to the same party program, in mobilizing fragmented executives and legislatures for unified programs of action.

In essence these are proposals for the re-invigorating and animating of popular democratic institutions through the prime organizing role of the political party. Why the political party for so crucial a role?

As mobilizers of majorities the parties have claims on the loyalties of the American people superior to the claims of any other forms of political organization. They have extended the area of popular participation in public affairs enormously and have given elections a meaning and importance never before thought possible. . . . Moreover, party government is good democratic doctrine because the parties are the special form of political organization adapted to the mobilization of majorities. How else can the majority get organized? If democracy means anything at all it means that the majority has the right to organize for the purpose of taking over the government.[6]

Only the parties, their supporters believe, are big, stable, extensive, and visible enough to carry this representational burden. As the only com-

[4] See Ranney, *The Doctrine of Responsible Party Government,* chaps. 1 and 2, for an analysis of what party government presumes about democracy.

[5] I am using "liberal" in the sense it is used in contemporary American politics; the liberal position favors popular, participatory democracy and positive government. Conservatism, on the other hand, generally connotes a preference for limited government and for the wisdom of political leaders and elites.

[6] E. E. Schattschneider, *Party Government* (New York: Rinehart, 1942), p. 208.

pletely "political" of the political organizations — and the only one with a public or "semi-public" character — the competitive political party alone has the capacity for developing the essential qualities of "responsibility."

The call for "responsible" political parties, therefore, is a call for political parties with new capacities and new goals. Specifically, the responsible political party must:

1. evolve and enunciate a reasonably explicit statement of party programs and principles.

2. nominate (despite the difficulties of controlling the direct primaries) candidates loyal to the party program.

3. conduct its electoral campaigns in such a way that voters will grasp the programmatic differences between the parties and make the voting decision at least substantially on that basis.

4. guarantee that public office-holders elected under the party label will carry the party program into public policy — and thus enable the party to take "responsibility" for their actions in office. This much seems necessary if the party is to "govern" and be responsible to the majorities which chose it to govern. The entire argument rests on the replacement of individual or group responsibility for governmental decisions with the placement of responsibility on the cohesive political party.

"Cohesion" is, indeed, the key to the responsible political party. It must be cohesive enough to enunciate a program which will distinguish it from its competitor. It must also recruit and elect a group of legislators and executives cohesive enough to unite in support of proposals carrying the party's pledges into public policy. Cohesion of that sort within the party as an organization and the party in office also presupposes clearly the development of a cohesive party electorate. And very clearly that pervasive cohesion can be built in only one way — through the development of an ideological politics with ideologically cohesive and ideologically differentiated political parties. It is precisely at this point that the scholarly advocates of party responsibility begin to seek the same goals as the non-academic advocates of party realignment (i.e., ideological realignment) and parties that prefer a "forthright stand" to "me-too-ism."

In fact, a strong case can be made that the infusion of some ideological concerns into an essentially non-ideological American politics is also the prime objective of the school of party government. As the report of the committee of the American Political Science Association argues in its very first paragraph:

While in an election the party alternative necessarily takes the form of a choice between candidates, putting a particular candidate into office is not an end in itself. The concern of the parties with candidates, elections and appointments is misunderstood if it is assumed that parties can afford to bring forth aspirants for office without regard to the views of those so selected. Actually, the party struggle is concerned with the direction of public affairs. Party nominations are no more than a means to this end. In short, party politics inevitably involves public policy in one way or another.[7]

The development of a concern for the policy views of candidates and the making of policy is, in other words, a necessary condition for the responsible party. Ideological politics — or at least a more substantial emphasis on policy issues in American politics — is thus both a crucial means and an important end for the advocates of party responsibility. For the whole idea of party government is inherently policy- and issue-oriented. It is concerned with capturing and using public office for predetermined goals and purposes — and not merely for the thrill of winning, the division of patronage and spoils, or the reward of the office itself. The winning of public office becomes no more than a necessary means to policy ends.

There still remains, however, a sizable platoon of American political scientists and political leaders who are, despite the persuasiveness of the advocates of party government, greatly unconvinced.[8] The journals of American political science were, in fact, dotted with rejoinders and exception-taking for several years after the publication of the report of the Committee on Political Parties in 1950. Their collective case against party government and responsibility divides into two related but independent arguments: the *undesirability* of party government and its *impossibility* (or at least its improbability). While the two points are related, both logically and polemically, no logic dictates that one must make both points if he ventures one.

On the grounds of undesirability the skeptics argue across a number of fundamental issues of political philosophy. They fear that an embrace of party government will stimulate a more ideological, politically "hyperthyroid" politics of intense, dogmatic commitment — one in which the softenings and majority-building of compromise will be more difficult. They fear, too, that by making the political party the prime avenue of political representation the advocates of party government will destroy the present richness and multiplicity of representational mechanisms in the American democracy. Interest groups and other non-party political organizations, they feel, are necessary means of political representation in a large and heterogeneous polity; to channel the representation of such a diversity of interests into the party system would "overload" its political and representational capacity. Furthermore, the skeptics are concerned lest party government destroy the deliberative quality of American legislatures, for legislators would cease to be "free," independent men and would become the mandated, committed representatives of a fixed party position. In

---

[7] *Toward a More Responsible Two-Party System,* p. 15.

[8] The bibliography critical of the concept of party responsibility is a very long one. Pendleton Herring's *The Politics of Democracy* (New York: Rinehart, 1940) early presented a view contra the reformers.

short, they fear what European critics often call "partyocracy" — the domination of politics and legislatures by a number of doctrinaire, unyielding political parties, none of them strong enough to govern and none willing to let others govern.

On the related grounds of realism (i.e., the questions of possibility and probability) the critics of responsible parties have argued that:

The American voter remains insufficiently involved in ideology to be coaxed easily into viewing politics and electoral choices in programmatic terms.

The complexity of American society, and the diversity of interests it generates, is too great to be expressed in the simple set of alternatives a two-party system can frame. Consequently, there is some fear that a more ideological politics would break the bounds of the two-party system and encourage the development of splinter parties.

The parties themselves are too diffuse and decentralized — too lacking in central disciplinary authority — to ever take a single, national ideological position and then enforce it on their assorted partisans and holders of public office.

The institutions of American government stand in the way at a number of crucial points. For example, the direct primary makes it difficult for the parties to choose nominees loyal to their programs, and the separation of powers (and bicameralism) often prevents the control of all executive and legislative authority by a single party.

At every point, in other words, the model of the responsible, governing political party appears to the critics to demand too much of the American voters, the major parties, and the institutions of American government. These points are not, of course, lost on the proponents of party government. They, too, recognize at least some of the practical difficulties in implementing their reforms. So, this aspect of the argument reduces in part to the question of whether the parties and the voters are being prepared for, or can be prepared for, government by "responsible" political parties.

If the major American parties are to meet the demands and roles of party government, they must find some source of unity and cohesion with which to overcome their egregious diffusion and disunity. The problem is really one of uniting the party organization, the party in the electorate, and the party in office in active and "responsible" support of a party program — and this despite their different political goals, their different political traditions and interests, and their different levels of attention, information, and activity. Three sources of the cohesion or unity necessary for governing parties appear possible within the range of democratic parties.

1. That cohesion may be promoted by *constitutional imperatives*. The

parliamentary system demands that the majority party maintain cohesion in the legislature — and to a lesser extent in the electorate and party organization — if it is to stay in office.[9] No such constitutional stimulus to party cohesion is at work on the American parties.

2. It may also be promoted by *organizational discipline*. A strong party organization may impose its discipline and cohesion on balky partisans in office if it can control renomination to office.[10] The American direct primary, however, makes that a questionable option. Alternatively, powerful party leaders or executives may enforce it through the manipulation of rewards they control (patronage, preference, access to authority, etc.). But the value of these rewards is shrinking, and popular political ethics in the United States no longer easily accept an enforced line-toeing. Although the available rewards and a tolerant political culture permit this kind of discipline in some American states and localities, it is an impossibility in many others.

3. Finally, the cohesion may be produced "naturally" by an all-pervasive, intra-party *agreement on ideology or program*. All three components of the party may reach some consensus on a basic party ideology or program — or at least on a "silent ideology" of interest. The activists and identifiers of the party then achieve a cohesion arising from common goals, and their relatively high cohesion is to a considerable extent a result of internalized and self-enforced commitment to those goals. Distasteful external constraints and restraints are thus less necessary.

Because it seems that only the third, the ideological, avenue to party government is a likely one for contemporary American parties, the issue of party government becomes one of ideological — or "more ideological" — politics and parties. For, if cohesion is the necessary condition for responsible, governing parties, a pervasive ideological commitment appears to be the necessary condition for cohesion. Organizational discipline may supplement and buttress it, but it does not appear to be a viable independent alternative to it.

IDEOLOGICAL PARTIES IN THE UNITED STATES

The complaint of the American ideologist with the major American parties is an old and familiar one.

[9] See Leon D. Epstein, "A Comparative Study of Canadian Parties," *American Political Science Review*, LVIII (1964), pp. 46–59.

[10] A highly centralized party such as the Indian Congress party can maintain control over nomination and renomination of candidates to the national parliament and thus exercise a potent sanction upon those parliamentarians of the party who break party discipline. In 1957, for example, the national Parliamentary Board of the party, the agency of the party which selects and approves the candidates for local constituencies, declined to renominate almost one-third of the party's incumbent members of Parliament.

The elections this November will prove totally irrelevant because the American electorate will have no substantive choice among the candidates. Naturally, there will be the traditional rhetoric about the "great liberal policies of the Democratic party" and the "great Republican tradition of fiscal responsibility," but if one pierces the rhetoric of each party, one sees that while each may say varying things, each pursues a common policy, *i.e.*, the preservation of the status quo.[11]

If the complaint is clear, its author and occasion are not. The admonition could be from the political left or the political right, and it could well have been spoken at virtually any national election since World War II. As it happens, it opened an article by a prominent spokesman of the New Left shortly before the 1966 congressional elections.[12] But some eighty years ago the American parties were similarly compared to Tweedle-dee and Tweedle-dum, and more recently their own partisans have accused them of "me-too-ism" and of generating only superficial differences. Consequently, the charges go, the Democrats and Republicans are guilty either of suppressing ideological alternatives subscribed to by significant numbers of Americans or of failing to promote a wide-ranging dialectic on public issues. In other words, they smother existing ideological differences, and they deny one important opportunity for others to develop.

Less ideologically disposed Americans have been largely willing to grant one part of the argument — and then make a virtue of necessity (or, more precisely, a virtue of reality). The American parties *are* relatively non-ideological parties of the political center. Since their mission is the organization of majorities, they cannot be deflected by the wishes of small ideological minorities. To organize the stable majorities that undergird the American polity — so the argument goes — the parties must often compromise, soften, or smooth over the issues that divide Americans. As competitive parties in the heterogeneous American society they must be pragmatic, brokerage parties, appealing for votes wherever those votes may be and regardless of the ultimate inconsistency of the appeal.

Yet, the celebration of the non-ideological character of the American major parties is not as logically secure as first it seems. For it vacillates between a view of the American electorate as ideologically neutral, centrist, and content with the status quo, and a sharply different one of a

---

[11] Edward M. Keating, "The New Left: What Does It Mean?" *Saturday Review* (September 24, 1966), p. 25.

[12] The following second paragraph of the essay is also illustrative:

Republicans and Democrats in 1966 are snarling and snapping at each other, vainly attempting to deceive the voter into thinking that there are choices, not echoes, on the political horizon. This is to dissemble. Both parties know that neither will attempt to alter basic American policy, which, on the national level, is to obfuscate the social sickness that is consuming us all, and, on the international level, is intended to extend Americanism to the rest of the world by military blackmail.

heterogeneous electorate containing such a wealth of interests and views that two parties could not possibly contain them. In other words, do the parties reflect a non-ideological satisfaction with the status quo, or do they soften and mediate among the conflicting, heterogeneous interests of the American electorate? Is it possible that they do both?

To a vast degree, the question of the amount of ideological involvement in American politics rests squarely on the definition and measures one adopts of ideology. It is possible to think of an ideology as a pattern or constellation of political attitudes (or values) and still beg the question, for the extent of the pattern and the objects of the attitudes remain unspecified. Certainly, however, no one expects to find in the American political context the kind of total *weltanschauung*, the all-embracing concern of an East European Communist party or an Asian Moslem party, for theirs is an ideology encompassing virtually all social relationships and thus a politics of limitless scope and total involvement. Nor, given the general American agreement on basic institutions, are ideological differences between the American parties apt to involve dispute over the constitution, the general outlines of the American economy, or the basic fabric of American society. Nor do American parties commit themselves dogmatically to *a priori*, fixed political ideologies in the manner of some doctrinaire European parties. And yet all of this may only be to say that ideological parties as one finds them elsewhere — and especially in the bitter class politics of the European democracies — do not exist in the United States.

It scarcely seems either fair or realistic, however, to accept the easy simplisms about the total unconcern of the American parties for issue or ideology. The American parties have often differed on the major political issues of the moment. In recent years their national platforms have differed over American foreign policy in the Far East, government medical insurance and aid for the aged, fiscal policy and the balanced budget, and government regulation of labor-management relations. Beneath these differences on the policy issues of the moment were the different constellations of attitudes, interests, and goals each party had embraced. Each party, in other words, developed a "silent ideology" based on the commonality of the interests and views (and in a few cases, the full-blown ideologies) of its activists and its party electorate. Its leaders constitute a group of "like-minded men" whose views on public issues separate them from the like-minded leaders of the other party.[13] Such a silent ideology stops short in only one main way from being an ideology in the more conventional sense; it is not usually codified or explicated — either by the party or the individual voter — into a systematic, coherent, and consistent pattern of political values. For the classic pragmatic American political

---

[13] Thomas A. Flinn and Frederick M. Wirt, "Local Party Leaders: Groups of Like Minded Men," *Midwest Journal of Political Science*, IX (1965), pp. 77–98.

style focuses the party's attention not on fixed, abstract principles of ideology but on the immediate, concrete issues of public policy that divide men at a particular time.

By these modest standards the American major parties have probably never been indistinguishable, but there are ample signs that attention to issues and even ideological concerns within the parties are on the rise. For example:

> Men and women are increasingly being drawn to party work out of their involvement with issues and ideologies. The triumph of political ideas and values thus becomes a major incentive to party activity, and to some extent it replaces the older incentives of patronage and preference.[14]

> Ideologically motivated partisans have increasingly been forming ideological organizations both within and parallel to the party structure. The club-style organizations of some urban Democrats are a case in point, and recently the Republicans have been proliferating extra-party organizations to the right (e.g., The Free Society Association, honorary chairman Barry Goldwater) and to the left (e.g., the Ripon Society).

> The labels of "liberal" and "conservative" are freely accepted and exchanged by increasing numbers of political activists, in contrast to the widely expressed belief of less than a generation ago that to accept the labels, especially the "conservative" label, was gross political imprudence. Behind those labels, too, there is an active, popular political discourse which reflects ideological differences over the proper role of government in the American society.

> In 1964 one of the major political parties chose an avowedly ideological candidate and wrote an unabashedly ideological platform, a move which one observer termed the end of the "reign of pragmatism" within the GOP.[15] It may even have been for many of the delegates to the 1964 Republican convention a conscious choice for ideological conviction over electoral victory and its inevitable compromises.

In the search for symptoms of the ideological renaissance, the recent politics of the nation's two largest states invite a special scrutiny. In the 1965 election of a mayor in New York City, conservative Republicans bolted their party's ticket (headed by the successful candidate, John V. Lindsay) to support the Conservative party and its candidate, conservative publicist and debater, William Buckley. And a number of reform club Democrats, including even some club leaders, left the Democratic candidate, whom they thought was too closely associated with the Democratic "bosses." Then at the 1966 general elections in the state, ideological,

---

14 See Chapter 4.
15 James Reichley, quoted by Theodore White, *The Making of the President 1964* (New York: Atheneum, 1965), p. 217.

third-party candidates blossomed out all over. Liberal and Conservative party candidates for the governorship siphoned off exactly 17 per cent of the popular vote, and assorted minor party candidates appeared in more than half of the state's congressional races. In California dissension continued in the Democratic party between the Democratic clubs and the regular Democratic organization, especially over the club activists' dissatisfaction with state and national party support of the Vietnam war. The liberal-conservative rift persisted in the GOP; the state's senior senator, Thomas Kuchel, refused to support the party's successful candidate for governor, Ronald Reagan.

Most of these signs of increased ideological concern are visible chiefly among the activists of the party organization. But what of the American voters, especially the less partisan electorate? Ideological political parties need not necessarily guarantee an ideological politics. It may very well be that only the small core of party activists are moving to greater ideological sophistication and concerns and that the broad American public is accepting them only selectively and cautiously. There is always the possibility, in other words, that more ideological party cadres and spokesmen will bring their new involvement to a deaf or hostile public, that their "ideologizing" will only bore or alienate the majority of the electorate to whom such matters are at best abstruse and only fitfully salient.

The issue of the differences in ideological concern between party organization activists and the electorate is, moreover, hardly an arid, scholarly one. The ideologists of American politics have long claimed that there is indeed a horde of ideological voters who are increasingly alienated by parties unwilling or unable to give them clearly defined ideological alternatives. Much of the 1964 pre-convention rationale of the Goldwater Republicans, for example, hinged on the argument that a frankly conservative Republican candidate would mobilize the disenchanted, "stay-at-home" conservative vote.[16] The entire question of whether the American parties are reflecting a non-ideological electorate or suppressing a latent ideological commitment rests on the stance of the American voter toward issue and ideology.

IDEOLOGY IN THE AMERICAN ELECTORATE

In the 1950's the authors of *The American Voter* found that by the most generous criteria only about 15 per cent of the American electorate employed an ideological framework or ideological terminology as either a primary or marginal means for evaluating parties and candidates. Only some 3 or 4 per cent saw American politics primarily in ideological

---

[16] It should be noted, of course, that none materialized in the 1964 elections and that no scholarly study of the American electorate, either before or since those elections, has confirmed the presence of such a body of voters.

terms.[17] That is to say that less than one in six American voters applied to the presidential politics of the time, some ideological abstractions greater than a single issue or group interest. A goodly portion of the ideologically disposed voters thought in terms of conservatism and liberalism, even though their manipulation of the terms may bespeak no particularly firm grasp of any philosophical subtleties. Beneath this thin stratum of ideologists and "near" ideologists, some 45 per cent of the electorate operated at an interest-oriented level — a level approximately of what we have earlier called the level of the "silent ideology." Their "sub-ideological" identifications and evaluations were non-systematic projections of the interests of a group or the fervor of an issue position. Theirs were, for example, the characterization of the Democratic party as the party of the "little" man, the Republicans as the party of "business" or "fiscal responsibility."

And who are the minority of ideologists? They are the better educated and the political activists; in fact, both educational attainment and political activism (measured by party work, membership, financial contributions, attendance at rallies, etc.) relate strongly both to ideological evaluations of politics and to a general knowledge of ideological terms and relationships.[18] So, one is led again to conclude that the men and women of the party organizations are far more intensely ideological about American politics than is the ordinary voter. But party activist and voter differ on more than the degree of ideological sophistication and commitment. The American voter tends also to remain closer to ideological center ground than does the activist. A study of the delegates to the 1956 Republican and Democratic national conventions found a greater ideological "distance" between these two groups of party leaders than between a national sample of the ordinary voters who identified with the two parties. The GOP rank and file, indeed, appeared to be closer, when asked their positions on current issues, to the leaders of the Democratic party than to the relatively isolated ideologists leading their own party.[19]

Increasing levels of ideological knowledge and information may well be marking the American electorate. The 1964 data of the SRC indicate that possibility; for example, 80 per cent of these respondents (who considered themselves informed) saw the Democratic party as more apt to propose governmental solutions of public problems than the Republicans.[20]

[17] See *The American Voter*, Chapter 10.

[18] Again see *The American Voter*, Chapter 10, and the article by Flinn and Wirt cited above in fn. 13.

[19] Herbert McClosky, Paul J. Hoffmann, Rosemary O'Hara, "Issue Conflict and Consensus Among Party Leaders and Followers," *American Political Science Review*, LIV (1960), pp. 406–427.

[20] However, since these ideological explorations were begun only in 1964 and since there are no comparable questions in the earlier studies of the national electorate, there are no bases for direct comparison.

But having the information is one matter, and acting on it is another. No information suggests that the greater ideological sophistication has been accompanied by rising levels of ideological involvement and action. To know the world and appeals of political ideology may very well be to reject it. No evidence suggests, for instance, that the American electorate is deserting its centrist position for the liberal and conservative (and left-right) poles of the conventional ideological continuum. In fact, the conservative renaissance in recent American politics — and especially among the activists of the Republican party — seems to have had little counterpart in the American electorate (see Table 1).

Table 1

IDEOLOGICAL POSITION PREFERENCES OF AMERICAN ADULTS,*
1945–1966

Date	Go Left	Half Way	Go Right	No Opinion
1945	18	52	21	9
1947	14	56	20	10
1955	19	52	17	12
1961	15	50	19	16
1962	21	42	21	16
1966	14	52	20	14

* The data are from the Gallup Poll (American Institute of Public Opinion). The 1966 figures were reported in the Minneapolis Tribune of January 12, 1966; the others were collected by Hazel Gaudet Erskine in "The Polls: Some Gauges of Conservatism," Public Opinion Quarterly, XXVIII (1964), pp. 154–168. The question was: "Which of these three policies would you like to have (the President, the government) follow? Go more to the right — by following more of the views of business and conservative groups? Go more to the left — by following more of the views of labor and other liberal groups? Follow a policy half-way between the two?"

In summary, then, there has probably been some increase in the absolute and relative number of adult Americans who perceive and act politically on the basis of ideological cues and frameworks. The reasons are not hard to adduce. Increased education and literacy among American adults — and the facilitation of new means of communication — make widespread political ideology possible, for ideology is by its nature abstract and intensely verbal. The growth of government responsibilities and programs — the advent of the "welfare state" or, if one prefers, "positive government" — creates the stuff and content of ideological and issue-oriented politics, for the raw materials of political ideology are the assorted demands for governmental action. The nationalization of American politics, too, promotes political ideology by focusing political attention on a single, dramatic set of issues or a single ideological dimension and by minimizing the often issueless politics of local traditions and personalities.

For a politics of ideology is abstract and remote, and it cannot easily thrive in the folksy, face-to-face politics of personal followings, family political traditions, and patronage and preference. It springs more naturally from a de-personalized, urbanized, group-centered politics of influence over governmental activity and programs.[21]

And yet, while sophistication about and involvement in things ideological may in general be on the increase, the major fact remains that the increase has not been evenly spread across the American polity. Ideology, and even consistent attention to political issues, has probably always been the political outlook of a minority. Not many voters can sustain the interest or provide the sophistication with abstractions that it demands; theirs is not the ideologist's view of American society. Recently in the United States that ideological minority has expanded, and it has entered the major party organizations for the first time. No longer is the ideological elite consigned to esoteric minor parties and genteel, reformist, even anti-party, associations. And its entry into the mainstream of party organization and activity raises a whole bevy of problems for the future of American parties and politics.

THE TRIALS OF IDEOLOGY

In general the uneven rise of ideology risks the development in American politics of a discontinuity between the ideological minority within the parties and the essentially non-ideological majority in the electorate. That electorate is at best only sporadically given to ideologies; it responds selectively to an issue, a personality, a deeply felt personal interest, a flair or style, a group loyalty, an ancient tradition. To that gulf between the ideological minority and the non-ideological majority, the parties and their candidates may respond with appeals on a number of levels — ideological arguments for some parts of the audience, non-ideological ones for others. But always there is danger of a political alienation among the majority who are irritated and ultimately repelled by a discourse which is to them obscure, irrelevant, and even fatuous.

More specifically than that, the increasingly ideological political activists and organization run the risk of alienating even that sector of the party in the electorate which is attuned to its ideological themes. Evidence is ample that the ideological position or positions of the activists need not be those of the party's electorate. McClosky's study, for example, documents the fact that Republican leaders and activists are far more

[21] I doubt very much that the psychological explanations are of great use in explaining the rise of ideology; those explanations, of course, range from sophisticated theories about popular paranoia and authoritarian personalities to the "garden variety" musings about "kooks" and eccentric little ladies in sneakers. These may well be valid explanations for some ideological responses, but they seem to me not to offer an explanation for the increase in the incidence of ideological involvement.

conservative, more unwilling to accept the social welfare reforms of the last generation than are the rank-and-file loyalists of the party.[22] Caught in the middle of these differences are the party's candidates and office-holders. The only alternatives open to them — conflict with the party's activists, lack of candor with the electorate, or defeat at the polls — are scarcely attractive.

So it is that a major American party, faced with the development of ideological activists, may develop an internal, "private" ideology or issue consensus different from the external, "public" one it shows to the voters. That ideological non-congruence exacerbates, in one more way, the tensions and strains among the party organization, the party in government, and the party in the electorate. The mid-1960's sees the agony within a Republican party whose organization is sympathetic in many quarters to Goldwater conservatism, whose electorate is less involved and less conservative, and whose Republican office-holders (headed by Republican governors) are trying to steer the party to "moderate" Republicanism and a matching presidential candidate in 1968.

For the party as an organization, however, the threats from ideological fervor are also internal. It may presage the factionalism of "true believers," perhaps the most virulent form of factionalism, since not even victory and victory's fruits will always heal it. It produces scenes of bitterness and irreconcilability such as those of the Southern delegations storming from the 1948 Democratic convention after the adoption of a "strong" civil rights resolution or the closing hours of the conservative triumph in the 1964 Republican convention. Furthermore, it threatens organizational divisions between the ideologists and the pragmatists. Those differences, of course, rest often on differences of incentive for activity in the party. And their organizational disagreements escalate as charges of "sell out" and "vote buying" fly past accusations of "dogmatism" and "extremism."

Party organizations, for all of these reasons and many more, seem incapable of containing an expanding ideological ferment. The ideologist quickly becomes disenchanted with the electoral pragmatism of party candidates and with the inability of party organizations to utter anything more than the most muted, even docile statements of principle. The American party organizations are indeed poorly adapted to the labors of ideology. They are decentralized and fragmented by American federalism and the separation of powers; lacking unifying structures, they speak in a Babel of ideological voices. They have no annual conference and no other instrument for arbitrating the conflicts and emitting a doctrine. They have no apparatus for political education or socialization; they have no way of propagandizing a doctrine or even an issue position. Their quadrennial platforms are instruments of the presidential campaign for votes rather

[22] See the McClosky, et al., study referred to above in fn. 19.

than a lucid declaration of party principles. And the institution of the direct primary makes it impossible for them to assure the ideological loyalty of their candidates. The major American parties, in short, are structurally incapable of controlling — much less monopolizing — the ideological content of American politics.

Discouragement with the party organization and its electoral pragmatism drives some ideologists out of the party and party activity. In some other cases it presses them into the "quasi-party" activity of the Democratic club reformers in New York and California; they man a separate organization affiliated with the party while expressing a distaste and reforming zeal for the "regular" party organization, and its "bosses" and other pragmatists. Other ideological activists shift the major part of their political concern to organizations less closely tied to the parties. Republican ideologists in the 1960's, for example, manned the following range of ideological satellites: [23]

The Ripon Society: a loose organization with some local chapters of young, liberal Republicans; its members tend to be college- and university-affiliated, and its strength is greatest in the academic environs of the Boston area.

The Free Society Association: a conservative "political education" group heavily peopled and oriented by the Goldwater forces of 1964; some surplus funds from the '64 race went to it and its president is Denison Kitchel, the Goldwater campaign manager; the candidate himself is the honorary chairman; it abjures the endorsement of candidates and other forms of political action.

United Republicans of America: conservative, too, but more devoted to political action than the Free Society Association; its funds go in part to support conservative candidates.

American Conservative Union: another conservative group predating the FSA and committed to an intellectual conservative position; it supports conservative candidates with money.

Republicans for Progress: a liberal and moderate GOP organization; its chairman is a long-time leader of the party's liberal wing, Charles P. Taft, brother of the late Senator Robert A. Taft (who is, of course, enshrined in the conservative pantheon).

At the least such organizations are institutionalized centers of ideological dissent and activity within the party organization or electorate. At the most they siphon off party resources (such as money, skills, and experi-

[23] These organizations have varying degrees of affinity for and informal relationships with the Republican party; the list does not include other ideological organizations (such as the John Birch Society) with ties less close. In all cases, of course, we are speaking about informal ties and relationships.

ence) and threaten party factionalism by supporting only selected party candidates.

Just as the spread of ideology over the past generation has not happened uniformly within the American electorate, the travails of ideology have not fallen evenly on the two major parties. The Republicans have clearly felt the greater burden. It was they who chose a forthrightly ideological presidential candidate in 1964 in an ideologically divided convention, and it is today chiefly the Republicans who suffer from the proliferation of ideological splinter organizations. In part the explanation lies in the fact that the Republicans have been a minority party — out of power in Congress and the Presidency and out of favor with a majority of the American electorate. Ideology is a natural instrument for raising alternatives to the status quo associated with the majority party. Its unambiguous principles are, furthermore, unhampered by the complex and heavy responsibilities of power. And within a persistently minority party, political disappointment invites the recriminations which exaggerate differences in principles or issue positions.

If that were the extent of the reasons for present Republican problems, it would simply be another case of the chronic ills of defeat. But the difficulties may very well go deeper. First of all, as we have already pointed out, the "ideological distance" between Republican activists and their electorate is greater by far than the comparable distance within the Democratic party. Secondly — and closely related — the views of the Republican activists themselves probably extend over greater ideological territory than those of their Democratic counterparts. The classic left-right spread of ideologists, in other words, is not necessarily a symmetrical, bell-shaped curve; it may be and probably is skewed to the political right. Consequently, there is greater ideological distance from center to right than from center to left. Thirdly, if one considers that the liberal-conservative ideological continuum really concerns the role of government in society, it is significant that the "breaking point" on the question — the point of division between those generally in favor and those generally opposed to positive government — does not fall between the two parties. It very probably runs through the Republicans. And finally, the Republicans probably have a greater number of ideological activists. Tendencies to ideological involvement, to political activity and participation, and to Republican identification are all found in the same well-educated, upper-SES groups.

Sporadically and unevenly, and often painfully, ideology appears to be coming slowly to the American major parties. And what is more, it comes at a time of unrivaled prosperity in American society and among the most affluent groups in a suffusing affluence. It remains, though, to return to the basic issue of this chapter: whether a politics of ideology or interest

— even "American style" — can provide the basic political cohesion for a heightened party responsibility.

PARTY RESPONSIBILITY, AMERICAN STYLE

The model of "the responsible political party" is an ideal type. One does not look for it in reality, for no political system yet has developed the cohesion, discipline, and unity that its pure form would demand. Even in Great Britain, home of the hopes of the American reformers, practice falls considerably short of the model. Party cohesion in the British parliament, while it is significantly greater than in the American Congress, is by no means perfect. British Cabinets and parliamentary parties, in fact, have long insisted that constitutional traditions forbade them to be bound by party decision or commitment. Even within the Labour party, traditionally committed to the binding discipline of party decisions, a series of Labour Prime Ministers have made it clear that while a Labour government would consult with the party's national executive, it could not be bound by it. Even in Britain, then, the model of the responsible party serves only to measure the distance of reality from the ideal.

American practice has fallen even further from the model. To be sure, one finds in some state legislatures a high order of party discipline behind and in opposition to the program of the majority and/or the governor. The programs or principles, however, spring not so much from a party organization or the decision of the electorate — there are rarely "mandate" elections — as from the initiative of the governor or the party's legislative leadership. What responsibility there is to the voters for their program is maintained *post hoc* at subsequent elections as the voters reward or punish their programmatic stewardship.[24] Under the best circumstances a sophisticated voter may be able to identify a past policy or decision with a party, but such a "quasi-responsibility" diverges from the model in one major way: there is little role in it for the party organization, since the legislative party or the executive originates the program and enforces discipline behind it through devices such as gubernatorial patronage or the perquisites of legislative leadership. It is a responsibility resting not on the overt decisions of party activists and organizations but on the homogeneity of interests of the voters, party leaders, and constituencies supporting each of the two legislative and executive parties. It is the "responsibility," or its approximation, which springs from the cohesion of a "silent ideology" of interest.

[24] This is substantially the point V. O. Key makes in *The Responsible Electorate* (Cambridge: Harvard Univ. Press, 1966). On the failure of the American voter to make the perceptions and decisions the goals of party responsibility would demand, see Donald E. Stokes and Warren E. Miller, "Party Government and the Saliency of Congress," in Angus Campbell, *et al.*, *Elections and the Political Order* (New York: Wiley, 1966), pp. 194–211.

Occasionally under the stress of crisis or catastrophe, American politics approach even more closely the model of party responsibility. A strong case can certainly be made that at the presidential election of 1936, the Democrats and Republicans were identified with sharply differing solutions to the nation's economic woes. If their positions were not truly ideological, they were at least determinedly programmatic. The burdens of the depression may also have focused voter attention on the hopes and remedies of policy to an unusual degree. Much of the campaign oratory centered around the Roosevelt program for social and economic change and his opponents' charges that he proposed a radical departure for the American polity and economy. The combination of programmatic rhetoric and identification, plus voter attention, may well have produced something close to a "mandate" election and a mandated congressional contingent of Democrats. If the supposition about the presidential election of 1936 is correct, it suggests the explanation that the kind of ideological or programmatic concern necessary for "pure" party responsibility has been a product of crisis conditions that have prevailed only for short periods of time in recent American experience. The necessary ideological concerns and attention are not ordinary expressions of American politics as usual; they are rather the product of occasional, heightened, extra-political crisis.

These sporadic expressions of a "party responsibility, American style," have not, however, satisfied the reformers. The quasi-responsibility of a silent ideology has prevailed only unevenly among the American states; vast regions (such as the South) have traditionally maintained an issueless politics incapable even of this degree of party government. And the occasions of nation-wide party responsibility have been sporadic and crisis-spawned. About the future of party responsibility in the United States, then, two questions remain. Are the political changes afoot in the American political system and within the parties inexorably bringing the conditions for a greater degree of party responsibility? And are there positive steps which anxious men can take to insure or speed the advent of government by responsible parties?

As for the first question — the possibility that the coming of ideology is leading to greater party government — it is true that a burgeoning group of ideological activists, a more sophisticated electorate, a slowly centralizing pair of party organizations, and even the development of nationally recognized issue differences between the parties may promise a trend to greater responsibility. But several sobering notes of caution ought to be mentioned:

The American institution of the direct primary (and its undermining of party control of nominations) combined with the decentralizing effect of federalism and the separation of powers continues to work against party responsibility even in the presence of ideology. It permits the non-ideological candidate to become a representative of and spokesman for a party program. It also permits the ideological candidate and office-holder to defend to the political death a program or ideology at odds with that of his party or his President or governor. He can be ideological and yet "irresponsible."

Much of the increasing ideological or programmatic commitment has not followed the single, uni-dimensional pattern necessary if ideology (or issue) is to provide the cohesion or unity essential for party government. If the divisions along SES lines do not coincide with those on Negro rights and civil liberties, or those on foreign policy, the resulting cross-cutting (multi-dimensional) ideologies divide much more than they unify. Then, for example, hawk-dove differences on Vietnam cut across, rather than reinforce, liberal-conservative lines on the welfare state. Only if multiple patterns of issue or ideological differences coincide do they offer the basis for two unified, cohesive programmatic parties.[25]

Ideology has thus far not been fully translated into party organizational strength. Especially, there are few signs of an important centralization of authority within the parties; the national committees remain essentially hostages to the traditional decentralization of the parties. The ideologists of state and local party organizations may turn increasingly to like-thinking candidates, but without some centralizing, arbitrating party authority, any significant measure of party government at the national level remains unlikely.

And thus, while the spread of ideology or issue orientation may be a necessary condition for government by responsible parties, it is anything but a sufficient one in and of itself. Especially in the context of fragmenting political institutions — most especially the institutions of federalism and the separation of powers — the growth of ideology may very well work to defeat the goal of party responsibility.

If the advent of ideology will not automatically (or willy-nilly) bring the party to a greater governing role, will the more conscious and overt proposals of the reformers? The breadth of the problem of converting the American major parties into prototypic responsible parties can be gauged by examining the scope of the reformers' proposals. The Committee on Political Parties of the APSA, for example, proposed: [26]

1. *A massive shoring up of the national parties and their organizations.* The Committee recommends that the national conventions meet at least biennially and exercise greater control over the national committee. Above

---

[25] Donald E. Stokes, "Spatial Models of Party Competition," *Ibid.*, pp. 161–179, develops this and related points.

[26] All of the quotations following are from the report of the Committee, *Toward a More Responsible Two-Party System* (New York: Rinehart, 1950). The italics in the original have been eliminated.

all it suggests a national Party Council of some fifty members who would draft a platform for the national convention, interpret and apply it to issues between conventions, make "recommendations . . . in respect to congressional candidates," make recommendations about "conspicuous departures from general party decisions by state or local party organizations," provide a forum for "the discussion of presidential candidacies," and coordinate relations among national, state, and local party organizations.

2. *A perfecting of the instruments of ideology.* The Committee in essence proposes that the platform mean something and that it bind the party office-holders and organizations. The platform ought to deal at least partially with the party's "permanent or long-range philosophy," and it ought also to be carefully prepared and systematically interpreted. Needless to say, "the party programs should be considered generally binding" on both office-holders and state and local parties.

3. *An asserting of party control over the Congressional party.* To achieve such a protean task the Committee recommends both a consolidation of the present congressional party organizations into a single party leadership group and the elimination of those practices (such as the seniority system and the traditional power of the House Rules Committee) which work against party discipline and ultimately against party responsibility.

4. *A remodeling of the American parties into membership, participatory parties.* The Committee's hope is perhaps best expressed in its words:

The development of a more program-conscious party membership may attract into party activity many who formerly stayed away, including public-spirited citizens with great experience and knowledge. It will thus be a factor in giving the parties a greater measure of intellectual leadership.

With increased unity within the party it is likely that party membership will be given a more explicit basis. Those who claim the right to participate in framing the party's program and selecting its candidates may be very willing to support its national program by the payment of regular dues. Once machinery is established which gives the party member and his representatives a share in framing the party's objectives, once there are safeguards against internal dictation by a few in positions of influence, members and representatives will feel readier to assume an obligation to support the program.

The Committee's report ranges beyond these general points. It tackles other basic inhibitors of party responsibility: the direct primary ("the closed primary deserves preference . . ."), the Electoral College (it "fosters the blight of one-party monopoly"), political finance, and barriers to full and meaningful adult suffrage (e.g., the long ballot). In short, it becomes clear that to achieve the goal of government by responsible parties the Committee would undertake — and probably would *have* to undertake — a wholesale reconstruction not only of the American parties, but of the American electorate and political environment as well.

Some of the other proponents of party responsibility have, however, been more modest in their goals. One of the most persistent and consistent, James MacGregor Burns,[27] touches many of the same themes as the APSA Committee. There is the same emphasis on the building of grass roots, membership parties, the buttressing of the national party (the presidential party), the reconstructing of a vigorous congressional party, the same recognition of the need for change in the parties' political environment (e.g., the present restrictions on adult suffrage and the status quo in political finance). The reforms Burns suggests are, however, less drastic and sweeping — and, therefore, more "realistic" — but their direction and their pin-pointing of the causes of the present lack of responsibility are not greatly different. Perhaps Burns' greater moderatism springs in part from his recognition of an essentially "Madisonian" political culture which has not tolerated any instrument — party or other — of national majoritarian political power. And in whatever form the proposals may appear, the argument for more responsible parties is exactly an argument for the parties as instruments for the more effective mobilization of national majorities.

The agenda of reform is, in conclusion, a very long one, and its measures touch the fundamentals of American political life. Even the basic American political institutions work against the development of more responsible parties — work, in other words, against a sweeping reorientation of the role of the parties in the American democracy. So also does a political culture suspicious of majoritarian political power marshalled behind programs of action, and so do the low levels of political knowledge and concern of the American electorate. Nor is there in the American political system a constitutional stimulus to disciplined, governing parties. American parties do not have to govern to maintain public office as they would have to in a parliamentary system. In fact, American institutions and traditions have always implicitly rejected the notion of "extra-constitutional" control of political power (as through a party responsible to an alert electorate) in favor of the intra-institutional controls of divided and opposing authority (e.g., the internal "checks and balances").

For the immediate future it seems likely, barring the special conditions of crisis, that the American parties will continue only a modest governing role — a *post hoc* responsibility for carrying out programs that generally promote the interests of the party's activists and loyal electorate. Neither the American parties nor the voters can meet the demands which the classic model of party responsibility imposes on them. But binding the

---

[27] See James MacGregor Burns, *The Deadlock of Democracy* (Englewood Cliffs: Prentice-Hall, 1963), especially chap. 14. Note also that Burns is dealing with the parties in terms of his own, somewhat different, frame of reference, most especially the distinction between the presidential and the congressional parties. See also Stephen K. Bailey, *The Condition of Our National Political Parties* (New York: Fund for the Republic, 1959).

various sectors of the party together — despite all that divides them — is an inarticulate ideology, a commitment to a set of issue positions which sets the activists, candidates, and voters of one party apart from those of the other. In a loose, often distressingly imprecise sense, the two parties are distinct groups of "like-minded" men. Out of that tentative and limited agreement on issues comes enough cohesion to produce a modest, if variable, degree of responsibility. The American approximation of party government does indeed fall far short of the model of party responsibility and the hopes of the reformers, but the role of the political party in organizing government and the debate on public issues cannot be ignored.

If a concern with political ideologies continues to spread within the American electorate, and especially if it motivates a new activism within the party organizations, we may well see a greater degree of responsibility within the American parties — but with an important difference. It may well be contained within and relevant to only an ideological minority. Party responsibility, even under the most receptive conditions, is very likely only "responsibility" to an involved, alert, informed minority. It is one pattern of relationship the political party develops with one segment of the electorate. To the non-ideological segment the party continues to make appeals on other than ideological grounds: on a mixture of traditions, interests, and personalities. Even in the classic ideological-responsible party systems, one suspects, ideological debate and discourse dull the political nerve-ends of the majority who would rather be involved with a dynamic political personality or a "gut" issue. The danger for parties caught in such a conflict or mixture of appeals — as the parties of Europe have been for at least a generation — is that they either alienate the ideological minority by compromise or bore the majority by dogma.

In any event, the entire issue of party responsibility and government is chiefly one of the entire role of the political party in the political system. Any attempt to change or reform the American parties to assume a new governing responsibility — to monopolize the avenue of political representation, in other words — is at once a question of how political organizations develop patterns of structure and activity and of how one goes about changing them. What, indeed, determines the peculiar and special nature of the American major parties and their place and role in the totality of the American political system? To these questions the final two chapters are devoted.

PART SIX

The Political Parties: Role and Theory

It is in the nature of a book on political parties to treat them more or less in isolation, to lift them from their context in the political system for a special scrutiny and examination. And yet, necessary though the isolation may be, it may give the impression that the political parties are autonomous political structures, moving freely within the political system as they and their leaders will them to. In the emphasis on the parties alone, we can easily overlook all of the political and non-political forces in the "environment" of the political parties which shape both their form and their activities.

Ultimately the development of a theory of political parties must be preceded by a spelling out of the relationship of the parties to the striking events, the social currents, the major institutions, the legal regulations, and the values and goals which shape the loyalties of American partisans and fix the outline and responsibilities of the political parties. This combination of limiting and shaping forces, both political and non-political, one may conveniently sum up in the term "environment." It is to changes in the environment that one must look to explain variations in the parties. The parties are results of these aggregates of forces impinging on them, and a theory of the political party is finally little more than an identification of these forces (or variables) and their relationships among themselves and to the party. To be sure, influences from within the party (e.g., strong personal leadership) may have an impact on its structure or activities, but in the long run the influences external to it are the main and important ones.

The quest for a theory of political parties is a quest for explanation of the influences which shape them and which, therefore, explain their variety and development. In its broadest sense a theory of parties ought to explain the special characteristics of the American parties which set them apart from the parties of the other Western democracies. It ought also to illuminate the causes of the different forms and patterns of activity one finds within the American parties themselves. The American major parties have changed considerably in organizational form and in their activities or their functions within the last sixty to one hundred years; similarly, at any particular point in time one may observe differences in structure and in activity in the parties of one state and another. The task of theory and analysis is to explain this variation across time or place.

These two final chapters will consider in order the two great analytical issues in the study of the American parties: the nature and shaping of the political parties themselves, and the role of the major political parties in the American political processes. Chapter 17 will be concerned primarily with the question of the theory of political parties — with those questions of the influences on the party structure and party activities. It will thus be concerned with the party as a dependent variable as it is acted upon by exogenous independent variables. In Chapter 18, the final chapter, the focus will be on the party as an independent variable — on the party's role in, impact on, and contributions to the American political system as a whole. That chapter will also in passing touch on the question of a theory of political organizations, both partisan and non-partisan, especially as it concerns the relationships and competitions of the parties with other political organizations.

For no real purpose, other than that of organizing a body of prose, can one separate the questions of the political party as independent and dependent variables. What the party is as a dependent variable — its resulting capacity for effective political mobilization — very much determines and limits what it will be and what it will accomplish in the political system as a whole. The degree of its dependence on the influences of its environment determines in turn the freedom and the force with which it may act as an independent variable in the broader political processes of the total system. Understandably, therefore, the materials of Chapter 17 flow easily and logically into those of the final chapter.

Chapter Seventeen

TOWARD A THEORY
OF THE POLITICAL PARTY

Even the most cursory awareness of the history of American politics since the Civil War suggests the enormous range and variety of changes in the major American parties. The classic urban machine, and especially its armies of disciplined party workers, motivated by pursuit of the patronage job, flourishes today in only a few American urban centers. The party boss, famed and fabled for the heady autocratic power he wielded, is clearly and obviously on the decline. The tireless door-to-door canvassing and the extravagant torchlight parades have generally been replaced by the more subtle appeals of the mass media, the handshaking tour of the shopping center, and the deliberately low-key campaigning of the coffee party. And all across the country a more intensive two-party competition replaces old one-party domination.

One does not, however, have to examine one hundred years' development in order to find change and variation in the American party system. That variation is readily apparent from one part of the country to another, even from one state or one part of the state to another. Party organizational forms and activities which Chicagoans or Philadelphians take very much as a matter of course might seem both unusual and somewhat shocking in communities an hour or two's drive away.

It is precisely the question of these variations or differences to which a theory of the competitive political parties must be addressed. In the more formal and conventional language of correlation, the political party is here the dependent variable, and one searches for those independent variables outside of the party whose change and variation is accompanied by change and variation in the parties. It is, in other words, an attempt to explain the variation by relating it to variation in those outside factors we have called the "environment" of the political party.

Ultimately, of course, any attempt at explanatory theory is also an attempt at prediction. There is no surer way of verifying one's explanatory propositions or theories than to submit them to the test of prediction. If we are confident that we know which independent variables will affect either the structure or the activities of a political party, then we must be equally confident that if we change those variables, those elements of the environment of the parties, that we will produce a change in the parties themselves.

The time for announcing a full-blown theory of the political parties, or even of the American political parties, is by no means here. For all of its current theoretical interests, and even its theoretical pretensions, the field of political science is some distance away from identifying the variables and relationships necessary for an intricate and sophisticated theory of the political system, or indeed for a theory of any part or process within it. The problem of formulating political theory in general is, in fact, exemplified by the problem of developing a more narrow and particular theory of political parties. The problem begins far short of the sophisticated questions of measurement and concepts, for we face a severe shortage of mere descriptive data. Most of the literature on party structures and organizations, for example, is limited to a small number of urban and metropolitan centers. The paucity of even sketchy descriptions of rural, small town, and suburban parties is as striking as it is discouraging. In general we also know a great deal more about one sector of the party, the party in the electorate, than we do about either the party organization or the party in government. In view of such rather basic shortages of important data, anything more than the most preliminary suggestions or tentative outlines of a theory of the political parties would be premature.

The reasons for the shortage of information on the American parties are not hard to find. Two chief ones predominate. First, there is the inexorable operation of the scholarly "laws" of available instruments and data. Those laws decree that scholars prefer to work with data that come in handy, readily accessible forms, or with data which their methodological instruments equip them to acquire easily.[1] Thus the information on the party in the electorate comes conveniently either from published vote totals or from the available data of opinion surveys.[2] Information on the organizations and intra-organizational activities of the major American parties is far more difficult to come by. Secondly, we have too often been prisoners of our reluctance to take a structural approach to the political parties, and conversely, of our eager readiness to infer their existence as structures from their activities and functions. For example, both scholars

[1] For the statement of the "law of the instrument," see Abraham Kaplan, *The Conduct of Inquiry* (San Francisco: Chandler, 1964), pp. 28–29.

[2] Scholars generally have easy access to sample survey data on American electorates through the Inter-University Consortium for Political Research.

and political practitioners often examine the vote totals in a district and from them infer something of the organizational characteristics and strength of the parties. (It becomes a commonplace, therefore, to observe that the party defeated badly at an election was either organizationally weak and ineffective in its campaign activities, or remiss in its attempts to "turn out the vote.") Similarly, it is easy to infer something of the caucuses and leadership of the legislative party from the mere fact of the voting cohesion of its members.

A SUMMARY VIEW OF POLITICAL PARTIES

Throughout the course of this book we have viewed the major American political parties both as structures and as sets of activities. In structure they are loose and conglomerate tri-partite organizations. In a rough and approximate way they embrace a party organization, a group of partisans in public office, and an associated electorate of varying degrees of loyalty. Each of these three sectors attracts to itself its own men and resources with its own blend of goals and incentives. The very different structural characteristics and the possibly conflicting goals of these three sectors combine to make the competitive political party a rather special phenomenon among the vast array of American political organizations. It is in part a limited organization able to control its internal processes and its membership, but the nature of the restraints under which it must operate and the nature of its mobilizing activities force it at the same time to be in part a public, inclusive, and easily permeable association.

In the examination of the activities of the major parties, the emphasis has been on their mobilization of political power and on their competition with each other and with other political organizations. All political organizations, the political parties included, are engaged in unending attempts to mobilize the political power and influence of individuals and small groups of individuals behind the securing of public office or the influencing of those already in office. They are great political brokers or intermediaries which organize, manage, and structure the democratic political processes; that is to say, they compete to organize and aggregate political influence in support of a limited number of salient political options.

The fact that the major political parties mobilize predominantly through the electoral process, in contrast to non-party political organizations, does not set them completely or even largely apart. They have more in common than in difference with other political organizations; they seek in similar ways to achieve similar goals in a competition which ranges over two broad fronts. Political organizations compete for scarce political resources, for the services and skills and money that are always in short supply. They compete secondly for the approval and support of groups in the electorate, for it is only with the aid of these supporting groups that the core of party activists can reach its political goals. Ultimately, of course, those two sets of competitions are united in the final competition in the political process for the scarce and controversial goals of public policy.

The diagram of Figure 1 suggests that the political party may be thought of as a self-contained structure, recruiting its own resources and expending them in the performance of its activities or functions. It maintains its varied incentives for attracting the resources, and those incentives depend directly on its success in achieving its political goals — on, in other words, its success in mobilizing an aggregate of political influence sufficient to achieve those goals. The party must help the individuals of all three of its sectors to reach their special, and often different, political goals. The activist of the party organization may seek the triumph of a liberal or conservative ideology, or perhaps simply the intra-organizational satisfactions of participation and social fellowship; the members of the party in government, on the other hand, are more apt to be guided by the single goal of electoral victory; the party's loyal voter may be moved by little more than a traditional loyalty to the party, an emotional tie to its fortunes, or affection for a candidate. But whatever the goals, incentives, or motives, there must inevitably be some direct relationship between the resources a party recruits and the activities it expends — some relationship between the partisan inputs and outputs, and between goals sought and goals achieved.

In viewing the party's structure and activities as a whole (see Figure 1 again) it is clear that the competitive political parties among all other political organizations enjoy a special set of relationships to the total American electorate. In the first place, the major parties must, as must the other political organizations, view the electorate as the reservoir of political resources. They must recruit the manpower, skills, and money they need from it, but unlike the other political organizations, they must operate much more broadly within the electorate. They are even forced by state laws, in effect, to accept the contributions and the participation of individuals they might have preferred not to accept. Secondly, since the political parties are regulated and controlled to a far greater extent than any other of the American political organizations, the norms and interests of the electorate create the pressure for that regulation; the electorate is in effect the regulator and, thus, the creator of a very important part of the party "environment." Finally, the electorate is for the parties, as it is for all political organizations, the consumer of their activities, the source of the aggregates of support the parties are trying to piece together.

Most of what seems the special character of the American political party stems from this peculiar relationship to the total electorate. The fact that the parties seek political power traditionally through the contesting of elections forces them to cater to a clientele of majority propor→

Figure 1

THE POLITICAL PARTY: STRUCTURE & ACTIVITIES

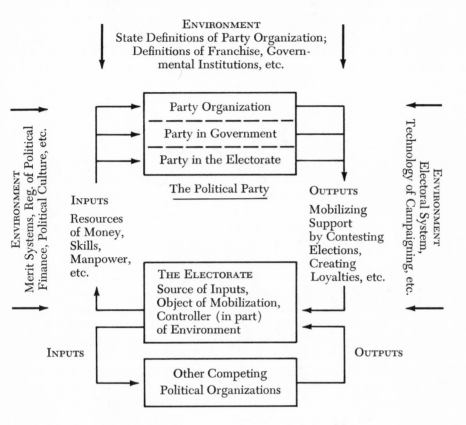

tions; the interest group classically relies on the influence of the involved minority rather than the sheer political weight of numbers. Its electoral relationship to millions of only marginally involved voters heightens the party's importance as a stable, enduring reference symbol. Not even its organizational activities and processes are its own; the direct primary, for example, invites the broadest participation by the electorate in the crucial nomination decisions. For all of these reasons, then, the political party must endure a special dependence on broad, poorly defined, and fickle groups in the American electorate. This is its special problem and the source of its special characteristics as the special political organization of mass, popular democracy in the United States.

As one approaches the problem of explaining the relationship of the parties to their environment — the relationship of dependent variable to the independent variables, and, therefore, the basic relationship undergirding a theory of the political party — one more observation seems in order. The classic tradition of theorizing about political parties has been one which has emphasized the party as an organization or a structure. (One need only mention the tradition established by Ostrogorski and Michels, and in our time by Maurice Duverger.) [3] But for some reason a structural approach to the American parties has not really dominated the work of American scholars. With notable exceptions,[4] their work has focused on party electorates and on party activities. Perhaps that has been the case because the American parties have been notoriously weak as organizations and slavishly committed to the contesting of elections. American scholars have seemed afraid that the conventional organizational approach to the parties may mislead more than it illuminates; the strictures of Michels about oligarchy within the party structure, for example, scarcely seem to apply to the American parties.

At the very least it is important to realize that the organizational sector does not in the American parties dominate the other two sectors — or does not overlap the other two sectors — to the extent that it does in most other competitive parties. Or, to put the matter a little differently, it is important, even crucial, to remember that the three sectors of the American parties are more separate, even more antagonistic than they are in most other political parties. Because the American party organizations are not usually membership organizations, they do not overlap greatly the party in the electorate, and the party in government in the United States is very likely more independent of the control and discipline of the party organization than it is anywhere else among the democracies. Party organization in the United States has not been able to dominate the other sectors of the party or to control the use of the party symbols. Within the American parties the three sectors remain apart, even estranged and competitive, to an extent which would be hard to duplicate elsewhere. The resulting tensions and divisiveness among the party sectors would be equally hard to match.

THE PARTY ENVIRONMENT: MATERIALS FOR A THEORY

It is possible to let analysis and logic run riot and to posit a party environment which includes every other structure and process in the political system and a good deal outside of it. But despite the superficial truth (the truism, indeed) of such a reductionism, there are clearly those particular influences on the political party which are more powerful and more immediate. It will suffice to limit this discussion to them.

[3] Moise Ostrogorski, *Democracy and the Organization of Political Parties* (New York: Macmillan, 1908), Roberto Michels, *Political Parties* (Glencoe: Free Press, 1949), and Maurice Duverger, *Political Parties* (New York: Wiley, 1954).

[4] One notable exception is Samuel Eldersveld, *Political Parties: A Behavioral Analysis* (Chicago: Rand, McNally, 1964).

THE POLITICAL INSTITUTIONS

Very little in the American political system escapes the influence of the American federalism and the separation of powers. No single factor seems to affect the American legislative parties, for example, as much as the overriding presence of a legislature constitutionally separated from the executive. Among the party systems of the world the legislative parties with greater discipline in voting and with greater ties to the regular party organization are found chiefly in those countries with parliamentary systems. The very institutions of parliamentary democracy promote the legislative party's cohesive support of (or opposition to) a cabinet drawn from one group of partisans in the legislature. Even among the fifty American states, each one committed to some form of the separation of powers, variations in one or another branch or in the relationships among them will affect the parties. Strong gubernatorial power can be mobilized to promote cohesive legislative parties; it may also centralize the party organization within the state. Similarly, the presence of a strong and autonomous committee system in the legislature may very well undermine the efforts of party leadership to produce a modicum of party discipline.

The decentralization of American federalism has also left its imprint on the American parties, engraining local political loyalties and stimulating generations of localized, often provincial, political traditions. It has spawned an awesome range and number of public offices to fill — and thus created an electoral politics which in size and diversity dwarfs that of other political systems. By creating local political rewards, local traditions, even local patronage systems, it has sustained and even created a whole set of semi-autonomous political organizations within the national framework of the two parties. American federalism itself has thus created an institutional milieu in which one-partyism could arise and persist. And, ironically perhaps, even though the federalism that gave rise to the decentralization of the parties now is going through centralizing modifications itself — especially with a centralization of power and attention in the affairs of the national government — the party decentralization appears well enough established to resist even those centralizing tendencies.

Any discussion of the institutional influences on the parties might with ample reason consider all of the other major American political institutions. It suffices here to add just one more: the executive or administrative institutions. Traditionally the American parties have, to an extent unknown elsewhere, drawn their organizational rewards from the administrative establishment — patronage jobs, high-level executive appointment, preferences in purchasing or contracts, special treatment in public services (new roads, easy access to welfare benefits, etc.), or special exemptions from public penalties (the "fixed" ticket, for example). But those kinds of access and favoritism clearly depend on the nature of the administrative agencies and their procedures. The advent of merit, civil service systems, for instance, closes off the supply of jobs for the party faithful. The supervision of state welfare programs by federal agencies (as a necessity of their receiving federal grants-in-aid) may diminish that source of favors. Or, to take a third example, United States government and some states close off to the parties an important source of activists by forbidding their civil service employees to take an active role in the affairs of a political party.

STATUTORY REGULATION
OF THE PARTY AND ITS ACTIVITIES

The point has already been made several times that no parties among the democracies of the world are as bound up in legal regulations as are the American parties. The form of their organizations are prescribed by the states in endless, often finicky detail; the statutes on party organization set up grandiose layers of hierarchically organized party committees, and they often also chart the details of who shall compose them, when they will meet, and what their agenda will be. State law also defines the parties themselves, at least for determining their ability to place candidates on the ballot. The progressive raising of those standards has effectively denied a number of small parties a place in the electoral processes of the states. Finally, a number of states undertake to regulate the activities of the parties — many, for example, regulate their finances, and most draw at least some limits to their campaign practices. Some, such as those which forbid some or all pre-primary endorsing, touch more crucial areas of activity.

Whatever the form or object of the regulation, however, it can and usually does seriously affect the parties of the state. At the least it may force them into evasive actions — such as the setting up of extra-legal party organizations — to escape the worst burdens of regulation.

ELECTORAL INSTITUTIONS AND PROCESSES

In a broad but realistic way the election machinery in a state may be thought of as an extensive regulation of the party's chief political activity. At least it is often difficult to know where regulation of the party ends and electoral reform begins, so closely are the two related. Consider, for example, the direct primary. It is both a sharp limitation on the business of a party — its selection of the candidates who will bear its label in an election — and a significant addition to the machinery of the electoral processes in the United States. But whatever it is, it has touched and influenced almost every aspect of the party. More than one major scholar of the American parties has traced the progressive atrophy of party organization from the loss of organizational control over nominations.[5] Even

[5] V. O. Key, *American State Politics* (New York: Knopf, 1956), Chapter 6.

the relatively minor differences in primary law from one state to another — such as the differences in the time of the year in which it occurs — are not without their impact.

The collective electoral mechanisms of the nation and the fifty states set a matrix of rules and boundaries within which the parties compete for public office. Their various components are not neutral, for they give advantages and strategic opportunities to some contestants. The basic American commitment to plurality elections within single-member districts doubtless works, as decades of scholars have suggested, in favor of the largest, most competitive parties and against the marginally competitive ones. (It should be noted, however, that the advantages in the American experience to the larger parties have never been as great as elsewhere; in 1951, for example, the Congress party of India won 73 per cent of the seats in the national legislature with only 45 per cent of the popular vote.) Similarly, population inequality and gerrymandering in constituencies distort the strength and composition of the party electorates, and the institution of the Electoral College shapes virtually every aspect of American presidential politics. Even the smaller details of the electoral law of a state may fundamentally alter the parties and the party system. The strength of the Liberal party in New York politics developed largely because of the section of the state's election law which permits one party to list as its candidate the candidate of another party.

THE DEFINITION OF THE ELECTORATE

Because of the importance of the relationship of the electorate to the political party, its definition is one of the central elements of the party's political environment. The addition of new groups to the electorate — for democratic electorates expand rather than contract — affects party composition and party appeals. Even those remaining limitations on the American suffrage — residence requirements, limits on absentee voting, literacy tests — are not unimportant; the last of the three, for example, diminishes political participation among lower SES groups and thus primarily affects the Democratic party electorate. Apart from controls and restraints on the "right" to vote, there are those less formal changes in the American society which alter the political perceptions and information, the political norms and interests, and the basic political involvement of the American electorate. Changes in educational levels, in the patterns of political socialization, in the American class and status structure have all led to significant changes in the political behavior of the electorate.

THE POLITICAL CULTURE

It is one thing to specify such tangibles as regulatory statutes, electoral mechanisms, and even political institutions and electorates, but it is quite another to pin down so elusive a part of the party environment as its political culture. The political culture is the all-enveloping network of the political norms, values, and expectations of the aggregate of American adults. It is, in other words, their conglomerate view of what the political system is, what it should be, and what their place is in it. Furthermore, it varies regionally and among different strata of the American population in what one might think of as political "sub-cultures." Party campaign tactics that the big city takes for granted might very well outrage the nearby country cousins.

Observers of American politics have for most of American history commented on the ingrained mistrust of Americans for politics, especially for partisan politics. The feeling that partisan politics is a compromising, somewhat "dirty" business has long seemed to be one of the major and persistent components of the American political culture. Since the advent of public opinion sampling — the technique that has made scholarly investigation of political culture possible for the first time — the indicators of that hostility toward partisan politics have multiplied. For example, a number of polls have found that American parents would prefer that their sons and daughters not choose a full-time political career; politics as a vocation, in their estimation, compares unfavorably with even the semiskilled trades.[6] Much of the popular vocabulary on politics also reflects the predominant view — party activists or officials are "party hacks," the party leader may be called the "boss," his followers "pols" or "politicos"; even the straightforward word "politician" has come to connote a person given to self-serving motives and covert, amoral methods. The consequences of that popular suspicion of the parties are not hard to find: the spread of non-partisan elections, the intense regulation of party organizations and processes, and the determinedly non-party politics of much of American suburbia,[7] for example.

Suspicion of things partisan, however, is only one element in a multifaceted political culture which impinges on the American parties. The views of Americans on such broad points as representative democracy itself are relevant. Very likely a prevailing "Burkean" view of representation, the view that the representative ought to decide public questions on the basis of his own information and wisdom, retards the development of party discipline in American legislatures. Even the widespread, if latent, American fear of aggregates of political power disposes Americans to rely on the controls of formal political institutions (such as the division of power among three combative branches of government) rather than on those controls generated through public opinion by a vigilant opposition

---

[6] See William C. Mitchell, "The Ambivalent Social Status of the American Politician," *Western Political Quarterly*, XII (1959), pp. 683–699.

[7] On the non-party politics of suburbia, see Robert Wood, *Suburbia* (Boston: Houghton Mifflin, 1958), Chapter 5.

party. More detailed attitudes will govern even such matters as the incentives for party activity and the kinds of campaign tactics a party or candidate chooses. Unfavorable public reaction, or its anticipation, will forestall the use of public office for patronage purposes, for example; similar hostility may also limit the effectiveness of campaign canvassing or the effectiveness of a candidate's vituperative attack on the qualifications of his opponent.

More careful and systematic studies of the American political culture now suggest, however, that we may well have overestimated its hostility to politics and political participation while underestimating its contradictions and complexities. Almond and Verba in their comparative study of the political cultures of the United States, Britain, West Germany, Italy, and Mexico,[8] find that the American political culture is the least cynical and least disaffected about the political system and the most accepting of the necessity for political involvement and participation. In this "participant civil culture" the American citizens

report political discussion and involvement in political affairs, a sense of obligation to take an active part in the community, and a sense of competence to influence the government. They are frequently active members of voluntary associations. Furthermore, they tend to be affectively involved in the political system: they report emotional involvement during political campaigns, and they have a high degree of pride in the political system.[9]

And yet the five-nation study explores little about the preference or rejection of the political party *per se* as a mechanism of political activity. One careful study of attitudes toward the party system in one state (Wisconsin) points to a curious popular ambivalence toward the parties. There is support for vague salutes to the two-party system and competition (68 per cent of the respondents agreed that "democracy works best where competition between parties is strong"), but other responses would appear to negate a good deal of such support (e.g., 53 per cent agreed that the political system would work better "if we could get rid of conflicts between the parties all together [sic]").[10] Partisan politics in the United States may thus enjoy only a tentative and somewhat ambiguous support at best within the American electorate.

Regional and local variations in political culture — a set of imprecisely described "sub-cultures" — further complicate the analysis of the effect of political culture on the parties. The Wisconsin study quoted in the paragraph above, for example, finds that only 19 per cent of the Wisconsin sample favored the tax deductibility of political contributions; but shortly

[8] Gabriel A. Almond and Sidney Verba, *The Civic Culture* (Princeton: Princeton Univ. Press, 1963).

[9] *Ibid.*, p. 440.

[10] Jack Dennis, "Support for the Party System by the Mass Public," *American Political Science Review*, LX (September, 1966), pp. 600–615.

before, in its 1964 sample, the Survey Research Center found that 26 per cent of its national sample favored the same proposal. (Both figures, of course, say a good deal about general American attitudes on money in politics.) Alternatively, one can infer the presence of an anti-party sub-culture in the northwest quadrant of the country (largely the states of the greatest Populist and Progressive influence) from much greater incidences there of institutions such as the open primary, the non-partisan judiciary, and ballot forms which do not facilitate straight-ticket voting.

THE NON-POLITICAL ENVIRONMENT

Much of the parties' non-political environment works on them through the elements of the political environment. Changes in levels and kinds of education, for example, affect the political culture, the skills of the elec-torate, even the levels of political information. Great jolts in the economy alter the structure of political issues and goals in the electorate. Educa-tion, and probably socio-economic status, seems also related to elements of the political culture; one excursion into the problem suggests that less well-educated Americans are more accepting of party loyalty and disci-pline than are their better educated countrymen.[11] Even general social values are quickly translated into political values. Acceptance of a Catho-lic candidate for the American Presidency had to await changes in more general social attitudes about religion in general and Catholicism in par-ticular.

Whether the impact of the non-political environment is direct or in-direct, however, may be quite beside the point. The impact is strong and often disruptive. Just a rise of several percentage points in the level of unemployment in the American economy, for example, may have im-portant repercussions on the parties. It may make it more difficult for the parties and candidates to raise money. It will very certainly make pa-tronage positions more attractive and perhaps even shift the incentive patterns on which the party organizations rely. It will define a very im-portant SES issue or political dimension for the party in the electorate and for the electorate as a whole. It may well affect the political futures of the party office-holders in government. If the crisis is especially severe — as was the Great Depression of the 1930's — it may even fracture and reorganize the pattern of basic, enduring party loyalties.

Change and Variation: The Problem of Causality

For whatever solace it may be, scholars of political parties are not alone in their troubled doubts over the causal implications of their general-izations and theoretical probings. All of the social sciences struggle desperately with the problem of raising statements of relationship (or cor-

[11] *Ibid.*

relation) to statements of cause and effect. We are able to relate changes or variations in the parties to changes or variations in their environment; we can say, for example, that identification with the Democratic party is inversely related to level of formal education, or that the elaborateness and discipline of party organizations are related to urbanism. But correlation is not cause. If A and B are related, it may be that A causes B, that B causes A, or that they both are the effect of one or more outside causes. In fact, most scholars would agree that the relationship of Democratic loyalty to low levels of educational attainment is best explained by the outside cause of socio-economic status. The Democratic party appeals to the interests of lower SES groups whose SES has also reduced their opportunities for a college education.[12]

As a starting point, it is very probable that the lines of influence and "cause" move from the parties' environment to the parties. The parties are the dependent variable; they are shaped and pummelled by all that is around them. They cannot escape the bounds and limitations of the institutions, controls, attitudes, and strivings which surround them. At least no one seems to defend the proposition that the parties primarily shape and control those elements of the political system and culture. But even so, it is not *entirely* a one-way relationship. Take the small example of two-partyism in the American South. An increasing percentage of Southerners, as reported by the Gallup poll, think that the South would be "better off" with a two-party system rather than a single dominant party: [13]

Year	Better off	Not better off
1939	57%	43%
1951	60	40
1961	63	37
1963	71	29

Is one to infer that the development of two-party competition led to this alteration, this reshaping of an element of the political subculture, or that changes in the political subculture encouraged, or at least permitted, the development of a Republican challenge to Democratic dominance? Or both? Or that an outside factor — the Republican espousal of a new brand of states' rights philosophy — produced both? The answer is not clear from the time series above; that is to say, it is hard to say which comes first. But there is a strong case that elements of the political culture such as this one both shape and are shaped by the activities and

[12] The reader may find it useful to think of the same problem in the biological sciences. A statistical relationship has been established between heavy cigarette smoking and the incidence of lung cancer in males. However, no direct causal relationship can be established since we do not yet know the cause of cancer.
[13] *Minneapolis Tribune,* June 9, 1963.

competitions of the parties, that they are, in other words, both cause and rationale.

In these muddled questions of cause the temptation is always strong to seek the most tangible (and most easily observed and measured) variable as the explanation. As we discussed in Chapter 2, the temptation has been to explain the occurrence of the two-party system in terms of the political institutions found with it — in the case of the American two-party system, in terms of the single executive and the tradition of plurality election from single-member constituencies. In fact, Americans, both citizens and scholars, have for a long time placed a tremendous confidence in the efficacy of institutional change; they have seen the political institutions of the American political system as a major key to change in other institutions and in the many political processes. Hence, they tried to work reforms in the American cities by importing the primary, the non-partisan election, and the city manager form of government. Others have promoted the nurturing of more disciplined, more "responsible" parties as the key to representational change and reform. But the political environment is composed of more than political institutions, and change in the institutions alone has often not achieved its goal.

Assuming that the primary direction of influence or "cause" moves from the environment to the parties (rather than outwardly from them), we might refine our thinking and generalizations by determining at what point in the structure and activities of the parties the environmental impact is felt primarily. Do the external forces of the environment work chiefly on the parties' activities, on their organizational forms, or on the resources which are their inputs? Or on all three more or less simultaneously? Do the styles of American political campaigning change because of changes in the money and skills available, because of changes in the organizational capacities of the parties, because of new skills and methods available (a new technology of campaigning), or because of new methods being exploited by competitors and new expectations in the electorate?

All of the dilemmas and problems of explaining variation and change among the American parties are present in the illustration of the gradual decline of the urban political "machine" in this century. Using the scheme of Figure 1, it is clear that one can see changes in the party environment touching all related dimensions of the party structure and activities as the urban machine gradually passed away in most large cities. The advance of merit systems deprived the old organizations of patronage, their major incentive for activists; but at the same time increasing literacy and education and full employment levels were making it a less desirable incentive and, thus, a less effective recruiter of resources. Changes in the American electorate and its values were at the same time undermining the ethos on which a patronage-based party rested. Concurrently, new expectations and new methods and techniques of campaigning for office made the kind of campaigns based on the skills and contacts of the classic "machine" both less palatable and less necessary. Furthermore, shifts to a greater issue-content and a more national focus in American politics made the local and issueless politics of the machine more and more an anachronism. So, as one tries to assess the major "causes" for the decline of the classic style of urban political organization, he sees changes in the environment impinging on the recruitment of resources, on the party structure itself, and on its activities.

There are countless generalizations and relationships one could examine in the same way — both changes across time and variations from state to state at the same point in time. And yet one cannot escape the major analytical puzzle, for it is really the central question for any theory of political phenomena. Clearly the environment can work on the parties at all points, and clearly, too, the pressures felt at any one point will ricochet throughout the entire party structure and its pattern of activities.

The parties are goal-oriented political organizations, however, and the major point at which they are molded and shaped is the point at which they compete in their activities with other political organizations to mobilize a part of the electorate behind their aims. If the parties' environment limits their capacity to act (e.g., by legal limitations on their fund-raising, or by elaborate and rigid stipulations of their organizational form) without altering the demands on their competitive activities, the parties will desperately try to re-adapt, to regroup, even to avoid the new restrictions. Much of the successful adaptation of the American parties to the regulations of the states is of that variety. But if the environment directly affects those activities — say, through the introduction of new competitors, new expectations in the political culture about the "proper" kinds of behavior, or a new technology of action — the party must submit or lose its ability to achieve its goals.

All of this is not to say, however, that no change or variation in the parties can result from forces "internal" to them. It is certainly possible, and even inevitable, that strong and skillful leadership, for example, or simple organizational efficiency, may generate changes in either party structure or activity. But these "internally fueled" influences are generally short-run, and they must operate within the grosser limits set by the external environment. More than one ambitious and confident party functionary with grandiose plans for reviving a dormant or tired party has discovered that fact. It is the sobering lesson of the intractability of great and enduring political structures.

THE AMERICAN PARTIES TODAY: CONTINUING CHANGE

Variations in both party structure and activity continue to mark the parties of the fifty states. The American party system remains a decentralized one and thus one in which response and adaptation to local environments is both necessary and desirable. The degree of party discipline in the state legislatures, for example, continues to differ considerably among the states; so do party practices in nominating and electing candidates for office. We have attempted some tentative explanations for the variations throughout the chapters of this book, and they need not be repeated here. At best, however, explanation of the variations among the fifty American party systems falters from lack of basic information about both the parties and their different environments.

The changes that have taken place in the American parties over the years of the 20th century have been more marked, more commented upon, and probably more significant. Within the period since the 1880's or 1890's, the following fundamental changes in the American parties have occurred:

a decline and even atrophy of the older, hierarchical forms of local party organization (and of the incentives on which they rested and the activities which they generated).

an increasing inability of the party organization to control the nominations and electoral campaign for public office (and the converse freedom of candidates and the individuals of the party in government to pursue their own electoral goals).

a declining effect of party loyalty on the decisions of the party in the electorate (i.e., the loss of the party's monopoly of the political reference symbols on which the electorate depends) and a converse tendency of voters to seek other avenues of political information and to react to other political stimuli (e.g., candidates and issues).

Above all, these recent developments have opened new distances and new antagonisms among the three, semi-autonomous sectors of the American parties. They are no longer bound, to the extent they once were, by agreement on the supreme, overarching goal of electoral victory for the party and on the electoral pragmatism that that goal demanded. Party activists of the organization depend less on patronage and the other incentives which flowed from the winning of office and more on the satisfactions of ideology and issue concern. The electorates increasingly choose among the candidates of "their" party and other organizations; their increased split ticket voting is one clear result. And since it is not in the nature of the party in government to surrender its electoral pragmatism and its concern for victory, it must increasingly separate its activities from those of the rest of the party structure.

The increasing separatism among the three sectors of the American major parties may — at the risk of some oversimplification — be thought of as a crisis in the party organization. It is no exaggeration to say that only parties in which a virile, well-staffed, and on-going party organization integrates and dominates the sectors of the party are capable of genuine political effectiveness. The parties we call "strong" for their ability to dominate or monopolize certain forms of political activity have been those led by the organizational sector. Only the party organization has the breadth of skills and resources and the commitment to the full range of party goals to fill this leadership role within the party. Party organization in the United States has always had problems maintaining its superiority within the broader party; statutory limitations, an unfriendly political culture, the direct primary, and a paucity of resources have all hampered its development. More recently and immediately the organizations have fallen on worse times by losing control over both political rewards and political skills and resources — a control the classic political "machines" once enjoyed. Without the unifying, integrating force of a healthy party organization, the three sectors tend to drift apart to greater independence and antagonism.

Many of these changes in the American parties, it must be pointed out, grow from general changes in the American society — rising levels of education and literacy, greater economic affluence, and greater economic and social mobility, for example. The American political culture is an offshoot of the wider American culture; if we develop a cult of youth and "cool" detachment, that cult will affect our image and expectations for party leaders and candidates. Much of American politics, including partisan politics, is also related to and grows out of socio-economic class differences. Even the changes in style of campaigning are related to class differences, just as surely as are those in popular music or popular art. The supermarket and coffee-hour campaigning are a case in point. Many issues, ideologies, and party loyalties are related to status differences and their concomitants, and so too are patterns of political activity. Therefore, those basic shifts in the society and economy that affect SES are very likely the basic stuff of which changes in our parties and politics are crafted. It may hurt the political scientist to admit it, but the political institutions and processes of the party's environment are largely only mechanisms for transmitting and reinforcing the impact of these nonpolitical changes to the parties.

Recent changes have also thrown the American parties into the classic dilemma of democratic parties — the conflict of electoral goals and the goals of issue and ideology. It is a conflict that has long plagued the European parties but one which the American parties long avoided by reason of their almost total devotion to electoral politics and its pragmatic imperatives. The activists of the party organizations now increasingly concern themselves with issues and ideologies and with the making of public policy. But whatever the explanation or the occasion of the change, it brings an especially serious tension to the tripartite American parties. The party in government and its candidates cannot give up their total commitment to electoral victory. And as the party organizations and electorates — or some parts of them — do so, the only result can be a further alienation and splintering within and among the three sectors of the party. For the American parties, unlike their counterparts in the other democracies, because of their decentralization and organizational weakness, have no real machinery for reconciling such basic divergences within the party structure.

All of these developments also have an importance beyond the parties themselves. They presage changes in the activities of the parties in the entire political system as well as changes in their competitive relationships with other political organizations. That is to say, they result in changes in the ways in which the parties affect the total mobilization of political resources and political influence in the American political system. Those considerations are the concern of the final chapter.

Chapter Eighteen

THE POLITICAL PARTIES
IN THE POLITICAL SYSTEM

American writers about the political parties have not been modest in their claims for the major political parties. They have celebrated them as agents of democracy and as the chosen instruments through which a diffuse and heterogeneous electorate governs itself. Some have gone a step further to proclaim them as the very originators of the democratic processes they now serve. E. E. Schattschneider opened his classic and influential study of the American parties this way in 1942: [1]

> The rise of political parties is indubitably one of the principal distinguishing marks of modern government. The parties, in fact, have played a major role as *makers* of governments, more especially they have been the makers of democratic government. It should be stated flatly at the outset that this volume is devoted to the thesis that the political parties created democracy and that modern democracy is unthinkable save in terms of the parties. As a matter of fact, the condition of the parties is the best possible evidence of the nature of any regime. The most important distinction in modern political philosophy, the distinction between democracy and dictatorship, can be made best in terms of party politics. The parties are not therefore merely appendages of modern government; they are in the center of it and play a determinative and creative role in it.

The reformist report of the American Political Science Association on more responsible parties also begins with its declaration of faith that the parties are "indispensable instruments of government" and that the party system "serves as the main device for bringing into continuing relation-

[1] *Party Government* (New York: Rinehart, 1942), p. 1.

ship those ideas about liberty, majority rule and leadership which Americans are largely taking for granted." [2]

It is not difficult to imagine the reasons for such confident claims. In part they grow out of the natural tendency of scholars to identify with the subjects of their study. Just as medievalists often find the late Middle Ages the high point of Western civilization, scholars of the parties come to be convinced of the essential contributions of the major parties to democratic political systems. In part, too, the claims reflect an increasing awareness among both scholars and laymen that one must look beyond the formal institutions of government to find the mechanisms by which the business of the entire democratic system is carried on. They reflect also an awareness of the distinctive features of the two-party system, of its obvious stability, and of its long identification with an ongoing democracy. They may also reflect an understandable protectiveness of the parties against what many observers have long thought was an antiparty sentiment in American opinion and in the regulation of the parties which it spawned.

Whatever the reasons, however, it is difficult to deal only in terms of the relationship of the parties and their activities to the political system. The issue has become — and perhaps must become — one of the relationship of the parties to a democratic political system, and thus to the American democracy. It is also a question of the importance, and even the indispensability, of the political parties in that democracy. For very clearly the democratic politics of the American system are for many observers unthinkable without the political parties and the two-party system as we know them.

THE ISSUE OF PARTY PRIMACY

Despite the enthusiasm of the claims, it is very doubtful that the political party can be viewed as a creator or an initiator, or even as a guardian, of democracy. This chapter in its entirety argues that the party is a product and a result of the political institutions and processes around it. The party has no life or existence apart from the phenomena and influences of the broader political system. The kinds of general social change that bring the conditions for and expectations of democracy also affect the parties; the case is overwhelming, in fact, that the political party as we know it today is the product of the same forces and conditions that led to modern democracy. [3]

In short, one cannot extract the political party from its enveloping environment in order to win a little more leverage for it on the system and

---

[2] Committee on Political Parties of the American Political Science Association, *Toward a More Responsible Two-Party System* (New York: Rinehart, 1950), p. 15.

[3] See the brief section in the first chapter on the origin of the parties.

its components. It is probably even too much to think of the party as some prime agent of political reform, as the school of party responsibility does. The fallacy of these claims of party primacy is to imagine that the political party — virtually alone among political structures — can escape the kinds of influences which resist and retard innovation in the rest of the political system. One cannot "will" a change in party structures or activities, or a new "role" for the party, without there being accompanying, supportive changes in the political environment. The history of state legislation on party organization, for example, suggests that we have not been able to create active ward and precinct units by legislative fiat.

If we reject the claims of party primacy and abandon notions of the party as the initiator of fundamental political change, what remains to be said for its place in the political system? Basically the political party is engaged in organizing influence in a democracy. Its obvious tasks and its own goal-oriented behavior involve the winning of governmental power, whether by contesting elections, fighting on behalf of ideas and issues, or organizing the holders of public office. In an open and reasonably public way the parties combine three groups or sectors — each with separate political goals — into a grand symbiotic alliance through which all three may achieve their goals. But all three can reach those goals only through some aspect or part of the party's success in aggregating units of political power. If the party is to provide the rewards its personnel claims, it must mobilize large parts of the electorate behind public political options.

At the same time, the political party's mobilizing activities produce a number of unintended consequences. They contribute to the political socialization of young Americans into the dimensions of party competition and into the prevailing values of the American democracy. They provide useful organizational avenues for coalescing both majorities and opposing minorities. They simplify and organize the buzzing confusion of political conflict for the weary and only somewhat interested citizen. Their label and their personages are his clue to an identification of his interests, his traditional loyalty, or his vision of political morality. Their activities run as a constant, clear, easily perceptible thread through the confusing jumble of political conflict and institutions and the baffling proliferation of American elections. They recruit much of the American political elite, for theirs is the major avenue to public power. But these are not so much "unintended consequences" as they are corollaries, or even requisites, of the central party activity: the mobilization of power aggregates to achieve public goals. Even their competitions among themselves and with other political organizations are the necessary mechanisms or methods of that mobilization.

Clearly, therefore, by the standards and requisites of democracy, the political party is a "valuable" political structure. By its organizing and mobilizing of political power it helps to effectuate and achieve the exer-

cise of popular political power which is in the long run exactly what democracy is all about. But there are those who are not content to say it is a
valuable and useful political intermediary; for them it is the most valuable, even the single indispensable political organization, in a popular
democracy. Writes Maurice Duverger: [4]

A regime without parties ensures the permanence of ruling elites chosen by
birth, wealth, or position. . . . A regime without parties is of necessity a conservative regime. It corresponds to the property suffrage or else to an attempt
to cripple universal suffrage by imposing on the people leaders who do not
come from their ranks. . . . Historically speaking parties were born when the
masses of the people really made their entrance into political life; they provided the necessary framework enabling the masses to recruit from among
themselves their own elites.

Such an identification of the political party with democracy depends on
how one defines democracy and on what postulates one draws from its
axioms. It is true that the parties are usually more open, more easily permeable than the other political organizations; they are also more fixed and
stable and less personalized as structures and symbols. But the kind of
cues and loyalties they bring to the millions are often so reduced, so
simple, that they are blind to the significance of candidates and issues.
The parties clearly do not promote the rational democracy of the market-
place of ideas, and it is by no means sure that they achieve a democratic
responsibility or accountability greater than do national interest groups
or the office-holders in their direct relationships with constituents. The
democracy of the mass political parties is not necessarily democracy's
pure or final realization.

But much of this argument is futile. Like one of the classic "my father
can beat your father" arguments, there is little or no reliable data on the
basis of which to settle it. Perhaps it suffices to make two assertions that
question the myth of party superiority and indispensability. We have, first
of all, managed to organize popular consent and power without the parties in countless non-partisan elections across the United States. It may
very well be that those elections have their "undemocratic" aspects; they
have often worked to favor middle-class and better educated groups in
the electorate (i.e., those able to make effective choices without the cues
of the party symbol). But the democratic processes, even if hampered,
have proceeded without serious compromise or impairment. Here and
elsewhere the other political organizations facilitate by their mobilizings
the same democratic processes that the parties do. Secondly, democracy
changes and so do its corollaries. The political parties may have been
more essential, as Duverger suggests, at a time of the initial politization
of the uneducated, economically disadvantaged masses than they are at a

[4] *Political Parties* (New York: Wiley, 1954), pp. 425–426.

time when education and affluence open new channels of political information and new means of political mobilizations.

The question, however, is hardly one of party or no party. It is, more precisely and accurately, a question of relative changes and adjustments in party role; it is not one of the dismissal or abolition of the parties. It is a question of whether for the sake of democracy the parties must monopolize or dominate the mobilization of political power within the democratic electorate. Can they lose some of their traditional control of those mobilizations without threatening democracy itself? And to return to an earlier point, are not any such changes in party mobilizing a reflection of changing conditions which affect both the parties and the democracy?

THE FUNCTIONAL ALTERNATIVE

All of the comments of this chapter, and indeed of this entire book, on the question of the parties' activities in the political system have been based on a view of the parties as mobilizers and organizers of political support. The view has been of the parties as political organizations seeking goals in the political system, and generalizations about them have been based on empirical observation of the overt and explicit activities of very tangible people and social structures. But there is an alternative view of the political world and the place of the parties within it. It centers about the "functions" that must be performed in the political system and on the parties' contribution to their performance.

The language of "functions" has been with the study of American parties from its infancy.[5] The texts and treatises on political parties have referred to "functions" such as the contesting of elections, the organizing of holders of public office, or the socializing of electorates. In such instances the usage would appear to refer to little more than the obvious behavior or activity of the parties. At times, however, "function" has referred to the unintended activities or consequences of activities of the parties — to those happy by-products or "dividends" which result from the parties' going about their usual intended activities.[6] Depending on whose list of functions one consults, the parties have been said to simplify political issues and alternatives, organize majorities and oppositions, recruit political elites and leadership, moderate the political conflict, promote compromises and consensus, and unify the assorted centers of governmental authority.

The use of "function," unfortunately, is confusing in its variety and imprecision. Is "function" merely another term for behavior or activity?

[5] Theodore Lowi has brought together a number of the various functional usages in his article, "Toward Functionalism in Political Science: The Case of Innovation in Party Systems," *American Political Science Review*, LVII (1963), pp. 570–583.

[6] These are the "latent functions" to which Robert Merton refers in *Social Theory and Social Structure* (Glencoe: Free Press, 1951).

For some writers it clearly is, especially when they refer, for instance, to the function of contesting elections. For others it has come to mean something close to place or "role"; the literature on the American parties is dotted with general references to the parties' function (not functions) in the American political system or process. For still others "function" refers, in a narrower and more precise sense, to the results and consequences (usually unintended) of behavior — for instance, to the function of promoting compromise.

Even among these latter, more specific references to function there is a deep and important division. One group among the functionalists merely uses the term to refer analytically to any group of unintended consequences that contribute to the operation and on-going activities of some wider social system. Hence, it is possible to refer to the parties' function of recruiting a broadly based political elite within the American democracy or helping to integrate new groups into the electorate. A second group of functionalists, however, begins with functional assumptions about the entire political system; they posit the necessary performance of specific functions if the system is to persist (or even exist). This approach to the parties thus examines which of these functions the parties perform and how they perform them. If, as one pair of authors suggests, one finds (*inter alia*) the functions of political communication and the articulation of interests performed in every political system, does the party perform these or other functions? And do the functions the American major parties perform differ from those performed by the minor parties or by the competitive parties in, say, Britain or India? [7] At this level of a closed, total system functionalism one comes close to a quasi-biological, organic relationship between a structure such as the party and the political system as a whole.

Confusion begets confusion, and this instance is no exception. We confront a term, a usage, that means a great many things to a great many different people — and thus very little to people in general. Basically the confusion springs from two chief questions: whether function implies something more than mere activity, and if it does, whether it can refer to *any* unintended consequence or result of activity. If function is to mean something more than activity (i.e., some perceived result or effect or consequence of the activity) one then confronts an imposing problem in measurement. How does one compare the extent that the parties of two political systems perform the functions of political communication or

---

[7] The specific reference is to Gabriel Almond and James Coleman, *The Politics of the Developing Areas* (Princeton: Princeton Univ. Press, 1960). For a more general discussion of functionalism in the social sciences, see the collection of essays edited by Don Martindale, *Functionalism in the Social Sciences*, Monograph 5 in a series of the American Academy of Political and Social Science (Philadelphia, 1965), especially the essays on functionalism in political science by William Flanigan and Edwin Fogelman and by Robert Holt.

interest articulation? Are there observable manifestations of functions, or does one "intuit" their performance? How, indeed, does one merely determine that a function is being performed? If the variety in lists of functions attributed to the American parties is any indication, serious and careful scholars viewing the same parties may and do come up with strikingly different lists of attributed functions.

These are serious problems for any theoretical approach, for the formulation of generalizations and theories of parties — or of any other social structure or process — depend on measurement. Measurement in turn depends on the establishment of specific categories and concepts and on an ability to fit empirical data to them. It is one thing to say as a matter of logic or impressionistic knowledge that function "x" (e.g., the organizing of majorities) is performed by the American parties. It is quite another to compare the extent to which two parties in two systems perform it and the ways in which they do. For functional categories, of whatever type or form, have the distinct disadvantage of being defined in terms other than those of the actual behavior and activity one most easily observes.

Hopefully, it is clear to the reader that this book has not been cast in terms of functional analysis. It has, indeed, sedulously avoided the uncertainties of functional terms. Here we have looked at the party activity itself: the contesting of elections, the organizing of public officials, the stating of ideas and issue positions. We have looked, in broader and generic terms, at the intended, goal-oriented activity of the parties as they seek to mobilize aggregates of political power. When we sought explanation it was in terms of the traditional forms of relationship and variation (or, if one prefers, correlation), and ultimately in terms of cause and effect. Functionalism, on the other hand, even though it can accommodate the usual forms of correlational and causal analysis (e.g., why does party A perform function X when party B in the same party system does not?), is basically involved with relationships that are consequential (rather than causal) and that deal, therefore, with contributions made and impact felt. It is an analysis which always relates the activities (and thus the functions) of the parties to the needs and healthy operation of some larger structure or system.

Without any doubt a functional analysis brings important and even striking insights to the study of the political parties. It unquestionably offers a useful heuristic framework for relating the activities of the political parties to the broader political system. Its strength is its concentration on the relationship of the part to the whole, while other ways of looking at social phenomena deal more comfortably with the relationship of part to part (e.g., of the political party to the legislative process, to the structure of legal regulations, or to the system of social stratification). It is, therefore, a very useful supplement to the more conventional modes of analysis. Yet the conviction remains that any explanatory statements — or even any simple generalizations — can be more easily stated in terms of intended, goal-seeking behavior. That is perhaps an act of methodological faith, but it is one buttressed at least in part by the history of difficulties scholars have had in so using the functional categories.[8]

COMPETITION IN ORGANIZING

Any assessment of the place of the parties in the political system must ultimately reckon with their competings with other political organizations. Theirs is not only the competition of party against party, but of party with non-party political organizations. They compete for the support of groups in the electorate in order to win success for their political goals by enlisting the support of aggregates of political power. Before that they compete for the political resources out of which to make the organizational capacity with which to compete for broader support. Each party and other political organization thus struggles continuously to recruit the resources and the support it needs to counter the appeals and effectiveness of its competitors.

Americans have long prized the competition of a vigorous two-party system. They have always worried vaguely about the consequences of a failure of competition within the party system — reduced party responsiveness to popular wishes, self-serving party leaders and organizations, even cynical and corrupt political goals. Much of what we accept as the conventional American regulation of the parties was initiated partly in response to the excesses of dominant parties; it is no accident that the direct primary, non-partisanship, and the regulation of the internal business of the parties began at a time of almost unparalleled one-partyism in American politics. We fear the irresponsibilities, the shoddy performance, the insensitivities to popular demands, the sheer lack of choice that monopoly produces — whether it is the monopoly of one-partyism or, more serious, a monopoly of all the political organizations, such as that a local power elite might achieve.

Active competition among the parties and political organizations insures the large number of citizens a continuing number of relevant political options. An active, responsive competition maximizes both their opportunities for participation in political organizations and their opportunities for influencing the staffing and conduct of government. It affords the electorate the greatest opportunities for participation in the processes of selecting and influencing a governing political elite. And it best insures

[8] For an example of an ingenious attempt at functional generalizations about political parties and party systems, see the Lowi article cited in footnote 5 of this chapter. See also the editors' first chapter in Charles G. Mayo and Beryl L. Crowe (eds.), *American Political Parties: A Systemic Perspective* (New York: Harper and Row, 1967).

that political organizations will not permit their private goals to suppress a responsiveness to the goals of the electorate.

To carry out the analogy to the economic model, competition among political organizations allocates political resources in a way most consistent with the assumptions of democracy. It maximizes choice and participation. It forestalls the undemocratic implications of the monopoly of political power. Given the necessity of organizing the complex business of decision-making in large representative democracies, competition among political organizations is necessary if meaningful choice is to be preserved for the individual. For suppression of choice at this step in the political system is effective suppression in the entire political system.

The competition may, of course, be very imperfect, for men will at times prefer political collusion to competition, and the sheer problems of mobilizing resources may prevent the rise of new competitors. To some extent it is as difficult for a new "producer" to enter political competition as it is for a new maker of automobiles to break into that "market." Very probably competition among political organizations has seen the same concentration of power among a smaller number of "producers" that the competition among business firms has. Witness the decline of the smaller "third" parties. Probably, too, the concentration has resulted for parallel reasons: the competitive advantages of size (especially at a time when the new "political technology" requires a greater and greater concentration of resources), the necessity for "national marketing," and the tendency of successful political organizations to merge and combine. But competition among giants remains a form of competition, and it continues to produce at least some of its sought-for results.

The place of the political party in the democratic politics of the American political system is, therefore, best estimated through an assessment of the competition of political organizations. Democracy itself presupposes some degree of citizen participation and choice. It involves, by definition, a breadth in the distribution of political power, and some organizational intermediaries must mobilize the political power of individuals if it is to be effective. Most of the "functional" statements about the parties, indeed, can be considered as variants or consequences of that very simple proposition. The party's "role" in democratic politics is very much a matter of its competitive position and its competitive activities in the various aspects of this mobilizing.

To a considerable extent, therefore, the question of the "natural superiority" of the political party is decided by the electorate's choices among competitive alternatives. If the voters or groups of them choose other organizational instruments than the parties, they indicate a preference for their efficacy as political mobilizers. It is possible that the result will be or will reflect changes in the processes of democracy. If so, the experts and philosophers can argue not over the political party, but over which form or state of democracy is preferable. It may be true, for instance, that the major American party has traditionally minimized ideology and social conflict. That is not primarily a question concerning the political parties so much as it is one of the desirability or necessity of fully articulated ideologies, explicit representation of political conflict, and campaigns and choices based on issues and ideas in democratic systems.

The traditional case for the superiority of the party among all other political organizations rests on its breadth of appeal, its stability (and the stability of the cues and symbols it emits), its openness of recruitment, and its ability to organize and moderate the political goals of large, heterogeneous groups of Americans. Parties have thus provided a broad base for the recruitment of a political elite while they have provided stable cues for political choice, and hopefully, for ultimate political responsibility. Because of their tri-partite and inclusive form they have involved the political mass and related it to the political elites of activists and office-holders in a way which no other political organization can match. But to say that the parties have done so in the past or present is no assurance that they will do so more efficiently and more effectively for all time. New competitors arise with new organizational forms, new appeals, and new political skills. The needs and demands of the electorate change. And the competitive status quo may be easily disturbed.

CHANGES IN THE PATTERNS OF COMPETITION

Two striking changes in the competitive positions of the major American parties are becoming increasingly evident. They have, first of all, entered a period of unparalleled two-party competitiveness. With the fall of the South to at least an erratic form of two-party competition, no region or even substantial pocket of one-partyism remains on the American political landscape. Second, and even more dramatically, the parties appear to have lost at least part of their dominance over the mobilization of political power in the American polity. Most noticeably, they have lost a considerable degree of control over the nomination and election of candidates for public office. The result can only be a shift in role for the parties; in part that shift is increasingly evident in the greater party concern for issues and ideology. In short, the parties appear to have suffered an over-all net decline in their competitive position among the political organizations. They have lost a one-time monopoly over the electoral processes without gaining any comparable footholds in other avenues of mobilization.

The over-all loss of competitive position to other political organizations is not difficult to explain. It is largely the result of three deeper political changes:

1. Old and new political skills (the "political technology") are no longer controlled by the parties. A new technology of media skills, and related opinion skills, has broken that party control. New avenues and skills are available to political organizations wanting to enter the electoral processes; the parties can be engaged in their arena of strength even by new private entrepreneurs of political organization.

2. A more politicized, informed, and sophisticated electorate seeks more specialized cues and loyalties than the parties can offer. Voters prefer not to "invest" all of their activity or political loyalty in an omnibus, undifferentiated party; they prefer to pick and choose, supporting, even working for, a candidate here or an issue there. As they become more attuned to issues and candidates they hesitate to make the gross commitment to an "umbrella" organization such as a party. Hence, for example, the decline of straight ticket voting. Voters may also now easily find alternate sources of political information and guidance in the mass media and other political organizations.

3. The activists of the party organizations have also drifted to incentives (such as issue and ideology) that are no longer purely electoral; they may wish to act only selectively on behalf of candidates whose issue positions are congruent with theirs. They, too, do not wish to invest all of their activity in an omnibus party; rather than support all of its causes and candidates, they may be more selective in their activity, reserving the right to work through other (and often competing) political organizations. Their selectivity tends, therefore, to make the party organizations into "pools" of potential activists rather than disciplined corps of ready workers. They are thus only partially recruited into party activity.

So, the political party now faces external competition armed with new political skills, a new and "choosy" electorate, and a less unified, multipurpose party organization.

In all of these changes, the key is differentiation. The parties seem increasingly to be too omnibus and too undifferentiated in their demands; the simple, issueless, almost "blind" loyalties they exact may have been more suitable to the levels of political sophistication of several generations ago. Today the parties labor under the disadvantage of size, simplicity, and bluntness as political instruments; an organizational form that succeeded with millions of recent immigrants at the turn of the century seems less suitable for an educated, socially integrated middle class today. The more politicized and informed the individual becomes, the more specialized must be the organizations competing for his resources and support. He will be more willing to give time and money, for example, to a specific cause or candidate than to the "bag" of causes and candidates the party represents.

But is there not an irony, even an inconsistency, in suggesting that two-party competitiveness is increasing at the very moment in which the parties, taken together, are losing some of their competitive pre-eminence among the full range of political organizations? Not necessarily, for the very kind of total commitment — with its lack of differentiation and specialization — that underlies the single, dominant party and that characterizes one-partyism is exactly what is fading from the American political scene. The very reasons for which the parties are no longer able to dominate the non-party political organizations are the reasons why one party can no longer easily dominate another.

These changes in competitive position and role cause internal problems for the parties. Always faced with the necessity for holding its three, disparate sectors together by a delicate diplomacy, party leadership now confronts an increasing divide between the party organization and the party in office. The organization activists become more ideological and less concerned about electoral victory — to the dismay of the men of the party in government for whom victory is a career necessity. The partisans in government also find that their long-time dominance of the party organization is passing to leadership not interested in seeking public office; like the office-holders of the European parties, they face attempts by the party organization to discipline their public activities. At the same time these public officials discover that the party organization is no longer indispensable for election or re-election, and they set out either to form their own campaign-oriented political organizations or to make alliances with other political organizations (such as interest groups). The party in the government is, therefore, increasingly drawn to political organizations who will and can help it organize the electoral processes. The cohesion and integrity of the political party as a political structure is by that much compromised.

WHITHER THE AMERICAN PARTIES?

The last and most speculative question — and in many ways the most troubling one — concerns the future of the American parties. Does the recent loss of competitive position presage a continuing decline in the ability of the major American parties to mobilize the power of the American electorate? Are the parties becoming semi-obsolete artifacts of an earlier and simpler political age? Ultimately the questions merge into a final speculation over whether it is possible to imagine a democratic politics without political parties, or at least without parties resembling those we know in the last third of the 20th century.

An assessment of the future of the parties suggests the projection of recent trends into the future. The recent gradual decline of the parties' position as mobilizers gives one reason to wonder if the development will continue. On a broader level it invites a speculation over whether in general the parties of the democracies change or develop through periods or stages — whether there is, in other words, a series of forms which parties go through as they respond to the more general changes in the politics of democracies. If there is a developmental pattern into which one can fit the natural history of the democratic parties, it will not be easily discernible in the development of the American parties. As the oldest parties in the oldest representative democracy, they would, if anything, be on the "leading edge" of change. Their changes would only suggest the direction other parties might follow, but one would have to wait and see if they do in fact follow.

To begin the speculation, it would seem unlikely that the parties would in any real sense "disappear." They are deeply rooted in American law; the advantages they afford in the business of political organizing, in considerable extent a result of their statutory and ballot status, would alone guarantee their continued life. They also remain deeply set as cognitive realities in the political "worlds" of countless citizens; they have a very real and enduring life for them as important reference symbols. Thus, too many political processes and too many political expectations are too deeply set for the parties to simply pass away. Much more likely is the possibility that the parties will change to accommodate changes in the political processes and structures which make up their all-surrounding "environment."

As a guide to "party watching" in the American political system, the reader may wish to consider whether the American parties are not moving into a third general stage in their development — and whether, indeed, those stages might not also be observable in the other mature democracies.

1. Initially the parties began in most of the Western democracies as parties of limited access. Originated at a time of a limited, aristocratic suffrage, they began as political organizations limited in personnel, limited largely to merely electoral activities, and largely closed to mass political participation.

2. As the electorates expanded, the parties, too, expanded their organizational forms to include larger numbers of activists and members (even though the American parties resisted to a greater extent than most the development of mass membership bases). But whether the parties of this stage are truly mass parties or not, they are largely characterized by a dominance of political mobilization. These are the parties which arise in the beginnings of mass, universal suffrage and which dominate the political loyalties and even the political socialization of the new, mass electorate. As the dominant political organization of an electorate marked by relatively low levels of

political information and sophistication, they come to be the chief repositories of political loyalties and the chief givers of political cues. (In many of the new nations of Asia and Africa, which begin with virtually complete adult suffrage, the parties enter stage two very quickly.)

3. Finally, as electorates mature along with democratic processes, as political loyalties and interests become more complex and more heterogeneous, there results a new differentiation and pluralism in political organization. The political party in this stage becomes something more of a *primus inter pares;* at the least its virtual monopoly of the mobilization of power ends amid the new challenges of growing organizational competitors. The party still remains both a potent political organization and a powerful reference symbol, but it loses its monopoly of political resources, political skills, and political support.

These stages in party development reflect no internal, "organic" growth, no quasi-biological "life cycle." They are direct responses to changes in a combination of the quantity and the quality of the democratic electorate. As the "quantity" of the electorate moves to total adult suffrage, and as its "quality" moves from political naiveté to political sophistication, so does the nature of the major party and its activities — and so, especially, does its position in the competitive pattern of the politics of democratic organizing intermediaries.[9]

There may possibly be other stages in party development to follow the third. But for the moment the American parties appear to be entering that third period in which they must adapt to a more complex electoral politics. The politics of the second stage, the one in which the parties dominate the mobilization of power, is based on a simple set of political loyalties and political cues. The ability of the parties — or any other single set of political organizations — to dominate its politics results from the simple, undifferentiated set of political loyalties and political cues which guide its electorate. But as that electorate develops more complex, differentiated interests, and loyalties, it comes to respond to more complex and differentiated loyalties and cues. It responds to party loyalties, but it also responds to candidate perceptions, to ideas, issues, and ideologies. It responds, furthermore, to specific elections and political levels differentially. It is a far more complex and sophisticated politics. No single set of loyalties, and thus no single set of political organizations, can easily organize and manage it.

[9] In many ways this analysis is largely consistent, especially in the parallels to the first two stages, with Duverger's assumptions in his *Political Parties* that parties tend to move from the aristocratic cadre parties to mass, popular, membership parties and that the latter form is pre-eminently the form of a mass, popular democracy.

INDEX

431

DATE DUE

SEP 18 '98			
GAYLORD			PRINTED IN U.S.A.